AF449247

ARCHIVAL
REFLECTIONS

ARCHIVAL REFLECTIONS

Postmodern Fiction of the Americas
(Self-Reflexivity,
Historical Revisionism, Utopia)

Santiago Juan-Navarro

Lewisburg
Bucknell University Press
London: Associated University Presses

Associated University Presses
440 Forsgate Drive
Cranbury, NJ 08512

Associated University Presses
16 Barter Street
London WC1A 2AH, England

Associated University Presses
P.O. box 338, Port Credit
Mississauga, Ontario
Canada L5G 4L8

The paper used in this publication meets the requirements of the American National Standard for Permanence of Paper for Printed Library Materials Z39.48-1984.

Library of Congress Cataloging-in-Publication Data

Juan-Navarro, Santiago, 1960–
    Archival reflections : postmodern fiction of the Americas (self-reflexivity, historical revisionism, utopia) / Santiago Juan-Navarro.
        p.   cm.
    Includes bibliographical references (p.   –   ) and index.
    ISBN 0-8387-5427-9 (alk. paper)
    1. Historical fiction, Spanish American—History and criticism.
2. Historical fiction, American—History and criticism.   3. Spanish American fiction—20th century—History and criticism.   4. American fiction—20th century—History and criticism.   5. Postmodernism (Literature)—Latin America.   6. Postmodernism (Literature)—United States.   I. Title.
PQ7082.H57J83   2000
863—dc21
                                                                        99-40562
                                                                        CIP

To Enrique García Díez,
In Memoriam

Contents

Acknowledgments

I would like to thank all those who have contributed their time and effort during the numerous stages in which this book was written. To Jaime Alazraki, Félix Martínez-Bonati, Eloise Quiñones-Keber, and George Stade, who supervised the elaboration of the initial drafts in Columbia University. To Mary Schwartz, Rick Shain, Jenaro Talens, and the anonymous reader from Bucknell University Press for their incisive observations and insightful recommendations regarding the final revision of the manuscript. To James López and Patricia Santoro for their untiring and effective editorial work. The Florida International University Provost Foundation and the Latin American and Caribbean Center provided me with grants and financial assistance to advance the work of this study. And lastly, this book would not have been possible without the support and encouragement of my wife, María Asunción Gómez, who also had the patience to read and revise the manuscript during the course of its writing.

I gratefully acknowledge permission from the Editors of *Revista Iberoamericana* to reprint material in chapter 2 that originally appeared in Vol. 62, No. 174 ("Sobre dioses, héroes y novelistas: La reinvención de Quetzalcóatl y la reescritura de la conquista en 'El mundo nuevo' de Carlos Fuentes"). A previous version of chapter 1 was previously published as a monograph in *Eutopías*, Vol. 196/197 (*La metaficción historiográfica en el contexto de la teoría postmodernista: una perspectiva interamericana*), reprinted with the permission of the publisher of Ediciones Episteme and the Editors.

Introduction: Prospects for an Inter-American Approach to Postmodern Fiction

In all the years I have dedicated to the study of the Spanish-American and U.S. literary traditions, I have always been puzzled by a question constantly put to me by my colleagues in both English and Spanish departments alike: Why the Americas? At first, I associated this attitude of thinly veiled distrust with a lack of sensibility regarding comparative literary studies. However, this initial intuition was disproved as I discovered that comparative studies among works produced in the Western hemisphere and their European "models" were not only abundant but rarely questioned. Whenever the cultural traditions of North and South America have been discussed together, the tendency has been merely to point out their differences rather than their similarities. As Gustavo Pérez Firmat acknowledges, inter-American literary studies are still "terra incognita," a critical field yet to be developed.[1] This scarcity of comparative pan-American literary studies is caused by the rigid borders that exist between academic disciplines. In both U.S. and Latin American universities, departments of English and Spanish rarely interact and encounters between "Americanists" and "Latin Americanists" are unusual.[2] "Americanness" is frequently approached from a narrow nationalist and Anglophone perspective, which can be seen in the appropriation of the word "America" as a synonym for the United States. Many Latin Americanists, in turn, look with suspicion on any attempt at connecting their own literary tradition to that of the United States, arguing that a history of economic and cultural domination stands in the way of any positive interaction between the two regions. Americanists and Latin Americanists in the United States seem more concerned with establishing the uniqueness of their respective cultures than with initiating a dialogue that would allow for an understanding of these cultures beyond their own limited, nationalist contexts.

The field of postmodern historical fiction in the Americas is particularly problematic in this respect. Because Latin American literature does not always conform to the models of Western literary history, most Hispanists have been reluctant to deal with the issue of postmodernism. Moreover, given its use of a highly subjective and relativistic epistemology, contemporary narrative production is considered to be at odds with the notion of historical consciousness. As a consequence, existing studies of postmodern fiction tend to read like decontextualized primers, dealing mainly with formal features and relying strictly on U.S. literature for examples. Latin American texts are either excluded from their studies or mentioned solely as exotic illustrations of a theory built upon U.S. or European models.

This book, which focuses on historical fiction written in Spanish America and the United States during the 1970s, attempts to correct these imbalances. Many New World historical novels of this period are characterized by a paradoxical combination of self-reflexivity and historiographic meditation; they foreground the act of writing, while simultaneously asserting their own historical condition. Linda Hutcheon has coined the phrase "historiographic metafiction" to refer to this practice, one of the most extensive within postmodern fiction. Informed by her poetics of postmodernism, as well as by Lucien Dällenbach's theory of the self-reflexive text, and new trends in the philosophy of history, I will examine this problematic narrative articulation in four American authors: Carlos Fuentes of Mexico, Julio Cortázar of Argentina, and Ishmael Reed and E. L. Doctorow of the United States. While these four writers approach historical issues from a highly reflexive perspective, they all exemplify dominant tendencies in the theory and practice of historiographic metafiction: the discovery of significance in the marginal, the use of political philosophies that accommodate heterodoxy and dissent, the concept of literature as a communal experience open to the reader's participation, and the parodic rewriting of historical and literary traditions in order to demystify the dominant forms of representation. Through a textual analysis of the major historical texts of these authors, I will attempt to establish some of the distinctive features of this kind of fiction in New World literatures.

The first chapter examines the intellectual and literary background of historiographic metafiction in light of the current debate on postmodernism. While the first half of the chapter discusses the nature of this debate in the Americas—with special attention given to the concepts developed by Anglo-American critics and to the controversial use of the term "postmodernism" in Hispanic letters—the last two sections discuss recent theories of reflexivity and history and their relationship to postmodernism. The goal of this introductory chapter is neither to survey all possible approaches to this question nor to create a whole new concept of postmodernism, but to provide an outline of those theoretical outlooks that inform my readings.

Chapter 2 analyzes Fuentes's oeuvre in the context of postmodern historical fiction. The chapter focuses on *Terra Nostra*, and covers the three main historiographic themes of the novel: Fuentes's reconsideration of imperial Spain and its imposition onto Latin America ("The Old World"); the novel's reinvention of pre-Hispanic myths and chronicles of the conquest ("The New World"), and the oppositional movements that confront monolithic Spanish institutions ("The Next World"). The analysis of these three historical motifs is carried out against Fuentes's historical essays, as well as in contrast to both his acknowledged sources and to contemporary works that confirm or deny the novel's claims. This historiographic analysis is followed by an examination of how these topics are expressed through self-reflexive metaphors and how they relate to the author's cultural vision.

Chapter 3 explores Ishmael Reed's historical revisionism as a means of displacing the dominant assumptions about the role of blacks in history. In *Mumbo Jumbo*, Reed constructs a new mythology that seeks to undermine stereotypes of African-American cultural inferiority. Historiographically, the chapter focuses on two issues: the origins of African-American culture and its varied expression during the Harlem Renaissance of the twenties. Like Fuentes, who rewrites the history of Spain from the perspective of the colonized, Reed inverts the dynamics of cultural imperialism by imposing a peripheral and marginal perspective upon the dominant Judeo-Christian culture. I will examine the radical self-reflexiveness of the novel's metafictional strategy, which is created by the intensive use of paradoxical duplications. By means of its self-reflexive structure, *Mumbo Jumbo* foregrounds the textual nature of its referential universe, including the historical referent itself.

Chapter 4 scrutinizes the work of two authors, Julio Cortázar and E. L. Doctorow, both of whom present an experimental prose style laced with moral and political concerns. Unlike the chapters on Fuentes and Reed, whose encyclopedic scope requires extensive clarification, this chapter's focus is restricted to the analysis of two of the most striking features of *Libro de Manuel* and *The Book of Daniel*: Cortázar's politicization of the modernist collage and Doctorow's allegorization of the acts of history and fiction writing. The analysis of specific historical motifs in these two novels (Argentina under military rule and the United States during the Cold War) is accompanied by a discussion of their epistemological concerns.

Both Cortázar and Doctorow struggle to accommodate historical skepticism within their search for a corrective historiography, a historical narrative with the power to overcome political repression and effect social changes.

Chapter 5 addresses the similarities and differences among the authors in their use of historically conscious fiction. Four features, which tie the works under discussion to their New World context, are here identified: utopianism, the search for cultural identity, hybridity, and the attempt to create a political pedagogical culture. The chapter summarizes the paradoxes revealed by textual analysis and lays the foundations for an inter-American approach to historiographic postmodern fiction.

Although their internal organization varies according to the topic under discussion, the three central chapters (the textual analysis of the selected authors) conform to a similar pattern. First, the career of each writer is discussed in terms of the presence of history and self-reflexivity in his works to establish its historical and aesthetic context. A major historiographic metafictional work of each author is then analyzed from this dual perspective (historical and self-reflexive). I will focus on the ways in which specific historical motifs are portrayed in each work, and on the historical vision implied by it. Contrary to the opinion that tracking down sources and evaluating historical novels vis-á-vis academic history are irrelevant, I believe in their pertinence to the understanding of works that, while not purporting to be faithful to the historical record, nevertheless use history as their organizing principle. In fact, some of these novels suggest that fiction is a system of knowledge that surpasses empirical historiography in cognitive power, a claim that will be tested through both literary and historiographic analysis.

The study of the metafictional component is influenced by Lucien Dällenbach's grammar of the *mise en abyme*, the literary and artistic device by which an element within the work mirrors the work as a whole. Dällenbach's concept of specular texts provides a systematic analysis of the different types and levels of reflection that is especially useful for the analysis of self-conscious fiction. My interest, however, is not in describing this specular dimension of the text as a realm that differs or is separate from historiographic concerns, but rather in demonstrating that self-reflexive metaphors and structures are repeatedly employed in these novels in order to highlight and succinctly present a particular historical vision. Through the use of self-referential syntheses, content quotes, philosophical debates, and mythic plots, these works reflect not only upon themselves, but also upon the discursive—and therefore mediated—nature of their historical referents.

Since this study deals with the way a narrative problem (that is, how postmodern fiction articulates self-reflexivity and historiography) is resolved within a particular context (that is, the Americas), its approach combines both formal and contextual analysis. By examining the cultural impasse in which these works were produced, I will try to answer some of the most important (and largely unexplored) questions raised by contemporary theory. As González Echevarría rightly suggests, it has become an almost uncritical cliché to refer to the importance of self-consciousness in contemporary narrative, but few have investigated its distinct functions in particular works.[3] Something similar can be said in relation to the new historical novel. Although it is quite common to hear of a new interest in history, it is not nearly as common to find studies addressing the functionality and consequences of the use of concrete historiographic subjects. The present study approaches the treatment of these two elements in Spanish-American and U.S. postmodern historical fiction. Unlike much of the theory written in this field, which either celebrates or rejects the global phenomenon of postmodernism, *Archival Reflections* provides a critical evaluation of the achievements and contradictions of this new aesthetic sensibility.

ARCHIVAL
REFLECTIONS

1

Historiographic Metafiction in the Context of Postmodernism Theory

In spite of the initial mistrust of many critics, the term "postmodernism" has grown increasingly popular since the early 1970s. Used to express a sequential relationship to modernism, the prefix "post" has acquired different shades of meaning in each critic's work. For some it designates a radical break with the aesthetic field of modernism, for others an extension of the premises of modernism itself.[1] If there is little agreement about postmodernism's relationship with previous movements, the same can be said about its chronology. The 1950s (Jameson), 1960s (Hutcheon), and 1970s (Harvey) have been given as its inaugural dates.[2] All of these issues are further complicated by differences in the critical perspective and ideological orientation of each analyst. While some consider postmodernism a style that may exist independently of the historical moment, others claim that it is the cultural expression of a particular stage in the development of world economics. Given the ubiquity and mutability of this term and its close association with historiographic metafiction, it seems useful to begin with an exploration of some of its current theorizations.

Anglo-American Concepts of Postmodernism

Ihab Hassan: The Heroics of Unmaking

One of the first critics to establish a concept of postmodernism from a literary-oriented perspective was Ihab Hassan.[3] In the epilogue to the second edition (1982) of his essay *The Dismemberment of Orpheus* (1971), he offers his most comprehensive systematization of a concept of postmodernism.[4] After underlining the basic continuity between modernism and postmodernism, Hassan provides a list of names coming from the most varied disciplines (philosophy, history, psychoanalysis, political theory, dance, music, fine arts, architecture and literature) that help to illustrate a possible concept of postmodernism.[5] As Hassan himself points out, the variety and heterogeneity of these names make their inclusion within the same movement, paradigm, or school impossible. They do, however, "evoke a number of related cultural tendencies, a constellation of values, a repertoire of procedures and attitudes" of what we call postmodernism.[6]

The dominant feature that Hassan sees in the representatives of postmodernism is the exacerbation of a tendency already existing in modernism and the avant-garde: "the will to unmake." However, while the elitism of the avant-garde became institutionalized and modernism leaned toward cultism, Hassan links this deconstructive impulse to the one that Leslie Fiedler (1969) sees in postmodernism: the recuperation of popular culture.[7] For Hassan, these two impulses—the will to (self-) dissolution and the challenge to institutionalized high art—constitute the articulating axes of the postmodern universe.

Before discussing the postmodern repertoire, Hassan elaborates on several conceptual problems that simultaneously hide and constitute postmodernism. The first of these problems refers to definition. The word "postmodernism" evokes modernism itself, that which it purports to overcome or suppress. It contains within its etymology its own enemy. As with other categories, postmodernism suffers from what Hassan terms semantic instability: What some critics call postmodernism others call avant-gardes and still others neo–avant-gardes or, simply, modernism. The historical ambivalence of all literary concepts has lead to overlappings and superpositions of modernism and postmodernism throughout their history. Hassan repeatedly emphasizes the impossibility of radically separating these two currents and notices that, throughout their careers, many authors will make use of techniques that could subscribe to both tendencies.

The remaining conceptual problems discussed underline the difficulties of all periodizations. For Hassan a period must be perceived in terms of *both* continuity *and* discontinuity. Postmodernism, in particular, carries within itself a "double vision" in which Apollonian and Dionysian impulses coexist: equality and difference; unity and rupture; filiation and revolt. Like any other period, postmodernism is a synchronic and diachronic construct that requires historical and theoretical definition. Inaugural dates are, therefore, arbitrary. For Hassan it would be possible to find antecedents of postmodernism in authors as dissimilar as Sterne,

Sade, Blake, and Rimbaud. He favors a dialectical and pluralistic vision that contains both continuities and discontinuities, diachronies and synchronies, one in which the defining features would not be excluding.

In what is undoubtedly the best known part of his essay, Hassan offers a table of thirty-three schematic differences that separate postmodernism from modernism:

Modernism	*Postmodernism*
Romanticism/Symbolism	Pataphysics/Dadaism
Form (conjunctive, closed)	Antiform (disjunctive, open)
Purpose	Play
Design	Chance
Hierarchy	Anarchy
Master/Logos	Exhaustion/Silence
Art Object/Finished Work	Process/Performance/Happening
Distance	Participation
Creation/Totalization	Decreation/Deconstruction
Synthesis	Antithesis
Presence	Absence
Centering	Dispersal
Genre/Boundary	Text/Intertext
Semantic	Rhetoric
Paradigm	Syntagm
Hypotaxis	Parataxis
Metaphor	Metonymy
Selection	Combination
Root/Depth	Rhizome/Surface
Interpretation/Reading	Against Interpretation/ Misreading
Signified	Signifier
Lisible (Readerly)	Scriptible (Writerly)
Narrative/Grand Histoire	Antinarrative/Petit Histoire
Master Code	Ideolect
Syntomp	Desire
Type	Mutant
Genital/Phallic	Polymorphous/Androgynous
Paranoia	Schizophrenia
Origin/Cause	Difference-Differance/Trace
God the Father	The Holy Ghost
Metaphysics	Irony
Determinacy	Indeterminacy
Transcendence	Immanence[8]

Hassan tries to escape the charge of taxonomic rigidity at all cost, vindicating a dialectical and pluralistic vision. Modernist forms continue to exist alongside postmodern forms, and some elements of both can be glimpsed in previous artistic manifestations.

Hassan ultimately defines postmodernism as "indetermanence." This neologism refers to the two theoretical elements that form the episteme of postmodernism: indeterminacy and immanence. Indeterminacy responds to the will to unmake that characterizes postmodern artists. Within this complex referent, he includes ambiguity, discontinuity, heterodoxy, pluralism, randomness, revolt, perversion, and deformation. In literature, this tendency manifests itself in a questioning of those canonized concepts regarding our ideas of the author, book, and audience, as well as genre, literary criticism, and literature itself. Hassan mentions the critical examples of Roland Barthes, Wolfgang Iser, Paul de Man, and Geoffrey Hartman to support his valorization of indeterminacy as an indispensable component of the act of literary creation. According to these critics, indeterminacy does not necessarily obstruct communication but, on the contrary, activates the reader's participation in the construction of meaning.

The second tendency Hassan sees in postmodernism—immanence—is defined as the increasing capacity of the mind to generalize itself through symbols, to intervene in nature, to act upon itself through its own abstractions, and to end up becoming its own environment. This intellectualizing tendency may also be evoked by concepts such as diffusion, dissemination, pulsion, communication, and interdependence. Behind the different manifestations of a fluctuating postmodernity (as revealed by history, science, cybernetics, and technologies), we find the immanence of language. As Hassan comments in a later essay, "languages constitute the paradigmatic example of this dynamic of immanence, since they reconstitute the universe . . . into signs of their own making, turning nature into culture, and culture into an immanent semiotic system."[9]

Not surprisingly, some critics have attacked the evaluative hierarchy that is implicit in Hassan's set of contrasting characteristics. In his representative table, modernism is associated with authoritarian principles, whereas postmodernism stands for a sort of libertarian utopia ruled by the unrestrained power of imagination. It is ironic, however, that in order to convey his anarchic message, Hassan uses a binomial nomenclature, which is a highly hierarchical way of perceiving reality. As Steven Connor has incisively noted, "interestingly, one term that we might have expected to turn up in Hassan's sinister column of dishonor is 'binarism'; the fixation upon strict and homogenous contrasts. Hassan here has to rely upon this binary logic to promote the very things that appear to stand against binary logic, the ideas of dispersal, displacement and difference."[10]

Brian McHale: Ontologies in Collision

Like Ihab Hassan, Brian McHale begins with the presupposition that postmodernism is a discursive construction and not a category with empirical value. Unlike other theorists of postmodernism concerned with different disciplines such as architecture, photography, cinema, or mass culture, McHale centers his analysis on postmodern fiction. Under this label, he discusses literary movements as diverse as North American metafiction, magical realism, the *nouveau roman*, and some of the most recent forms of science fiction and concrete prose. For McHale the change from modernism to postmodernism is characterized by a shift in the "dominant." The concept of the "dominant" is taken from Tynjanov and Jakobson.[11] These critics conceive the dominant as that central component of a work that governs, determines, and transforms all the other elements in the work. Poetic evolution takes place as a consequence of a change in this hierarchy. Advancing possible objections to the determinist or monolithic character of his model, McHale notices that Jakobson's concept is in reality plural. There are many dominants within art in general, within cultural history, and even within one single text (depending on which aspect we are analyzing).

While the dominant of modernism is epistemological, postmodernism originates, according to McHale, from ontological concerns. Rather than problems of knowledge and interpretation that inspired modernist authors, postmodern writers prove to be more interested in reflecting upon the nature of literature and its problematic relation to the outside world. These concerns are articulated on three levels: 1) the ontology of reality: What kind of world is this? How is it structured? What can we do in it?; 2) the ontology of literature: What is a literary work? What is the structure of the world projected by the work?; 3) the confrontation between reality and literature: What happens when different worlds—the so-called empirical reality and the reality of the literary work—confront each other or when their structural frames are violated? What is the mode of existence of a text in the world?

By comparing the early and late work of authors such as Beckett, Robbe-Grillet, Fuentes, Nabokov, Coover, and Pynchon, McHale describes this shift in the dominant. He ascribes Beckett's *Molloy*, Robbe-Grillet's *La Jalousie*, Fuentes's *La muerte de Artemio Cruz*, Nabokov's *Pale Fire*, Coover's *The Origins of Brunists*, and Pynchon's *V.* to a modernist and stylized perspectivism that is close to the postmodern sensibility, while still embedded in the epistemological concerns of modernism. All of these works seek an answer to epistemological questions: How can I interpret the world of which I am a part? What can be known? How do we know it? How is this knowledge transmitted? What are its limits? The most recent works of these same authors, however, reflect their changing concerns. McHale perceives both a foregrounding of their respective ontologies and a conflictive relationship with extratextual reality. *The Unnamable*, *La Maison de rendez-vous*, *Terra Nostra*, *Ada*, *The Public Burning*, and *Gravity's Rainbow* are, from this point of view, exemplary of the postmodern repertoire.

In order to support his theory, McHale makes an eclectic use of semiotics (Eco), poststructuralism (Foucault), Bakhtinian criticism, and phenomenology. Given his interest in exploring the ontological concerns of postmodernism, he is particularly attracted to the analytical model developed by Roman Ingarden, whose work has been one of the first to extricate the "intrinsic ontological complexity" of the fictional work.[12] Departing from Ingarden's two basic postulates (the heteronomous character of the work and its polyphonic constitution), McHale describes the four strata that configure the structure of the literary work: sounds, units of meaning, represented objects, and schematized aspects. Of particular relevance to his analysis of postmodern fiction is the third of these strata (represented objects). For Ingarden, fictional texts not only carry information through signifying chains, they also project objects and worlds. Purely intentional objects are projected by words, as well as by higher units of meaning (clauses, sentences, etc.). These represented objects constitute an "ontological sphere," a world that is always partially indeterminate. Indeterminacy, as discussed in Hassan, is one of those features that—although present in the structure of all literary works—becomes accentuated in postmodern texts. These indeterminate spaces are either permanent or temporary (until they are resolved by the reader in the act of concretizing the aesthetic object). When ambiguity is consistently sustained, an ontological oscillation—a flickering effect that Ingarden labels "iridescence" or "opalescence"—occurs. Two worlds, the reader's and the work's, are locked in a struggle for supremacy, which neither is able to win.

In *Postmodernist Fiction* McHale describes the strategies that contemporary fiction uses to highlight the ontology of the text and of the world.[13] His analysis emphasizes the mode in which postmodern texts establish and then transgress the ontological borders between discourses. To that effect, he adopts Hrushovski's tridimensional model of semiotic objects: the reconstructed world, the textual continuum, and the dimension of the speakers, voices and positions. With regard to the first of these dimensions, McHale is interested in the postmodern concern for the construction and deconstruction of fictional spaces. Unlike realist and modernist novels, which are organized around the perspective of a character or a detached narrator, the "heterotopic" space of postmodernism is simultaneously constructed and deconstructed by a series of strategies that he calls "juxtaposition, interpolation, superimposition, and misattribution."[14]

The second dimension in Hrushovski's analysis (the textual continuum) openly adopts metafictional forms in literary postmodernism. According to McHale, postmodern works of fiction are principally concerned with "the order of things," and thus are discourses that reflect upon discursive worlds. This intense self-consciousness is enhanced by its polyphonic and carnivalesque value. McHale adopts these two concepts from Bakhtin in order to make one more distinction between postmodern fiction and the previous narrative modes. Although heteroglossia—the plurality of discourses manifested by the juxtaposition of languages, styles, and diverse registers—is a characteristic of modernist authors such as T. S. Eliot or Dos Passos, it is held under rigorous control by a unifying monologic perspective. Modernist texts integrate the multiplicity of discursive worlds on a single ontological level, a consequence of the projection of a unified worldview. Postmodernism instead works to achieve discursive plurality. In Burrough's *Naked Lunch*, for example, the dialogical confrontation between the antilanguage of the criminal subculture and the languages of the "straight" or official reality leads to a polyphony of voices involved in a dialectical relationship. Postmodernism, as McHale points out, also recuperates all of those popular genres associated with the tradition of carnival and, especially, Menippean satire and the picaresque.

McHale identifies Hrushovski's third dimension (corresponding to the speakers, voices, and positions) in terms of "construction," and discusses the indeterminacy that is characteristic of this level of "represented objects." Unlike real objects, which are universal and unequivocally determined, "represented objects" show spaces of indeterminacy that tend to be filled in provisionally through the cognitive mechanisms of reading.[15] Most of the recurring strategies in postmodern fiction (Chinese box structures, *mises-en-abyme*, trompe-l'oeil effects, or infinite regresses) foreground and consequently subvert the structural frames of the literary work. Unlike modernist perspectivism, postmodern fiction presents an ontological perspectivism based on the "iridescences" or "opalescences" commented on by Ingarden. This "flickering effect" mediates between the language and style of the text and the reconstruction of this textual world carried out by the reader.

Finally, McHale analyzes the way in which postmodern forms exploit for their own benefit the work's ontological foundations. He points out how the ontological structure of the literary work ultimately rests on the material book and its typography. Unlike realism, which tends to deny its "technological reality," postmodern texts openly display that reality. The use of titles, headings, concrete prose, photographs, illustrations, texts in multiple columns, and the nonchronologic enumerations of chapters conform to what McHale calls the "schizoid text" in which visual and verbal discourses cross each other in polymorphic attitudes. Against the mirage of determinacy that realism proposes, postmodern fiction bestows "model kits" that disclose before the reader the interstices of its materiality.

Regardless of the persuasiveness of many of his readings, McHale's basic definition of the postmodern as ontologically dominant is not convincing. In fact, many of his examples may be easily used against him. For example, the four authors discussed here (Fuentes, Reed, Cortázar, and Doctorow), incorporate epistemology as a major and growing concern in their works. Fuentes's *Terra Nostra* and Reed's *Mumbo Jumbo* question the ontological boundaries between fiction and history, as McHale states; however, they also pose epistemological questions about the nature, origin, and transmission of knowledge. Similarly, Cortázar's *Libro de Manuel* concerns itself with epistemological and political issues more than most of the fiction he had previously written. The same could also be said about Doctorow's *The Book of Daniel* or *Ragtime*. In all of these works, the consistent combination of self-conscious reflexivity and metahistorical reflection point rather toward a correlation of ontology and epistemology, without either of the two being predominant. McHale's approach is, however, paramount to the study of the ontological level of postmodern historical fiction. His description of the strategies of postmodernism's revisionism of history illuminate the way historiographic metafiction seeks to revise both "the content of the historical record" and "the conventions and norms of historical fiction itself."[16]

Fredric Jameson: The Cultural Logic of Late Capitalism

While Ihab Hassan and Brian McHale focus on the formal techniques and properties of postmodern literature, Fredric Jameson has produced one of the most influential views of the relationship between postmodern culture and socioeconomic postmodernity. Jameson's purpose is to reveal the existing connections between the emergence of new artistic forms (dominated by pastiche and schizophrenia) and the new economic order, to which he refers as late capitalism. In an early essay, "Postmodernism and Consumer Society" (1983), Jameson contemplates the global phenomenon of cultural postmodernism as a reaction against the institutionalized forms of high modernism.[17] This phenomenon would comprise examples such as John Ashbery's poetry, seen as a reaction against the complex forms of modernist poetry that were defended in academic circles; the pop buildings celebrated by Robert Venturi in his manifesto *Learning from Las Vegas*, a reaction against the monumentality characteristic of the International style; pop art; photorealism; the music of John Cage, Philip Glass, and Terry Riley; the punk and new wave in rock music; Godard's films; and the novels of William Burroughs, Thomas Pynchon, and Ishmael Reed.

According to Jameson, two distinctive features are inferred from the creative practices of these individuals: the reaction against the established forms of high modernism, and the rise of an aesthetic populism sympathetic to mass culture and kitsch. In Jameson's view, we discover as many postmodernisms as modernisms, since postmodernism is always envisioned as a reaction against a phenomenon that has already occurred. Therefore, the unity of postmodernism is found not in postmodernism itself, but in the preceding modernism that it purports to displace. Postmodern artists cross the boundaries among various disciplines and movements—and, especially, between high and popular or mass culture. They do not hide their fascination for those forms that traditionally have been marginalized or ignored by the cultural elite in control of academic power. Thus, these artists regularly incorporate kitsch, TV series, Hollywood B-films, paraliterature, and subgenres (romance, mystery, science fiction, and fantasy) into their repertoire. Jameson emphasizes the difference between a modernist literature (confined mostly to academic circles and prone to "quote" these marginal texts) and postmodernism's tendency to make such texts the basis of its art in spite of their purely commercial origin.

A similar tendency toward the effacement of key boundaries can be appreciated in the circumvolutions of contemporary theory. Unlike modernism, which believed in limitations among disciplines (philosophy, political science, sociology, and literary criticism), the new critical discourses of postmodernism are grouped under the ambiguous denomination of "theory." A paradigmatic example of this tendency is, for Jameson, Foucault's unclassifiable work, for which labels such as philosophy, history, social theory, or political science prove to be insufficient.

In Jameson's view, the term "postmodernism" is not a style but a periodization concept that serves to connect the emergence of new cultural forms to a new type of social life and economic order. This new economic order has received names such as "modernization," "postindustrial society," "consumer society," "mass media society," "society of the spectacle," or "multinational capitalism." Chronologically, Jameson situates its origin in the postwar period of the United States. The 1960s represent a period in which this order—characterized, among other things, by neocolonialism, the green revolution, computerization, and the electronic revolution—would be simultaneously consolidated and questioned by its own contradictions. According to Jameson, the new postmodernism expresses "the inherent truth to the new social order of late capitalism." At this point, he proceeds to examine the two features that define postmodern experience in time and space: pastiche and schizophrenia.

In his discussion of pastiche, Jameson distinguishes this phenomenon from parody, with which it has been frequently associated. Both terms imply the imitation of a peculiar or unique style. Yet if parody establishes a distance from which the author derides the defects, stylistic mannerisms, or eccentricities of other styles, pastiche lacks this ulterior motive. Pastiche is, from Jameson's point of view, "blank parody," that is, parody without a sense of humor, without satiric impulse, without laughter.

In order to understand this change in the use of parodic forms, Jameson introduces a motif recurrent in postmodernism: "the death of the subject," or the end of individualism as such. The modernist aesthetics was associated with the existence of a unique subject, of a style of its own as an expression of individual identity. Jameson's postmodernism relegates this kind of individualism and cenobitical cult of the self to the past. In the age of corporate capitalism, of financial bureaucracies, and of demographic explosion, there is no place for the bourgeois individual subject. Poststructuralist criticism takes this process much further, to the point of affirming that the so-called bourgeois individual subject has never actually existed, and can only be seen as "a philosophical and cultural mystification."[18] From this argument, it follows that pastiche is the perfect aesthetic correlative of this socioeconomic impasse. In a contemporary world that distrusts stylistic innovation and creative originality, the only cultural alternative is the imitation of dead styles, the cannibalization of styles in the museum of history.

A brief analysis of the so-called "nostalgia film" (*American Graffiti*, *Chinatown*, and *The Conformist*) and of the new historical novel (E. L. Doctorow's *Ragtime*) leads Jameson to see the recurrent use of pastiche in the representation of history as an "alarming symptom" of the inability of the culture of late capitalism to deal with the issues of time and history. We are condemned, in Jameson's view, to seek the historical past in the images and stereotypes that popular culture has created around that past, without being able to capture the past in itself.

Jameson's treatment of schizophrenia originates in Lacan's linguistic anthropology. According to the Lacanian model, schizophrenia basically consists of the breaking of the relation between the signifiers. Since signifiers follow one another in a temporal chain, the rupture of this chain condemns the schizophrenic subject to live in a perpetual present. Schizophrenic experience is an experience of isolation, disconnection, and discontinuity between signifiers that fail to organize into a coherent whole. In their isolation, however, such signifiers achieve a greater material intensity, a more vivid nature. The dissociation of the signifier within the linguistic chain and the consequent loss of meaning lead to the transformation of the signifier into images, into pure representation whose referential value remains fluctuant.

The formal features of postmodernism (the transformations of reality into images and the fragmentation of time into a series of perpetual presents) correspond, in Jameson's view, to the emergence of a new phase of capitalism. Unlike modernism, which was often critical of its society, postmodernism is, according to him, a force that replies and reinforces the logic of a consumer society. Jameson concludes "Postmodernism and Consumer Society" expressing his skepticism about the emergence of new forms that resist this logic.

In the two versions of his already classic essay "Postmodernism, or the Cultural Logic of Late Capitalism" (1984 and 1991), Jameson takes this question up again and, although he does not offer a satisfactory answer, he sketches a brief program of what we could call an oppositional aesthetics to multinational capitalism.[19] The two most important innovations in this new essay are the greater depth of his analysis of socioeconomic postmodernity and the attenuation of the negative tones through which cultural postmodernism was originally represented.

Closely following Ernest Mandel's analysis of the present socioeconomic impasse, Jameson believes that a change in the organization of a global economy has taken place. This change does not supersede capitalism, as some conservative analysts suggest; instead, it implies an intensification of capitalism's forms and energies. Jameson adopts Mandel's periodization of capitalism, which distinguishes three different stages: market capitalism, monopoly capitalism or imperialism, and multinational capitalism. Multinational capitalism—known also as late capitalism or consumer capitalism—is, according to Jameson, the purest form of capitalism yet to have emerged. The analysis of this new economic organization for the world of culture is of great importance, because, while the cultural forms of the past aimed at hiding or distorting economic relations, under late capitalism the production of these forms has become the center of economic activity. Jameson talks about a prodigious expansion of the world of culture in the social realm, to the extent that everything in our lives has become "cultural."[20] This situation forces Jameson to reformulate his initial condemnation of postmodernism and to accept its existence as an inescapable fact to be approached without either facile celebration or condemnation. Rather than breaking with the cultural forms of postmodernism, the task of the revolutionary intellectual should be oriented to seek a cultural model that would enable the opening of new spaces of participation within postmodernism itself. Jameson ends his revised essay with a despairing call, in clear apocalyptic tones, advocating for the creation of a pedagogic political culture that would allow for the creation of a new space for the articulation of the private and the public, a cognitive map in which the individual will understand his or her place within the social organization. This new political art, according to Jameson, will need to adjust itself to the truth of postmodernism (the world of multinational capitalism), even as it systematically fights that truth.[21]

Linda Hutcheon: Postmodern Metafiction

A more favorable vision of postmodernism is offered by Linda Hutcheon. In a sense, her essays about the poetics and the politics of postmodernism can be seen as a reaction against Jameson's charge that postmodernism is nostalgic in its critical revision of history. Hutcheon is also one of the critics who has analyzed the relationship between the new tendencies of metafictional narrative and the global phenomenon of postmodernism in greater depth. However, her treatment of the relation between the two has evolved through time.[22] In the preface to the second edition of *Narcissistic Narrative* (1980), Hutcheon considers metafiction another manifestation of postmodernism. At the same time, she focuses her study on the architectonic forms in which it originated. Following the guidelines established in architecture by Charles A. Jencks and Paolo Portoghesi, Hutcheon sees in architecture a "double code," similar to that of postmodern fiction: Both manifestations respond to modern codes, but also to those of popular and local character. The interest of postmodern architects revolves around historical memory, the urban context, participation, the public realm, pluralism, and eclecticism. In a similar fashion, postmodern fiction seeks to create a democratic space in which the reader's participation is made possible. In Hutcheon's new schema of literary communication, the reader ultimately assumes a composite identity with the writer and the critic. Postmodern metafiction is also highly experimental, hence its interest in playing with the possibilities of meaning and form. The use of self-reflexive narrators and of techniques of defamiliarization has also made possible a greater ideological consciousness in contemporary literature.

In *A Poetics of Postmodernism* (1988), Hutcheon studies this increasing historicization of postmodern discourse. In the preface to her essay, she declares her intention to avoid equally an unconditional celebration and an uncritical rejection of postmodernism. She therefore refuses to see in this movement either a revolutionary change or the agonizing expression of late capitalism. Her intention is to show those common elements between theory and practice that lead to the creation of a poetics of postmodernism that is flexible enough to contain both postmodern culture and our discourses about it. The goal of this poetics is to account for the paradoxes that result from the encounter between the self-reflexive forms of modernism and the new interest for the historical, the social, and the political that characterizes postmodern culture. Her diagnosis of this culture is, therefore, radically different from that of Jameson, who sees the present cultural impasse as ahistorical, antisocial, and apolitical.

Hutcheon discusses the dichotomy that Lentricchia sees underlying current literary studies: the oscillation between the need to essentialize literature and its language and the no less urgent demand to place them both within larger sets of discursive contexts.[23] According to Hutcheon, there are no dialectics in postmodernism: What is self-reflexive remains distinct from what is traditionally considered its opposite (the historical and political), with no resulting synthesis.[24] She recognizes that this dual tendency (opposition between self-reflexive and historical forms) is not an invention that is exclusive to postmodernism. We can find this duality in works as early as *Don Quijote*. What is new, according to Hutcheon, is the pervasiveness with which postmodernism rethinks and exposes this paradoxical relationship.[25]

For Hutcheon, postmodernism is principally a contradictory and political movement.[26] It poses questions about all those things that we accept as natural, but does not offer univocal answers or simple solutions. Hutcheon regards postmodernism as a "problematizing force" in contemporary culture. Its works are characterized by duplicity and undermining. Concepts are stated and foregrounded only to be immediately questioned. The purpose of this deconstructive craving is to denaturalize the dominant features of our way of life and thinking, to defamiliarize those entities that we had always admitted as natural, so that we will be able to perceive their purely cultural value.

In the first part of her *Poetics*, Hutcheon studies the background in which this artistic current originates. Its most immediate source is traced back to the challenge to liberal humanist culture that took place in the 1960s. Postmodern artists and thinkers were formed, therefore, in the markedly antiempiricist (and sometimes antirationalist) atmosphere that characterized that period. They concentrate their energies in questioning and demystifying both the established notions and the tendency to systematize and standardize. The limits between academic disciplines, artistic practices, and literary genre become more and more fluid. The very distinction between theoretical and literary discourse is challenged. The rejection of totalization, centralism, and homogenization has as its consequence the vindication of all that which is provisional, decentered, and heterogeneous. Those groups that had been secularly excluded from both the artistic and theoretical realms are given voice. Issues of ethnicity, race, gender, and sexual orientation come to the foreground as part of a new discourse that favors difference and eccentricity. In challenging those theories and practices that ignore the situational character of discourse, this new orientation seeks to redefine literature at all levels (historical, social, political, and aesthetic). Hutcheon's use of examples from different artistic practices and various theoretical perspectives attempts to avoid the habitual vagueness and simplification of these kinds of studies.

In a second part, Hutcheon focuses on "historiographic metafiction," which she considers the most representative form of postmodern narrative. The works that she ascribes to this fictional mode respond to a paradoxical impulse: They purport to be self-referential but they are presented as ultimately subject to history. In reflecting upon themselves and upon their own process of production and reception, these works initially convey the false impression that the literary work enjoys fictional and linguistic autonomy, a mirage that the text itself finally dispels. Likewise the inclusion of historical characters and situations within the fictional context of these works aims at undermining the pretensions of objectivity and empiricism traditionally held by historiography. No matter how self-referential and reflexive they might seem, these works end up asserting their subjection to history, but history itself is depicted as equally unable to escape from the limitations of all cultural constructions (an assertion that is very much in tune with the new philosophers of history such as Hayden White, Lionel Gossman, Louis Mink, and Dominick LaCapra).

Hutcheon establishes a problematic equation between postmodernism and historiographic metafiction, which moves her to consider as "ultramodernist" all those practices that do not fit in her historicist scheme. Although the paradigmatic condition of historiographic metafiction within literary postmodernism can be accepted as a premise, it is clearly reductionist to see in it the only possible manifestation of the postmodern sensibility. Concluding, as Hutcheon does, that all postmodern fictions are historiographic, would leave out of the postmodern mainstream many experimental authors in both the North American context (John Barth, William Gass, Donald Barthelme, among others) and Latin America (Severo Sarduy, Guillermo Cabrera Infante, and Salvador Elizondo, for example), who have contributed in different ways to the postmodernism debate. Although not primarily concerned with history, these writers could hardly be identified with a cultural project (modernism) they systematically parody and question. It therefore seems more accurate to consider historiographic metafiction as the term that best describes those postmodern fictions that are historically oriented.

The present analysis departs from the point at which Hutcheon's essay ends. Her poetics of postmodernism seeks, above all, to provide a global concept of international postmodernism. A vast number of works coming from very different cultures are mentioned to support her transnational theory, and are then abandoned without further analysis. This study attempts to recontextualize postmodern historical fictions in the New World, focusing on the specific conditions of their production. Rather than being confined to the narrow perspective of a particular theory, the four writers analyzed here are contextualized within the cultural and theoretical framework in which they originated. The four concepts discussed—although at times dissimilar—illuminate different aspects of a composite postmodernism characterized by a penchant for open, plural, and flexible forms; ontological and epistemological concerns; a new reflexive sense of history; and a political stance marked by the emergence of resistant cultures opposed to the new forms of hegemony.

The Postmodernism Debate in Latin America

The four concepts discussed thus far are closely associated with Anglo-American postmodernism. They deal with Latin American works and authors only occasionally and usually neglect to analyze the idiosyncrasies of Latin American culture. Hassan and McHale include some of the best known Latin American authors (Borges, García Márquez, Fuentes, and Cortázar) within their taxonomies, but without a clear contextualization. These writers are automatically labeled postmodern because of their use of certain formal strategies. Even Hutcheon, who emphasizes the need to place postmodern narrative practices within a larger framework, fails to explain the specific forms that this framework may take in postcolonial societies.

Fredric Jameson: the Third-World Novel as a National Allegory

If Latin American postmodernism is present—albeit unsatisfactorily—in the work of these three critics, Jameson does not even contemplate such a possibility. His concept of postmodernism as the "cultural logic of late capitalism" forces him to limit his approach to the most aggressive forms of this logic. His study focuses, therefore, on the United States, the country in which that culture supposedly originated. Jameson contrasts that U.S. culture with the cultural impasse in which he sees the rest of the world. In his essay "Third-World Literature in the Era of Multinational Capitalism" (1986), he undertakes a study of this situation.[27] What seems at first sight a laudable attempt to appreciate voices outside of the U.S. dynamic, gives way to more problematic generalizations. Even Jameson himself recognizes the controversial nature of the very term "Third World." More controversial still, however, is his theory that all novels in Asia, Africa, and Latin America invariably conform to an allegorical pattern. According to him, "all Third-World texts are necessarily allegorical, in a very specific way: they are to be read as what I will call national allegories, even when, perhaps I should say, particularly when their forms develop out of predominantly western machineries of representation, such as the novels."[28] "Third-World" texts, he goes on to say, "necessarily project a political dimension in the form of a national allegory: the story of the private individual destiny is always an allegory of the embattled situation of the public Third-World culture and society."[29] Jameson seeks an alternative to the apocalyptic impasse that he envisions in U.S. culture. The production of a culture of resistance in the "Third-World" thus becomes a utopian alternative to the political quietism and representational simulation of "First-World" postmodernism.[30]

The study of Latin American postmodernity has proved to be a highly controversial field. In some cases, Latin American critics reject the term "postmodernism" because it tends to get conflated with the "modernista" movements led by Ruben Darío in the Spanish American context and by Mario de Andrade in Luso-Brazilian literature. Others point to the anachronism of adopting the expression "postmodern" to refer to societies that, in some cases, have not even gone through the stage of modernity. The use of these terms is thus seen as an extrapolation of a phenomenon alien to the sociohistorical reality of the Hispanic world, if not as a new case of cultural imperialism.[31]

Among those who defend the relevance to Latin America of the postmodernism debate, attitudes differ depending on the critical orientation of each theorist. On the one hand, there are those who define postmodernism in terms of a poetics (that is, as a group of techniques that define the style of a group of authors). On the other, there are those who propose a sociohistorical approach in which postmodernism would be the cultural manifestation of the most recent social developments. No systematic theories have yet been produced on this topic, however. As has been already noted, the field of Latin-American postmodernism studies has only recently emerged and is still in the process of defining itself. Although the volume of critical production has grown vertiginously in the last five years, the lack of agreement on its basic premises is still overwhelming.[32]

Julio Ortega: Toward an International Postmodernism

A representative example of a formalist perspective is Julio Ortega's essay on postmodern literature (1988).[33] Ortega supports the use of the terms modernism and postmodernism in Latin America. In order to avoid confusion, he distinguishes between what he labels "international modernism" (the artistic movement led by Pound, Eliot, and Joyce, but also coinciding with the programs of the avant-garde in Spanish America), and "modernismo hispanoamericano" or "nineteenth-century modernism." Ortega sees postmodernism not as a rupture with, but as an extension of modernism, owing to the influence of the avant-gardes in both movements. According to him, although the avant-gardes originated in international modernism, they have since managed to survive the modernist debacle and have kept the innovatory spirit alive within postmodernism.

Ortega takes his defining characteristics of postmodernism from two very dissimilar critics: John Barth and Fredric Jameson. From Barth, he adopts some of the formal devices of the postmodern repertoire and their treatment of the problem of representation. In works such as *Cien años de soledad*, language does not limit itself to problematizing its relationship with reality (as happens in modernist texts), rather it questions "natural logic itself, the very presence of the word and its laws in the book . . . it does not seek to reveal, replace, or reformulate reality, but aims to show how it can both represent and undo a variety of realities."[34] Language is seen as a modus operandi, whose transformations simultaneously constitute "a game and an inquiry" that the reader can evaluate, on the basis of its innovative power. Unlike realist texts, *Cien años de soledad* induces a new kind of reading that is submitted to a permanent state of revision and in which all realities cancel each other out (including the reality of the novel itself).

While Barth establishes a continuity between what he calls Cervantes's premodernism, Borges's *dernier cri* modernism, and García Márquez's postmodernism, Ortega supports this continuity but questions Barth's categorization. According to Ortega, Cervantes's modernity is unquestionable. Like Rabelais and Sterne, Cervantes is in many senses more modern than Tolstoy or Balzac. Ortega bases his concept of modernity on an author's use of self-conscious irony and the parodic possibilities of a novel. Correspondingly, Borges is for Ortega the author who allowed Latin-American postmodernism to emerge.[35] Although his literary beginnings were closely linked to the avant-garde and, especially, to *ultraísmo*, Borges moved away from these positions to eventually become the main transgressor of institutional modernism. His fiction and essays tend to replace the modernist vision of a totalizing text by "the notion of the work as a deferred entity, to be annotated and commented upon."[36] The two distinctive characteristics of postmodern culture in Jameson's view (the transformation of reality into images and the fragmentation of time into a series of momentary presents) were already part of Borges's annotatory style. In "El Aleph," for example, Borges rewrites the epiphanic tradition, making a small object into an image that is capable of revealing the entire universe; an image that resists transcription and implies a vision of time that is knowable only as a series of perpetual presents.

Ortega concludes by stating that the great Latin American novels (*Pedro Páramo, Rayuela, Los ríos profundos, Cien años de soledad, Tres tristes tigres, Terra Nostra,* and *Paradiso*) all sprang from international modernism. In addition to applying techniques and motives adopted from foreign traditions, those novels also confront the modernist vision and practice with their own literary and historical context. In so doing, they problematize high modernism, conferring on postmodernity a more critical accent on both the aesthetic and social level.

Néstor García Canclini: Hybrid Cultures

A less celebratory approach to this phenomenon is offered by cultural anthropologist Néstor García Canclini. In *Culturas Híbridas* (1989), García Canclini examines the paradoxes resulting from transnational politics and cultures, and their influence on the postmodernism debate.[37] He is critical of the two most common attitudes regarding Latin American postmodernism: those who spurn a postmodern perspective in a continent that has yet to be fully modernized; and those who regard a hybrid Latin America as the geographical paragon of postmodernity.[38] García Canclini rejects both the paradigm of imitation and of originality. He considers the view of the Latin American intellectual as an imitator of metropolitan models a rough stereotype. And yet, he finds it is equally misleading to mystify Latin American cultural and socioeconomic hybridity. García Canclini's proposal, while accepting the usefulness of postmodern discourse in Latin America, acknowledges the need to develop a critical model that would account for the relationships between tradition, cultural postmodernity, and the Western socioeconomic modernization of which Latin America is a part.

Among the aspects that make an understanding of postmodernity difficult, García Canclini refers to the lack of synchronicity between the social realities of the "First" and the "Third" worlds. Thus, while postmodernism is hegemonic in the art, architecture, and philosophy of Western developed countries, most sectors of

Latin America's economy and politics display an uneven modern-ization. This leads many Latin American intellectuals to an ironic underestimation of the postmodernism debate ("Why should we go about worrying about postmodernity if on our continent modern advances have not yet arrived completely, nor for everyone?").[39] A significant part of Latin America has enjoyed neither a solid indus-trialization nor an extended mechanization of its agriculture. Even the relative advantages of political liberalism have been denied to many of its countries, which have suffered the consequences of suc-cessive military rules.

Although modernization arrived late and was unequally distrib-uted, its impact is noticeable in most of the urban centers where the most diverse stages of economic and cultural evolution overlap. García Canclini believes that Latin America should be treated as a complex articulation of traditions and modernities, "a heteroge-neous continent made up of countries in which multiple paths of development coexist."[40] García Canclini sees in the antievolutionist reflection of postmodernism a valid and useful instrument with which to explore Latin America's heterogeneous reality. Postmo-dernity is understood "not as a stage or tendency that would replace the modern world, but as a way of problematizing the equivocal links that that world forged with the traditions it sought to exclude or to supersede in order to constitute itself."[41]

While cultural modernity was based on the division between high, popular, and mass culture as radically different spheres whose relationship was frequently conflictive and antithetical, postmodern relativism facilitates the revision of such boundaries and the con-templation of these three manifestations of culture as constitutive of the collective sensibility of Latin American contemporaneity. García Canclini sees in postmodern thought a starting point for the constitution of "nomadic social sciences" that would be able to cir-culate through all the levels of this artificial division of culture and even to reorganize these levels in a horizontal and democratic way. These mechanisms would allow us to follow the trace left by the dissemination and transnationalization of culture effected by new technologies and the mass media.

The model that García Canclini seeks, while different from Jame-son's generalizations about Third World culture, coincides with Jameson's view in its urgent need to create an oppositional model that could be applied to the social totality. For, as García Canclini suggests, "in this time of postmodern dissemination and democratic decentering, we are also seeing the strongest manifestations of the accumulation of power and of the transnational centralization of culture that humanity has ever known."[42]

George Yúdice, John Beverly, José Oviedo, and Neil Larsen:
Reconceptualizing Postmodernism from a New Left Perspective

García Canclini's work cleared the path for a number of essays that take a similar sociocultural approach. A sympathetic response to his call for the creation of nomadic social sciences can be found in the works on postmodernism by George Yúdice, John Beverly, José Oviedo, and Neil Larsen. Like García Canclini, Yúdice insists on the need for a critical perspective when studying Latin American postmodernism. In his view, postmodernity is not a poetics or an episteme that has replaced modernity. On the contrary, it should be defined as "a series of conditions variously holding in different social formations that elicit diverse responses and propositions to the multiple ways in which modernization has been attempted in them."[43] This viewpoint contemplates the relationship between modernity and postmodernity in terms of critical revisionism rather than of rupture. In Latin America postmodernism is characterized by the rearticulation of tradition within new cultural patterns that neither reject nor celebrate the past, but critically assume it.

Beverly, Oviedo, and Larsen have evaluated Latin American postmodernism from a similar oppositional perspective. For Beverly, in Latin America the hegemonic cultural dominant—what Jameson calls the cultural logic of late capitalism—intermingles with distinct local forms of expression.[44] The resulting transculturation compels the critic to adopt new forms of analysis and to renovate the dated critical tools of the old left. In a similar fashion, Larsen (1990) champions the existence of a Latin American "left postmodernism," as exemplified by testimonial literature, Liberation Theology, Ernesto Laclau's neo-Marxism, and the work of the Cuban critic Roberto Fernández Retamar.[45] Larsen's effort, like Yúdice's and Beverly's is mainly directed to present postmodernism as a heterogeneous phenomenon, a consequence of the interaction between a global omnipresent world system and local resisting cultures. Beverly and Oviedo (1993) take this proposition to the extreme by inverting Jameson's model. In their view, what the Anglo-American critic labels postmodernism might be better understood other than a movement that emanates from a supposed center (advanced capitalist societies) toward neocolonial periphery (the "Third World"). Postmodernism is "precisely the effect in that center of postcoloniality," and is not so much the "end"of modernity as the end of Western hegemony.[46] In their attempt to reshape a concept of postmodernism that would account for the liberatory potential of local cultures, these critics tend to favor discourses more akin to the political project of the new Latin American left (testimony, feminism, and popular culture). Such expressions are usually presented in opposition to the traditional elitism of the Latin American intelligentsia, and parallel to the new forms of grassroots organization that have emerged in recent years.

The Self-reflexive Text

One of the most distinguishing features of contemporary narrative is its tendency to focus on its own processes. This self-reflexivity responds to a general trend in the realm of contemporary discourse. The human sciences (such as history, sociology, psychology, linguistics, and anthropology) as well as the more traditional disciplines of the humanities (such as philosophy, rhetoric, and aesthetics) have grown increasingly subjective and figurative, making explicit the questions and assumptions that ground their own methods. Metafiction echoes this tendency toward self-representation and makes it a part of its own structure. Consequently, the distinction between separate discourses becomes blurred, as does the borderline between art and theory, fiction and reality.

The Metafictional Paradigm

The earliest discussions on metafiction date back to 1970. Although terms such as "metatheater" and "metapolitics" had already been used, "metafiction" originated in William H. Gass's *Fictions and the Figures of Life*.[47] For Gass, metafiction is an expression of a dilemma found in all works of art: "In every art two contradictory impulses are in a state of Manichean war: the impulse to communicate and so to treat the medium of communication as a means and the impulse to make an artifact out of the materials and so to treat the medium as an end."[48] Many of the so-called antinovels are, in Gass's view, metafictions, that is, fictions that emphasize the process of narration over the referent itself.

Following Gass's suggestion, Robert Scholes uses the term "metafiction" to refer to those narrative works that deal primarily with mechanisms of representation. Scholes distinguishes among four basic dimensions of fiction: fiction of forms (romance), fiction of existence (novel), fiction of ideas (myth), and fiction of essence (allegory). Each of these types corresponds to four kinds of criticism (formal, behavioral, structural, and philosophical). Although metafiction may emphasize one or several of these dimensions and perspectives, it incorporates them all into the fictional process itself. In *Fabulation and Metafiction* (1979), Scholes suggests a similarity between metafiction and the fable.[49] Both are narrative forms that show a particular delight in design, strong authorial control, and a didactic quality.[50] Scholes's essays ultimately fail to offer a general theorization of metafiction. He actually uses this term synonymously with "modern fabulation" and "experimental fiction," without establishing a clear distinction among the three.

A convincing definition of metafiction is offered in Robert Alter's *Partial Magic* (1975): "A self-conscious novel, briefly, is a novel that systematically flaunts its own condition of artifice and that by so doing probes into the problematic relationship between real-seeming artifice and reality."[51] Alter sees the self-conscious novel as an expression of dominant trends in modern intellectual culture, such as critical-philosophical awareness, a skeptical approach about the nature of fiction and reality, and the supreme affirmation of art as a reaction against prevalent chaos and dissolution. *Partial Magic* chronicles self-conscious fiction from Renaissance Spain to contemporary France and the United States. Although admitting the presence of the self-consciousness in even the most realistic novels, Alter reserves this label for more radical manifestations: "A fully self-conscious novel . . . is one in which from beginning to end, through the style, the handling of narrative viewpoint, the names and words imposed on the characters, the patterning of the narration, the nature of the characters and what befalls them, there is a consistent effort to convey to us a sense of the fictional world as an authorial construct set up against a background of literary tradition and convention."[52]

Alter's definition of the self-conscious novel has been refined by other critics, such as Patricia Waugh: "Metafiction is a term given to fictional writing which self-consciously and systematically draws attention to its status as an artifact in order to pose questions about the relationship between fiction and reality."[53] In unveiling its own artificiality, metafiction reveals the process through which our idea of the world is similarly constructed. Both Alter and Waugh consider metafiction not as an exclusive phenomenon of contemporary narrative, but as a part of an old tradition. In fact, more than half of Alter's book is devoted to early premodernist self-conscious novels and, although Waugh's essay focuses on contemporary works, she too acknowledges that "the practice is as old (if not older) than the novel itself."[54] What distinguishes the self-consciousness of much contemporary fiction is the new sense that "reality or history are provisional: no longer a world of eternal verities but a series of constructions, artifices, impermanent structures."[55]

Other critics who have dealt extensively with these topics include Gerald Graff (*Literature Against Itself*, 1979) and Linda Hutcheon (*Narcissistic Narrative*, 1980). Graff's book is written as a reaction against antimimetic theories that, he believes, have trivialized literature and criticism and tried to deprive these of their educational power.[56] In Graff's opinion, there is no escape from mimesis: All art represents nature. Even the most radical forms of antirealism and metafiction are paradoxically mimetic, since they mirror a reality in which there seem to be no stable referents: "Where reality has become unreal, literature qualifies as our guide to reality by derealizing itself."[57] In Graff's moral view, literature must bring understanding and order to—and not be a mere celebration of—an increasingly nihilistic culture.

Hutcheon's book also deals with antirealism, although from a very different perspective. While Graff condemns what he considers the postmodern relativistic attack on meaning, Hutcheon celebrates the transgressive impulse of contemporary metafiction. Unlike the forms of nineteenth-century realism, which were based on what Hutcheon calls a "mimesis of product," modern metafiction is "a mimesis of process" in which readers are creatively involved.[58] Drawing on reader-response theories, Hutcheon sees metafiction as a narrative form that allegorizes the process of its own creation, while reflecting on its linguistic nature. The dominance of one of these two mimetic impulses leads Hutcheon to classify metafictional texts into two groups: diegetically self-conscious texts (those that emphasize their own creative process) and linguistically self-reflexive texts (those that foreground the limits and powers of language). In both cases, metafictional works are trapped in a paradox: They invite the reader to participate in the creation of meaning, while simultaneously distancing that reader through their very self-reflexiveness.

The ambiguity and all-inclusiveness of the metafictional models have provoked several reactions. In *Beyond the Metafictional Mode* (1984) Robert C. Spires proposes a more selective approach.[59] Based on Spanish fictional texts and Scholes's theory of genres, Spires defines metafiction as a narrative mode bordering on theory and diametrically opposed to reportorial fiction, which is at the very edge of nonfiction in the form of history. Unlike the previous models, which identified every self-conscious work of fiction as meta-fictional, Spires's model reserves the former term for the self-referential novel (that is, the novel that above all refers to itself as a process of writing and reading). Spires bases his analysis of meta-fiction on a linguistically oriented theory of modes. Although he focuses on the metafictional forms that emerged in Spain during the sixties and seventies, he believes that modes are atemporal. Unlike genres or movements, which have a diachronic value, modes are synchronic structures that can occur in any period of history.

Although postmodern historical novels problematize Spires's view of metafiction as contrary to documentary fiction, his approach succeeds in emphasizing the need to establish a more accurate use of critical terms. Spires's attribution of the term "metafiction" to those narrative forms that are self-conscious as well as consistently self-referential is valuable in the study of the self-reflexive component of the works under discussion, even though in the case of historiographic metafiction the referent goes beyond the strict limits of the work itself.[60]

Lucien Dällenbach's Grammar of the Mise en Abyme

Among the specular devices by which a novel can be made to mirror itself, critics have paid special attention to the *mise en abyme*.[61] This term was originally adapted by André Gide from the language of heraldry, and was used to describe the image of a shield that showed in its interior a miniaturized replica of itself.[62] In his novel *Les Faux-monnayeurs*, Gide adapted this concept to literary practice by presenting a character who is himself a novelist working on a novel entitled *Les Faux-monnayeurs*, in which there is also a self-conscious author similarly involved in the writing of a novel with no other subject than itself. The forms and possibilities of this major form of textual reflexivity have been thoroughly studied by Lucien Dällenbach in *Le récit spéculaire* (*The Mirror in the Text*). In his examination of the ways in which one element of a work can mirror the work as a whole, Dällenbach establishes a typology of both the modalities of duplication and of the structural levels of re-flection. On the basis of examples drawn from painting (Van Eyck and Velázquez) and literary works (the New French novel), he de-fines the *mise en abyme* as "any internal mirror that reflects the whole of the narrative by simple, repeated or 'specious' (or para-doxical) duplication."[63] Simple duplication occurs when a sequence maintains a similarity with the work that encloses it, as in Gide's shield within a shield. In the case of infinite duplication, this relationship is endlessly multiplied in a way that evokes an image reflected by two parallel mirrors (the mirroring fragment bears within itself another mirroring fragment, and so on). Finally, the paradoxical—or aporetical—duplication consists of a sequence that seems to enclose the work that encloses it in an endless spiral.

In addition to these three types of duplication, Dällenbach distinguishes among four structural levels of reflection that rarely occur in a pure form, but frequently overlap. By fictional *mise en abyme*, he refers to the "intertextual résumé or quotation of the content of a work."[64] This is the device being used when, for example, a narrative offers a compilation of the events or motifs that have been thus far presented, or when it anticipates a synthesis of the events about to occur. The *mise en abyme* of the enunciation, in turn, 1) makes present in the diegesis the producer or receiver of the work; 2) reveals the production or reception per se; or 3) manifests the context that determines this production / reception. The third level of reflection in Dällenbach's taxonomy is the *mise en abyme* of the code ("metatextual"), which reveals the form in which the text functions, "but without being mimetic of the text itself."[65] This level operates as a set of instructions that allow us to read the novel in the way it "wants" to be read, and it usually encompasses an aesthetic theory or debate, a manifesto, a creed, or any "indication of the purpose assigned to the book by the author or by the book itself."[66] To these three basic levels Dällenbach adds a more obscure one, which he calls transcendental *mise en abyme* or fiction of origin. By these terms, he refers to that which reflects "what simultaneously originates, motivates, institutes, and unifies" the narrative and determines in advance what makes that narrative possible. It also implies the question of how a work conceives its relationship to mimesis and truth.

Dällenbach's grammar of the *mise en abyme* provides a useful guideline for the exploration of reflexivity in fiction. By means of his complete categorization, we can grasp the complexities of the novel's self-representation. Rather than overuse a term that does not exist in English, I will henceforth use the following four English equivalents (depending on the level of reflection involved). "Reflections of the Utterance" refers to the ways in which the novel summarizes and/or quotes itself; "Reflections of the Enunciation" indicates the representations of the text's producer and/or receiver; "Reflections of the Code" denotes the representations of its functioning principle (either narrative or linguistic); and "Fictions of Origin" designates those mythic constructions that reveal the origin and effect of the work's writing. These descriptions and functions will be studied within the particular context of each of the four major texts under consideration, since self-reflexivity is ambivalent and may therefore be used to different—and sometimes even opposite—ends. For example, critics have mentioned the totalizing effect that results from the use of these miniature scale reflections. In presenting images of totality, the narrative work seeks to overcome its own representational limitations. However, this longing for totality is denied by some of its most characteristic forms, such as the aporetical duplication, in which the reflecting and the reflected elements exchange positions. The use of these levels of reflection in postmodern fiction is intrinsically paradoxical, since they give an air of totality to narrative models that are deliberately discontinuous and purport to resist totalization.

Other conceptual problems emerge from the analysis of these reflexive devices. For example, the question of to what extent the *mise en abyme* is self-consciously used, or is merely the result of the critic's obsessive allegorical reading; whether it is a device that guarantees the literariness of the fictional text or maintains a connection with extratextual reality. Dällenbach eludes these problems by adopting the New Critics' position on the intentional fallacy, according to which there is no need for explicit evidence of the author's intention in order to discover the work's modes of self-representation. From this perspective, authorial intention and extratextual relationships lack interest and relevance. Dällenbach's work is best understood within the context of an aspect of formalism that seeks to make reflexivity the defining characteristic of all literature and art. As David Carroll suggests, "the *mise en abyme* has largely been considered a tool of formalist critics used to ensure the purity of the literary and to exclude the extra-literary from having any significant impact on literary texts."[67] For its part, historiographic metafiction reacts against this aesthetic closure, and opens the work up to the impact of the historical and the sociopolitical, without having to reduce its self-conscious dimension. Because of its hybrid nature—between self-referentiality and historical meditation—this new form of historical fiction demands a different approach. The chapters that follow will combine textual analyses with the study of the cultural project of their authors and the literary and historical context in which they were produced.

WRITING HISTORY IN A POSTMODERN ERA

Many of the tendencies of the theory of self-conscious fiction may be equally appreciated in the contemporary philosophy of history. Like other branches of the humanities, the study of history has benefited from intellectual developments in other discursive realms (especially in philosophy and literary theory). Of special interest is the increasing tendency among philosophers of history to question basic assumptions about the goal and method of history. As Keith Jenkins points out, philosophy, literature, and history "have engaged very seriously with the question of what is the nature of their own nature."[68]

The relativism and skepticism that characterize postmodernism have had a strong impact on the epistemological practices of many contemporary historians, to whom the search for truth in the past appears even more unrealistic.[69] We can hardly speak today of an exclusive historical discourse. Instead, there only seem to be positions, outlooks, models, and angles that fluctuate according to different paradigms. The postmodern thinkers resort to various discursive forms and interpretations while simultaneously reflecting on both the way they use them and their possible limitations. This vision of history is based on the assumption that one can observe a single phenomenon from multiple perspectives, without considering any of the resulting historical narratives as having a necessary permanence or as being expressive of any particular essence.

One of the greatest efforts of postmodern historians is directed toward breaking the myth of an identity between the past and history. The past is obviously the historian's domain, but such a past can only be approached through limited and necessarily inconclusive discursive practices. This critical reconceptualization of history may have a democratizing effect, since it allows even the most marginal sectors to produce and validate their own versions of the past: "Querying the notion of the historian's truth, pointing to the variable facticity of facts, insisting that historians write the past from ideological positions, stressing that history is a written discourse as liable to deconstruction as any other, arguing that the 'past' is as notional a concept as 'the real world' to which novelists allude in realist fictions—only ever existing in the present discourses that articulate it—all these things destabilize the past and fracture it, so that, in the cracks opened up, new histories can be made."[70]

Postmodern thinkers in different fields have thoroughly revised traditional visions of history. The idea of the historian as a witness, for example, has been dismantled by contemporary epistemology.[71] This concept was based on the need for immediacy between the historian and the narrated events. New discoveries in the philosophy of science, however, demonstrate that there are no bare facts. Those past events that enter our knowledge (even those that are apparently empirical) are already perceived in a certain way and thus are not "natural" but theoretical.[72] Positivistic visions of the historian as a scientist have equally been disputed. At the end of nineteenth century, philosophers and historians such as Taine, Michelet, Comte, and Ranke tended to consider that facts spoke by themselves, and from the scientific analysis of these facts, inevitably emerged the rules that governed them. In unveiling the process of mediation inherent in the writing of history and its inescapable ideological component, postmodern historiography invalidates the assumptions of positivism. Following the direction pointed to by Nietzsche in *The Use and Abuse of History*, new philosophers of history state that facts do not exist in themselves. For a fact to exist we first need to introduce meaning: "history is never itself, is never said or read (articulated, expressed, discoursed) innocently, but . . . it is always for someone."[73] Every historian guides the text in a specific direction. As Paul Veyne points out, facts do not exist in isolation, but are always part of a plot created by a particular historian.[74] The façade of objectivity supported by empiricism and positivism in historiography loses all its value when we are aware of the fetishism of the document and its consequent naively realistic methodology.[75] Even the personality more recently adopted by historians—that of the reconstructor of a past mystery through a detective plot—is likewise submitted to revision.[76] This view of history implies the resolution of a previous enigma through the collection of evidence. In making manifest the multiplicity of possible versions of the past and unveiling both the historian's ideological manipulation and the impossibility of any final closure, postmodern philosophers of history show the artificiality and limitations of this new fiction of the historian. Above all, the postmodern vision of history seeks to problematize the concept of referentiality, which had traditionally been presented in mechanistic—if not simplistic—terms.

Two tendencies play a crucial role in the postmodern revision of history: the substitution of organic views of history by fragmentary views and the reevaluation of narrative in history writing. The former finds one of its most radical formulations in Michel Foucault's work, whereas the latter has been taken to its limits by Hayden White's formal analysis of history. Both seek to disclose the mediation inherent in the textualization of the past. Foucault's work unravels attempts to formulate a global theory of history, and instead proposes the writing of fragmentary narratives (microhistories) that focus on differences rather than on continuities. White's works, in turn, reveal the poetic (tropologic) and cultural character of all histories. Both of these theorists offer self-reflexive alternatives to the so-called crisis of historical representation.

Michel Foucault: The Genealogy of Microhistories

As happens with the analysis of any aspect of his thought, a study of Foucault's historical vision will encounter a series of obstacles due to his radical contempt for all forms of systematic theoretization. One's attention is inevitably drawn to the incredible number of paradoxes, ambiguities, and interruptions in the course of his argument. In Foucault's fragmentary discourse, ideas often follow one another with no clear logical causality, remain temporally suspended, or are obscured by a multiplicity of metaphors. This heterodox and provocative aspect of his style is a substantial part—as well as the formal manifestation—of the historical vision that he theorized in "Nietzsche, Genealogy and History" (1971) and put into practice in works such as *Discipline and Punish* (1975), and *History of Sexuality* (1976).[77]

Following Nietzsche's *On the Genealogy of Morals*, Foucault proposes "genealogical analysis" as an alternative to traditional history. Unlike historians concerned with finding the story that will inexorably lead to the present, Foucault's history seeks to delegitimize that present by questioning the causality that binds it to the past. In Foucault's analysis, there is no place for the concepts of continuity and progress fostered by historiographic empiricism. On the contrary, in focusing on all those aspects that are different, he counteracts the notion of historical inevitability through which all historians seek to justify their ideas and strengthen their intellectual authority. Foucault's philosophy of history unmasks the epistemological naiveté of empiricist historians, who were traditionally represented as truth seekers. The historian's search does not aim at truth, but at knowledge, which is understood as a source of power. Historical writing thus becomes a means of taming the past with specific legitimating effects: "Historical writing," Foucault contends, "is a practice that has effects, and these effects tend, whatever one's political party, to erase the difference of the past and justify a certain version of the present."[78]

The genealogist's historical method, on the contrary, is based on the methodical observation of differences: "it must record the singularity of events outside of any monotonous finality; it must seek them in the most unpromising places, in what we tend to feel is without history—in sentiments, love, conscience, instincts."[79] The Nietzschean historian starts from the present and goes back to the past until he spots a difference. At that point, he begins to describe the evolution of such an anomaly and the transformations it undergoes through time, always taking into account the need to preserve continuities as well as discontinuities: "These alien discourses/ practices are then explored in such a way that their negativity in relation to the present explodes the 'rationality' of the phenomena that are taken for granted. When the technology of power of the past is elaborated in detail, present-day assumptions which posit the past as 'irrational,' are undermined."[80]

In his study on Nietzsche, Foucault proposes three alternative uses of the historical sense that oppose the three Platonic modalities of history. The first is parodic and directed against reality (opposes history as reminiscence or recognition). The second is dissociating and destroys identity (opposes history as continuity or tradition); and the third is sacrificial and undermines truth (opposes history as knowledge).[81] These three transgressive uses contribute to the formation of an alternative history to which Foucault indistinctly refers to as "effective history"and "genealogy." From his point of view, "history becomes 'effective' to the degree that it introduces discontinuity into our very being—as it divides our emotions, dramatizes our instincts, multiplies our body and sets it against itself. 'Effective' history deprives the self of the reassuring stability of life and nature, and it will not permit itself to be transported by a voiceless obstinacy toward a millennial ending. It will uproot its traditional foundations and relentlessly disrupt its pretended continuity. This is because knowledge is not made for understanding; it is made for cutting."[82]

As a global theory of history, Foucault's work is obviously insufficient and obscure. His refusal to deal with epistemological problems—and the vagueness of many of his basic concepts—makes its reading especially difficult and its evaluation nearly impossible. His is, above all, an oppositional work that offers a scathing criticism of some of the basic assumptions held by historical realism. The greatest achievements of Foucault's thought are thus not in theory but in the realm of practice. His most brilliant pages are those referring to the microhistory of specific phenomena, such as the history of prisons or the history of sexuality. In these studies, he forces us to rethink the notions of knowledge and power that we have been taking for granted.

Hayden White: A Tropological Approach to Historical Discourse

A different approach to history—although equally representative of postmodern skepticism—is that offered by Hayden White. Following the relativization of historical knowledge initiated by European continental thinkers from Valéry and Heidegger to Sartre and Lévi-Strauss, and the refutation of the scientific nature of history undertaken by Anglo-American philosophers (Mink, Dray, and Danto), White proposes a formal analysis of the historical work's narrative structure. This approach originates in the consideration of the historian as narrator and of all writing as inherently poetic. In White's opinion, the historical work is, above all, a verbal structure whose form responds to the stylistic imperatives of narrative prose.[83] All historiographic activity is thus limited to metahistory; that is, to a reflection made a posteriori, organized on the bases of other texts and according to the rhetorical conventions of poetic discourse. In his works, White underlines the process of mediation that characterizes each of the steps in the construction of historical discourse. The very process of the selection and exclusion of events and evidence is inevitably conditioned by the historian's prejudices and interests, hence White's emphasis on the structure of exclusion that characterizes the narrativization of the past: "Our explanations of historical structures and processes are thus determined more by what we leave out of our representations than by what we put in. For it is in this brutal capacity to exclude certain facts in the interest of constituting others as components of comprehensible stories that the historian displays his tact as well as his understanding."[84]

In his attempt to refute the empiricist pretensions of traditional history, White questions the purely archeological value of historiography and, instead, emphasizes its narrative component. The data contained in the historical archive, and present in the form of documents and chronicles are organized by the historian according to their signification and their relationship to the rest of his work. To this construct the historian adds particular observations that allow us to understand an event in the light of his or her ultimate project. The writing of history becomes an act in which invention which was originally reserved for fiction is not completely absent, and actually plays a dominant role in most cases.[85]

In *Metahistory* (1973), White distinguishes among five levels of historiographic conceptualization: chronicle, story, mode of emplotment, mode of argumentation, and mode of ideological implication. The historical work is conceived of as an attempt to mediate between what White calls a historical field (the unprocessed document) and a public. In this scheme, chronicle alludes to the disposition of events in the order in which they occurred. Chronicles therefore constitute a phase previous to history that lack closure (Danto calls them "preparatory exercises").[86] They also lack inaugural and climactic parts; they simply start when an author begins to chronicle the events, and can be continued indefinitely. The transition from chronicle to story occurs when the writer begins to combine the events as part of the components of what While calls a "spectacle"—or process of happening—to which the historian assigns a beginning, a middle, and an end. While in chronicles an event constitutes a position in a series, in the story, that event becomes significant as an element of a narrative. Unlike chronicles, stories trace the sequence of events that lead from inaugural to conclusive—although always provisional—phases of social and cultural processes.

The arrangement of events drawn from chronicles and their incorporation into a story give rise to a series of questions that the historian has to anticipate and respond to in the course of constructing his narrative: What happened at that moment in time? How did it happen? Why did it happen in precisely this way, and not some other? These questions permeate the historian's total narrative project and are answered in several ways. White limits these possibilities of explanation to three types: 1) explanation by emplotment; 2) explanation by formal argument; and 3) explanation by ideological implication. Within each of these interpretative strategies he distinguishes among several possible modes of articulation respectively: 1) romance, satire, comedy, and tragedy; 2) formalism, organicism, mechanicism, and contextualism; and 3) anarchism, conservatism, radicalism, and liberalism. The historian's style results in his particular combination of these modes. Historiographic style is the result of an essentially poetic act that prefigures the historical field and constitutes the structure in relation to which the different interpretations of the past will be undertaken. The narrative modalities chosen by the historian are ultimately elaborated by the use of certain rhetorical figures. In order to theorize this rhetorical dimension of historiography, White resorts to the four basic Aristotelian tropes of poetic language: metaphor, metonymy, synecdoche, and irony. The dominant tropes in historical narrative contribute in a very special way to support the author's theses and produce particular effects on readers.

In his metahistorical analysis, White comes to the following conclusions: 1) there is no "history" that is not at the same time a "philosophy of history;" 2) the historiographic modes are formal-

izations of previous poetic perceptions that sanction theories used
to give the historical account the appearance of an "explanation";
3) the demand of a scientific history reveals only a preference
among the multiple modalities of historical conceptualization; 4)
the choice of one or another historical perspective is not of a moral
or aesthetic, but of an epistemological, order.[87]

As might be expected, White's theories were soon celebrated by
literature departments and strongly criticized—when not ignored—by an important part of the historiographic establishment.
One of the most balanced evaluations of White's work has been undertaken by Dominick LaCapra. As a confessed supporter of interdisciplinary perspectives in the study of history and literature,
LaCapra admits the necessity for traditional historiography to open
itself to new developments in philosophy and literary theory. He
does suggest, however, that it should do so critically. Although opposed to the objectivism of empiricist historiography, LaCapra similarly rejects the radical inversion of that model, which leads to a
reductionism of the opposite sign. For LaCapra, White's initial
model (the one prevalent in *Metahistory*) is characterized by a gen-
erative structuralism that presents the figurative or "tropologic"
component as determinant of the other discursive levels. In White's
theory, form seems to determine content and ideology. On the other
hand, White's initial work assumes the possibility of "neutral" documentary forms upon which the historian would impose a narrative
form. White's subjectivist relativism emerges, according to LaCapra, from a neo-idealist and formalist vision of history as a formal
imposition on an inert documentary register. LaCapra, on the contrary, suggests the textuality of all documentary forms: "the documentary record is itself always textually processed before any given
historian comes to it."[88] On the basis of Bakhtin's concept of dialo-
gism and Freud's notion of "transference," LaCapra poses that the
writing of history implies a permanent exchange between the historian and the texts of the past, which in their turn maintain a similar
interaction with other texts. In his vision, the document is not something that inertly awaits the historian's manipulation, but also exercises an impact on the sociohistorical context in which it is
produced and reproduced. In this sense, LaCapra's theoretical
model—although tenuously outlined—allows an effective alternative to both the extreme objectivism and subjectivism that dominate
contemporary visions of history.

The theories by White and LaCapra are symptomatic of the so-
called revival of narrative that has occurred in the philosophy of
history over the last two decades.[89] Most of the thinkers who sup-

port the eminently narrative nature of the historical work tend to contemplate the difference between history and fiction as an intentional—rather than a formal—problem. From the point of view of their tropological resources, both fiction and history present no substantial differences. However, this consideration of historical discourse as a narrative construction neither opens the door to all possibilities nor places all historical works on the same level. As Roland Barthes pointed out in a pioneering essay on this tendency ("The Discourse of History," 1967), even though past can be represented by a broad variety of tropes and modes, some are less mythological or mystifying than others.[90] In particular, Barthes proposes self-consciousness as an important standard in the evaluation of historiography. Those historical works that unveil their own processes of production and expose the artificial and constructed nature of their referents are more reliable than those that present themselves as indisputable.[91] This need for a reflexive methodology (self-conscious and scrutinizing of other textual practices) is one of the most recurrent claims in the postmodern philosophy of history. The main contribution of the works of Foucault, White, and LaCapra consists of the radical historization of history. Through their problematizing models, we can examine how previous or contemporary histories were constituted and received at a particular moment. Their works offer skeptical but critically reflexive approaches that allow us to explore the world in which we live and the forms of history that have contributed to producing it.

2
Heretical History:
Carlos Fuentes's Theater of Memory

HISTORY AND SELF-REFLEXIVITY IN THE WRITINGS OF CARLOS FUENTES

From his first short-story collection, *Los días enmascarados* (1954), to his most recent books, Fuentes has shown an almost obsessive concern for the rewriting of history. In his texts the past is not a closed and passive realm waiting for purely archeological investigations, but is multidimensional, open, reinterpretable, and alive in our contemporary world. For Fuentes the ideal medium to explore this past is not the discursive province of history, but the imaginative space of fiction. His goal is to bring to light the dark areas of the historical register, or as Fuentes himself writes, "to give voice to the silences of our history."[1]

As early as *Los días enmascarados*, Fuentes began to describe the Mexican past and its conflicting relationship with contemporary reality. In two of the stories included in the collection, "Chac Mool" and "Por boca de los dioses," the pre-Hispanic world lies dormant behind Mexican reality. In "Tlactocatzine," on the other hand, Carlotta, the wife of the nineteenth-century emperor Maximilian, reappears in present-day Mexico. Although forgotten in our daily lives, the past in these three stories is always on the lookout, waiting for an opportunity to burst into our lives and recover possession of its rights. In his remaining early stories, Fuentes sets the action at significant times of Mexican history in order to reflect upon the unavoidable conflict between past memories and present perception. The title of the collection itself, *Los días enmascarados*, alludes to the five final "nameless" days of the Aztec solar calendar, illuminating the importance of the pre-Cortesian traditions to contemporary Mexican culture.

With *La región más trasparente* (1958) Fuentes begins experimenting with the totality of Mexican culture. The main goal of this voluminous novel is to offer a great mural of modern Mexico. To that effect, he resorts to the technique of collage. Adopting John Dos Passos's literary artifices of panoramic montage and "camera eye," he portrays a large number of characters representing different social types of Mexico City. The work's central consciousness, Ixca Cienfuegos, provides a link with the Aztec past. Along with Teodula Moctezuma, Ixca shows his contempt for the mediocrity of modern Mexico and looks to the country's pre-Hispanic roots for a sense of identity. This search is ultimately frustrated, since in Fuentes's novels myths of origin are often incomprehensible to the modern mind. From these early works on, Fuentes's efforts are directed to recuperating this past in a critical way, and especially to understanding its part in the construction of the mestizo culture that constitutes the Mexico of today.

The later publication of *La muerte de Artemio Cruz* (1962) consolidates Fuentes's tendency to reflect upon historical motifs with innovative literary patterns. In what is, until now, his sharpest criticism of post-revolutionary Mexico, Fuentes analyzes the psychology of a representative member of the oligarchy who emerged from the shadows of the Mexican Revolution. Events in the life of the protagonist, Artemio Cruz, correspond to significant episodes in Mexican history. The Revolution, which broke out in 1910, is contemplated here as a mere succession of names in power, one that did not solve the secular injustices that the Mexican nation had suffered. The interest of *La muerte* is historical as well as epistemological. The influence of Dos Passos, which is noticeable in *La región*, is enriched by that of William Faulkner.[2] The former's influence can be appreciated in the use of three narrative voices to describe the same event, while that of Faulkner manifests itself in the use of juxtaposition and multiplication of perspectives to convey both the multiplicity of the self and the subsequent impossibility of achieving definitive versions of the past.

At the same as *La muerte de Artemio Cruz* Fuentes published another work: *Aura*, a short novel in which history and fantasy mingle in a disquieting fashion. The protagonist, a historian who dreams of writing a monumental history of Spain and the Americas, accepts an offer to write the biography of a dead Mexican general and, under the spell of the general's widow, assumes the personality of the deceased. What at first sight appears to be a fantastic plot in the best gothic tradition serves Fuentes, at a deeper level, to present a reflection on both the deceitful mechanisms of memory and the difficulty of reconstructing a personality in a world where identity is endlessly exposed to doubling and dissemination.

This emphasis on the protean quality of the human personality reaches higher levels in Fuentes's following novel, *Cambio de piel* (1967). Once again the pre-Hispanic past, represented by the awesome landscape of Cholula, serves as the background. The novel's opening thematizes the tension between contemporary Mexico and its pre-Hispanic past that characterizes Fuentes's works. Throughout the early part of the novel two parallel narratives intersect: the description of the characters' arrival in contemporary Cholula and Bernal Díaz's account of the Spaniards' entry into the Aztec city in the sixteenth century. The collagelike effect resulting from this violent superposition is enhanced by other devices. For example, in this novel Fuentes introduces with greater intensity than ever before numerous allusions to Mexican and U.S. popular culture. In a similar fashion, the experiments with multiple perspectivism of his previous novels are here taken to such extremes that they sometimes make its reading particularly difficult. The volatility of characters and events, the interest in undermining the logic of discourse and the attribution of the narrative voice to a disturbed mind produce a novel in which the gratuitous experiment at times puts the global design of the novel in danger.

This experimental line has its most recent manifestation in *Cristóbal Nonato* (1987). A work of epic proportions, Fuentes again conceptualizes the novel as an immense historic mural. As in *La región más transparente*, Fuentes resorts to a great display of characters who represent different facets of Mexican society, and the city of Mexico again becomes the protagonist and the space that encompasses the country's reality. As in his earlier works, pre-Hispanic myths reveal their presence in twentieth-century Mexico. However, the almost thirty years that mediate between *La región* and *Cristóbal Nonato* have left their imprint on this latest work. The view that Fuentes offers now is mostly apocalyptic, parodic, and even grotesque. The self-reflexive discourse—which manifested itself only occasionally in his first works, was consolidated in *Cambio de piel*, and reached its limit in *Terra Nostra*—becomes disproportionate in *Cristóbal Nonato*. In this novel of rewarding excesses, the protagonist, an embryo first and then a fetus in the process of gestation, reflects ironically about the process of the novel's production and maintains a playful dialogue with the reader. *Cristóbal Nonato* represents in many senses the apotheosis of the pastiche novel. It is a fiction about fictions that explicitly confesses and reflects upon its borrowings.[3] In it Fuentes portrays the apocalyptic reality of Mexico in a carnivalesque future, which is already past— October 12, 1992, the five-hundredth anniversary of the so-called discovery of America. Fuentes's novel both dramatizes and parodies what Fredric Jameson sees as a recurrent concern about national identity in a postcolonial society, and connects it with the problems of writing. Furthermore, *Cristóbal Nonato* challenges our assumptions that historical statements are objective, neutral, or impartial. Through his self-conscious first-person narrator Fuentes mocks the traditional concept of history as a disinterested and utilitarian enterprise that responds to coherent designs. It views the construction of nation-states in the same terms as the production of novels: Both are acts of fabulation that look for legitimacy in a manipulated past.

Similar concerns recur also in Fuentes's brief dramatic production. His two plays published to date, *El tuerto es rey* and *Todos los gatos son pardos*, discuss Latin American historical problems from a very different perspective. To the Beckettian two-character minimalism of *El tuerto* (1970), *Todos los gatos* (1970) opposes an anti-epic reconstruction of the conquest of ancient Mexico. Both show, however, a common interest in a topic to which Fuentes will return in *Terra Nostra*: the criticism of power and authority. Of the two plays, *Todos los gatos* contains a great number of historical elements that would be elaborated later in *Terra Nostra*.[4]

A survey of Fuentes's creative work would be incomplete without a commentary on his essays. Following the long Spanish-American tradition of the literary essay, Fuentes has frequently underlined the two major concerns of his work: the search for innovative literary forms and historiographic revisionism. In *La nueva novela hispanoamericana* (1969), Fuentes proposes the invention of a new language that would free Spanish-American literature from the limits of documentary and naturalist representation. According to Fuentes, this documentary tendency had its origin in the need to register and evaluate the tensions of a continent that, while searching for an identity, lacked the mechanisms of expression to represent it. The lack of both democratic channels of expression and an emancipated intellectual class forced the novelist to play the role of legislator, reporter, revolutionary, and thinker, as well as novelist.[5]

With the novel of the Revolution and, especially, with the historical revisionism represented by Agustín Yáñez and Juan Rulfo, Fuentes sees an important change taking place in Spanish-American literary history: the introduction of the necessary ambiguity to represent the modern world and, in the case of Rulfo, the articulation of the subject of Revolution with the great universal myths. In Fuentes's view, *Pedro Páramo* laid the groundwork for the new Spanish-American narrative. The new novel was no longer simply a mirror image of the reality of the continent. On the contrary, its narrative created a parallel reality through myth and a new language in order to give literature the voice that history silences. To the monolithic forms of power, Fuentes proposes a language of dissidence, "in short, the language, of ambiguity: of a plurality of meanings, a constellation of allusions: of openness."[6]

While *La nueva novela* represents the first effort at systematizing Fuentes's literary utopia, the essay collection *Tiempo mexicano* (1971) may be defined as the first detailed exposition of his social utopia. Adopting a highly oratorical style, Fuentes analyses Mexican society in its broadest historical perspective. He is particularly interested in the confluence of three great concepts of time in present Mexico: the circular time of pre-Cortesian Mexico, the linear time of European history, and the hybrid forms of time that emerged from *el mestizaje*. In its most critical aspect, Fuentes's essay protests against the monolithic power structures embodied by the Mexican PRI (Institutional Revolutionary Party) and diagnoses the country's history as a succession of "subverted Edens," that is, as a permanent frustration of the dreams of change that have recurred throughout time.

Fuentes's literary and historical revisionism achieves its highest degree of synthesis in a work that is highly important to the study of *Terra Nostra. Cervantes, o la crítica de la lectura* (1976), an essay contemporary to *Terra Nostra*, presents a compendium of Fuentes's aesthetic and historiographic program. The bibliography included at the end of *Cervantes*, "Bibliografía conjunta," applies to both the essay and *Terra Nostra*, published one year before. On an aesthetic level, Fuentes establishes a double literary tradition that corresponds to two antithetical world views: the epic vision, either classical or medieval, that he associates with institutional power and the univocal reading of reality and the heretical view that is opposed to power, subverts order, and aims at perspectivism, openness and ambiguity. Within this framework of conflicting worldviews, Fuentes turns to *Don Quijote* and *Finnegans Wake* to exemplify his multivocal theory of reading and writing. Cervantes's and Joyce's works are seen as reactions of openness in moments in which traditional modes of representation had reached an unbearable degree of closure.

In historical terms, in *Cervantes* Fuentes reflects upon the evolution of Spanish society from the Middle Ages to the death of Charles II, the last of the Spanish Hapsburgs. It is the same historical period on which *Terra Nostra* is focused. This fact, along with the contemporaneity of the two works, makes the essay an invaluable tool in the exegesis of the novel. At this point in his literary career, Fuentes's historical view points in the same direction as his literary program. According to Fuentes, historical events in the Hispanic world subscribe to one of these two great tendencies: one that is stagnant, isolationist, funereal, monolithic, and repressive, and whose paradigm is Philip II (although it had other manifestations throughout history) and another that is dynamic, multicultural, playful, diverse, and liberating, and whose origin is in the interethnic coexistence of medieval Spain. Although constantly repressed by power, the second of these two tendencies emerged periodically in the form of oppositional movements, such as religious heresies, democratic upheavals, and the scientific and cultural revolutions initiated in the Renaissance.

The same view regarding the historical evolution of the Hispanic world can be inferred from one of Fuentes's last macrohistorical essays. In *El espejo enterrado* (1992), Fuentes aims at systematizing his historical meditations of the last forty years. This work, originally conceived as a television series on the occasion of the five-hundred-year anniversary of the "discovery," may be defined as Fuentes's new attempt at reaching a larger public. While historical reflection in *Terra Nostra* was oriented to a small readership, frequently labeled elitist, now Fuentes had an opportunity to answer to these accusations, and so he did by converting a substantial part of the historical material of the novel into both a far-reaching television program and a popular essay widely distributed by a commercial publisher. However, Fuentes's rewriting of the Hispanic past is very similar in both novel and essay, hence my use of *El espejo enterrado* to elucidate Fuentes's treatment of historical elements in *Terra Nostra*. Although the message of *Cervantes* is substantially the same, *El espejo enterrado* offers the advantage of a clearer chronological and thematic organization, as well as the incorporation of additional material dealing with pre-Hispanic history.

Terra Nostra (1975)

Among all of Fuentes's writings, *Terra Nostra* (1975) represents the culmination of his formal and historical pursuit. Several of his novels have experimented with metafictional forms or have inquired deeply into Mexico's past, but in none of them is the paradoxical intertwining of these two tendencies so intense and so successful.

Written during a period in which Spain and much of Latin America suffered the repression of totalitarian regimes (1968–

1975), Fuentes's novel attempts to explain the historical condition experienced by the Hispanic world during the second half of this century.[7] To do so, the Mexican novelist rewrites a good deal of Western history, focusing on the cultural confrontation between imperial Spain and pre-Cortesian Mexico. However, the novel's most outstanding and surprising feature is its recurrent use of an apocryphal history that ends by displacing the vision we have inherited from the official chronicles. In *Terra Nostra* the traditional history of exact chronologies, dynastic successions, and heroic deeds yields to a chaos of characters and narrative voices in which it is at times impossible to establish historical agency. The result is an alternative version of the past where the fantastic elements often turn out to be real, and the apparently real frequently are the product of the author's imagination.

The sense of chaos we experience during the first stages of our reading recede as the reading progresses and finally yields to the opposite impression: All in the novel responds to an all-encompassing design in which the reader is invited to establish connections between the most disparate elements. As Goytisolo has pointed out, *Terra Nostra* subscribes to a great movement in the contemporary novel that does away with the patronizing attitude of orientation and indoctrination, assuming, on the contrary, the existence of an adult and intelligent reader, willing to participate in the enjoyable match play of "reconstructing" the text.[8]

Terra Nostra is divided into three major parts: "The Old World," "The New World," and "The Next World." The novel begins and ends in the apocalyptic Paris of 1999 (chapters 1 and 144). The remaining 142 narrative segments are set mostly in sixteenth-century imperial Spain and in its spheres of influence (America and the Mediterranean). Chapter 1 introduces Pollo Phoibee, an armless youth who witnesses the most extravagant events—among others, the birth of a child with six toes on each foot and a red cross marked on his back. He receives a letter signed by "Ludovico and Celestina" informing him that the child's coming had been foretold by ancient prophecies and compelling him to give the child the name of Iohannes Agrippa. At the *Pont des Arts* Pollo meets a girl with tattooed lips, Celestina. His subsequent fall into the Seine turns out to be a symbolic plunge into sixteenth-century Spain. Celestina throws a sealed green bottle after him and repeats a reversible set of sentences. Thus begins the telling of the stories that make up the novel.

The arrival of three young castaways in northwestern sixteenth-century Spain unleashes a series of enigmas in the first part of *Terra*

Nostra. Each of them bears the same odd characteristics as the child Pollo helped to deliver in the first chapter: six toes on each foot and a red cross on his back. The three shipwreck victims, who are found along with three green bottles, are rescued successively by La Señora, Elizabeth (El Señor's wife), the Mad Lady (El Señor's mother), and Celestina (the page-boy drummer of the queen mother). The first of the castaways becomes Elizabeth's lover, is later transformed into Don Juan, and ends his days as a statue. The second assumes the personality of Philip the Fair, the Mad Lady's deceased husband, and becomes the Idiot Prince, proclaimed inheritor by the Queen consort and forced to marry the dwarf Barbarica. The third is the Pilgrim, taken by Celestina to the palace, where he will relate to El Señor his adventures in the New World (Part II of *Terra Nostra*).

In "The Old World" events and people coincide in El Escorial, the palace-necropolis where El Señor, an imaginary version of Philip II of Spain, waits for the arrival of thirty coffins containing the remains of his ancestors. The characters tell each other stories, enabling the reader to reconstruct their past and the origin and the nature of their conflicts.

The novel's second part, "The New World," is the Pilgrim's story of his journey to ancient Mexico. It reproduces to a great extent the chronicles of the discovery and conquest of the new continent. The first chapters describe his ocean voyage along with Pedro (a former believer in social utopias), the arrival of both on the Beach of Pearls, Pedro's death, the Pilgrim's meetings with the natives of the region and, especially, his trip from the Gulf of Mexico to Tenochtitlan, the capital of the Aztec empire. Throughout his journey, the Pilgrim successfully overcomes a series of trials. Upon arriving in Tenochtitlan he is received by the Aztec sovereign as the long awaited god Quetzalcoatl. During his stay in the capital he kills the Aztec emperor and has to escape in a barge made of serpents.

Part III of the novel, "The Next World," deals with threats to El Señor's monolithic power, as represented in Part I. In "The Next World" many of the enigmas, such as the origin of the three shipwreck victims, are solved. The three youths turn out to be sons of Philip the Fair, El Señor's father, although they were conceived by different mothers. The first is the son of Celestina, raped by the king father the day of her wedding; the second is the son of a she-wolf; and the third is Elizabeth's. Their reappearance at significant moments in Western history is explained in one of the manuscripts that El Señor finds in the mysterious green bottles: Before dying, the Roman Tiberius had cursed his assassin, Agrippa Postumo, to be reborn sometime in the future with the above-mentioned marks. To neutralize the threat represented by his three brothers, El Señor orders their imprisonment: the Idiot Prince with the dwarf Barbarica in the monastery of Verdín, Don Juan with Inés in a glass-covered cell, and the Pilgrim in a dungeon along with Ludovico and Celestina. El Señor also decrees the nonexistence of the New World and represses, by means of his secretary Guzmán, the popular rebellion of Castilian townships.

Unlike "The Old World," in which everybody came to the palace, at the end of "The New World" all the characters abandon El Señor. Elizabeth returns to England where, in trying to avenge the misfortunes of her marriage, she plans the destruction of the Spanish Armada. Ludovico and Celestina also escape from the palace, as do Inés and Don Juan, who sail for the New World in Guzmán's caravels. Once in America, the novitiate becomes Sor Juana Inés de la Cruz. Guzmán continues his repressive activities and, at the opposite extreme, Fray Julián takes over the personalities of Fray Bartolomé de las Casas and Fray Bernardino de Sahagún. Attacked by Guzmán's falcon, which devours one of his arms, the Pilgrim is also forced to flee seaward. In a manuscript found in another bottle, El Señor reads a passage about the U.S.-Mexican war, in which a young guerrilla fighter resembling the Pilgrim is the protagonist. Julián, the court painter, confesses to the Chronicler (Miguel de Cervantes) that he is the narrator of all these stories and asks him to write them down, together with the chronicle of El Señor's last days. This same chronicle is presented to the reader in the final chapters. Hounded by both his own ghosts and the specters of the dead kings buried in El Escorial, El Señor rehearses his own funeral, experiences the decomposition of his body, and is aware of his own embalming. While in his coffin, he is called forth by a ghost, ascends magical stairs, and finally reappears at the Valley of the Fallen, the necropolis Francisco Franco built in the mountains of Castile.

The last chapter of the novel takes us back to Paris on the eve of the second millennium. In a hotel room Pollo Phoibee, one of the last survivors of the human species, witnesses the same kind of events narrated in the first chapter. In this final moment of *Terra Nostra* he is surrounded by several of the most significant objects that recur throughout the novel: the green bottles, the chronicles, a pair of tailor's scissors, a basket filled with pearls, a collection of various kinds of mirrors, ancient boxes filled with bones and skulls, and a mask of brightly colored feathers. There is a knock on the door. It is the girl with the tattooed lips, Celestina. Pollo and Celestina make love at exactly the same time that the old millennium ends and a new one begins. Their bodies fuse into one androgynous organism from which the narrator hopes a new humanity will be born.

Not only does this reconstruction of the story line leave aside many characters and situations, the sequential organization of this account is in itself a violation of the spirit of the novel, which resists linearity and systematization. What in *Terra Nostra* is presented as a series of flashbacks and scattered narratives has been ordered chronologically and connections have been made that the novel only hints at. However, it is appropriate to establish a general pattern of events against which to discuss the metafictional and historiographic components of Fuentes's work. Such an analysis will be organized around the novel's three major parts.

"The Old World" discusses the monolithic power structures embodied by El Señor and his palace. The historiographic correlation in this first part is enshrouded by an authoritarian, lugubrious, and dogmatic Spain; it spans the expulsion of the Jews in 1492 to Franco's death in 1975. Both the novel and the analysis focus on imperial Spain, and especially on Philip II's rule. The section on "The New World" studies Fuentes's reinvention of pre-Hispanic myths and the chronicles of the conquest. Unlike parts I and III, "The New World" presents a chronological sequence of events, hence this analysis corresponds more faithfully to the novel's story line. Finally, "The Next World" comprises all those oppositional movements that are present in *Terra Nostra*, with special emphasis on the heretical power of imagination represented by intellectuals (writers, artists, and scientists).

THE OLD WORLD: THE ETHICS OF EMPIRE

In his essay on Cervantes, Fuentes specifies the three major dates that establish *Terra Nostra*'s temporal coordinates: 1492, 1521, and 1598.[9] The first of them, 1492, alludes to four events that changed the historical and cultural panorama of Renaissance Spain: the expulsion of the Jews, the fall of Granada, the "discovery" of the New World, and the publication of the first Spanish grammar. The expulsion of the Jews and the Inquisition's persecution of false converts meant the end of a fruitful multicultural coexistence of seven centuries, and also had serious implications for the economic future of Spain. The Jews were at the forefront of the country's economic progress. Holding key positions in the national economy (as bankers, money lenders, merchants, administrators, tax collectors, and ambassadors), Jews constituted, according to Fuentes, "the avant-garde of the nascent capitalist class in Spain."[10] The expulsion occurred when their help was most needed, for, once the reconquest of the peninsula was over—after the fall of the Moorish kingdom of Granada—the expansionism of the Catholic monarchs, Ferdinand and Isabella, faced new horizons. Both the maritime enterprises of the Spanish crown (accelerated by the recent discoveries) and its European military campaigns needed prodigious financing. Paradoxically, the money was borrowed from those foreign powers that were Spain's political, military, and economic rivals. The publication of Antonio de Nebrija's grammar (the first grammar of a vernacular European language) contributed greatly to the unifying effort of Isabella and Ferdinand, since the Spanish language was for the first time conceived not just as a vehicle of official communication in the peninsula, but more importantly as an instrument of imperial domination.[11] The four above-mentioned events point to the crown's major goal at the middle of the fifteenth century: the consolidation of national unity and the creation of foundations for the future Spanish empire.

The imperial project of the Spanish monarchy was not consummated until the reign of Charles V. Two events of special significance for Fuentes occurred under his rule: Hernán Cortés's conquest of Mexico (1521) and the repression of the revolt of Castilian townships (1519). The Spanish conquistadors' march to the Aztec capital is one of the main topics of Part II of *Terra Nostra*. The rebellion and repression of the Castilian *comunidades* (townships), on the other hand, presented in "The Next World" (Part III), is also an important object of analysis in his essays, especially in *Cervantes* and *El espejo enterrado*.[12] The date of 1598, finally, refers to Philip II's death and the subsequent decline of the Spanish empire.

During the reign of the remaining Hapsburgs, political organization lapsed into forms of increasing decadence. Fuentes's portrayal of these historical events reflects his global view of the Hispanic world. Specifically, he underlines how difficult it was for modernity to penetrate first the Spanish soil and then into Spanish America. The entrance of modernity was hindered at three levels: economic, by the expulsion of the Jews; political, by the repression of the *comuneros*; and religious, by the systematic proscription of heretical ideas. The conquest of America implied, therefore, the export, at an official level, of an obsolete and deficient model that was closer to medieval obscurantism than to the openness of thought offered by European Renaissance. However, from a positive perspective, the concept also meant the introduction into America of a multicultural reality that remained hidden and opposed to the official policy of religious persecution.[13]

Historical Background

In order to understand the character of El Señor in *Terra Nostra* it is necessary to review the account of the Hapsburg empire that Fuentes presents in his essays. According to Fuentes, Charles V introduced the expansionist ideal of the Holy Roman Empire into Spain. This concept of a central state of continental dimensions, along with the Catholic monarchs' efforts to unify Spain, put an end to the pluralist and democratic tendencies of a medieval Spain that was already heading toward modernity and was also looking for a compromise between its own cultures and forms of autonomous government.[14] In his portrayal of Charles's personality, Fuentes offers details that help us to understand El Señor's personality. In *El espejo enterrado*, he comments on the emperor's divided nature.[15] Fuentes describes him as confident and insecure, tough and gentle, divided by national alliances and trapped between his Erasmian education, which made him lean toward conciliation, and his imperial inclination, which moved him to fight his declared enemies (the Indian nations, the Ottoman empire, France, and German Protestantism). Burdened by the political problems of his reign, Charles V retired to the monastery of Yuste, where, surrounded by clocks and rehearsing his own funeral, he died in 1558.[16]

When his son Philip II ascended the throne, Spain was in need of urgent changes. Not only did those changes fail to take place, but political and economic situations grew worse. Instead of modernizing the apparatus of power, Philip II showed a stubborn desire to maintain the organic structure of the medieval imperium.[17] Instead of opening the country to the reforming ideas of the Renaissance, he isolated Spain from the rest of Europe. In fact, during the reign of Philip II the crown's imperial orientation ceased to be European (as it had been with Charles V) and directed itself instead toward the Atlantic.[18] Military campaigns did continue in Europe, but their objectives were strategic and religious (fighting the Reformation) rather than strictly economic. The sources for financing those campaigns and the New World adventures did not change substantially. Northern European bankers and money lenders were still the crown's major creditors, and Philip II added new debts to those already contracted by his father, Charles V. How was the crown going to repay those loans? The answer could have come from the launching of a solid and competitive economy through the improvement of national industry.[19] Instead, the crown preferred to rely on something as unstable as the bullion coming from the Americas. The metals from the New World served to pay both the interests on the loans and the manufactured goods coming from the industrial centers of the Low Countries. Thus, Spain was indirectly financing the same Protestant Europe it purported to fight, and more regrettably, it was also contracting debts with foreign powers. As Fuentes suggests, "Spain became the colony of capitalist Europe, and we in Spanish America became the colony of a colony."[20]

According to Fuentes's historical view, the end of Philip II's rule replicated the last years of Charles V. Like his father, Philip II isolated himself behind the walls of a monastery.[21] In the middle of the Castilian sierra, he erected a colossal monument to the orthodoxy of faith that would also serve as a mausoleum to the kings of Spain, as well as a memorial to honor the victory over the French at Saint-Quentin (1557). Surrounded by royal corpses and relics of saints collected throughout Europe, Philip II spent his last years, in Fuentes's account, plunged into solitude and doubt. The portrayal of Philip II that Fuentes presents in his essays revolves around several traits of the king's mysterious personality such as his insecure character, his extraordinary capacity for work, his bureaucratic obsessions, and his ascetic life.

The reigns of Philip III (1598–1621), Philip IV (1621–1665), and Charles II (1665–1700) are contemplated by Fuentes as the beginning of the political ruin of Spain. During this period, the country became a nation of beggars in which bankruptcies followed one another. While describing the decline of Spain in the reign of the late Spanish Hapsburgs, Fuentes amuses himself with the physical decadence of these kings, from Charles V's prognathous jaw to the mental retardation of Charles II, euphemistically called "the Bewitched." However, in the middle of this generalized degradation, the seventeenth century witnessed a paradoxical flourishing of culture in what has been known as the Golden Age. The work by Velázquez, El Greco, Zurbarán, and Murillo, in the visual arts; Lope de Vega and Calderón de la Barca, in drama; and Quevedo and Góngora, in poetry, leads Fuentes to state that it is precisely in those moments of political decadence and corruption that art at times reaches its highest levels of creativity.[22]

History in the Novel

As in the rest of *Terra Nostra*, the historiographic view that Fuentes presents in "The Old World" does not attempt to objectively reflect the past or use it as mere background for a fictional plot. Fuentes's historiographic project instead rewrites the past in order to illuminate the dark areas of the historical register. In the case of "The Old World," he looks for the origin of the power structures that dominate the modern Hispanic world. It is essential to bear in mind that during the years *Terra Nostra* was being written (1969–1974) Spain and Latin America were living either under the rule of totalitarian regimes or in fragile democracies where the forms of popular representation were subordinated to the interests and will of national oligarchies and foreign capital. The first part of the novel inquires into the roots of this situation, that is, into the moment in which the bases for the present condition of dominion and dependency were established. To do so, Fuentes sets the principal action of the novel in sixteenth-century Spain, a period in which the peninsula reaches its imperial zenith and then begins its decline, and in which Latin America begins to suffer the consequences of a deficient colonization.

Among the many characters and voices, it is El Señor who receives preferential treatment in this part of the novel. Although this character combines the features of various members of the Hapsburg dynasty, Fuentes models him on Philip II, with some elements from Charles V.[23] From the latter Fuentes adopts some extravagant biographical data (his accidental birth in a latrine at Ghent, his bedroom walls covered in black, and his last days spent tinkering with clocks and rehearsing his own funeral), as well as some elements of major historical relevance, such as his repression of the revolt of Castilian townships or the conquest of Mexico that took place during his reign. From Philip II, Fuentes borrows his insecure and meticulous personality, his asceticism, his restless fight against religious heterodoxy, and the melancholy of his last years. The description of El Señor's physical birthmarks responds to those of both sovereigns, who suffered from prognathism and hemophilia. El Señor's isolated life in his palace-necropolis repeats the legendary isolation of both Charles V in the monastery of Yuste and Philip II in El Escorial. The construction of El Escorial is obviously taken from biographies of Philip II, as is the description of El Señor's long agony, which in some details even foretells that of the Spanish dictator Francisco Franco.[24]

On the other hand, many elements of El Señor's characterization are purely fantastic. As a result of compressing a long historical period into only one generation, chronologies are violently altered. America is discovered one century too late. El Señor, represented mostly as Philip II, is the son of Philip the Fair and Joanna the Mad, when he was in reality the son of Charles V and Isabella of Portugal. El Señor's experiences as a former heretic have no historical foundations in any of the Spanish Hapsburg kings. The battle that instigated the construction of El Escorial (Saint-Quentin), which is described in Chapter II, was not against Northern European heresies, as it is presented in the novel, but against France.[25] In the novel El Señor marries Elizabeth Tudor, but he never consummates his marriage.[26] Offended by the overly courteous treatment she receives from her husband, Elizabeth, historically known as "the Virgin Queen" but a nymphomaniac in the novel, returns to England and prepares the destruction of the Invincible Armada. The fantastic element in El Señor's characterization culminates in his final metamorphosis into a wolf.

As with the rest of the characters in *Terra Nostra*, Fuentes incorporates both historiographic collage (several historical figures and historiographic sources) and literary fabulation (imaginary, even fantastic elements) in order to portray this character. El Señor initially evokes the figure of "the solitary of El Escorial," but also a whole tradition of reactionary tendencies that form the collective consciousness of Hispanic nations: obscurantism and orthodoxy at the political, religious, and cultural level.

From a political point of view, El Señor represents authoritarian power concentrated in the figure of the absolute sovereign. His concept of himself as the last of kings, the ultimate incarnation of power, impels him to leave no offspring. Permanently engaged in a paranoid fight against everything that threatens his authority, new ideas and discoveries are denied by law. The three shipwreck victims, his brothers, who represent succession to the throne, are confined to his enormous mausoleum. Dissidents like the Chronicler or Mijail-Ben-Sama (Miguel de la Vida) are either severely punished or annihilated. However, El Señor fails in his efforts to keep his reality under control. His power recedes as the novel progresses. From the very first time he appears in the novel (in a hunting incident where his vassals ignore his orders), we witness the impotence of a sovereign defeated by events, vanquished by a reality that he is ultimately unable to understand. Through the representation of this progressive loss of political and personal power, *Terra Nostra* depicts, at an immediate level, the decadence of the Spanish empire that is shadowed by the reign of Philip II. At a deeper level, however, Fuentes's novel dramatizes the failure of all imperial systems to submit reality to their control. One of the lessons that follows from *Terra Nostra* is that power, as Foucault suggests, is not a property, but a strategy, not a privilege one possesses, but a dynamic "network of relations, constantly in tension, in activity."[27]

At a religious level, the world view El Señor embodies is in the tradition of medieval theocentric thought. Unlike the rest of Europe, where, according to Fuentes, there was "a successful confluence of critical thought, capitalist expansion and religious reform," the Spain of Philip II was still subjected to the hierarchical and univocal perspective that was characteristic of scholasticism.[28] According to this perspective, systematized by Thomas Aquinas, human law should be based on natural law, which is, in its turn, the perfect image of divine law. In this worldview, the state has to be subordinated to the directions of the church, since the church is the only institution that can facilitate human beings' ultimate goal: their union with God.[29] In *Terra Nostra*, Fuentes makes El Señor into a spokesman for Thomism. In a theological disquisition, El Señor establishes the principles of this medieval world view: "El libro de Dios sólo puede leerse de una manera: cualquier otra es locura . . . la visión del mundo es única . . . todas las palabras y todas las cosas poseen un lugar para siempre establecido y una función precisa y una correspondencia exacta con la eternidad divina" (624) ["The Book of God can be read only in one manner; any other reading is madness . . . the vision of the world is unique . . . All words and all things possess a forever established place, a precise function, and an exact correspondence with divine eternity"] (619).

In the cultural sphere, El Señor is opposed to the esthetic revolution of Renaissance perspectivism or to the openness represented by Erasmian humanism. Scientific revolutions that succeed in Europe do not have room in El Señor's stagnant world. For him, the earth is still the center of the universe and is not round but flat. When he finds out about a New World, he decrees its nonexistence. El Señor supports an impossible unity in a world dominated by multiplicity and the expansion of physical and intellectual horizons.

As a consequence of failing in his crusade for total orthodoxy, El Señor orders the construction of a fortress that can serve as a microcosm of his obsolete world. His fortress ultimately becomes a necropolis, not just because it is intended to be his own mausoleum, but also because it is a museum of inert objects. El Señor seeks to embalm and enshroud Spanish reality and imprison it within the walls of his palace. In a final necrophilic fantasy, he tries to overcome death itself and, to a certain extent, he succeeds, since he ends ruling literally from a tomb, El Escorial, and witnessing his own flesh rotting in an obvious reconstruction of Philip II's long agony. The novel's final irony is that El Señor's absolute government is circumscribed to the world of death. Hence, when he climbs the magical stairs that bridge his palace with the future world, he finds himself transported to another mausoleum, the Valley of the Fallen, the fascist monument and tomb that Franco ordered to be built after the Spanish Civil War.

Metafiction

Essential to the discussion of the referential aspect of a novel such as *Terra Nostra* is the analysis of its metafictional nature, that is, the novel's systematic tendency to disclose its status as an artifact, the double spiral movement, centrifugal and centripetal, that characterizes the relationship between text and referent in historiographic metafiction. In this fictional mode reflection on the dark areas of history runs parallel to speculation on the mechanisms of representation. The novel reveals a labyrinthine specular design in which the mirrors of fiction capture images from outside reality, while reflecting the interior reality they themselves help to create.

Within the inner world that is progressively built in the first part of *Terra Nostra*, Fuentes adopts a dualistic organization in which each of the elements is defined in relation to its opposite. To the view of Genesis that opens the novel, Fuentes opposes the Parisian apocalypse that is described immediately afterwards.[30] The chaos and dynamism of these initial images contrast with the static order of Philip II's Spain, which Fuentes introduces in the following chapter. The world of heresy described in chapter 3 ("Victory") contrasts in turn with the stubborn orthodoxy of the Spanish sovereign. The long list of oppositions results in a common pattern: The confrontation between the world of power represented by El Señor and the world of imagination emblematized by heterodox thinkers. Although in "The Old World" the two conflicting universes meet, authoritarian paraphernalia that surrounds El Señor is emphasized. It is not until the third part of the novel that we understand the challenge that political, religious, and cultural dissidence represent in the novel.

Several metafictional elements correlate the reflection on power that is carried out in "The Old World." Among them, the palace-necropolis of El Escorial is the most outstanding. Critics have frequently pointed out the value of El Escorial as a metaphor of the aesthetic project against which the novel is opposed.[31] Conceived as the materialization of the spirit of the Counter-Reformation and as a mausoleum for the kings of Spain, El Escorial is Philip II's monument to both the orthodoxy of faith and the Hispanic cult of death. El Escorial works as the antithesis of the world view that Fuentes proposes in *Terra Nostra*. This lugubrious mausoleum symbolizes, for the Mexican novelist, the worst of the Spanish heritage: disproportionate asceticism, religious obscurantism, denial of sensuality, isolationism, stubborn stagnation, and absence of difference.

In chapter 35 ("El Señor Sleeps"), a dream of the sovereign offers the opportunity for a detailed analysis of the totalizing and oppressive nature of the palace-necropolis. It does so by means of one of the most complex reflexive structures that proliferate in *Terra Nostra*. After taking a narcotic, El Señor falls into a deep sleep. In his dream, he sees himself in the middle of a fantastic landscape, an oneiric transposition of the topography where El Escorial stands. Besieged by eagles and falcons, he looks desperately for a way out of a reality that is depicted as labyrinthine and prisonlike: "el valle era una prisión al aire libre, un sólo vasto y profundo calabozo de escarpados muros" ["the valley was an open prison, a vast, deep jail with steep, sheer walls"] (144; 138). In his nightmare, the sovereign dreams of himself split into three different subjects. As he approaches the first of them, he sees scenes of death and destruction reflected in each of his eyes (or "windows"). In the face of another he recognizes himself in an old man lying in the sun and in a state of decay. Reintegrated to his former identity, he ends his dream with a new vision of a prisonlike universe ruled by sterility: "Alta cárcel, helado sol, carne de cera, carnicería, el soñador sollozó: ¿dónde, mis hijos; a quién heredar lo que yo heredé?" (145) ["Lofty jail, icy sun, flesh of wax, charnel house the dreamer sobbed: Where, my sons; to whom shall I bequeath my inheritance?"] (139).

El Señor's nightmare combines Dällenbach's two basic levels of reflection: the level of the utterance and the level of the enunciation.[32] It is a reflection of the utterance in that it summarizes previous events (El Señor's adolescent years and the slaughter at his father's citadel) and foresees other events that will occur later on (the sovereign's death and decay and his final metamorphosis into a wolf). It is a reflection of the enunciation as well, since its *énoncé* also mirrors aspects of the text's production and reception. The dream presents us with the megalomaniac creator trapped in the labyrinth of his own creation: A monumental, but sterile, work in which only fear, violence, and decay have room. El Señor reveals himself in this passage as the reader or interpreter who fails in his aim to produce meaning. Even his own monolithic reality resists an univocal interpretation. As happens in many other moments in the novel, his attempts at establishing connections between the multiple events ultimately fail, unleashing anxiety and bewilderment.

To the sterility of power represented in El Señor's nightmare, Fuentes opposes the fertility of imagination assigned to the sphere of art. "The Old World" develops this dichotomy from the very beginning. In chapter 8 ("All My Sins"), El Señor contemplates an anonymous triptych from Orvieto (later we will find out that its author is Fray Julián). Descriptions of the triptych, which represents moments in Christ's life and are inserted in the novel under the title of "The Painting," intersect with passages commenting on the architecture of El Escorial, which appear under the title of "The Palace." "The Painting" and "The Palace" form a new opposition that incorporates, in its turn, a detailed set of radically confronted concepts: heterodoxy / orthodoxy; anthropocentrism / theocentrism; hedonism / asceticism; affirmation of the present / denial of time; perspectivism / two dimensionality; dynamism / rigidity; metamorphosis / fixity; open world / sealed world.[33] The painting encompasses the majority of the elements in Fuentes's aesthetic program. The palace, on the contrary, is presented as its antithesis.

Many of the elements briefly commented on in chapter 8 acquire greater consistency in other passages of the novel. For example, the story of the painting confirms its protean condition, in contrast to the palace's rigidity of forms in chapter 132 ("Fifth Day"). Fray Julián dissolves the forms of the triptych with a magical mirror and they reappear in the New World, in new combinations. The now empty canvas will be replenished with different forms that will progressively make a new work, another painting that suggests Hieronymous Bosch's "The Garden of Earthly Delights." As opposed to these multiple metamorphoses, the palace is from beginning to end "un cuadrilátero de granito," "una fortaleza," "un probo castillo con ángulos de bastión," "implacablemente austero," "tallado como una sola pieza de granito gris" (99) ["A granite cuadrangle," "a fortress," "a straight, severe castle with a bastion on each corner," "implacably austere," "carved like one solid piece of gray granite"] (93).

Among all the features contrasting these two cultural artifacts, perhaps the most significant is the communication with their addressee that they establish or deny. The painting's ambiguity, representative of the indeterminacy that Fuentes seeks in *Terra Nostra*, forces the beholder to participate in the production of meaning. The spectator/reader in *Terra Nostra*, becomes an active protagonist in the work of art. This relationship between work and receiver is thematized through the play of glances that is established between the painting's contemplators (El Señor, La Señora, and Guzmán) and the characters represented in it (a humanized Christ who looks at a group of naked men with their backs turned to the spectators). The complexity of the dynamics of the ceaseless exchange of gazes, in which the beholder is perceived by a figure in the painting, culminates with the final breaking of the structural frames between the work of art and outside reality: "el cuadro lo mira a él" (96) ["the painting is looking at him"] (90). Fuentes has recently discussed this inversion of roles in the act of perception in relation to Velázquez's *Las Meninas*. According to Fuentes, when we contemplate Velázquez's painting, "we are free to see the painting, and by extension the world, in multiple ways, not in one dogmatic, orthodox way. And we are aware that the painting and the painter are watching us."[34]

The palace, instead, denies any participation to the beholder.[35] Like El Escorial in Ortega y Gasset's description, it is the hermetically sealed work that curls in upon itself, scorning all that is alien to it.[36] It is a work made in El Señor's proportion, where the sovereign, terrified by any sort of change, strives to keep reality under his absolute control.[37] It is this same will to power, this feverish desire for control, that moves him to set down his world in the written discourse. The act of writing is thus described as a necessary activity to infuse an object or idea with life. "Escribe," El Señor orders Guzmán, "nada existe realmente si no es consignado al papel, las piedras mismas de este palacio humo son mientras no se escriba su historia" (111) ["write: nothing truly exists if it not be consigned to paper, the very stones of this palace are but smoke if their story not be written"] (106). The construction of El Escorial and the writing of history that El Señor promotes respond to the same impulse. They are ways through which the sovereign seeks to dominate reality and reduce it to his own power space.

El Señor finally fails in his goals. His role as guardian of the only text is undermined by the democratizing consequences of the introduction of the printing press in Spain.[38] His plan of encapsulating Spain within the limits of his palace runs up against a fragmentary reality that resists his totalizing project. In one of the last portrayals of El Señor, the novel underlines his incompetence as reader of a protean reality: "La historia era un gigantesco rompecabezas; entre las manos transparentes del Señor, sólo había dejado unas cuantas piezas quebradas" (714) ["History was a gigantic puzzle; it had left only a few broken pieces in El Señor's transparent hands"] (710).

Historiographic reflection in "The Old World" probes into the failure of this Escorial-like view of history. In his frustrated attempts to comprehend historical reality El Señor makes use of the same aesthetic notions used in the construction of El Escorial: univocal view of reality, intolerant orthodoxy, oppressive monumentality, rigidity of forms, and dogmatism of contents. While on an aesthetic level his project becomes a monument to death, and therefore denies the function of art as a vital expression, on a historiographic level, his work turns out to be a highly selective register in which those events threatening his power are denied existence.

The construction of the palace and the writing of history sponsored by El Señor are intended to function as antitheses of Fuentes's project. However, some critics have pointed out the striking similarities between these two levels of "The Old World" (aesthetic and historiographic) and some of Fuentes's global postulates in *Terra Nostra*.[39] El Escorial may be perceived as an unintentional *mise en abyme* of *Terra Nostra*; rather than an antithesis of Fuentes's aesthetic and historiographic view, its unconscious embodiment. This perspective will also be useful to clarify several paradoxes that have have surfaced in my reading of *Terra Nostra*, and that have attracted most of the criticism.

It was Robert Coover who first pointed to the novel's most striking irony: "In mass, rigidity of design, hostility toward individual character, doctrinal devotion and seigniorial hubris, the making of *Terra Nostra* parallels the laborious construction of El Escorial, and like Philip's necropolis, the book seems largely to have been a labor more of duty than of love."[40] Since Coover was reviewing the novel only briefly, he did not enter into details. However, his hypothesis is of the greatest importance in interpreting Fuentes's aesthetic project, as well as for the study of *Terra Nostra* in the light of the present debate on postmodernism.

As noted, an early novel such as *Aura* already shows symptoms of its author's interest in gigantic designs. Its protagonist, Felipe, is a historian obsessed by the creation of a total work:

> Si lograras ahorrar por lo menos doce mil pesos, podrías pasar cerca de un año dedicado a tu propia obra, casi olvidada. *Tu gran obra de conjunto* sobre los descubrimientos y conquistas españolas en América. *Una obra que resuma todas las crónicas dispersas*, las haga inteligibles, encuentre las correspondencias entre *todas las empresas y aventuras del siglo de oro*, entre los prototipos humanos y el hecho mayor del Renacimiento" (emphasis added).

[If you can manage to save at least twelve thousand pesos, you can spend a year on nothing but your own work, which you've postponed and almost forgotten. *Your great, inclusive work* on the Spanish discoveries and conquests in the New World. *A work that sums up all the scattered chronicles*, makes them intelligible, and discovers the resemblances among *all the undertakings and adventures of Spain's Golden Age*, and all the human prototypes and major accomplishments of the Renaissance (emphasis added)].[41]

This impossible novel is, in many senses, *Terra Nostra*, a historical novel that seeks a difficult synthesis between dispersion and monumentality.[42] As happens with other postmodern encyclopedic novels, this synthesis reveals itself to be unattainable, hence the tension in which both elements (fragmentation and totalization) coexist.[43]

Fuentes's novel proposes fragmentation and multiplicity, rather than linearity and monologism. However, the novel's design, in Coover's view, seems quite rigid: three parts ("The Old World," "The New World," and "The Next World") correspond to three different realms (El Señor's medieval Spain, the discovery and conquest of America, and the oppositional movements that emerged in the wake of Renaissance) and dramatize a particular view of historical progress. Thematic cycles, complex symbolic webs, and recurrent images and episodes tend to stress this tendecy toward totalization. If we add to this unifying tendency the long series of binomials that cause characters and situations to be defined in relation to their opposites, the result is a general impression of absolute order and hierarchical structure, an order and a hierarchy that rather than creating an endless constellation of perspectives, favor the author's exclusive point of view.

In this context, it is rather disappointing that the most detailed analysis of the metaphor represented by El Escorial (Raymond Lee Williams's recent book on Carlos Fuentes) arrives at conclusions even more paradoxical than those expressed in *Terra Nostra*.[44] According to Williams, El Escorial operates as the novel's *mise en abyme*, a suggestive idea first proposed by Coover in his *New York Times* review, and one I have been arguing throughout the present chapter. However, while for both Coover and I, El Escorial constitutes a metaphor not desired by the author (that is, the embodiment of all that Fuentes claims to reject: totalization, exclusion, dogmatism, repression), in Williams's view it becomes the materialization of Fuentes's democratic and postmodern vision. In his attempt to justify the most contradictory aspects of *Terra Nostra*, Williams converts Phillips II's necropolis into the image that consolidates the novel's multicultural project, which is a hypothesis that any cultural historian would be hard pressed to defend. According to Williams, El Escorial is, together with *Terra Nostra*, a multicultural object that encompasses and reflects the heterogeneous cultural forces at play in sixteenth-century Spain, and represents the culture exported to the colonies over more than three centuries.[45]

It is obvious to anyone who has visited El Escorial and survived the educational system under Franco, that this monument, together with the reign of Phillip II, represents the exact opposite of that which Williams proposes. How is it possible that Phillip II's palace / necropolis / monastery be a celebration of Spanish cultural heterogeneity, as Williams constantly suggests, when it was constructed as a fortress for religious dogma and has remained in the Spanish collective consciousness as a symbol of the intolerance and backwardness of the Counter-Reformation? Moreover, when speaking of culture, it is useful to discern among hegemonic culture, popular culture, and oppositional culture. The very notion of national culture is doubtful in a Spain in which to this day historical communities conserve autonomous forms of government, and in which cultural manifestations, which fortunately had nothing to do with the concept of culture imposed by El Escorial, thrived. The mere fact that this monument may or may not represent the hegemonic culture sustained by its creator, in no way means that it embodies "Spanish culture" in all its heterogeneity. El Escorial may very well be interpreted as a microcosm, as William suggests, but not "a microcosm of sixteenth-century Spanish society," but rather a microcosm of the dark personal utopia of Phillip II.

Williams's misreading of El Escorial does reveal some interesting facts, but ultimately it falls prey to a widespread tendency within contemporary criticism: the manipulation of texts according to poststructuralist clichés. It is important to keep in mind that postmodernism goes beyond the simple blending of styles, and postmodern criticism would do well to also go beyond the acritical mystification of heterogeneity and its subsequent imposition upon any cultural artifact. To hope to find postmodern characteristics in an architectural monument constructed in an ultraconservative context such as that of Phillip II's Spain is absurd. For many Spaniards who suffered under Franco's dictatorship, El Escorial represents, together with the Valley of the Fallen, the most flagrant manifestation of a historical vision that is not postmodern, but rather antimodern and Fascist; something that Fuentes emphasizes throughout *Terra Nostra* (although maybe not in his official speeches as of late).[46]

A new paradox comes from the fact that, although *Terra Nostra* purports to stand for nameless beings, minorities, and masses, and against authority and the elite, the protagonist is doubtlessly an outstanding figure of Spanish history: Philip II. Thus, while El Señor has the richest and most complex personality in the novel, the so-called group of "the workers" (Jerónimo, Martín, Nuño, and Catilinón) is presented in a stereotypical way: They are coarse, rude, sometimes brutal, and always ignorant and susceptible of being manipulated by those who hold power.[47] On the other hand, although devoid of psychological insight, the intellectuals occupy the other privileged space in the novel. While El Señor rules over "The Old World," in the last part of the novel he has to share power with artists, heretics, and *comuneros*. These oppositional groups form the most distinguished elite in *Terra Nostra*, the one that, according to Fuentes, should—but could not—have led the march toward modernity in Spain and Spanish America.

On a historiographic level, the novel accuses El Señor's history of hiding events and, therefore, of manipulating truth. But, due to its own fictional condition, the process of selecting events in *Terra Nostra* is even more arbitrary. Such arbitrariness is perfectly admissible in a work of fiction. What is less admissible is the novelist's pretension of turning his work into a cognitive instrument that purports to be superior to historiography: "Because the history of Spain has been what it has been, its art has been what history has denied Spain . . . Art gives life to what history killed. Art gives voice to what history denied, silenced or persecuted. Art brings truth to the lies of history."[48] Imaginative literature can say what history silences, but it also frequently silences what history says. Similarly, the discourse of a novel does not have to be devoid of group interests nor to oppose institutional power. This opposition between literature (which Fuentes associates with openness and progress) and official history (which represents, on the contrary, closure and obscurantism) leads to an easy idealization of creative activity when removed from its own cultural context.

Some of these paradoxes are resolved in the current debate both on postmodernism and the Hispanic literary and historiographic tradition. The desire for and suspicion of totalizing views of reality are two antagonistic tendencies that tend to appear together in many contemporary historical novels. According to Linda Hutcheon, historiographic metafictions respond to a paradoxical impulse that moves them to install, and simultaneously subvert, "the teleology, closure and causality of narrative, both historical and fictive."[49] For Hutcheon, this double impulse aims at dismantling the process through which we both represent reality and make our representation look like an ordered and coherent whole. In disclosing the mechanisms of representation of literature and history in all their arbitrariness, these postmodern historical novels question the claims to truth of traditional historiography, as well as the objectivistic epistemology of literary realism.

As noted, both in his essays and in his novels Fuentes insists on the need to build models of total representation. Nevertheless, it is necessary to clarify the concept of totalization that he proposes. For Fuentes, a total novel is not a narrative that presents itself as coherent, continuous, and unified; nor is Fuentes's aesthetic program to impose an exclusive view of reality upon us. Both tendencies are present in *Terra Nostra*, not as cult objects, but as a merciless parody of authorship. On the contrary, Fuentes's total novel is posed as "a program of an open book, of a common writing."[50] From these words, used to describe Joyce's poetics in *Finnegans Wake*, we can deduce the antiauthoritarian intention that Fuentes assigns to his concept of totalization. He attempts to make of the novel a great "field of possibilities" in which no voice should feel excluded; to open the work in order to allow the coexistence of "all contrary views simultaneously seen from all possible perspectives"; to transform the production of the text into a communal activity, one that extends beyond the author's full stop.[51] This same inclination to inscribe and subvert the traditional mechanisms of representation also helps us to understand Fuentes's interest in the great characters of history. In "The Old World" he novelist conducts an exploratory investigation into the tyrannical power that has devastated Hispanic nations for centuries.[52] In order to do so, he focuses on Philip II and depicts his complex personality through a collage of various sources and inventions. Fuentes's approach works mostly by means of amalgamation. He reproduces in the novel entire passages and anecdotes from several of the most conservative and moralistic of the chronicles written about the Spanish king and mixes them with a fantastic plot of his own invention.[53] In literally inscribing these chronicles in their most grotesque and fantastic aspects, and allowing them to mingle with fiction, Fuentes denies both their authority and the reactionary view they convey.

Finally, Fuentes's favoring of fiction over history as the basis of truth must be understood in light of the repeated contempt that the intellectual establishment has traditionally manifested for the literature of creation.[54] The opposition against creative literature on the part of the Hispanic intelligentsia (both clergymen and secular humanists) was so virulent that the export of novels to the New World was even banned several times in the sixteenth century, and all the works of imagination in the peninsula were subjected to vigilant censorship.[55] More recently, this initial rejection of fiction was compounded by the scorn of positivist epistemology for the narrative component in the transmission of knowledge. It is also contemporary culture that has inverted the evaluative criteria of history in relation to fiction.

In this context, Fuentes's intentions are understood as an attempt to recuperate the dignity of creative literature, inverting the terms in which the dichotomy "novel equals lie" versus "history equals truth" was traditionally posed. For Fuentes, novels, and art in general, should offer something new to reality, complete it, and not limit themselves to pure documentary reflection.[56] On the historiographic level, this means giving a voice to those groups traditionally silenced in the historical register, and in this sense, some of the master lines of Fuentes's novelistic project are connected to the new currents in contemporary historiography. From the French School of the Annals to Foucault's genealogical analysis, new historiographers seek to leave a large space for everything that is dispersed, heterogeneous, and marginal, that is, to everything that has been denied a history.

In short, we can affirm that El Señor's palace works as the central *mise en abyme* of the first part of *Terra Nostra*. Whether we accept Fuentes's "official" version about this subject, or we adopt the critical perspective suggested by Coover, Kerr, or González Echevarría, it is evident that Philip II's monument has a determinant metaphoric value in the novel. El Escorial significantly occupies the repressive space of orthodoxy, the dominant subject in "The Old World." In the analysis of Part III, "The Next World," the other major *mise en abyme* of the novel, Valerio Camillo's Theater of Memory, will be discussed as a metaphor of the oppositional utopia to which Fuentes subscribes.

THE NEW WORLD: THE REINVENTION OF AMERICA

"The New World," the second of the three parts into which *Terra Nostra* is divided, focuses on the conflictive clash between Judeo-Christian culture and the Aztec world, an encounter that Fuentes anachronistically places in the reign of Philip II. The novel's first part ends with the arrival of the character known as the Pilgrim, the son of Philip the Fair and Celestina, to El Escorial. The entire section entitled "The New World" is filled by the Pilgrim's report to the king of his discovery and conquest of the New Continent. Unlike the radically nonlinear narrative of the first and third parts of *Terra Nostra*, the events described in "The New World" conform to the rather precise chronological pattern of initiation and discovery journeys. Its nineteen chapters establish the itinerary of the Pilgrim from his acquaintance with Pedro in a place on the Spanish coast (chapter 60), to Mexico Tenochtitlan, the very core of the Aztec empire (chapters 76 and 77).[57] The last two chapters (78 and 79) narrate the protagonist's flight and his reappearance on the same coast from which he had departed. In his description of the Pilgrim's circular and eventful journey, Fuentes creates a vast network of allusions in which two different levels interact: several of the best known episodes in the saga of Quetzalcoatl (the Nahuas' god-hero and one of the most complex figures in Mesoamerican religion) and Hernán Cortés's trajectory in his conquest of Mexico Tenochtitlan.

The following discussion of the reinvention of the past in "The New World" focuses on the (supposedly) pre-Hispanic legend of Quetzalcoatl and on its relation to the vision of the conquest that is implied by the novel. The first part discusses some of the most authoritative versions of the myth, as well as the view that Fuentes has developed about this topic. The historical and mythical background that Fuentes uses to re-create in a fictional way the different variants of the legend are established here. The second part is a textual analysis of "The New World" oriented to Fuentes's use of documentary materials pertaining to the pre-Hispanic past and the conquest period. His is a threefold focus: Nahuatl texts written directly after the conquest; histories, chronicles, and stories by the conquistadors and Spanish missionaries; and modern secondary sources from the fields of cultural anthropology and ethnohistory. The last section addresses those metafictional devices through which Fuentes connects the mythical intertext with his inquiry into the act of literary communication.

Historical Background

Quetzalcoatl is one of the most multifaceted figures of Mesoamerican religions. According to Davíd Carrasco, his cult started at the great cultural center of Teotihuacan (A.D. 100–750) and persisted until the fall of the Aztec capital in 1521.[58] For H. B. Nicholson, the name Quetzalcoatl ("the serpent of quetzal feathers") is usually associated with a double identity: a god-creator (Ehecatl Quetzalcoatl) and a quasi-legendary Toltec ruler (Topiltzin Quetzalcoatl), who adopted the god's name.[59] The former, Ehecatl, has an important demiurgic value in the cosmogonies of Central Mexico. Among the four suns or eras in which the Nahuas divided the past, the second was ruled by Ehecatl Quetzalcoatl, who participated as well in the formation of the Fifth Sun or present era.[60] The name "Ehecatl," "wind" in Nahuatl, alludes to his relationship with this natural force, and he is represented with a buccal mask through which he blew the wind of creation.[61] Linked to the concepts of creation and fertility, Ehecatl Quetzalcoatl was also the patron god of the commercial and religious center of Cholula. From an archeological point of view, the cult of Ehecatl Quetzalcoatl was, according to Nicholson, extended throughout Central Mexico, Western Oaxaca, and the Gulf Coast.

Besides the god Quetzalcoatl (Ehecatl) there exist numerous documentary references to a Toltec ruler and priest who held the title of Topiltzin ("our dear Lord") Quetzalcoatl. Some documents written immediately after the conquest contain transcriptions of Aztec history that refer to this legendary figure who ruled over the city of Tollan. Drawing mostly from sixteenth- and seventeenth-century documents, H. B. Nicholson has reconstructed a basic history of the myth as it flourished in Mexico at the time of the Spaniards' arrival in 1519.[62] According to Nicholson, Topiltzin Quetzalcoatl is a historical character who existed at an early stage of Toltec history and whose figure was confused with that of Ehecatl Quetzalcoatl, the ancient god of fertility, and of the rain and the wind. Son of one of the main Toltec conquerors, Topiltzin avenged the death of his father and rose to become one of the leaders of a group at Tollan. During his rule he introduced many religious and cultural practices of the Toltecs.[63] These reforms provoked a conflict that ended with Quetzalcoatl's flight from Tollan in the company of some of his followers. Heading eastward, with a long stay in Cholula, he disappeared beyond the known horizon. In addition to revealing his religious and cultural innovations, the documents analyzed by Nicholson reveal Topiltzin Quetzalcoatl's importance as a political leader and legitimator of Mexican and Guatemalan dynasties of Toltec origin.[64]

The mixed figure of a cultural hero and god, Quetzalcoatl is closely related to the phenomenon of the conquest, or at least, to many of the versions that have come down to us. In order to explain how a small group of Spanish conquistadors could rapidly subdue a whole empire, several hypotheses have been proposed from the sixteenth century on. One of the most popular arguments was, and it still is, the paralyzing fear that omens and prophecies exercised on the Aztecs, and especially on their emperor. There existed a pervasive belief in the return of Quetzalcoatl to reclaim his throne, and the arrival of the Spaniards at the moment announced by those prophecies spread panic throughout the Aztec empire.

When dealing with Nahua myths, however, we should take into account the absence of a preconquest written literature, as well as evidence that could determine the reliability of many of the sixteenth-century documents to which we have access. The first attempts to systematize oral Nahua mythology, by both Indians and Spaniards, were undertaken in the decades that followed Cortés's arrival, that is, after the fall of the Aztec empire. This fact, along with the process of transculturation that resulted from the conquest and the many personal interests that were at stake, led to historiographic versions of the indigenous world that at best differed one from another, when they did not openly contradict each other.

Regarding the mythical figure of Quetzalcoatl, some historians have grown increasingly suspicious about the pre-Hispanic nature of some parts of the myth. Scholars such as Jacques Lafaye, Anthony Pagden, J. H. Elliott, Victor Frankl, Susan Gillespie, and Werner Stenzel question the decisive role conferred on the prophecies in the conquest of New Spain, and even their authenticity.[65] Lafaye, Pagden, and Elliott, for example, suggest that the two speeches in which Moctezuma recognizes in Cortés a prophesized god, and that Cortés himself reproduces (or "produces") in his *Cartas de relación*, are apocryphal. This fact is essential since Cortés's *Letters* were the main source of information for López de Gómara, who, in his turn, became the most important source for the seventeenth-century historians. For Lafaye, the versions of Quetzalcoatl's myth that have come down to us are not of exclusive pre-Hispanic origin, but are rather the result of the religious and cultural syncretism that developed in New Spain during the sixteenth century. To indigenous apocalyptic thought was added Judeo-Christian Messianism, and both traditions, in Lafaye's view, looked for the myth of Quetzalcoatl "to extricate them from a situation that their religious conscience found intolerable, the situation of living a moment of history—and henceforth to be their common history—not foreseen by their respective prophets."[66] From the point of view of Pagden, Elliott, Frankl, Gillespie, and Stenzel, Cortés's manipulation could be explained as an attempt to legitimate his conquest and to ingratiate himself with Charles V, who had never authorized Cortés to speak for him.[67] Thus, the encounter between Cortés and Moctezuma is portrayed in the terms of the political and legal tradition of sixteenth-century Spain: the vassal, in this case Moctezuma, welcomes his "natural lord," Cortés, who, in his turn, describes himself as an ambassador of the king.[68] Yet, the connection between the prophesied return of a Quetzalcoatl and the conquistador's arrival was not accomplished by Cortés but by the Franciscans Fray Toribio de Benavente (Motolinia) and Fray Bernardino de Sahagún. Elliott has pointed to the influence of the apocalyptic tradition on Franciscan missionaries, who came to the New World with the utopian hope of founding a new church far from the ecclesiastic corruption that prevailed in their time. It is possible, according to Elliott, that Motolinia and Sahagún initially, and other missionaries afterwards, could have overstated the value of omens and prophecies as manifestations of their own providential plan.[69] In short, the multiple versions of the legend favored particular agendas that could be summarized in a generalized interest in legitimizing and justifying the attitudes held by both Aztecs and Spaniards at the time of the conquest.

Fuentes's version of the saga of Quetzalcoatl does not follow any of these skeptical proposals. In *El espejo enterrado* (1992), Fuentes depicts a Quetzalcoatl in which the elements of the god and the ruler are conflated. Furthermore, his description of the narrative of Quetzalcoatl does not discriminate among the numerous and contradictory versions at our disposal. For Fuentes, Quetzalcoatl, the plumed serpent, was the creator of mankind, of agriculture, of village life, and the inventor of architecture, song, writing, metallurgy, and craftsmanship. Quetzalcoatl gave men his tools and taught them to work precious metals and feathers and to grow corn. Because of the scope of his teachings, Quetzalcoatl came to be identified with the Toltecs, and with *Toltecayotl*, a word that means "the totality of creation."[70] His moral value in ancient Mesoamerica leads Fuentes to compare him with Prometheus:

> And so Quetzalcoatl became the moral hero of ancient Mesoamerica, in the same way that Prometheus was the hero of the ancient time of the Mediterranean—its liberator, even if liberation cost him his freedom. In the case of Quetzalcoatl, the freedom he brought to the world was the light of education—a light so powerful that it became the basis for legitimation of any potential successor state to the Toltec legacy.[71]

Although Fuentes's vision is inclusive, the Mexican novelist tends to privilege certain aspects of the representations of Quetzalcoatl. For example, he values Quetzalcoatl's role as a demiurgic god and cultural hero over his role as a military conqueror that some versions of the myth attribute to Topiltzin Quetzalcoatl.

In the prologue to one of the editions of *Todos los gatos son par-*

dos (1980), an epic drama of the conquest, Fuentes offers a description of the fall of Quetzalcoatl [Topiltzin] that he will develop in later fictions, especially in *Terra Nostra*.[72] The prologue begins in this way:

> Cuéntase en los anales de Cuauhtitlán que los llamados Tezcatlipoca, Ilhuimécatl y Toltécatl (todos ellos mágicos certificados) decidieron expulsar de la ciudad de los dioses a Quetzalcóatl, la serpiente emplumada, el creador de los hombres y el instructor en las artes básicas: el cultivo del maíz, el pulimento del jade, la pintura del mosaico y el tejido y tintura del algodón. Pero necesitaban un pretexto: la caída. Pues mientras representase el más alto valor moral del universo indígena, Quetzalcóatl era intocable. Prepararon pulque para emborracharlo, hacerle perder el conocimiento e inducirlo a acostarse con su hermana, Quetzaltépatl.

> [It is said in the *Anales de Cuauhtitlan* that Tezcatlipoca, Ihuimecatl and Toltecatl (all of them certified magicians) decided to expel Quetzalcoatl, the plumed serpent, the creator of men and the instructor of the basic arts, the growing of maize, the polishing of jade, mosaic painting and weaving and dying of cotton—from the city of gods. But they needed a pretext: the fall. Since, while he represented the highest moral value of the indigenous world, Quetzalcoatl was untouchable. They prepared pulque to make him drunk, sink into a stupor, and induce him to lie down with his sister, Quetzaltepatl.]

However, the magicians cannot find a way to make Quetzalcoatl give in. It is Tezcatlipoca, the "smoking mirror," who invents the definitive plan: to bring a mirror to Quetzalcoatl and show him his own mortal body. Since he was a god, Quetzalcoatl did not know his appearance; he thought he had no face. When he saw it reflected in the mirror, the feathered serpent felt fear and shame. Out of his senses from facing a human image, that night he drank and committed incest with his own sister. The following day he departed toward the sea, in the direction of the sunrise, saying that the sun was calling him, and promising to return. Fuentes finishes his "free" version of the myth saying: "Quetzalcóatl se fue sin saber que había sido el protagonista simultáneo de la creación y de la caída. Sembró, en la tierra, el maíz; pero en las almas de los mexicanos sembró una infinita sospecha circular" ["Quetzalcoatl left without knowing that he had been the simultaneous protagonist of both the Creation and the Fall. He sowed the fields with maize; but in the Mexicans' souls he sowed an infinite circular suspicion."][73]

This version of the myth of Quetzalcoatl's fall shows the amalgamating eclecticism that characterizes Fuentes's writing. Although his version is said to be based on the *Anales de Cuauhtitlán*, the way he describes the hero's flight does not correspond to this source, but to the alternative ending proposed by Sahagún in his *Historia General*. As opposed to the *Anales* where Quetzalcoatl dies by immolating himself, Sahagún's *Historia General* shows the hero heading eastward in a boat of serpents and promising to return.[74] Fuentes's details about the god's fall also depart frequently from the original source. The *Anales* neither mention nor suggest that Quetzalcoatl's horror was due to metaphysical reasons, but to the monstrous deformation of his face.[75] A simple revision of the episode, as presented in the Garibay's translation of the *Anales*, allows us to see the differences in relation to Fuentes's version:

> Y al momento se vio Quetzalcoatl: se llenó de pavor, dijo:
> —¡Si mis vasallos me vieran a correr echarían!
> Porque sus párpados estaban muy inflamados,
> hundidos los ojos en las cuencas, y la cara por doquiera
> toda llena de abolsamientos, *¡no tenía figura humana!*
> Cuando vio el espejo dijo: —¡Nunca me verán mis siervos
> aquí he de estarme solo! (emphasis added)

> [And at once Quetzalcoatl saw himself: he was filled with terror, and said:
> —If my vassals could see me they would run away!
> Because his eyelids were all inflamed,
> his eyes sunken in their sockets, and his face
> all covered with blisters, *he did not have a human form!*
> When he looked into the mirror, he said: —My servants will never see me
> I will remain here alone! (emphasis added)]

The *Anales* do not depict the fall taking place in the mechanistic way depicted by Fuentes. Terrified by the discovery of his own ugliness, Topiltzin Quetzalcoatl decides to seclude himself in his quarters, away from his people's gaze. It is only after a third trick (played this time by Ihuimecatl and Toltecatl, not by Tezcatlipoca), and several complications that Quetzalcoatl succumbs to drink. Even the episode of the incest on which Fuentes places so much emphasis in his reinvention of the myth is presented in the *Anales* in a very subtle way. One of the few suggestions is given by these lines of moving lyricism:

> Y después de embriagarse, ya no dijeron:
> ¡Si nosotros somos ascetas! Y no bajaron ya nunca

> al baño ritual al río, ni tampoco se punzaron con espinas,
> ni nada hicieron cuando la aurora aparece.
>
> [And after becoming intoxicated, they no longer said:
> But we are ascetics! And they no longer descended
> the ritual baths at the river, neither did they pierce
> themselves with thorns,
> nor did they do anything when dawn appeared.][76]

After a long pilgrimage, Quetzalcoatl arrives at the edge of the sea, where he ends his days by cremating himself. All the birds of beautiful plumage come to see his ashes, and his heart ascends into heaven and is transformed into the planet Venus.

According to the version of the myth that Fuentes offers in *El espejo enterrado*, Quetzalcoatl had announced that he would return at a particular time: *Ce Acatl*, the year "One Reed" in the Aztec calendar; "when fate and nature coincided under the sign of fear, the Indian world would be shaken to its very roots, and the whole world would be afraid of losing its soul."[77] The arrival of Cortés, on Holy Thursday, 1519 (the year One Reed), coincided with the prophesied moment, which made Moctezuma associate the conquistador's arrival with the god's return. According to Fuentes, the coming of the Spaniards was announced by supernatural omens. Signs in the sky, natural catastrophes, and all kinds of strange phenomena. Throughout the Aztec empire it was known that the prophecy was soon to be fulfilled: Quetzalcoatl was going to return. The time of the Fifth Sun was coming to its end. When Moctezuma received the news that floating fortresses were approaching his lands from the East, bearing white bearded men dressed in gold and silver who were like six-legged monsters, he knew that the end was unavoidable (118; 110).

Among the sixteenth-century sources for Quetzalcoatl that Nicholson considers the most complete and reliable, only one directly refers to the omens and the prophecy of Quetzalcoatl's return: Sahagún's *Historia General*.[78] According to the native informants who helped Sahagún, ten years before the Spaniards landed in Mexico a long series of ill omens began to follow one another. Sahagún specifies eight of them: 1) a huge flame that burned for one year; 2) the temple of Huitzilopochtli burst into flames without provocation; 3) the temple of Xiuhtecuhtli was struck by lightning, although nobody could hear the thunder; 4) a comet streaked across the sky and then exploded into three pieces; 5) the waters of the lake churned up waves that toppled the houses; 6) a woman roamed

the streets in the night crying for the fate of her children; 7) some
sailors rescued from the lake a strange bird with a mirror on its
head; 8) deformed men and monstrous beings were seen.[79] Fuentes
almost literally reproduces these omens in *Todos los gatos son pardos*, *Terra Nostra*, *Ceremonias del alba*, and *El espejo enterrado*.
The influence that Fuentes confers on the myth in the exchanges
between the Aztecs and the conquistadors also may have been taken
from Sahagún's *Historia General*, where Moctezuma welcomes
Cortés as *"el esperado"* ("the awaited one") and yields the throne
up to him with exactly the same words that Fuentes will reproduce
in his works:

> —Señor nuestro: te has fatigado, te has dado cansancio: ya a la tierra tú
> has llegado. Has arrivado a tu ciudad: México. Aquí has venido a sen-
> tarte en tu solio, en tu trono. Oh, por tiempo breve te lo reservaron, te
> lo conservaron, los que ya se fueron, tus sustitutos.

> [—Our Lord: You have fatigued yourself, you have exhausted yourself;
> but you have come to your own land. Your have reached your city:
> Mexico. Here you have come to be seated upon your throne. Oh, it was
> a brief time that they kept it for you, those who are already gone, your
> substitutes.][80]

According to Sahagún's version, as the conquest progressed the
Aztecs realized that the Spanish were not gods but men of flesh and
blood like themselves, and even in the times of Sahagún (late sixteenth century) were still waiting for the return of Quetzalcoatl.

There are other elements that make Sahagún's *Historia General*
one of the main sources not only of Fuentes's narrative of Quetzalcoatl, but also of his vision of the pre-Hispanic world described in
Terra Nostra. Moreover, Fuentes shares with Franciscans like Sahagún the search for a synthesis between utopian and apocalyptic
thought.[81] In any case, we should take into account that Fuentes's
view of history is always personal. His manipulation of existing
sources regarding the conquest and the myth of Quetzalcoatl
achieves its most original expression in *Terra Nostra*, where he proposes an original rewriting of the indigenous and Christian traditions. Fuentes uses a number of versions in order to offer an all-
encompassing synthesis, behind which we can glimpse his own cultural design: the creation of a mythology of *mestizaje* and the presentation of the writer as the standard-bearer of cultural and
political change in Latin America.

History in the Novel

In "The New World" the Pilgrim tells the king the story of his journey to Mesoamerican lands. Two motives intersect throughout this section of the novel, shaping a double structuring axis: the saga of Quetzalcoatl and the discovery and conquest of America. Both the mythical and the historical components are submitted by Fuentes to a process of selection and distortion that gives way to an original universe, where the Mexican writer dramatizes his vision of the traumatic encounter between the two civilizations. The following analyzes the evolution of the representations of Quetzalcoatl within Fuentes's own text and the articulation of this evolution with the history of the conquest. The Pilgrim's adventures in the New World correspond, on one hand, to the principal stages in the life of Topiltzin Quetzalcoatl and, on the other, to the itinerary of Cortés in his conquest of Mexico. The study of these two components is coordinated with the documentary sources used in the novel.

In the first three narrative sections (chapters 60–62), the Pilgrim describes his journey of discovery in the company of Pedro, a journey that begins under the sign of Venus, one of the emblems of Quetzalcoatl.[82] However, the formation of the Nahua web of mythic references is only detected *a posteriori*, after a close reading of the first nine chapters of "The New World." References to the chronicles of the discovery and conquest dominate these three chapters. The narration of the voyage, especially the relationship between Pedro and the Pilgrim, at times evokes the narratives describing Columbus's first voyage. The following three chapters (63–65) narrate their arrival to the coast of Mexico after a shipwreck, and their lives in a place described as a "lost shore of renewed Creation" (380; 373). The Pilgrim's first descriptions of this "new world" correspond to those of Columbus, Amerigo Vespucci, Peter Martyr, and Pérez de Oliva, who all depict the recently discovered continent as a utopian "Golden Age."[83] Regarding their movement along the New World coastline, they repeat—sometimes literally—moments in the story of Pedro Serrano's shipwreck, which the Inca Garcilaso includes in his *Comentarios Reales*.[84] Chapter 63, "The Exchange," portrays the first meeting with the natives of the continent, a meeting in which Pedro dies and the Pilgrim survives thanks to his participation in the rules of exchange and negotiation that rule the life of the Indians. The Pilgrim's behavior in this episode, along with his subsequent integration in the indigenous community and ulterior transformation into a Messianic leader, points to Cabeza de Vaca's *Naufragios* as another possible intertext, and his description of this utopian community reflects the "anarchist utopias" that were described by the first explorers of the New World.[85]

The transition from Spanish chronicles to pre-Hispanic mythical narratives only occurs after the Pilgrim's encounter with the so called "ancient of memories." In chapter 69, "The Ancient's Legend," an old man gives the Pilgrim a reconstruction of Nahua cosmogony, focusing on the creation of earth, of men, and of the sun. According to the Ancient, the earth was created by two gods who transformed themselves into two great serpents and tore off the limbs of an earth goddess, from whose dismembered body all things were born. As the goddess saw that the fruits born from her skin grew and rotted away but had no reason for being, she summoned three gods—one red, one white, and the third black—and said that one of them must sacrifice himself in order for men to be born. Only the humpbacked and leprous black god threw himself into the belly of the earth goddess, which was pure fire, and from the flames came the first man and the first woman. The sacrifice of the black god was rewarded with his ascension to the sky and his transformation into the first sun of humanity.

Although the ancient does not directly mention Quetzalcoatl, his cosmogony is based on different versions of the creation myth in which Quetzalcoatl plays an important role. The first part of the Ancient's account coincides with one of the legends edited by Angel M. Garibay in which the protagonists are Quetzalcoatl and Tezcatlipoca.[86] The second part of his legend is based on the myth of the origin of the fifth sun. According to the Nahua text of the *Códices Matritenses*, the Fifth Sun was the result of the sacrifice of the god Nanahuatzin, "the scabby one."[87] León-Portilla has pointed out the extraordinary importance of this myth in understanding one of the most disturbing aspects of Nahua mysticism: "sun and life exist through sacrifice; only through sacrifice will they be able to save themselves."[88]

After the story of the creation of the earth, human beings, and the sun, the Ancient's account continues with the narrative of the invention and organization of time. He explains the Nahua calendar to the Pilgrim, the cyclical conception of time and the birth and death of the suns, or eras, in which Aztecs divided history from the first creation of the world. An important difference in relation to the Nahua model is Fuentes's placement of the Pilgrim's events in the fourth sun, strategically underlining the apocalyptic significance that the conquest would have for Nahua civilization, since it implied its destruction. The form in which the Ancient describes the death of the fourth sun is similar to the way Fuentes's novel portrays the catastrophe of the conquest: "El cuarto sol, que es el de la tierra, y que desaparecerá en medio de terremotos, hambre, destrucción, guerra y muerte" (400) ["The fourth sun, which is the sun of the Earth, which will disappear like the others, in the midst of earthquakes, hunger, destruction, war, and death"] (394).

At the end of his speech the Ancient introduces himself as "he who remembers," the guardian of "the book of destiny" and of memory (402; 396). It is most likely that the Ancient is Fuentes's literary invention, since there is no single figure in the Nahua pantheon with these attributes. In any case, this character represents a crucial motif in *Terra Nostra*. Memory, not only individual, but especially collective, is the originating force that sets in motion the rewriting of the past that Fuentes accomplishes in his novel. That explains why the figure of this emblematic character frames the Pilgrim's experiences in the Mexican land. The old man is the first who welcomes him, and he reappears at the end of his journey in the plaza of Tlatelolco to bid him farewell on his voyage back to Spain.

All the Pilgrim's experiences in Aztec Mexico occur between these two apparitions of the Ancient. The structure of this progression conforms to the pattern of funerary ceremonies customary among the Nahuas. According to Séjourné, the dead had to overcome seven difficult trials lasting four years before being able to rest. The last of these trials consisted of confronting the feared god of the dead, and the land of the dead could only be reached if the deceased could escape the god's rule and trickery. Séjourné relates these trials to different stages of Quetzalcoatl's life after leaving Tollan. Both the narrative of this phase of Quetzalcoatl's story and the funeral rites that, according to Séjourné, reenacted them, dramatized man's passage toward higher spheres of spirituality that would culminate in his union with the transcendent.[89]

Throughout his mysterious journey, the Pilgrim also faces a series of trials that he overcomes thanks to his inventiveness and adroitness. In the first he is trapped in the middle of a whirlpool. He escapes only after a careful observation of the mechanism of this natural phenomenon. In a second trial he confronts a group of natives ("the people of the jungle") after landing on the Mexican coast, and in this case, he saves his life by exchanging a pair of scissors for some gold. After being urged by the ancient to offer a new tribute, the Pilgrim shows him a mirror, escaping again from death in this way. In a later episode the Pilgrim is thrown into a sacrificial *cenote*, from which he emerges after manipulating the subterranean water channels. In the midst of the forest he meets a

monstrous woodsman (through a subsequent commentary we will
learn that he was one of the diverse manifestations of Tezcatlipoca).
The woodsman challenges the Pilgrim to seize his palpitating heart,
a deed the valiant Pilgrim will perform. In a new trial the so called
"Lady of Butterflies" (a synthesis of the Nahua goddesses Tlazol-
teotl and Itzpapalotl) offers him one of two possibilities before he
dies: either to enjoy a year of pleasure or to resume his aimless
wandering. The Pilgrim chooses the second of these alternatives,
escaping what otherwise would have been a certain death.[90]

After successfully overcoming these preparatory trials, the Pilgrim-Quetzalcoatl must face the last one, consisting of his descent
into the underworld and his confrontation with the sovereigns of the
Land of the Dead. This descent takes place in the following chapter
("Night of the Volcano"). Fuentes again presents a ritual of death
and rebirth through the character's symbolic descent and ascent.

For the narrative of the Pilgrim's descent Fuentes draws from one
of the legends that describe the creation of man, and the participation of Quetzalcoatl as demiurge. The *Leyenda de los soles* tells
how the gods assembled in Teotihuacan recognized the need to create a new human species. For this purpose, they entrusted Quetzalcoatl with the task of descending into Mictlan in search of the bones
that would create this new race. Once there, with the help of his
double or *nahual*, Quetzalcoatl overcame a series of trials conceived by the Lord and Lady of the Land of the Dead, and escaped
with the bones to Tamoanchan, where he infused life into them by
sprinkling them with his own blood.

Apart from minor details, Fuentes's account substantially follows
this legend. The main difference, however, is that the *Leyenda de
los soles* describes the creation of the men of the fifth sun, that is,
the men of the current era, whereas in Fuentes's novel the bones the
Pilgrim rescues create the first mestizos of the New World.[91] Instead
of sprinkling the bones with blood, Quetzalcoatl infuses life into
them with his tears. The bones are immediately transformed into
ten boys and ten girls who run together with the Pilgrim, who are
described "as if newly born," and who speak Spanish "with a much
sweeter tone."

This rewriting of Aztec cosmogony allows Fuentes to express his
foundational myth of *mestizaje*. Thus, the origin of Mexican mixed
blood in the novel is just the opposite of what it was in reality, that
is, not the fruit of violence and of rape, but a gift of the gods. Instead of the "cruel father," Cortés, Fuentes gives to the New World
a "generous father," Quetzalcoatl. The strategy is the same as that
articulated in Valerio Camillo's Theater of Memory: to show the

past that could have been but was not. In Part III of *Terra Nostra* ("The Next World"), Camillo himself describes his theater in terms that help us to understand both Fuentes's use of history and his concept of a textual utopia. The images projected in Camillo's theater encompass all the possibilities of the past, not only the ones that were fulfilled, but also those that could have been (567; 561). The goal of this great utopian machinery is to show a way out of the fatalism of history, an alternative to the endless repetition of that "permanent catastrophe" that we associate with Spanish-American history.[92]

"The New World" opposes the mythical pattern offered by the narratives of Quetzalcoatl to the epic of the conquest. It opposes utopia to apocalypse. We have already seen how these two components intersect in several of the existing versions of the myth.[93] Fuentes seems to follow closely Sahagún's account of how the Aztecs identified Cortés with the returning god. Through the multivalence and multifariousness that he confers on the Pilgrim, Fuentes takes this superimposition of Quetzalcoatl's return and the conquest of the New Spain to a fantastic extreme. It would be naive to establish a simple Pilgrim-Quetzalcoatl identification, since many other personalities can be perceived in this character. The Pilgrim's association with Cortés-Quetzalcoatl is, however, the most pervasive and is established from his first contacts with the natives of the continent. On many occasions, the Pilgrim is welcomed with expressions, such as "Has regresado, hermano. Has llegado a tu casa. Ocupa en ella tu lugar" (401) ["You have returned, brother. You have come home. Take your place in your house"] (395).[94]

The chapter entitled "Day of the Lagoon" describes the Pilgrim's march through Mexico Tenochtitlan along with the group of twenty mestizos who had been created by him in the Underworld. This new conquest of Mexico, corresponds in many details with Bernal Díaz del Castillo's narrative in his *Historia verdadera*. In fact, the Pilgrim, as narrator, also incorporates the personality of Díaz del Castillo himself.[95] The text reproduces, for example, the famous passage in which the chronicler recalls his awe when seeing the city in the lake for the first time.[96]

In "The New World" the arrival of the Pilgrim-Quetzalcoatl-Cortés to the Basin of Mexico coincides with the apparition of premonitions that follow those described by Sahagún. As the Pilgrim approaches Mexico-Tenochtitlan "a great thorn of fire" ascends to the sky as "a pyramid of pure light" (Sahagún's first omen); the waters of the lake "boiled and foamed and rose to great heights" (fifth omen); a "comet extended across the sky, and from it were born three other comets" (fourth); "lightening was flashing without the warning of thunder" (third); "a woman emerged from the haze" was weeping profoundly and sorrowfully lamenting the fate of her children and of her city (sixth); two-headed monsters were announcing the end of the world (eighth); and, finally, a crane with a mirror in its head is killed by the boatmen of the lake, and the mirror projects images of the conquistadors landing in Mexico (seventh). In the Pilgrim's meeting with Moctezuma (who is never mentioned by name), the Aztec ruler repeats word for word the above-quoted welcome speech that Sahagún reports in his *Historia General* (463; 455).

In the description of the time spent by the Pilgrim-Cortés in the Aztec capital Fuentes borrows from the information given by Cortés himself in his *Letters*, as well as to the writings of Gómara and Díaz del Castillo. The narrative of Quetzalcoatl's fall intermingles with these events. The reasons for the hero's fall as interpreted by Fuentes—drunkenness and fornication—recur here in an original form. Instead of Tezcatlipoca, it is the Lady of Butterflies, in her third apparition—this time as a decrepit old woman—who invites Quetzalcoatl to drink. Instead of the incest Fuentes sees in the *Anales*, in the novel the sexual transgression is manifested at first in the rape of the old woman. However, a few moments later the Pilgrim in his incarnation of Quetzalcoatl is accused by the lame prince (Moctezuma-Tezcatlipoca) of drunkenness and incest, which leads the reader to believe that the apparent encounter with the goddess could have been an act of sorcery or a new trick of the god-magician Tezcatlipoca. The latter's words repeat the version of the myth of Quetzalcoatl's fall that Fuentes appropriates and proposes in his essays and plays: "véanlo; vean al joven señor del amor y de la paz; vean al creador de los hombres; vean al educador manso y caritativo; vean al enemigo del sacrificio y de la guerra; vean caído al creador; vean su vergüenza desnuda y borracha; véanle embriagado, recostado con su propia hermana." (473) ["See him; see the Young Lord of love and peace; see the creator of men; see the gentle and charitable teacher; see the enemy of sacrifice and war; see the creator fallen; see his naked and drunken shame; see him intoxicated, lying with his own sister."] (464).

As in the legends of Topiltzin Quetzalcoatl, flight follows transgression. In his march, the Pilgrim stops for a time in the great plaza of Tlatelolco, where a poignant encounter with the ancient of memories and the Nahua poets and artisans takes place.[97] The end of "El mundo nuevo," with its description of the Pilgrim's flight and the references to Venus as a manifestation of Quetzalcoatl, poses a return to the dominion of the mythical narrative.[98]

The Pilgrim's story loosely follows the archetypal pattern in seven stages that Nicholson deduces from the narratives about Topiltzin-Quetzalcoatl: birth, youth, enthronement, apogee, fall, flight, and death or disappearance. 1) The Pilgrim's awakening in the New World works as his birth (he is ignorant of his origin). 2) His initiation into adulthood and subsequent acceptance by the community take place in the company of the People of the Jungle, from whom he learns their life and customs, and by whom he is accepted as a member. 3) After the apparent death of the ancient of memories, the Pilgrim occupies his place (although this enthronement is presented in ambiguous terms); 4) the apogee of the Pilgrim occurs after his overcoming of the seven trials that culminate with his descent into the underworld, his creation of a new race and his victorious march over Mexico Tenochtitlan. 5) The Pilgrim's fall is produced, as in several versions of the myth, as a result of Tezcatlipoca's temptations. 6) His fall is followed by the departure narrated in the section "Day of Flight." 7) The last stage in the Pilgrim's progress consists in his disappearance into the sea in the direction of the east and under the sign of Venus.

The two main problems encountered in the analysis of "The New World" are the fragmentary nature of transcribed pre-Hispanic mythology and the ambivalence of Fuentes's characters. In the realm of Nahua religion it is difficult to come to definitive conclusions. The fragmentation of Nahua myths has been attributed to their oral transmission, which precludes access to original sources, free from the transculturating effects that resulted from the conquest. The problem becomes more pronounced in the tracing of Quetzalcoatl's saga, which has acquired different value depending on which interest groups is exploiting it. The most important functional value derived from the present analysis of the myth is its explanatory and legitimizing power. Quetzalcoatl's myth acts as a supplement to history, covering a space that remained empty in the teleological thought of both Aztecs and Spaniards. All the elements of the conquest that otherwise were considered inconceivable could be explained in light of this myth. For the conquistadors the legend of a sovereign-god's return favored their pretensions of judicial legitimation as natural lords of the New World. For many of the missionaries it implied either the fantastic idea of a preconquest evangelization, or a reflection of their own apocalyptic mentality (an announcement, for example, of the new church that they wanted to found in the New World). For many of the vanquished it justified their defeat, not for lack of courage or military capability, but as the rule of fate. For those who were at odds with the Tenochcas, like the inhabitants of Tlatelolco who helped Sahagún in his *Historia General*, it allowed them to discredit the figure of Moctezuma, presenting him as a weak and inadequate emperor.

Fuentes's use of Quetzalcoatl's myth is inspired by a similar legitimizing interest. He builds an amalgamating vision in which the elements of Quetzalcoatl the god (Ehecatl) and of Quetzalcoatl the hero (Topiltzin) are fused.[99] His inclusive collage is fed from the numerous versions of the myth and the legend, a strategy that affords him a great functional flexibility in the fictional application of both. Among all the values attributed to Quetzalcoatl, Fuentes shows a particular preference for his demiurgic and cultural aspects. The element of terror implied in the figure of Ehecatl or in the warlike attributes present in some versions of Topiltzin's tale are absent in Fuentes's narrative.

The vision of the conquest that follows from "The New World" exalts the concept of *mestizaje*. The conquest is presented as a catastrophic phenomenon that nevertheless produced a positive element: the creation of a new multiethnic and pluralistic civilization. In dealing with the protagonists of this historical moment, Fuentes follows the line established in *Todos los gatos son pardos*. Fuentes opposes Cortés's power of will to Moctezuma's power of fatality. Both leaders are portrayed in a negative way. The anti-epic Cortés is presented as the "cruel father," hence Fuentes frequent borrowing from Bernal Díaz's *Historia verdadera* and Sahagún's *Historia general* rather than from Cortés's *Cartas de relación*. From the indigenous perspective, Moctezuma is presented in a marginal way, to the extent that he is not even directly mentioned. The Aztec ruler is portrayed with the attributes of Tezcatlipoca, the god of darkness, wars, crossroads, and disputes. On the other hand, "The New World" idealizes both common people (especially the Indian communities that were subjected to Aztec rule) and Nahua craftsmen and artists. To that effect, Fuentes makes a free use of Sahagún's work, which includes this vision of the vanquished.

Metafiction

"The New World" lacks the great unifying image such as El Escorial in Part I and the Theater of Memory in Part III that would exemplify one of the two poles of the aesthetic conflict dramatized in *Terra Nostra*: the struggle between repressive power and creative imagination. The focus of Part II is rather on the analysis of the conflict itself and on its transplantation to the Americas. Hence, the metaphors associated with the above-mentioned poles alternate throughout "The New World," without one completely dominating the other.

Although the text reflects and foresees the signs of the utterance and of the enunciation that characterize the rest of the novel, the abysmal structure of "The New World" is principally built upon mythical bases. The use of myth with reflexive intentions aligns "The New World" with Dällenbach's category of "transcendental *mise en abyme*." This is a level of reflection that presents, usually through myth, a fiction of origin, a metaphor of the reality that generates the world of the work. Its goal is to reflect within the text itself "what simultaneously originates, motivates, institutes and unifies it."[100]

The originating motif of *Terra Nostra*, as reflected in the Pilgrim's story, is the above-mentioned struggle between the sphere of absolute power and death, embodied by the god Tezcatlipoca in his multiple manifestations, and the world of imagination and life, epitomized here by the Pilgrim in his role of Quetzalcoatl as a Messianic cultural hero. This confrontation, which in "The Old World" revolved around El Señor and his prisonlike palace, on the one hand, and the alternative movement represented by the heterodox groups, on the other, is transplanted to the New World and invested with the attributes of pre-Hispanic mythologies. Thus, "The New World" vindicates the multivocal figures of anonymous poets and artists who defy the tyrannical power of the Aztec emperor, the *Tlatoani* or the Lord of the Great Voice.

In addition to the major fiction of origin, which corresponds to the global development of this second part, "The New World" presents several examples of Dällenbach's three other levels of reflection: fictional, enunciative, and metatextual. In order to exemplify the use of these three categories in "The New World" three of the moments of highest reflexivity will be considered: the first meeting with the ancient of memories ("The Ancient's Legend"), the episode in which the Pilgrim faces the staff of mirrors of the god Xipe Totec ("Night of Reflections"), and the final reencounter with the ancient in the Plaza of Tlatelolco ("Day of Flight"). In all three of these cases the different structural levels of reflection overlap. They are all fictions of origin channeled through consistent references to myth; however, they also contain summaries of the story (reflections of the utterance), meditations on the act of writing or reading (reflections of the enunciation), and representations of the poetics, aesthetic credo, or manifesto underlying the novel and conditioning its interpretation (reflections of the code).

While "The New World" generally follows the archetypal pattern of the narratives of Quetzalcoatl, Fuentes consistently introduces original elements so as to convey his own view of the Hispanic world and literature. In the case of Quetzalcoatl's fall, Fuentes introduces an innovation that links "The New World" with the reflexive universe of the two other parts of *Terra Nostra*: the immediate reason for Quetzalcoatl's flight is not drunkenness or incest, but the terror produced by a specular image.

In this episode, "Night of the Reflection," the Pilgrim asks Tezcatlipoca about those moments in his journey throughout Mexican lands that he has forgotten; the god-sorcerer gives him as response the staff of mirrors of Xipe Totec. Each of those mirrors reflects an image of death in which the Pilgrim has been the protagonist. The reflections allude to the general destruction perpetrated by the conquistadors, focusing on violent actions carried out both by Cortés and Pedro de Alvarado in the conquest of New Spain and by the Pilgrim in *Terra Nostra*. The Pilgrim believes that the mirrors reflect what he did during those forgotten days, but Tezcatlipoca warns him that "the mirrors of this staff see into the future" (479), implying in this way both a past of desolation and a prophecy of destruction for Mexico. Such omens are fulfilled when in his flight the Pilgrim witnesses a massive killing in the plaza of Tlatelolco, an event whose description evokes three different historical incidents: the past slaughter ordered by Pedro de Alvarado in the *Templo Mayor* of Mexico Tenochtitlan, the great Tlatelolco battle that was the last stand of the Aztecs after their capital had already fallen, and the premonition of the future massacre of university students in Tlatelolco in 1968.

"Night of Reflections" fulfills the compiling task that Dällenbach confers on the reflection of the utterance. This kind of specular structure allows the reader to summarize what has happened and foresee what is to come, as well as to glimpse that which precedes, follows, and runs parallel to the *énoncé* itself. As a consequence, the novel expands beyond its physical frames in an attempt to defy closure and to approach Fuentes's utopia of the total novel.

In addition, this passage presents several features that allows it to work as a reflection of the enunciation. On the one hand, the mechanism of projection of specular images evokes one of the novel's major devices.[101] On the other, the staff of mirrors of Xipe Totec recalls two memorable examples in the Spanish American literary tradition: Fitón's orb in Ercilla's *La Araucana* (1569) and Borges's

"The Aleph" (1945). In his epic poem about the conquest of the Araucanians, Ercilla introduces several supernatural mechanisms to provide a simultaneous view of the historical events of imperial Spain. The best known of them is a glass orb that the magician Fitón uses to show Ercilla, the poet, images of the Battle of Lepanto (Canto XXIV) and then the whole world, country by country (Canto XXVII). Apart from the obvious intentional differences between Ercilla's and Fuentes's works, it is striking that in both of them history is often communicated through supernatural agents (Fitón and Tezcatlipoca) who use an all-encompassing mirror mechanism (a glass orb and a staff of mirrors) and that a writer's surrogate is the one who witnesses and then tries to communicate this experience (Ercilla's *persona* and Fuentes's Pilgrim).

However, Fuentes's most immediate reference in this episode is probably not Ercilla but Borges. In his short story "El Aleph," Borges presents one of the most famous *speculum mundi* in the Hispanic tradition, an object (the Aleph) that magically comprises the whole universe. Furthermore, the totalizing power of this fantastic object has three related manifestations that link the search for totality to the act of writing. The two main characters of the story, Carlos Argentino Daneri and the narrator called Borges, are writers involved in the impossible task of verbalizing their experience of totality. They struggle in vain to express the fullness of reality, which is simultaneous, in words that are successive. Although they try different solutions (maximal in Daneri's case, minimal in Borges's), both finally give up. In search of literary recognition, Daneri devotes himself to more futile enterprises, and Borges the narrator acknowledges that his memory of the Aleph is blurred by the passing of time.

But the Aleph is not only a fantastic object. As the narrator of Borges's story notes at the end, the Aleph is also the first letter of the Hebrew alphabet, a letter that for the cabalists means unlimited and pure divinity, the sign that encompasses all the other signs of human language.[102] Borges's use of the cabalistic Aleph foretells the poststructuralist concept of the universe as a text, and this causes us to read the story as a metaphor for the act of writing and a reflection upon the limits of literary representation. In this short story Borges ironically toys with the idea of conveying the whole of reality through literature. The irony of Borges's irony is that, although his story parodies the futile attempt to grasp totality, it shows the reader a way to approach it. We glimpse, however imperfectly, the simultaneity he is trying to convey by means of the narrator's chaotic enumeration. Fuentes's work is in many senses both a rewriting of this struggle with language and an attempt to counter-act the forgetfulness expressed by Borges's narrator at the end of the story.

We are faced, therefore, with three specular metaphors that in three moments in Spanish American history and literature have repeated a similar eagerness for totalization. While Fitón's glass orb serves a structural purpose in Ercilla (the presentation of events that are simultaneous or immediately posterior to the conquest of the Araucanians), in Borges the Aleph communicates the author's deeply skeptical view of the boundaries of representation and about the incapacity of human intelligence to penetrate into a chaotic universe.[103] In Fuentes, instead, the different reconstructions of the Aleph (the staff of mirrors of Xipe Totec and Valerio Camillo's Theater of Memory) present a utopia of simultaneity, not only with structural intentions (as in Ercilla) or ironical purposes (as in Borges), but also with aesthetic and political motives. Reality, in Fuentes's view, is endlessly multiple, and only an equally multiple perspective will successfully attempt to disclose its secrets. This multiplicity will never achieve the infinitude that is implicit in the concept of the Aleph, but the writer should make of that total plurality the utopian goal of his work.

As with the images reflected in the staff of mirrors, the intervention of the ancient of memories refers to events that precede and follow the present narrative. Given that "The Ancient's Legend" portrays a Nahua cosmogony in which Quetzalcoatl plays a leading role, in identifying the young Pilgrim as the god-hero, the ancient inscribes the character into the myth's web. In this way that which is part of the past (the legend of Quetzalcoatl) is also seen as destiny with regard to the Pilgrim. These implications are fully developed in the episode that portrays the Pilgrim's final encounter with the ancient of memories. Directly in the center of the immense plaza of Tlatelolco the Pilgrim meets the old man again, and is welcomed with the usual words, except for a small change: "Sé muy bienvenido, mi hermano (. . .). Te hemos esperado. Te esperaremos siempre" (482) ["You are welcome, my brother. We have awaited you. We shall always await you"] (474). The last sentence alludes to the need of a permanent belief in this myth as a source of utopian hope. It also suggests its circularity and its inextinguishable nature: The Pilgrim is awaited to fulfill Quetzalcoatl's promise, but at the same time that he fulfills his promise, he destroys it, he escapes, and his return is awaited again. The ancient's cryptic message refers also to a new facet of that is of capital importance for Fuentes: The Pilgrim is recognized by the ancient as Quetzalcoatl in his role as cultural and political leader, as the inventor of writing, guardian of memory, and standard-bearer of progress and change. The ancient's words summarize the martyrlike and Messianic role that Fuentes attributes to the Latin American intellectual and, in particular, to the writer throughout the continent's history:

> Tu destino es ser perseguido. Luchar. Ser derrotado. Renacer de tu derrota. Regresar. Hablar. Recordarles lo olvidado a todos. Reinar por un instante. Ser derrotado de nuevo por las fuerzas del mundo. Huir. Regresar. Recordar. Un trabajo sin fin. El más doloroso de todos. Libertad es el nombre de tu tarea. Un nombre con muchos hombres (484).

> [Your destiny is to be pursued. To struggle. To be defeated. To be reborn from your defeat. To return. To speak. To remind men of what they have forgotten. To reign for an instant. To be defeated again by the forces of the world. To flee. To return. To remember. An endless labor. The most painful of all labors. Freedom is the name of your task. One word represented by many men] (475).

As a reflection of the utterance, the ancient's last words summarize the dynamics of Quetzalcoatl's myth, foretell the hero's fate, and trap him in the circular view of time that characterizes Nahua cosmology. The ancient's message also carries the attributes of a poetic and political manifesto, one that coincides with Fuentes's cultural project, as expressed in his essays.[104]

The metatextual nature of this passage is reinforced by another event that contemplates both the Messianic role of the writer and of the power of the word as part of a continuum that in Mexico has its origin in the pre-Cortesian tradition. The ancient's political harangue about the role of the writer as a permanent rebel is followed by his passionate homage to the ignored side of the Nahua world: not the cruel aspect of the empire, but the world of craftsmen who meet in the plaza of Tlatelolco (484; 476). In this universe of the Bakhtinian encounter and exchange of the plaza, the Pilgrim hears a series of enigmatic phrases of uncertain origin that underline this need for the writer to persist in his writing:

> No cesarán mis flores . . .
> No cesará mi canto . . .
> Lo elevo . . .
> Nosotros también cantos nuevos elevamos aquí . . .
> Deléitese con ellas el grupo de nuestros amigos . . .
> Disípese con ellas la tristeza de nuestro corazón . . .
> Tus cantos reúno: como esmeraldas los ensarto . . .

Adórnate con ellas . . .
Es en la tierra tu riqueza única . . .
¿Se irá tan solo mi corazón como las flores que fueron pereciendo?
¿Nada mi nombre será algún día?
Al menos flores, al menos cantos (484)

[My flowers will never cease . . .
My song will never cease . . .
I raise it . . .
We, too, raise new songs here . . .
Also, new flowers are in our hands . . .
With them delight the assemblage of our friends . . .
With them dissipate the sadness of our hearts . . .
I gather your songs; I string them like emeralds . . .
Adorn yourself with them . . .
On this earth they are your only riches . . .
Will my heart fade away, solitary as the perishing flowers?
Will my name one day be nothing?
At least, flowers; at least, songs] (476)

All these verses come from different poems collected in the six-teenth-century Nahua manuscript of the *Cantares mexicanos*.[105] Thus, what is presented as an organic unity is, in reality, a collage of poems that deal with recurrent motifs in Nahua poetry, especially the transience of our lives on earth and the need to enjoy this mortal life. A great many of these poems are praises and eulogies that the poets addressed to each other, something that fits very well into the tribute that Fuentes pays to the figure of the writer in *Terra Nostra*. The above-quoted fragments from Fuentes's novel are presented as phrases that the Pilgrim hears by chance in the bustle of the plaza, without having a definite and individual addressee. The multiplicity of voices that make up the poem contributes to create the poly-phonic and democratic impression that Fuentes establishes as a uto-pian proposal opposed to the despotic power of the Lord of the Great Voice (the Aztec emperor).[106] In contrast to the monologic discourse of the tyrant, the author of *Terra Nostra* presents the transgressive value of a community based on the equality of expres-sion: "Diste la palabra a todos hermano. Y por temor a la palabra de todos, tu enemigo se sentirá siempre amenazado" (485) ["You gave the word to all men, brother. And your enemy will always feel threatened"] (476).

However, the image of Nahua poetry that Fuentes offers does not correspond to historical reality. On the one hand, poetry among the Nahuas was not exactly a popular and democratic form of expression—or, at least, not in the sense we give to these concepts today, but rather it was a vehicle of expression of Aztec nobility.[107] On the other hand, a motif in Nahua poetry is the comparison of the poem with the flower, both for its beauty and for its ephemerality. Although Fuentes's selection maintains this flower-poem comparison, he opposes the transience of life with the permanence of art. Let us compare the last lines of the above-quoted passage with what seems to be their original source: the poem that Garibay suggestively calls "The Poet's Mission":

> De modo igual me iré
> que las flores que fueron pereciendo,
> ¡Nada será mi renombre algún día!
> ¡Nada será mi fama en la tierra!
> ¡Al menos flores, al menos cantos![108]
>
> [In the same way I will be gone
> as the flowers that were perishing,
> My name will be nothing one day!
> My fame will be nothing on the earth!
> At least the flowers, at least the songs!]

By means of a clever manipulation of punctuation, Fuentes modifies the original sense of the poem. What in the Nahuatl text is an acceptance of the evanescence of all earthly things, becomes in Fuentes's text a utopian defense of the permanent value of art and of the transforming power of the word. Fuentes's manipulation of documentary sources in *Terra Nostra* is a function of his own cultural and political design.

This design is communicated through the ancient, who ends his speech with a new affirmation of the utopian value of the New World. His words summarize the Pilgrim's arrival and experiences in America: "La libertad fue la orilla que el hombre primero pisó. Paraiso fue el nombre de esa libertad. La perdimos palmo a palmo. La ganaremos palmo a palmo" (485) ["Freedom was the shore that man first trod. Paradise was the name of that freedom. Inch by inch, we lost it. Inch by inch, we shall regain it"] (477). The ancient concludes his speech with a declaration of faith in the need to fight for social transformation, even though the fight is seen as doomed to fail. At that precise moment, they hear the uproar of the massacre at Tlatelolco, and the Pilgrim begins the last steps of his flight.

Fuentes emphasizes Quetzalcoatl's role as a giver of life and as a cultural leader of his people. Both aspects of Quetzalcoatl (demiurge and liberator) find an original synthesis in "The New World" through the Messianic value that Fuentes confers on the Latin American writer. His reinvention of the myth reveals, behind the figure of Quetzalcoatl, that of the man of creation and, in the Mexican case, that of the mestizo novelist as one of the leaders of cultural and political change.

"The New World" is presented as a model for the great utopian enterprise that, according to Fuentes, Latin Americans must face: the creation of a great synthesis of their deeply heterogeneous reality. On the literary level, this synthesis manifests itself in open and encyclopedic forms that allow the coexistence of "todos los contrarios vistos simultáneamente desde todas las perspectivas posibles" ["all the contraries seen simultaneously from all possible perspectives."][109] This "utopian heresy" is the most important weapon that Fuentes proposes in order to subvert the discourse of power that is expressed in the epic visions of the past. In this context, Fuentes rewrites the Nahua epic as well as the conquest epic, stripping both of their old univocal meaning. Disposessed of their precise ritual function, pre-Hispanic myths acquire a great plurality of meaning, turning into paradigms of the open work that Fuentes proposes as the aesthetic ideal of art in our century. Deprived of their bureaucratic or evangelizing goals, the chronicles of the Indies rewrite the origin of mestizaje in Latin America. Myth and history intersect in this second part of *Terra Nostra* not to repeat the past, but to create a new world.

THE NEXT WORLD: COUNTERHEGEMONIC DISCOURSES

While "The Old World" focuses on the universe of orthodoxy embodied by El Señor and his necropolis, "The Next World" brings to the foreground those groups and traditions that stand against such a universe: the Spain of the three cultures (Christian, Moslem, Jewish), the heterodox currents of thought, the revolt of Castilian townships, and the Renaissance utopias. Although these forces were already active in the first part of the novel, it is in "The Next World" that they achieve a dominant role. "The Next World" revolves around a sphere of possibilities, possibilities that, although fatally crushed and negated in the Hispanic tradition, recur at periodic intervals. In order to find a way out of this deterministic and endless cycle of hope and destruction, Fuentes conceives a utopian machine—Valerio Camillo's Theater of Memory—that works as the novel's central metaphor. It is through this unifying *mise en abyme* that Fuentes's novel reflects on its own fictional methods and the aesthetic ideas from which they originate.

Historical Background

The Spanish tradition of ethnic and cultural coexistence among Christians, Jews, and Moors is one of the elements that El Señor's univocal and intolerant world clearly opposes. This tradition of multicultural commingling was aborted when the Spanish sovereigns decreed the expulsion of the Jews (1492), continued persecuting converts (especially in the reign of Philip II), and expelled the *Moriscos* under Philip III (1609). In his analysis of Spain's tricultural heritage, Fuentes closely follows the views of Spanish historian Americo Castro.[110] Castro inverts the traditional conception of the Christian world as superior to Hebrew and Islamic cultures. For Castro, the most valuable elements of Hispanic culture have their origin in the two expelled communities, in comparison to which Christianity always occupied a position of inferiority.[111] The Islamic influence was manifested principally in the flowering of science, philosophy, music, and literature, as well as in the sensual conception of art that was absent in the austere and mournful Christian Middle Ages. The Jewish community, in turn, contributed noticeably to the intellectual life of the country. Thanks to Jewish writers, the Spanish language became a vehicle of intellectual communication and acquired literary dignity.[112]

Fuentes recognizes his debt to Castro's theses regarding tricultural Spain. In his "Bibliografía conjunta" he mentions three titles of the Spanish historian: *El pensamiento de Cervantes*, *España en su historia*, and *La realidad histórica de España*. However, the mention of these three in *Cervantes* is somewhat baffling. González Echevarría has pointed out the major divergences between these three essays, divergences that in the case of the first two works become incompatibilities.[113] In fact, in *El pensamiento de Cervantes* (1925), Castro discusses the influence of Italian humanism on Spanish writers. Castro's concern at this early period in his career is to understand Spanish culture within the currents of European thought. The publication of *España en su historia* in 1948 implies a dramatic shift in his interests. Since then, Castro's studies focus more and more on the singular aspects of Spanish culture instead of on its indebtedness to European models.[114] Castro finds this singularity in the intermingling of Moors, Jews, and Christians— among which the Arab world stands out.[115] As González Echevarría has correctly pointed out, *La realidad histórica de España* (1954,

1962) is not really a new work, but rather a thorough revision of *España en su historia*.[116] The revision is principally aimed at underlining the contribution of both Jews and converted Jews to the history and culture of Spain.

Fuentes's attraction to Castro's writings is found both in specific areas of his work and as the very basis of his historiographic vision. Just as Castro's great texts had emerged as a reaction against the kind of positivist historiography that had been practiced so far, so Fuentes declares that Latin American culture urgently needs to free itself from the burden of positivism, which has proven to be so counterproductive in literature.[117] In addition, Castro proposes a global view that accounts for both relevant political events and the gestation of Spanish culture during the Middle Ages and the Renaissance. This overall perspective, which moves away from the privileged castes in order to favor the marginalized groups, suits Fuentes's simultaneously totalizing and decentering conception of history. Both Castro and Fuentes base their historical view on a subverted original harmony: the Spain of cultural and religious coexistence that reached its apogee in the thirteenth century, with Alfonso X's court of intellectuals.[118] Alfonso brought to his court Arab and Jewish men of letters who worked together to translate the Bible, the Koran, the cabala, the Talmud, and the Panchatantra into Spanish. Castro's theories concerning the problems of interethnic comingling are ultimately used in *Terra Nostra* as a genealogy of Fuentes's concept of Latin American *mestizaje*, a topic that is discussed at several points in the novel.

The other great challenge to El Señor's monolithic orthodoxy comes from the heresies and millennial movements that flourished in the Middle Ages. According to Fuentes, heresy undermined the foundations of scholasticism. By presenting mutually exclusive versions of the Scriptures, heretics subverted the Church's unitarian dogma and pursued freedom of thought. As explained by Fuentes, Syrian or Egyptian Gnostics, Docetists, Ebonites, Sabellians, Arians, Apollinarians, and Nestorians rewrote Biblical tradition in a way that reflects his own literary utopia: the creation of a fictional Aleph, the work that contemplates all things from all points of view.[119] Similarly, the messianic groups, such as the Flagellants, Beghards, Free Spirit Brothers, Popular Crusaders, Cathars, Waldensians, and Adamites protested against the impositions of medieval orthodoxy and announced, according to Fuentes, the changes that later on would bring about the scientific revolution.

The violent synthesis of apocalyptic and utopian thought embodied by these groups fascinated Fuentes. Its traces can be found not only in *Terra Nostra* but also in *Cervantes* and *Cristóbal Nonato*. According to Norman Cohn, such movements originate in the confluence of general poverty in the Middle Ages and in the emergence of prophecies announcing the promise of a new Paradise on earth.[120] Fuentes mentions Cohn in both the acknowledgment section of *Terra Nostra* and his "Bibliografía conjunta," and repeats, sometimes word by word, several passages from Cohn's *The Pursuit of the Millennium* (1957). However, neither in *Cervantes* nor in *Terra Nostra* does Fuentes refer to what could be considered the most negative side of these movements. In the prologue to his essay, Cohn makes clear his interest in establishing a connection between the proletarian millenarianism of the Middle Ages and the great totalitarian movements of the twentieth century. The frequently gratuitous violence of these groups is only obliquely mentioned by Fuentes and is justified as the result of an intolerable situation of injustice. For Fuentes, these movements attempted to fulfill at a practical level the original meaning of "heresy," "to take for oneself, to choose."[121]

The revolt of the Castilian townships is another oppositional movement that has captured Fuentes's attention. In his consideration of this historical phenomenon as one of the first modern revolutions, Fuentes follows the version of the Spanish historian José Antonio Maravall.[122] According to Maravall, during the sixteenth century Castilian institutions were undergoing a process of political development that may have led to the creation of autonomous democratic organs of government.[123] In Fuentes's version, when Charles V came to the throne, Castilian townships saw their civil liberties and local institutions threatened. The new king's policy was oriented toward increasing centralization and concentration of power in the crown. Fuentes sees in both the social composition of the rebels and the language of their manifestos, a progressive movement of democratic intentions. From his point of view, the defeat of the *comuneros* in Villalar (1525) was a hard blow for the modernization of Spain. However, Fuentes's interest in this historical event pertains not to its local or national relevance, but to its repercussions in Spanish-American history. Charles V's crushing of the institutional reforms and public liberties in Villalar, only a few years after the conquest of Mexico (1521), implied, for Fuentes, a victory for the authoritarian machinery of the Spanish empire and the frustration of all democratic hopes for Spanish America.[124]

A brief analysis of Fuentes's use of historical sources dealing with the *comuneros* again reveals his simplification of complex historical phenomena. In *Cervantes*, Fuentes rejects the interpretation of this movement as an anachronistic outbreak of feudalism. In contrast with this negative evaluation of the revolt, Fuentes proposes Maravall's democratic celebration, since for Fuentes Maravall is "the author of the definitive book on the *comunero* revolution."[125] In a similar fashion, Fuentes emphasizes the work of a new generation of historians who, in the same line as Maravall, "has put things firmly in their place," depicting the townships as "the expression of unrest of the Castilian urban middle class."[126] Both the form and content of these statements are highly questionable. We can hardly talk about "definitive books" in historiography: to do so would imply to favor the univocal interpretations of history that historiographic metafiction and Fuentes himself purport to fight. Regarding the sharp identification of the *comunero* movement with the Castilian urban bourgeoisie, such identification does not necessarily have to put things in "their" place, but in "the" place that Fuentes would like them to be.

One of the obsessions in Fuentes's work is to account for the difficulties in creating a broad-based democratic bourgeoisie in Spanish America. The *comunero* revolt offers Fuentes an opportunity to explain the roots of the problem, which he finds in the events of imperial Spain. However, as happens with the rest of the historical motifs discussed so far, this specific event is open to other interpretations. Two of the most prestigious scholars of imperial Spain, J. H. Elliott and John Lynch, cast doubt upon the political transcendence that Maravall confers on the revolt. Specifically, Elliot underlines the initial lack of a unified political program among the insurrectionists, as well as the deeply traditionalist origin of the upheaval. Furthermore, Elliot points to the xenophobic nature of the movement in its early stages. He interprets the revolt as the culmination of the popular indignation against both a foreign king and a court that were threatening the interests of the Castilian low nobility.[127] Similarly, John Lynch points out the internal divisions among the *comuneros*, as well as the different stages of the uprising (from a revolt of the low nobility to a social revolution). The defeat of the *comunidades* in Villalar certainly meant the consolidation of absolutism and centralism in the peninsula, but its importance in the political future of the New World is a topic that remains to be studied.

This political catastrophe that Fuentes sees in the repression of the Castilian townships did not involve a cultural regression. While the Middle Ages were restrictive and dogmatic, the Renaissance brought a great expansion of knowledge, the prominence of ambiguity, paradox, and the plurality of meanings.[128] The Renaissance was also the age of utopias, the period in which the myth of a perfect society came alive, the moment in which the interests of community prevailed over those of power, and that utopian consciousness emerges, in Fuentes's view, as an immediate result of the New World discoveries. For Fuentes, America was founded as a utopia, and its destiny became and still remains inseparable from utopian ideals.[129]

History in the Novel

The four elements under analysis in the Next World (multicultural Spain, heretical millenarianism, the *comunero* revolt, and Renaissance utopias) form an alternative to El Señor's worldview. All of these forces develop a recurring pattern that explains how difficult it was for modern thought to penetrate Spain and Spanish America. This pattern may be summarized as follows: 1) presentation of a challenge to El Señor's absolute power; 2) repression of the transgressive movement; 3) consequences of this conflict for the New World; and 4) possibility of a utopia that would avert the repetition of these errors.

For Fuentes, the coexistence of Jews, Moors, and Christians in medieval Spain represents one of the embodiments of the cultural utopia he longs for. Following Américo Castro's theories, Fuentes presents, through the character of Mijail Ben Sama (Miguel de la Vida), a compendium of the three cultures that shared their lives and thoughts for centuries on the Iberian peninsula. Unlike the blood purity defended by El Señor and watched over by the Inquisition, Mijail is "dueño de todas las sangres" (252; 246), an affirmation that is frequently repeated throughout the novel.[130] This racial intermingling, which has its correspondence with a religious and cultural syncretism, is seen as part of the nature of Spain itself, which distinguishes it from all other European nations: "Sólo en España se dieron cita y florecieron los tres pueblos del Libro: cristianos, moros y judíos" (568) ["Only in Spain did the three peoples of the Book—Christians, Moors, and Jews—meet and flourish"] (562). According to Fuentes, the moments of simultaneous economic prosperity and cultural splendor occurred only when tolerance and cooperation were a reality in Spanish society. In the reign of Ferdinand III, for example, Castilian industry and culture thrived as never before: "moros y judíos aportaban a la barbarie goda, arquitectura y música, industria y filosofía, medicina y poesía . . . y así prosperaron las ciudades, se gestaron las instituciones de la libertad local" (635) ["the Moors and Jews brought to Gothic barbarism architecture and music, industry and philosophy, medicine and poetry . . . and thus cities prospered, and institutions of local liberty were taking shape"] (630). Religious dogmatism and fanaticism, which reached its culmination with the expulsion of Jews in 1492, constituted, on the contrary, one of the most insurmountable obstacles to the incorporation of Spain into the modern world.[131]

Mijail's death by fire, decreed by El Señor, symbolizes in the novel the negation of the possibilities embodied by the seven hundred years of fertile multicultural coexistence: the possibility of a common space of tolerance, the creation of democratic institutions, and the development of an energetic financial and trading class. This historical reality was to have important repercussions in Spanish America, where Spain's multicultural experience would constitute the foundations for utopian experiments, but where its repressive tradition would also be repeated in similar episodes of ethnic, social, and religious intolerance.

In Christian Europe the Middle Ages is the period of emergence and consolidation of scholastic dogma. However, it is also the moment of heresies and millennial movements, two phenomena that paved the way for the modernity and the expansion of intellectual horizons brought about by the Renaissance. In *Terra Nostra* Fuentes offers alternatives to the inertia of dogma in what may be considered a cycle of heretical thought. Chapters such as "Victory," "The First Testament," "Schwester Katrei," "Hetergenbosch," "The Free Spirit," "The Defeat," and "Seventh Day" give voice to an enormous number of interpretations of reality that are often contradictory, but that always undermine the point of view sanctioned by the religious hierarchy.

In "First Testament" the novel paradoxically discusses several of these heretical views through El Señor, the figure who embodies precisely the dogma against which these heresies rebel. El Señor dictates his secretary, Guzmán, a first version of his will, which is in reality a long series of divergent interpretations of Christian faith and, especially, of relevant episodes in the life of Christ. The testament basically moves between the exposition of actual theological controversies (the Gnostic view of the world's creation as the work of low powers [197; 192] or Basílides's negation of Jesus's crucifixion and resurrection [208; 202]) and the suggestion of blasphemous apocryphal possibilities (Jesus's presumed homosexuality [206; 200] or the Virgin's promiscuity [218; 213]). By establishing a written record of the potentialities opened by heretical thought El Señor does not seek, of course, to spread them, but rather to keep them under check. Since he believes himself to be the only one in possession of the privilege of producing and interpreting textual reality, he confines the subversive movements to the realm of writing, where he believes he has absolute control. However, subsequent events in the novel prove him to be wrong. El Señor's ultimate failure stems from a double defeat: on the textual level, new works are produced by those who sympathize with heresy and are spread by the recently invented printing press; on the level of the extratextual reality, new geographic and scientific discoveries deny the absolute closure imposed by El Señor.

The novel's exposition of a long series of theological possibilities responds to the same globalizing impulse that was discussed in the previous sections and will be reexamined in the analysis of Valerio Camillo's Theater of Memory: the presentation of the past from all possible perspectives. In offering a seemingly endless number of alternatives to the orthodox version of events, and in showing the arbitrariness behind its empowered status, official history ends by losing all legitimacy.[132]

For Fuentes, millennial movements exemplify the revolutionary tendencies that materialized in the Middle Ages. One of these groups, the Brethren of the Free Spirit, is the focus of chapter 119. "The Free Spirit" describes the unstoppable advance of an army of poor led by a nameless heresiarch and by Ludovico, a theology student and one of the novel's "dreamers." This heresiarch, who is described as "the prophet of Millennium," evokes the image of the Pilgrim (a blond young man with six toes on each foot and a red cross on his back). Ludovico, on the other hand, is associated with the novel's heretical movements. Both of them lead a crusade that seeks "to sweep away the corrupt Church of the Antichrist in Rome" and to abolish all social hierarchies. They deny, among other things, private property, authority, sin, marriage, chastity, and priesthood, and propose, instead, a community of goods, anarchy, innocence, free sex, and the unrestrained freedom of the spirit. In his description of the movement Fuentes reproduces the information given by Norman Cohn about this group, which both consider the most radical of the millennial sects. Cohn emphasizes in his essay the revolutionary potential of this Brotherhood, which was opposed to all forms of power and rejected the given rules of moral, religious, and political behavior. Similarly, Fuentes sees in this phenomenon an early manifestation of the social revolutions that came with the Modern Age.[133] They both quote the poet Suchenwirt, who invited the dispossessed men of the Middle Ages to act out the ultimate dream of heresy: "The coffers of the rich are full, those of the poor are empty. The poor man's belly is hollow . . . Hack down the rich man's door! We're going to dine with him. It's better to be cut down, all of us, than die of hunger, we'd rather risk our lives bravely than perish in this way."[134]

As in all the other movements belonging to this oppositional cycle, heretics and millennialists are crushed by the machinery of absolute power. The heretics' defeat is presented in the novel from two different perspectives. Chapter 3 ("Victory") shows the point of view of the supposed victors and is focused on El Señor's thoughts. Chapter 122 ("The Defeat") offers, instead, the perspective of the defeated, focusing on Ludovico. Both chapters describe the meeting between these two characters in the cathedral of the nameless city where El Señor's troops put an end to the heretical resistance. However, El Señor's victory is not represented as absolute. It is a political rather than a religious victory. Hidden behind the pillars of the cathedral, El Señor witnesses an atrocious act of profanation by his own mercenary troops, which makes him understand that the battle just fought was a battle of self-interest rather than one of ideas. His meeting with Ludovico takes place in this same unnamed scenario and it repeats literally a passage mentioned by Cohn in his study of the Brethren of Free Spirit. It is the vision through which the mystic Heinrich Suso was initiated into the precepts of the Brotherhood by an incorporeal image that appeared to him in the middle of his meditations.[135]

The view of heresy that Fuentes provides in *Terra Nostra* responds, once again, to the agglutinative impulse that characterizes his use of history. Thus, contradictory tendencies are integrated as part of the same movement, as happens with the austerity of the Cathars and the Waldensians, who preached asceticism and believed that all matter was evil, and the licentiousness of the Adamites, who supported promiscuity and recognized no sin.[136] What is important for Fuentes is to emphasize the transgressive role of these groups, which paved the way for the religious and social reforms of the Modern Age. Although ultimately subdued, in Fuentes's view, heresies and proletarian messianism heralded both the perspectivism and the dynamic, protean view of modernity inaugurated by the Renaissance. Their reappearance in Paris at the end of the Millennium, portrayed in the novel's first and last chapters, proves their persistence and projection into the future.

The uprising of Castilian townships is portrayed in chapter 135 of *Terra Nostra* ("La rebelión"). Two discourses, reproduced in two different kinds of type, intersect throughout this narrative segment: presumedly historical documents of the insurrectionists and dialogues between the fictional characters.[137] The connecting thread of this chapter is provided by a series of documents of and about the *comuneros*, which are fragmentarily inserted. The first of them is a proclamation in which the rebels explain their goals and ask for the support of other Castilian towns. The next three documents are of a different sign: In the first two the *comuneros* describe the repression of Medina del Campo by royal troops; in the last one, a noble comments to his kinsman, a Marquis, on the defeat of the rebels at Villalar (655; 650).[138]

Although these archival materials appear to be completely historical at first glance, a close analysis reveals that they are really a collage of fragments probably taken from different sources: Maravall's and Ferrer del Rio's books on this subject, fictional elements related to other events in the novel, and ideas that the author would have liked to have seen in the minds of the *comuneros*. The two Latin passages of the initial proclamation, for example, reproduce fragments from *De Motu Hispaniae*, a work written by the humanist historiographer Juan Maldonado in the sixteenth century: "omnia eo consulta tendebant ut democratia," "de libertate nunc agitur quam qui procurant nullas audiunt leges, omni virtuti pietatique renunciant" (636; 631). In fact, Maravall quotes these two fragments in his book to support his thesis about the democratic longings of the townships.[139] The passage of the proclamation that alludes to the social composition of the revolt also originates in Maravall's writings. In contrast to the supposition that the instigators belonged to the low nobility, Maravall and Fuentes (635; 630) propose the urban bourgeoisie as the principal force behind the movement. However, fictional and fantastic elements also penetrate into the realm of the apparently empirical, and so Fuentes turns his novelistic character Guzmán into the main agent of royal repression,[140] and allows the comuneros to express improbable claims in favor of converted Jews and Moors (and, therefore, against the Inquisition).[141]

In addition to this fictionalization of history, *Terra Nostra* dramatizes the effect that the revolt may have had upon its characters. The multiplicity of narrative voices, the lack of transitions, and the nearly complete absence of an omniscient narrator (most dialogues lack punctuation), contribute to create a great multivocal ensemble. The resulting polyphonic effect purports to reflect on the formal level the democratic and egalitarian spirit that Fuentes attributes to the uprising. The majority of the main characters take part in the events in one way or another. However, even though in his essays Fuentes proposes the urban bourgeoisie as the leading force of the movement, in the novel it achieves the proportions of a total revolution. The social composition of the revolt extends to all of the marginal sectors that are opposed to the king's orthodoxy: "obreros,

árabes, judíos, herejes, mendigos, sobrestantes, putas, eremitas"
(636) ["workers, Arabs, Jews, heretics, beggars, overseers, whores,
eremites"] (631). To the austere order personified by El Señor, the
rebels represent chaos and transgression. Fuentes underlines the
dramatic character of this confrontation by causing the revolt occur
in El Escorial.[142] In this way, the mausoleum of the Castilian kings,
erected as a fortress of orthodoxy and a monument to the Eucharist
turns for a few moments into the home of the helpless, the land of
heretics, and a scene of profanation. Fuentes consistently presents
a carnivalesque world in which the social pyramid is temporarily
inverted.

As in the actual historical revolt, in the novel the upheaval is ultimately crushed and the plotters are either killed or imprisoned. The
punishment of the leaders, Nuño and Jerónimo, is portrayed as a
violent nightmare, one in which the Inquisition's rituals of torture
mingle with the terrorist practices of any modern dictatorship.
Meanwhile the subduers, like Guzmán, are rewarded.[143] In recognition of his bloody but efficient repression, Guzmán requests from
El Señor the favor of leading an expedition to the New World. The
final moments of the chapter describe the preliminaries of Guzmán's journey. The status of the other participants in this journey
is critical since it dramatizes Fuentes's ideas regarding the impact
of the *comunero* revolt in Spanish America. On the one hand, the
expedition is led by Guzmán, who embodies the most negative values of obscurantist and reactionary Spain—the authoritarian view
of government, the privileges of feudal nobility, the merciless repression of dissidence, and the scorn for culture. On the other hand,
the members of the crew represent many of the most characteristic
strata of Spanish society: defeated *comuneros* (which for Fuentes
implies both the urban bourgeoisie and manual workers), criminals,
impoverished nobles, and false converts (656; 651). At the last moment the expedition is also joined by Fray Julián, the antithesis of
the values represented by Guzmán: the intellectual who defends the
dispossessed, the iconographer of heresy, and the missionary who
looks to the New World for the realization of Renaissance utopias.

Metafiction

"The Next World" contains the metafictional center of *Terra
Nostra*: the episode entitled "The Theater of Memory." Through
the metaphor of Valerio Camillo's theater, Fuentes thematizes both
his aesthetic and historiographic program and the novel's production and reception. The different levels of reflection in this powerful

mise en abyme summarize the ideas previously presented in a fragmented way, solve some of the enigmas and paradoxes that have been pointed out, and, above all, confer an exemplary unity to the novel.

This episode, which appears in chapter 103, describes the meeting of Ludovico with Valerio Camillo as a reflection of Frances Yates's work *The Art of Memory*.[144] After arriving in Venice, Ludovico looks for a job as a translator and is sent to Maestro Valerio Camillo, who is said to possess a huge library. In his new job, Ludovico begins by translating into several languages classic works by Cicero, Plato, Philostratus, and Pliny. They all have one subject in common: memory. Once Ludovico is initiated into the secrets of the memory arts, Valerio Camillo shows him a theater of his own creation in which the spectator can contemplate "all the possibilities of the past" (567; 561), the memory of what could have been, but was not.

The abysmal structure of the chapter originates in its pervasive allusions to the text's production and reception. Through the characters' debates, Fuentes exposes his own aesthetic theory. As in his essay on Cervantes, in this passage he discusses the acts of writing and reading, and, as in this essay, he arrives at problematic conclusions about production but more satisfactory ones on reception. More importantly, the analysis that follows seeks to answer the question that surfaced throughout the study of *Terra Nostra*: Is Fuentes's literary utopia just a utopia, or can it be made real?

Valerio Camillo's realm reflects the archetypal scene of reading.[145] His residence is initially described as "a paper fortress" whose windows are "blocked with parchments," and whose walls and columns are formed by accumulated manuscripts and documents (559; 553). As was seen in the first part of the novel with regard to El Escorial, Fuentes uses an architectonic metaphor to reveal his poetics of reading. This strategy is confirmed by Valerio Camillo and Ludovico, the two characters who inhabit this textual scenario. The former is portrayed as a compulsive decipherer. His stuttering is the result of his total dedication to reading, a dedication that has nearly led him to forget how to speak. The novel reveals Ludovico's previous experience as a reader and translator in Toledo, and reading and interpreting continue to occupy him while he is in Valerio Camillo's residence.

Yates's book offers a historical and intertextual model for these two characters. Valerio Camillo is based on the sixteenth-century historical figure of the Renaissance scholar Giulio Camillo, whose theories about the art of memory occupy a substantial part of

Yates's work. Ludovico refers to at least two other historical figures who are briefly mentioned in *The Art of Memory*: Ludovico Dolce, a translator of treatises on the memory arts who wrote the prologue to Giulio Camillo's works, and the Erasmian disciple Viglius Zuichemus, who has left us one of the few descriptions of the Theater of Memory.

All we know about Ludovico Dolce is that his work on the art of memory is a translation or adaptation of Johannes Romberch's essay *Congestorium artificiosa memoriae* of 1533.[146] Regarding Viglius, Yates quotes one of his letters to Erasmus in which he describes his meeting with Giulio Camillo.[147] As Yates points out, this meeting goes beyond the anecdote, since it represents the conflict between two different conceptions of the Renaissance: on the one hand, the rational humanism of Erasmus and Viglius and, on the other, the esotericism of Camillo. In this chapter, Ludovico adopts a rather skeptical attitude toward the utopian possibilities of the theater similar to that of Viglius. It is also similar to that of the reader of *Terra Nostra*. By inscribing the doubts and objections of the potential reader within the text and through one of its characters, Fuentes seeks to confer a dialogic quality on this important episode. Following the model provided by the Socratic dialogues, the reader's position is channeled through the questions of the disciple, in this case Ludovico, questions to which Camillo gives prompt responses. The portrayal of the dialogue between Valerio Camillo and Ludovico, which reproduces, in its turn, the historical encounter between Giulio Camillo and Viglius, has a greater specular implication, since it reproduces, on a symbolic level, the encounter of the virtual reader with *Terra Nostra*.[148]

In order to understand the implications of this reflexive web, let us look briefly at Yates's description of the original theater, which Fuentes reproduces in *Terra Nostra*. Yates defines Giulio Camillo's theater as a worldview and, at the same time, as a system of mnemonic mechanisms. In his posthumously published work *L'Idea del Teatro* (1550) Camillo had described the building according to the cabalistic tradition of the Renaissance. His theater rested on seven pillars, which represented both the seven pillars of Solomon's House of Wisdom and the seven Sephirots of the supercelestial world, containing the ideas or concepts of all things.[149] Other aspects of the theater's structure ruled by the cabalistic symbolism of the number seven were the seven grades presided over by the seven ancient deities: Diana, Mercury, Venus, Apollo, Mars, Jupiter, and Saturn; and the seven rows into which each grade was divided, each devoted to a major topic (Prometheus, the Sandals of Mercury, Pasiphae and the Bull, the Gorgon Sisters, the Cave, and the Banquet).

While the cabala and several other hermetical doctrines that were popular in the Renaissance offered the symbolic model on which Giulio Camillo built his theater, the construction itself reflected, and at the same time inverted, the structure of the classical theater. As in Vitrubius's traditional conception, Camillo's edifice was divided into seven parts, but Camillo located the stage where Vitruvius placed the audience. In Camillo's model there was no multiple audience contemplating a unique representation from their seats. On the contrary, Camillo's theater situated a single spectator in the place normally assigned to the stage and made him face a semicircle, where all the universe was represented in microcosm.

The principal function of the theater was to offer what Yates calls "a system of memory places" (144). As in other manifestations of the art of memory, orators were thus able to memorize a great amount of information. With the invention of the printing press, the memory arts lost most of their practical functions. However, they continued to have an important place in esoteric doctrines that did not rely on the written word. That was true of the Hermetism and Cabalism implicit in the ideas of the Neoplatonic philosophers of the Renaissance, such as Marsilio Ficino, Pico della Mirandola, and Giordano Bruno. However, from our contemporary perspective it is difficult to discern the ultimate purpose of Giulio Camillo's invention. In spite of Yates's exhaustive description and interpretation, some of the connections between the practical aspect (the tradition of memory systems, which dates back to Cicero) and the esoteric aspect of the theater (the hermetical tradition that originates in Hermes Trismegistus) remain unclear. Some authors attribute a magical or mystical nature to these connections. This is certainly not the most appropriate place to pursue this kind of enigma. Suffice it to say that Camillo's work contains motifs of exceptional importance for Fuentes: the utopian ideal of total representation, the inversion of the relationship between public and stage, and the implication of these two elements for a poetics of reading.

Although Fuentes's description of the theater in *Terra Nostra* is close to Camillo's original design, Fuentes's theater fulfills a function that is not contemplated in Yates's essay. Apart from its symbolic significance, the theater discussed by Yates played a practical role: the training of the orators' memory. In *Terra Nostra* the practical function of Camillo's theater is associated with the other aspect of memory, what Fuentes calls "la más absoluta de todas las memorias: la memoria de cuanto pudo ser y no fue" (566) ["the most absolute of memories: the memory of what could have been but was not"] (559). Fuentes's theater projects images of an apocryphal past. Thus, Ludovico witnesses a new version of history in which, for example, Calpurnia convinces Caesar not to attend the Senate during the ides of March; in the reign of Augustus, a girl is born in Bethlehem; Pilate gives his pardon to a prophetess and condemns Barabbas to be crucified; Socrates refuses to take the poisonous hemlock; Noah sinks with his ark; Lucifer returns to God and is forgiven; Columbus searches for the terrestrial route to Cipango and arrives in the court of the Great Kahn riding a camel; Oedipus lives contentedly along with his adoptive father; Pelagius wins his theological dispute with Augustine. The list goes on, covering episodes in the lives of Cicero and Catiline, Alexander of Macedonia, Homer, Helen of Troy, Job, Antigone, Polybus, Jocasta, Plato, Dante, Beatrice, Giotto, Demosthenes, and Judas (566–67; 559–60).

Fuentes's theater responds to a mechanism that is only implied in the theater of Giulio Camillo and that is developed through different versions of the Borgean Aleph: the presentation of all past possibilities. This apocryphal history fulfills, in Fuentes's view, a corrective function regarding the future: in knowing the alternative versions of history, we can prevent catastrophe from being repeated. As Valerio Camillo says, "la historia sólo se repite porque desconocemos la otra posibilidad de cada hecho histórico" (567) ["history repeats itself only because we are unaware of the alternate possibility for each historical event"] (561). Fuentes acknowledges taking this idea of a second opportunity for past events from Borges:

> What Borges achieves is this: an extraordinary opening for the deepest need of Latin America, which is to have the opportunity of a second history, not to remain with the history we have, the one we detest so much and has humiliated us. Thus, he writes a second history, like all Borges's characters in "La segunda muerte," and "Tadeo Isidoro Cruz," who always have a second opportunity, a second moment in their day, although they only deceive themselves, and that second moment having already passed and having been the first one, they keep on waiting for the second.[150]

In his dialogue with Ludovico, Valerio Camillo repeats this same idea. Camillo underlines the importance of his invention, especially for a country like Spain that "destruye todo lo anterior a ella y se reproduce a sí misma" (568) ["destroys everything that previously

existed in order to reproduce itself"] (561). An important component of the study of historiographic metafiction follows from this
statement. According to Fuentes, mere self-absorption leads to sterility and death if it is not accompanied by historical memory.[151] El
Señor's Spain, encapsulated in El Escorial and exported to Hispanic America, emblematizes this pure narcissism that denies exterior reality and curls up on itself. That is why Valerio Camillo
confesses to Ludovico that "no habrá en la historia, mi señor, na-
ciones más necesitadas de una segunda oportunidad para ser lo que
no fueron, que estas que hablan y hablarán tu lengua" (568) ["there
will not be in history, monsignore, nations more needful of a second opportunity to be what they were not than these that speak and
will speak your tongue"] (562). Valerio Camillo's speech is followed by the projection of images of plundering, destruction, and
starvation that summarize the history of Spanish America from pre-
Columbian empires to present and that confirm his diagnosis of
Hispanic history.

However, the most important aspect of the theater is not that it
reflects Fuentes's historiographic ideas, but that it also reflects the
process by which these ideas are expressed and the fictional devices
he uses in *Terra Nostra* to dramatize them. Valerio Camillo provides a further detail that reveals a key concept for understanding
the use and abuse of history in the novel. As a culmination of his
experiments, Camillo seeks to combine the elements of his theater
in such a manner that two different epochs coincide: "por ejemplo,
que lo sucedido o dejado de suceder en tu patria española en 1492,
1521, o 1598, coincida con toda exactitud con lo que allí mismo
ocurra en 1938, 1975 o 1999" (567) ["for example, that what happened or did not happen in your Spanish fatherland in 1492, in
1521, or 1598, coincide exactly with what happens here in 1938, or
1975, or 1999"] (561). This is Fuentes's project in *Terra Nostra*:
the superimposition of temporal levels that allows us to contemplate all the possibilities of the past in order to avoid committing
the same errors in the future. I have already commented upon the
first three dates in relation to "The Old World." Regarding the latter, 1938 corresponds in Mexico to the year in which President Lá-
zaro Cárdenas nationalized the Mexican oil industry, and in Spain
to the civil war, at a moment when the defeat of the popular army
by the Fascist troops seemed unavoidable; 1975, the year in which
Terra Nostra was published, was also the year that Francisco
Franco, the last member of El Señor's military offspring in Spain
(although not in Latin America), died; finally, 1999 signals the beginning and end of *Terra Nostra*, the last of the two thousand years

of Western history that Fuentes seeks to explain in the novel. What in *Terra Nostra* is presented as a superimposition of the immediate past on the future is, in reality, a revision of the remote past from the point of view of the present. Let us remember that Fuentes's historiographic analysis is based both on a reinvention of history from the perspective of the moment in which he is writing and on the utopian projection of history into an immediate future.

The totalizing drive in *Terra Nostra* is the source of multiple paradoxes. If we consider the act of writing in its traditional sense, that is, as an inscription of signs on paper that ends with the author's closing full stop, we will hardly understand the total work that Fuentes proposes. In fact, Borges, whose Aleph is a clear model for the Theater of Memory, has devoted a good deal of his work to destroying this idea of a representable simultaneity. In stories like "El Zahir," "El Aleph," and "El jardín de los senderos que se bifurcan," Borges parodies these attempts to write all-encompassing works, presenting them as ultimately futile. His theory is that total reality, because of its simultaneous nature, can never be grasped by language, which is always successive. On the contrary, Fuentes poses just this possibility, but he does so through a magical device based on the projection of images. In his essay on Cervantes he also insists on the creation of a work representing everything from every possible point of view. He refers to Joyce's *Finnegans Wake* as an example of this poetics of total writing. If we take Fuentes's words literally, his proposal, as proved by Borges, is clearly an impossibility. Neither *Terra Nostra* nor *Finnegans Wake* can represent in itself the totality of the universe. Of course, they do represent higher degrees of openness than traditional novels, and, due to their greater indeterminacy they also succeed in multiplying the number of interpretations derived from the texts. However, it is impossible to talk about totality if we consider the text in itself and as the work of a single author.

Something very different happens when we the text is placed in the communicative chain of which it is a part. If we consider the act of reading an additional component in the act of writing fictions, and imagine an endless chain of readers, then we may speak of the totality that Fuentes is looking for and which, according to him, Joyce longed for too. This consideration is crucial to understand the totalizing impulse in Fuentes's works in a positive way. From this point of view, the act of literary communication is not conceived of as an act of authorial imposition, but, on the contrary, as an act of communion with the reader.

The Theater of Memory as a machine for writing fictions is a literary chimera. No physical receptacle can encapsulate the totality of the universe, and Fuentes has, in fact, parodied this attempt in "The Old World." However, the theater becomes a plausible fantasy as an analog for the mechanisms of cognition that are activated in the act of reading. If we consider the totality of the reading community, a limited group of ambiguous images will produce an almost infinite number of realizations among readers.

This idea is in consonance with Eco's early inquiries into the so-called open work. For Eco, contemporary art and music tend to boost the production of meaning through ambiguity and incompleteness. Unlike traditional art, which is essentially unambiguous and directs the reader's responses in a particular direction, many forms of modern art are systematically indeterminate and stubbornly resist closure. However, the open nature of the work must be understood not as a given intrinsic quality, but as a potential capacity that is accomplished only in the act of reading. Openness, in Eco's view, is achieved not on the level of production, but on that of reception. A work is considered "open" because of the multiplicity and mobility of readings that it allows. A similar interpretation may be applied to the concept of totality that has been the source of so much confusion in Fuentes: "Neither openness nor totality is inherent in the objective stimulus, which is in itself materially determined, or in the subject, who is himself available to all sorts of openness and none; rather, they lie in the cognitive relationship that binds them and in the course of which the object, consisting of stimuli organized according to a precise aesthetic intention, generates and directs various kinds of openness."[152]

Fuentes has acknowledged Eco's influence, and many of his commentaries on Joyce in *Cervantes* clearly derive from *Opera aperta*. Indeed, Eco's theses help to explain some of the paradoxes commented on so far. In displacing the concept of totality form the work's materiality to the virtuality of the reading experience, both Eco and Fuentes leave the door open to the fulfillment of totalizing utopias in literature.

This fulfillment is also inscribed in the novel itself, as it approaches its end. The last chapter ("The Last City"), dramatizes the cognitive and creative power of reading. Pollo Phoibee's experience between the first and the last chapters of the novel is, in fact, an experience of reading. When Celestina visits Pollo's apartment in the Hotel du Pont Royal, she addresses him as Pilgrim and alludes to his adventures in imperial Spain and in the New World. However, Pollo insists that he has remained in that place during the six months that passed between their two encounters (July and December 1999). The apartment in which this encounter takes place contains the documents written by Fray Julián and the Chronicler. The controversy between Pollo and Celestina stems from the fact that Pollo believes that he has experienced the novel's events through his reading of those documents, while Celestina insists that they both have experienced those events firsthand, and that the texts only record a biography of their actual lives. In this way, the reader of *Terra Nostra* is again placed in a structure *en abyme* in which it is difficult, even impossible, to establish a clear distinction between being and reflection, the original and the representation. Thus, Pollo Phoibee is the reader of a story in which he appears as a fictional character under the name of the Pilgrim; but, this story is at the same time a historical biography that describes moments he himself has lived in reality. The dialogue between Pollo and Celestina expresses this dual possibility:

> —No es cierto, yo he estado encerrado aquí, no me he movido, desde el verano no abro las ventanas, me estás contando lo que ya he leído en las crónicas y manuscritos y pliegos que tengo allí, en ese gabinete, tú has leído lo mismo que yo, la misma novela, yo no me he movido de aquí . . .
> —¿Por qué no piensas lo contrario?, te dice después de besar tu mejilla, ¿por qué no piensas que los dos hemos vivido lo mismo, y que esos papeles escritos por fray Julián y el Cronista dan fe de nuestras vidas? (778)

> ["That isn't true, I've been shut up here, I haven't left this place, I haven't opened my windows since summer, your are telling me things I've read in the chronicles and manuscripts and folios I have here in this cabinet, you've read the same things as I, the same novel, I've not moved from here . . ."
> "Why not believe the opposite?" she asks kissing your cheek. Why not believe that we two have lived the same things, and that the papers written by Brother Julián and the Chronicler give testimony to our lives?"] (774)

Fuentes does not exclusively favor one of the two perspectives, for the simple reason that he does not see a contradiction between the two. Pollo Phoibee has simultaneously read and experienced the 142 central chapters of the novel, since the experience of reading in the novel is not conceived of as an escape from historical and textual reality but as a probe into the mechanisms of both.

Pollo's fall into the Seine and his final rebirth in Paris signal the beginning and end of an activity understood in both cognitive and experiential terms. From the experience of the two thousand years of history that he has lived in the brief span of six months (the time that a critical reading of *Terra Nostra* might last), he emerges with the necessary keys to interpret the apocalyptic reality in which he is living. The experience of reading is an experience of transformation that takes place both at individual and collective levels. A transformed subject comes forth from the reading, one who has discovered facets of his own mind that he has so far ignored. Other possibilities are raised from this experience of reading, including the possibility of effecting changes in historical reality. This virtual projection of fiction into the outside world, already contemplated by Borges in "Tlön, Uqbar, Orbis Tertius," is presented in *Terra Nostra* through the multiple transgression of its structural frames. Like the *hrönir* from Borges's imaginary region of Tlön, which end by invading historical reality, Pollo's apartment is invaded by objects belonging to representative episodes in *Terra Nostra*: the green bottles, the chronicles, the nauseating relics kept by El Señor, the multiform mirrors that reappear in the three parts, a basket filled with pearls, the treasures from pre-Cortesian Mexico, a collection of masks, and maps that delineate the historical and fantastic geography of *Terra Nostra*. But if in Borges's story modern reality was invaded by an idealistic world, the invasion Fuentes writes about is an invasion of the past, with all its promises and catastrophes— "hemos sido ocupados por el pasado" (775) ["we have been occupied by the past"] (771)—an invasion that is ultimately made possible by fiction.[153]

In the final moments of the novel Pollo recalls a moment of great specular intensity that took place in his apartment, now transformed into a new Theater of Memory. It is a curious game in which the protagonists of some of the greatest Spanish-American works of fiction take part: Borges's Pierre Menard, Cortázar's Oliveira, García Márquez's Buendía, Cabrera Infante's Cuba Venegas, Donoso's Humberto the mute, Carpentier's Esteban and Sofía, and Vargas Llosa's Santiago Zavalita.[154] The game, called *Superjoda* ("Superfuck") in homage to Cortázar's *Libro de Manuel*, consists of "una partida de naipes competitiva en la que ganaba el que reuniera mayor cantidad de oprobios y derrotas y horrores. Crímenes, Tiranos, Imperialismos, e Injusticias; tales eran los cuatro palos de esta baraja, en vez de tréboles, corazones, espadas y diamantes" (766) ["a card game in which the winner was the one who collected the most cards representing ignominy and defeats and horrors. Crimes, Tyrants, Imperialisms, and Injustices were the four suits of this deck, replacing clubs, hearts, spades and diamonds"] (761).

This card game works as a new *mise en abyme* of the novel. Through it Fuentes presents the doubly coded project of historiographic metafiction: On the one hand, the playful and hazardous element of fiction in which characters are part of the intertextual reality that feeds the literary work; on the other, the novel's drive to go beyond the mere formalist play of the avant-garde and high modernism, and to install itself within the historiographic context to which it belongs.

The invasion about which Fuentes writes is not, therefore, a fantastic intrusion, as in Borges, but an invasion of memory. In this sense, Fuentes confers a high cognitive value on fiction, since he proposes that it is through fiction and not through history that we will be able to understand past events and, what is more important, we may become aware of utopian alternatives that may be actualized in the future. This historical reflection is communicated by means of a deeply reflexive narrative that often asks us to look into literary history for the answers to many events in political history.

Literary communication is ultimately posed as an effective but not yet actualized potential. *Terra Nostra* is presented to us as a labyrinthine map in which orientation depends mainly on our cultural competence and our predisposition to participate in the rewarding if sometimes frustrating task of reconstructing the work. One of the theoretical problems that originates in this poetics is the possibility of establishing the terms and limits of the reader's participation. Although the novel purports to be incomplete and ambiguous, in the tradition of Eco's *opera aperta*, the resolution of indeterminacy and the actualization of the text's potential meaning require an endless searching for references in Fuentes's essays, where the novelist expresses similar historiographic and aesthetic views without the deformation and obscurity that characterize *Terra Nostra*. The novel is presented as open, an impression that results principally from its indeterminacy. Nevertheless, the underlying message is not ambiguous or vague, but particular and public: Fuentes's call for the political and cultural transformation of Hispanic societies, a transformation in which intellectuals, and especially novelists, are called upon to play a crucial role.

CONCLUSION

As in much postmodern fiction, Fuentes's novels articulate historical meditation and narrative self-consciousness. Although both history and the novel are contemplated as verbal constructs, Fuentes clearly favors the latter as an instrument of cognition. A hybrid genre from its very origins and highly capable of transformations, the novel becomes in his view the ideal vehicle to convey Spanish America's multicultural reality. Furthermore, novels, according to Fuentes have the power to unveil those phenomena that are traditionally silenced in history books. Unlike historiographic discourse, which is constrained by empiricist methodology, novels are flexible systems that not only account for what happened, but also for what might have happened but did not. By depicting the apocryphal and the possible, the novel—as Valerio Camillo's Theater of Memory— can provide an alternative to the eternal return of the past. It thus becomes a utopian space of infinite possibilities, a democratic arena where distant people, times, languages, and cultures interact.[155]

Fuentes's poetics of the open text reaches its highest expression in *Terra Nostra*, his most ambitious novel to date. In this work, he places the monolithic power of empires and the heretical power of imagination in antagonistic positions. The history of the Hispanic world is seen as an eternal struggle between the forces of despotism, isolationism, obscurantism, and dogmatism and those who defend participation, openness, progress, and dissidence. The first of these two sides is epitomized by El Señor, who is modeled on the image of a long tradition of intolerant rulers from Philip II to Spanish and Latin American dictators. The power of imagination is instead the privilege of intelectuals, writers, and artists, all of whom propose a worldview that, according to Fuentes, bloomed during the Rennaisance.

Two principle metaphors serve Fuentes to expose his view of two cultures at war: the monolithic and somber Escorial and Valerio Camilo's dynamic and open theater. Through these powerful images, the novel, while reflecting upon its own condition as an artifact, explores two antithetical traditions that have had an impact on Hispanic history and culture. El Señor's mausoleum and Camillo's theater function as the aesthetic embodiment of the projects Fuentes respectively attacks and supports. The struggle between their underlying worldviews also establishes the dilemma in which the novel is at times engaged: it seeks the impossible utopia represented by the Theater of Memory, but often recalls the monumentalism of Philip's mausoleum.

In order to support his historical vision, Fuentes resorts to various forms of documentation. Different—sometimes incompatible— sources are accommodated to his multicultural agenda. At times these sources are transformed—either by omission or commission—others are literally inserted into the novel. The resulting historiographic and literary collage—including mythic accounts, ancient chronicles, academic scholarship, esoteric theories, and apocryphal and fantastic versions of the past—seeks both to question the dominant systems of representation and to recuperate the value of hybridism and syncretism in the cultures of the Americas.

On a theoretical level, *Terra Nostra* frequently falls into paradox, if not into contradiction. However, it succeeds in exposing the revisionist aim of historiographic metafiction and serves as Fuentes's vehicle for conveying an overall heterodox view of Hispanic history. The novel is presented as a model of the utopian enterprise that, according to Fuentes, must be undertaken by Latin Americans: the creation of a final synthesis of a deeply heterogeneous reality.

3

Displacing the Official Record: Ishmael Reed's Reinvention of Western History and Myth

HISTORY AND SELF-REFLEXIVITY IN THE WRITINGS OF ISHMAEL REED

All nine novels that Reed has published to date are distinguished by their thematic and formal continuity. Each of these works develops from those preceding it in order to construct a personal mythology that has come of age over time. Reed's creation reveals several layers of meaning, from the apparent surface triviality—resulting from his use of popular genres like Westerns, science fiction, or detective novels—to the deepest and most complex, which are reached only after careful study of Reed's work and of the cultural context from which it emerges.

Throughout his career, Reed has demonstrated constant concern for historical issues and for their expression through reflexive narratives. This blend of the historical and the aesthetic is one of the many amalgamations achieved in his works. In terms of both form and ideology they are characterized by syncretism. In form, the nine novels overstep the boundaries among genres, as well as the gulf between academic and popular culture; in ideology, Reed supports multiculturalism as an expression of the plurality that constitutes U.S. society. Form and ideology are oriented toward the formation of a narrative hybrid that blends fiction and reality, satire and mysticism, the mass media and the African and Western literary traditions.

In his first novel, *The Free-Lance Pallbearers* (1967), Reed establishes some of the techniques and motifs present throughout his later works. If there is one single element that clearly stands out in this early narrative experiment, it is the use of satire and parody. At this early stage of his career, Reed focuses on a satiric portrayal of

1960s U.S. history and literature. The novel's plot reveals his caustic view of cultural and political history. Its protagonist, Bukka Doopeyduk, is a black youth who, after a life of sacrifice and humiliation, rebels against the Nazarene Creed (a parody of Christianity) and the absolute power exercised by Harry Sam (an embodiment of the United States). Although his revolt succeeds in deposing the tyrant, Doopeyduk is ultimately crucified in front of television cameras, and a new despot restores Sam's police state.

From a historical point of view, the satirical component of the novel is aimed at two main targets: U.S. political institutions and certain sectors of the black community. As a satire of political power, *Pallbearers* criticizes the monolithic power structures embodied by Harry Sam, who rules omnipotent over a wasteland. As a satire of black opposition movements, Reed reveals the corruption of some of their leaders and the "embourgeoisment" of North American black culture.[1] His humorous denunciation culminates in the novel's final scene, in which Doopeyduk is betrayed and crucified by his own people.

Reed's satirical thrust is similarly manifested through a caustic parody of both Western and African-American literary traditions. The novel's portrayal of Doopeyduk's passion and sacrifice and of Sam's death parodies the Gospel and the Book of Revelations. Rites of initiation and the great mythic voyage are distorted to the point that their original sacredness is grotesquely mocked. *Pallbearers* has also been interpreted as a multifarious parody of many other motifs, genres, and specific works. These include Ralph Ellison's *Invisible Man*, the popular subgenres (gothic, horror, fantasy, science fiction, B movies), African-American confessional narratives, the traditional American success-story, black popular literature of the sixties, literary criticism, and the academic profession in general.[2]

Numerous reflexive images and self-referential devices complete the dense web of intertextual allusions and give the book its metafictional dimension. One example of these reflexive techniques is the use of allegorical names. Thus, the novel's protagonist, Bukka (whose name is reminiscent of Booker T. Washington), encounters doom as a result of the wrong reading of the wrong books (especially the Nazarene Manual), and one of the most authoritarian characters is called Mr. Spellman, a thinly veiled allusion to what Reed considers the repressive power of writing codes.

In *Pallbearers*, episodes are superimposed to form a collage in which the linear sequence of events or cause-effect relationships lack the importance they may have in more traditional fiction. In fact, the novel's dynamic and lively language recalls cinematic and television montage rather than other more proper literary models.[3] Besides these media techniques, *Pallbearers* evokes the universe of cartoons and science fiction.[4] The general impression is that of a hybrid in which ultimate success depends not on specific components, but on the sum of its parts. It is precisely the successful interaction between the historical and experimental components that creates such originality and impact in Reed's first novel.

U.S. political and literary history and the myths of Christianity are again targeted in Reed's next novel, *Yellow Back Radio Broke-Down* (1969). However, unlike *Pallbearers*, which takes place in the sixties, in *Radio* the action is set in the far West during the nineteenth century. The work presents the adventures of Loop Garoo Kid, a black cowboy initiated into the secrets of voodoo, who must confront the aggression of tyrannical landowner Drag Gibson and his underlings in the army (Field Marshal) and in Congress (Pete the Peek). This basic story line conceals a complex discourse about the conflict between Judeo-Christian civilization and African-American culture. As in *Pallbearers* and each of Reed's subsequent novels, this conflict has important repercussions on both historical and esthetic levels.

From a historical reflectionist point of view, *Radio* presents a fantastic version of North American history, from the times of Cabeza de Vaca's extraordinary "pilgrimage" in the sixteenth century to the present. Among the myriad of events that take place between these two extremes, Reed proves especially interested in those elements ignored by official chronicles. *Radio* valorizes, for example, the presence of blacks in the expansion of the U.S. frontier and the importance of African heritage in the cultural tradition of the Americas. Reed contrasts the tolerant syncretism of African-American culture with the exclusive and authoritarian ideology of the U.S. establishment, represented in the novel by capitalism and Christianity.

Regarding the metafictional aspect, *Radio* continues the parody of popular genres begun in *Pallbearers*. In this case, the most obvious intertextual code is provided by Westerns and science-fiction novels; literary discussions also occur throughout the novel. In particular, *Radio* establishes Reed's position in relation to the type of black aesthetics advocated by critics such as Houston Baker Jr., Addison Gayle, and Amiri Baraka (Leroi Jones). A debate between Loop Garoo and the members of the so-called neo–social realist gang lays out Reed's aesthetic opinions within the text itself. Realist leader Bo Shmo's criticism of Loop Garoo closely parallels the type of charges made by the "new black aesthetic critics" against Reed: "The trouble with you Loop is that you're too abstract. . . . Crazy dada nigger that's what you are. You are given to fantasy and are off in matters of detail. Far out esoteric bullshit is where you're at. Why in those suffering books that I write about my old neighborhood and how hard was every gumdrop machine is in place while your work is a blur and a doodle" (35–36). Loop Garoo's response offers important clues to understanding Reed's aesthetic views, views in which literature is conceived as a ludic liberating activity, inclusive and not exclusive, open and not closed, in which the artist's creative freedom should be respected above all else: "What if I write circuses? No one says a novel has to be one thing. It can be anything it wants to be, a vaudeville show, the six o'clock news, the mumblings of wild men saddled by demons" (36). *Radio* is the first novel in which Reed associates his aesthetic and cultural program with voodooism, and from this point on, voodoo (hoodoo in the North American version) will recur in Reed's works as a metaphor for his amalgamating artistic utopia.

It is in his following novel, *Mumbo Jumbo* (1972), that Reed systematizes his historical view of the black world. Through a complex detective plot, *Mumbo Jumbo* allegorizes the search for a genuinely African-American aesthetics. The intricate web of references is skillfully articulated through endless reflexive motifs, which makes this novel Reed's masterpiece and his greatest experimental undertaking to date.

After a work as ambitious and innovative as *Mumbo Jumbo*, it is not surprising that critics were less enthusiastic about *The Last Days of Louisiana Red* (1974).[5] While *Mumbo Jumbo* is a groundbreaking novel that offers a complete view of African-American history and culture, *Louisiana* is limited in that it simply reelaborates (in a rather limited way) the mythical and aesthetic countersystem already established in Reed's previous novels. Like *Mumbo Jumbo*, this new novel is structured along a detective story line, in which two parallel plots are united in a final resolution. In the central plot, PaPa LaBas, *Mumbo Jumbo*'s hoodoo detective, investigates a murder in the town of Berkeley during the sixties. The victim, Ed Yellings, is representative of the industrious black bourgeoisie. The novel suggests that Yellings had been a member of a secret society at war with a conglomerate of multinational capitalism and Judeo-Christian culture known as the Louisiana Red Corporation.

Parallel to this central plot, the novel describes the fight of a character named Chorus to regain his importance in contemporary society. Chorus is representative of the situation of blacks in a white world, caught in a restricted role and permanently threatened with expulsion. According to Reed, the origin of this loss dates back to the Greek play *Antigone*, in which monologues first began to usurp the dominant place previously occupied by the chorus in Aeschylus's works. The progressive diminishing of the importance of the chorus in Greek drama allows Reed to reflect upon the inherent evils of Western culture. Besides PaPa LaBas's detective story and Chorus's aesthetic struggle, the novel creates an allegorical subtext in which each of the characters corresponds to the protagonists of Sophocles's play. However, Reed does not reproduce Antigone's drama but instead reworks it in his own personal way, making Creon the hero and Antigone the protagonist of an unjustified rebellion. In actuality, however, Reed is attacking the tragic sense of life that has permeated both Judeo-Christian culture and black liberation movements. Through the so-called Moochers, Reed criticizes the intolerant attitudes and gratuitous violence rampant among the most radical sectors of the black nationalist movements, something he had already condemned in each of his previous novels, and that now becomes the main focus of his satire.[6]

The publication of *Flight to Canada* in 1976 signaled a return to the levels of quality and originality in Reed's first three novels. In this great example of historiographic metafiction Reed once again uses parody to chronicle U.S. history. Published in North America's Bicentennial year, *Flight to Canada* contains Reed's response to two hundred years of official history. In its pages he attacks the most untouchable U.S. historical myths, focusing on the period of the Civil War. Both the Union worldview and the Confederate ideals are undermined by Reed's biting satire. Lincoln is portrayed as an illiterate opportunist who declares emancipation of the slaves in an act of cunning political pragmatism. Harriet Beecher Stowe is a snob who becomes rich at the expense of others' suffering (her *Uncle Tom's Cabin* was "lifted" from Josiah Henson, who appears in the novel as Uncle Robin). The new capitalist order introduced after the Union victory is personified by Yankee Jack, a plutocrat who controls the nation's destiny. Southern values are embodied by Swille, the ruler of a decadent empire that is haunted by Edgar Allan Poe's ghost and modeled on the image of King Arthur's Camelot. Along with nineteenth-century characters and situations, the novel introduces elements from twentieth-century technology (telephones, walkie-talkies, microphones, cassettes, Xerox machines, radios, TVs, videos, computers, cars, airplanes, and helicopters). Raven Quickskill, the protagonist, escapes to Canada in a jumbo jet. Lincoln's assassination is broadcast live and replayed as part of a TV broadcast of the play *My American Cousins*. The novel's language is not typical of traditional historical fiction, but is instead composed of contemporary colloquialisms and slang. The result is one of the most aggressive expressions of what Brian McHale has called the postmodern revisionism of the historical novel. In introducing twentieth-century material culture into the past, the novel undermines conventional chronology and thereby twists the linear logic of discourse that dominates canonical historiography. Above all, Reed's apocryphal version of the events allows the reader to witness a rewriting of U.S. political history that identifies the past's true protagonists and rescues its true victims.

Regarding its metafictional nature, *Flight to Canada*—together with *Mumbo Jumbo*—contains the greatest concentration of reflexive metaphors in all of Reed's works. This work presents a self-referential dynamic that likens its own basic situation to the "self-begetting novel," that is, the type of novel that takes credit for a character's development to the point at which he or she is able to begin writing the novel we have just finished reading.[7] *Flight to Canada* describes the process of its own writing. It begins with a poem called "Flight to Canada" that summarizes its main motifs. The first chapter then opens with the protagonist, Raven Quickskill, as he begins to write Uncle Robin's (Uncle Tom's) biography (Robin's story had been stolen and falsified by Harriet Beecher Stowe). The novel Quickskill writes is most probably *Flight to Canada*, and its narration takes up the subsequent pages. In addition to this proleptic reflection of the utterance, similar to the one that begins *Mumbo Jumbo*, from its first pages the novel offers all possible levels of reflection. Raven's poem incorporates *Flight to Canada* with its commentary (reflection of the enunciation), establishes the code according to which the novel must be interpreted (reflection of the code), and introduces the trickster (the cultural hero associated with myths of origin in Native American and African-American traditions). The spatial and temporal coordinates soon acquire an overtly metafictional quality. Quickskill's flight to Canada allegorizes the search for an aesthetic utopia represented by writing in a state of liberty, an ideal for which Reed has fought in all his works. The novel ends with its protagonist coming to an understanding of his own condition: Canada is only a state of mind, a desirable ideal the black writer has to strive for, no matter where he may be physically. The fact that Reed has his protagonist return to the South and devote himself to rewriting history is symbolic of the author's engagement with his immediate reality and contradicts the charges of escapism that social-realist critics have launched against him.

Flight to Canada is simultaneously a declaration in favor of creative freedom and a denunciation of the plunder of black culture by the white cultural establishment. In its pages Reed develops tendencies he had outlined in previous novels, especially *Mumbo Jumbo*. In terms of plot, however, Reed abandons the detective genre as the novel's structuring convention in order to focus on the re-creation of slave narratives. The successful result of this work (Reed's best after *Mumbo Jumbo*) stems from the multiplicity of its levels of interpretation, from the inexhaustible richness of its network of allusions, and, above all, from the effective interaction between parodic play and historiographic reflection.

Reed's experimental leanings, which culminated in *Mumbo Jumbo* and *Flight to Canada*, are interrupted in *The Terrible Twos* (1982). Although witty and humorous, this new work rehashes the basic schemes and ideas presented in Reed's early works, giving one the impression that his technical and thematic repertoire was starting to shrink. *The Terrible Twos* chronicles a conspiracy launched by big business and the White House to monopolize the Christmas market. Using this trivial plot as a pretext, Reed again dismantles the most sacred elements of U.S. politics (the presidency and lobbyists), economics (capitalism and large corporations), and folklore (St. Nicholas, Christmas, and Thanksgiving). The action in *The Terrible Twos* is set in the present and immediate future (the eighties and nineties), and at first glance may be considered a commentary on the Reagan era and its aftermath. Metaphorically, however, Reed's work censures the monopolizing tendencies in North American culture. The United States is portrayed as a self-centered two-year-old child who sees the world as an extension of himself; the diversity and depth of African-American legends and myths serves as a contrast to this narcissistic and egocentric view of contemporary North America.

Although in *The Terrible Twos* Reed recycles the detective plot of *Mumbo Jumbo* and *Louisiana Red*, in this case it is a new character, Nance Saturday, who must discover the intricacies that make up the novel's tangled plot. One of the central enigmas of the novel is "Operation Two Birds," a conspiracy organized by a gang of businessmen, corrupt politicians, mock missionary men, and paranoid militarists. The plan entails a holy war against the "surplus people" in the United States (the homeless, the poor, women, blacks, Hispanics, and Jews) and a West African country (most likely Nigeria, the original land of the Yorubas). In this way Reed continues his traditional inclination—initiated in *Pallbearers* but most extremely manifested in *Mumbo Jumbo*—toward a conspiratorial view of North American politics.

The Terrible Twos has a logical, yet somewhat disappointing, continuation in *The Terrible Threes* (1989), where the motifs and situations of the first are reintroduced seven years later. Reed's satire persists in targeting the same sectors of U.S. society: the military, the White House, feminists, Miltonian critics, writers of minimalist fiction, biblical scholars, TV evangelists, and anyone else with politically and culturally conservative leanings. Aside from several new characters and the humorous plot circumvolutions, *The Terrible Threes* does not offer any substantial changes in relation to Reed's previous work. The fact that it is a sequel limits the novel even more, since it presupposes the reader's familiarity not only with Reed's countersystem, as expressed in *Mumbo Jumbo*, but also with the characters and situations presented in *The Terrible Twos*.

Between the two *Terribles*, Reed published what seems to be his most straightforward—and probably most unsuccessful novel: *Reckless Eyeballing* (1986). The setting is an imaginary present where intellectuals are victims of an aggressive wave of neo-Nazism and a fanatic feminist conspiracy. Once more, Reed blends fiction and reality to make a fiery and impassioned statement against authoritarian attitudes within the cultural establishment. The novel's protagonist, Ian Ball, is a black playwright whose work (*Reckless Eyeballing*) reflects his own situation as well as Reed's actual creative problems. In this case, the metafictional effect is achieved through playful interaction on three levels: the diegetic (the story of Ball's misfortunes), the metadiegetic (the story told in Ball's play), and the extradiegetic (the author's well-known and long-standing dispute with feminists). However, other than the witty dialogues and a few clever comic scenes, Reed's satiric potential falls short. Too frequently *Reckless Eyeballing* seems to be an attempt to settle old personal scores with his personal enemies (the white intelligentsia, the social-realist critics, and the feminist movement).

Similar concerns provide the dominant motifs in *Japanese by Spring* (1993). In this work Reed takes on the subject of intolerance in the academic world. Neo-conservatism, racism, cultural imperialism, intellectual turncoats, literary fashions, political correctness, black and white nationalists, and radical middle-class feminism are now some of the objects of Reed's relentless satire. In each of these cases, *Japanese* proposes the celebration of multiculturalism that has its most irrefutable expression in the California setting of the novel.

In both ideological and formal terms *Japanese* is replete with metafictional devices. The novel as a whole is a reflection on the role of literature and criticism in North American society. It also raises ideas that occur throughout each of Reed's novels: the importance of the African influence on Western culture, the distortion of aesthetic ideals in contemporary society, the literary critic's overly important role in academia (which sometimes even overshadows the creative writer), and the need for a syncretic vision of North American cultural reality. A brief cameo appearance by the author also spotlights the novel's self-reference. When invited to lecture at the fictitious Jack London College in California, Reed discusses his work and again presents his own literary theory.

In general *Japanese* demonstrates the satirical features that have characterized its author's style thus far. It is unlikely, however, that his work would be of any interest for a reader who is not part of the academic world or who is not already familiar with Reed's other works. In fact, this last novel is a confirmation of his already noted tendency to condense his frame of reference and therefore limit his target audience. His basic aesthetics were already outlined in his first two novels and more definitely established in *Mumbo Jumbo*. In his later works, except for *Flight to Canada*, Reed has merely developed these elements further.

As noted at the beginning of this chapter, all of Reed's nine novels follow a process of continuity in terms of aspects of the postmodern historical novel. They frequently refer to the dark areas of the past in order to understand present reality. Indeed, history is seen as the eternal conflict between the tragic and repressive spirit of Judeo-Christian civilization and the ludic and liberating forces represented by African-American culture and the indigenous peoples of the Americas. Reed's historical revisionism causes him to reveal and question the conventions and norms of canonical history; it is a historiographic revisionism as well, aimed at demystifying and deconstructing the mythmaking mechanisms of cultural history.

In metafictional terms, Reed shapes his novels into scenarios where aesthetic and cultural projects are debated. By repeatedly dramatizing the acts of reading and writing and using all types of specular metaphors, Reed rejects the traditional forms of representation of both white monoculturalists and black social realists. What he ultimately proposes is an oppositional aesthetics free from any kind of formal or ideological constriction. This search for freedom on all domains leads him to experimentation with all genres—especially those of popular culture—remodeling them into a new blend of a hybrid and original nature.

In each of the nine novels that have been briefly reviewed, as well as in his poetry and essays, Reed has proceeded to outline a personal theory of art and literature that he refers to as Neo-HooDoo aesthetics.[8] In point of fact, terms such as voodoo, hoodoo, and Neo-HooDoo occur throughout Reed's fiction, poetry, and critical essays. Voodoo is a word that originated from the Dahomey language and originally signified "the unknown," "spirit," or "deity." For the purpose of this book, voodooism is defined as a set of beliefs and religious rituals practiced by most blacks who were brought to the New World and that is still alive today in many places in the Americas, especially Haiti and Brazil. Voodooism incorporates the language, mythologies, rituals, folklore, and knowledge of many cultures that came to the New World as a result of the slave trade. Yet, although most of its symbols and images originated in western Africa, it is actually a phenomenon characteristic of the Americas. Voodoo emerged from the cultural interchange that occurred when members of ethnic groups such as the Senegalese, Bambara, Quiamba, Wolof, Foulbe, Arada, Mina, Caplau, Fon, Mahi, Congo, Mondongue, Ibo, Loango, and Fula, among others, were split up and disseminated throughout Haiti and other Caribbean and New World countries.[9] Consequently, it is a combination of those beliefs and customs shared by a wide variety of African peoples and transplanted to an alien continent. In spite of the many ethnic differences, these groups had certain common beliefs—ancestor worship, the use of dance and music in their religious ceremonies, and the adept's possession by the god—around which they began to develop the ritual forms of what today we know as voodoo.[10]

The Haitian voodoo pantheon is divided into two classes of deities: the Rada and the Petro. Each group traces its roots to a different region of Africa. According to Hurston, Rada deities come from Dahomey and are benevolent gods commanded by Damballah (the supreme mystery whose symbol is the serpent).[11] Petro gods, conversely, are said to come from the Congo and have the power of evil. The most popular Petro deities are the three barons: Baron Samedi (Lord of the Saturday), Baron Cimitière (Lord of the Cemetery), and Baron Croix (Lord of the Cross).

Most voodoo rituals are acts of piety offered to particular *loas* (spirits) or long celebrations that take place in the *ounfó* (temple). Unlike other religions, voodoo lacks a complex hierarchy of celebrants. Although there is a priest (*houngan* or *mambo*, depending on whether a priest or a priestess is being referred to), the priest's function is simply to ascertain that the *loas* are properly fed. In this sense, sacrificial offerings and dances play a central role. Offerings generally consist of food, alcohol, and animals that are given to the *loas* to appease them and win their favors. Dances are performed in the center of the temple to the rhythm of drums. The climax of the ceremony takes place when one of the worshippers ("horses") is possessed ("mounted") by a *loa*.

As a result of the slave trade, voodooism arrived in the United States through New Orleans. The form practiced in North America is known as hoodoo, and it reached its peak during the 1890s. According to Reed, hoodoo challenged the civil authorities' ability to maintain control and was therefore forced to go underground, which explains its persistence in the U.S. black ghettos until the present.[12] Because it adds elements of North American culture to the already hybrid Haitian rites, hoodoo represents one more step in the syncretic tradition of voodoo. Its center, New Orleans, is also a multicultural paradigm, since its cultural personality was formed by the blend of French, Spanish, North American, and African-American traditions. In spite of the secretive character of its practices, hoodoo pervades the culture and folklore of the city, from its gastronomy to its music, as well as its festive carnivals. For Reed, New Orleans's carnivals exemplify the most flamboyant manifestation of hoodoo spirit and serve to further develop his concept of voodoo/hoodoo as a metaphor for his cultural utopia. While Reed emphasizes the syncretic and popular qualities of voodoo, he recognizes that Mardi Gras also exemplifies its participatory character, and this spectacle becomes the epitome of Reed's communal concept of art: "Mardi Gras is the one American art I have witnessed in which the audience doesn't sit intimidated or wait for the critics to tell them what to see. The Mardi Gras audience talks back to the performers instead of sitting there like dummies, and can even participate in the action."[13]

Reed's hypothesis about the voodooistic vision of culture does not stop here, because voodoo beliefs and practices are not simply a relic of the past invoked yearly in festive celebrations. Indeed, they have survived under new forms, one of which is Neo-HooDoo. With this label, Reed refers to the contemporary manifestations of hoodoo that are the result of the blending of its beliefs and practices with U.S. popular culture. The Neo-HooDoo aesthetic agenda is exemplified by Reed and other writers who belong to the "Manhattan Project" of writing.[14] In music, Charlie Parker is, for Reed, a prime example of the Neo-HooDoo artist as an innovator and improviser; to his name Reed adds a long list of jazz, blues, and rock-and-roll musicians. Among its theoreticians, Reed mentions Zora Neale Hurston and Julia Jackson, the former for her studies on Haitian voodoo and on hoodoo in African-American folklore, the latter for having "stripped" hoodoo of its oppressive Christian influences. Neo-HooDoo is, therefore, described as a highly flexible construct in which a common base—seen as multicultural, pluralistic, and participatory—is permanently enriched by new contributions. Its open character is best illustrated in Reed's poem "The Neo-Hoo-Doo Aesthetic," which ends with the exclamation: "The proportions of the ingredients used depend upon the cook!"[15]

This mythic configuration of Neo-HooDoo aesthetic doctrine is part of a sequence that Reginald Martin has organized chronologically into five stages: 1) the pantheistic and syncretic worship of Osiris in Ancient Egypt; 2) West African religions (especially Yoruba and Fon) until the beginning of the Arabian and European slave market; 3) voodoo, as the result of the transplantation of tribes from the Gulf of Guinea to the Caribbean in the seventeenth and eighteenth centuries; 4) hoodoo, as a consequence of the diaspora of African Americans in the United States during the nineteenth and twentieth centuries; 5) Neo-HooDoo, proposed by Reed as the syncretism between voodoo-hoodoo forms and U.S. popular culture.[16]

In each of these five stages, the different manifestations of voodoo have suffered persecution by fanatic followers of Judeo-Christian culture, which is represented as monolithic, hierarchical, rigid, foreboding, and repressive.[17] Neo-HooDoo sensibility, on the other hand, is plural, participatory, open, lively, and tolerant. In Reed's vision of religious history, Judeo-Christian civilization defends orthodoxy and cultural and religious dogmas. The Neo-HooDoo world view, in contrast, values dissension and syncretism on all possible levels. In opposition to the Western manipulation of the environment, Neo-HooDooism advocates absolute respect for Nature. Finally, if the Judeo-Christian world privileges rationalism and cold scientific analysis, Reed's countersystem favors intuition, mystery, and emotion.

Mumbo Jumbo is without question the work that best exemplifies Reed's Neo-HooDooism, as well as his adherence to the basic postulates of the postmodern historical novel. Reed submits the recognized versions of history to his revisions. To this end, he invites the reader to probe into the depths of the Western past and reveals those events covered up by official chronicles. In short, Reed constructs in *Mumbo Jumbo* an alternative vision of history that ends by displacing the canonical versions of the past.

Mumbo Jumbo (1972)

Most critics consider *Mumbo Jumbo* (1972) Reed's masterpiece.[18] Its pages contain an endless series of discursive modes, including, among others, fantasy, history, mythology, religion, and popular culture. Literary elements coexist alongside an array of visual paratextual materials, such as photographs, posters, drawings, graphics, symbols, tarot cards, telegrams, party invitations, headlines, and newspaper clippings. *Mumbo Jumbo* conveys the impression of an interdisciplinary collage and, in this way, informs the reader that the novel does not only refer to the literary tradition, but also includes a multifarious cultural context.[19] This complexity in the novel's nature requires a clarification of its structural level and story line.

Mumbo Jumbo is organized into fifty-four narrative segments of very different lengths, ranging from a simple paragraph to a chapter of more than thirty pages. The bulk of the novel is framed by a prologue (chapter 1) and an epilogue. The prologue offers some significant details about the plot and establishes its most important themes. After this false beginning, the novel lists its credits and provides a group of epigraphs that announce future events. Toward the end, it closes with an epilogue in which the action returns to the time when the novel was written, and several of the central motifs are recapitulated. A "Partial Bibliography," in which the author displays most of his documentary sources, concludes the narrative.

In terms of the story line, the action is initially set in New Orleans during the Roaring Twenties. An epidemic called Jes Grew has broken out and is spreading dangerously in the direction of the great urban centers of Chicago and New York. The infection's most obvious symptom is a frantic desire to dance. This inclination toward spontaneous frenzied dancing is often described in terms similar to those of "possession" in voodoo. From the beginning, the origin of this outbreak is identified with the reemergence of the "Text," which refers to the Book of Thoth, a sacred anthology that recounts the mysteries of ancient Egypt. However, the Text soon acquires a metaphoric value and is ultimately identified with the code of the new African-American aesthetics that Reed seeks. The central plot deals precisely with the search for the Text, a search that has two antagonists: PaPa LaBas, a hoodoo detective trying to find it in order to unleash the beneficial effects of Jes Grew, and Hinckle Von Vampton, a Knight Templar who wants to ritually destroy the Text and in this way stop the epidemic forever.

Parallel to this central story line, the novel develops several subplots whose mutual relationship is revealed as the reading progresses. In one of these subplots a powerful secret society, the Atonist Path, and its militant arm, the Wallflower Order (a pun alluding to the Ivy League), attempt to create a fake black intellectual—a Talking Android—to discredit the true protagonists of the African-American cultural Renaissance. At the other extreme of the ideological spectrum, another subplot introduces the activities of the Mu'tafikah, a multicultural urban guerrilla group that seeks to return artworks kept in museums (known in the novel as Art Detention Centers) to their places of origin in the Third World. The fictitious activities of the Atonist Path and the Mu'tafikah alternate with historical and pseudohistorical subplots, such as the ancestry, administration, and death of President Warren G. Harding and the occupation of Haiti by U.S. troops.

However, the central action in *Mumbo Jumbo* revolves around the history of the Text (from its origin in ancient Egypt to its reappearance in North America in the twenties), and LaBas's and Von Vampton's search for the text. In Von Vampton's possession since the Middle Ages, the book passes accidentally to the black nationalist Abdul Sufi Amid, who translates it and is killed soon after. Abdul dies grasping in his hands an epigram in which the key to locating the Book is encoded. LaBas deciphers this message and finds the Book, buried in the very center of the Cotton Club.

In an episode that parodies the "recognition" scene of traditional detective novels, LaBas reveals some of the novel's central mysteries: the nature and meaning of Jes Grew, the origin and history of the Book of Thoth, and the plots of several secret societies to exploit the book's wisdom. In front of an audience composed of the novel's main characters, LaBas ties up some of the novel's loose ends. Finally, he opens the box found in the Cotton Club and finds that the Text is gone. A letter written by Abdul just before his death and reproduced at the end of the novel tells us that Abdul himself had burned the Text on the grounds that it was obscene. We also discover that Abdul's translation had been lost in the labyrinthine postal service, after having been rejected by an editor who considered it outdated and not "Nation" enough. With the book's destruction the Atonists believe the epidemic has been extinguished, but, as LaBas finally reveals, the spirit of Jes Grew is invincible and will always make use of new texts to manifest itself. The epilogue of

Mumbo Jumbo presents LaBas as a hundred-year-old man giving a lecture on Jes Grew to a group of students in the sixties or seventies (the years during which the novel was written). After several decades of oblivion, Jes Grew begins to show signs of reemerging.

Mumbo Jumbo combines real historical events, documented—but probably false—gossip, and fantasies completely invented by Reed. Although most of the characters that are part of the main action (the search for the Text) are fictional, they are frequently representative of historical figures. The novel's two antagonists, for example, allude to mythical and/or historical characters. In terms of his name, physical aspect, and function, PaPa LaBas represents the voodoo trickster deity Papa Legba.[20] Labas is in reality the name that this Haitian *loa* (spirit) has been given in the United States.[21] This character is also described in the novel in the same way as Papa Legba—he is an experienced old man who likes to wear showy hats and sunglasses and walks leaning on a stick or crutch:[22] "He is a familiar sight in Harlem, wearing his frock coat, opera hat, smoked glasses and carrying a cane" (26).[23] In voodoo, Papa Legba is the lord of the crossroads, the messenger of the gods, the guardian of the threshold, who regulates traffic between the visible and the invisible worlds.[24] LaBas is, significantly, the character in charge of resolving the novel's principal mystery: the meaning and the origin of the Text. In order to do so, he puts the characters, and therefore the reader himself, in contact with the spiritual world of African-American tradition. LaBas is the guide who allows us access to the dark areas of myth and history.

LaBas's antagonist, Hinckle Von Vampton, is reminiscent of Carl Van Vechten.[25] Van Vechten was one of the controversial white patrons of the Harlem Renaissance who popularized the black arts through his articles in fashionable magazines, such as *Vanity Fair*; a novel (*Nigger Heaven*, 1926), praised by Alain Locke and James Weldon Johnson and strongly criticized by W. E. B. Du Bois; numerous soirees in which black artists, musicians, and writers interacted with art dealers, producers, and publishers; and many photographs of almost all well-known African Americans in the United States.[26] Van Vechten is representative of a wave of curious whites who invaded Harlem in the twenties in search of the exotic and primitive, and who then commercially exploited its creative potential.[27] In this sense, his fictionalization in *Mumbo Jumbo* enables Reed to attack not only the manipulation by this kind of patron, so typical of the time, but also something he considers endemic of the white intelligentsia: the tendency to exploit, manipulate, and enrich themselves at the expense of the black world's creative efforts.

Another character associated with Harlem patronage, in this case black, has escaped the attention of most of Reed's critics: the anonymous hostess at whose party LaBas solves the novel's main mysteries. This character is clearly a synthesis of Sarah Breedlove Walker and A'Leilia Walker Robinson, mother and daughter, respectively. The former, better known as Madame C. J. Walker, was the founder of the first dynasty of black plutocrats.[28] Although formerly a washerwoman, she became wealthy after discovering and marketing a hair straightening process (the "Walker system"). With part of her immense fortune, she built a sumptuous palace known as Villa Lewaro, where the novel's famous recognition scene takes place.[29] A'Leilia Walker Robinson was well-known in her own right for her sponsorship of young black artists. Her mansion on 136th Street became one of Harlem's social centers for many writers and artists. At her cultural gatherings she offered these young creators an opportunity to meet the influential whites who were sympathetic to the new trends in African-American arts.[30]

Some religious and political leaders of the time are represented by the dogmatic Abdul Sufi Hamid. Abdul's career primarily recalls that of Malcolm X. Both are ex-convicts who became self-educated while in prison, and both are Islamic black activists whose rhetoric has a wide audience among the black masses.[31] Gates also points to the figures of the editor Duse Mohammed Ali and W. D. Fard (Elijah Muhammad's mentor) as possible historical references for Reed's character.[32] However, all of Reed's critics overlook the fact that a Sufi Abdul Hamid actually existed. Known also as Bishop Conshankin, or just "the Bishop," Hamid was a charismatic cult leader in Chicago in the late twenties. He soon became involved with Muslim organizations and led a movement to force business owners in black neighborhoods to hire black employees. In 1932 Hamid moved to Harlem, where he tried to repeat the success of the Chicago campaign, yet there he found strong opposition from the Left and from conservative blacks. After being arrested in 1935, he became disillusioned with political activism and returned to his former mysticism. In addition to representing the flourishing religious cults in the Harlem of the twenties and thirties, Hamid has come to be remembered as the organizer of the first black consumer boycotts in the United States.[33] In *Mumbo Jumbo* the characterization of the fictional Abdul is quite ambivalent. While the novel openly mocks his deeply moralistic view and censures his dogmatic tendencies, it evaluates positively the recuperation and embracement of African origins that characterizes black nationalism.[34]

The character Benoit Battraville, a fictionalization of the historical leader of the fight against the North American occupation, is important for the novel's exposure of the dirty war the United States waged in Haiti. Through his dialogue with PaPa LaBas in chapter 42, we obtain several important keys to understanding both the significance of voodoo in the history of the Americas and the effect secret societies have had on U.S. politics. Among these societies, the Wallflower Order is the most active in *Mumbo Jumbo*. Its chieftain, Walter Mellon, to whom the novel refers often as "the Sphinx," is pointedly reminiscent of Andrew Mellon, the U.S. Secretary of Treasury during the twenties and early thirties, who had amassed one of the largest fortunes in North America. Mellon's inclusion within the conspiratorial schemes of the novel allows Reed to reinforce his fictionalized version of U.S. reality, in which the highest hierarchical power position is occupied by big business, with political and military groups offering behind-the-scenes support.

Some other minor characters are also vaguely reminiscent of historical figures of the times. Dutch Schlitz, for example, is a fictitious reconstruction of Dutch Schultz, a famous Prohibition era gangster. According to De Filippo, the name Harry "Safecracker" Gould suggests railway tycoon Jay Gould, while LaBas's assistant, Charlotte, evokes Mademoiselle Charlotte, one of the few white *loas* in the voodoo pantheon.[35] However, as Gates has rightfully pointed out, Reed's fictional characters serve to exemplify attitudes and personalities within the great cultural conflict they dramatize, because although their names and attitudes are sometimes reminiscent of historical or mythological figures, their personalities and interrelations are mostly fictional. Many of the historical characters, such as presidents (Woodrow Wilson, Warren G. Harding, Calvin Coolidge), black leaders (James Weldon Johnson, Booker T. Washington, Marcus Garvey, W. E. B. Du Bois), black musicians (Scott Joplin, Louis Armstrong, Charlie Parker), and European thinkers (Sigmund Freud and C. G. Jung), help make up the historical background of the novel, but are not main agents in its major story line, which is the search for the Text and the deciphering of its mysteries.

REED'S REWRITING OF HISTORY AND MYTH

In *Mumbo Jumbo* Reed rewrites myth, history, art, and religion from an African-American perspective. In this way, he refutes the traditional charges that blacks in the Americas have always lacked a tradition and that their "high" cultural manifestations have been modeled after those of the white world. Reed radically inverts this vision and portrays black culture as the real victim of the plunder and piracy of whites. In the novel, the cradle of Western civilization should not be found in Greece, but rather in the black world.

A superficial reading of the novel could lead to the conclusion that Reed is simply replacing the dominant perspective with an alternative worldview that represents the same kind of essentialism and racial chauvinism that he wants to displace. However, far from advocating a dominant civilization, Reed's works conveys a multicultural message.[36] His attitude must be understood within the postmodern context of the "homeopathic" fight against the dominant forms of representation. As Jameson points out, one of the few forms of political action within reach of the contemporary intellectual is to undermine the dominant cultural logic from within, that is, to neutralize it by using its own forms of expression. This combative attitude is ever present in the novel, as well as in Reed's essays and interviews. His remarks about his previous novel, *Yellow Back Radio Broke-Down*, arc also applicable to *Mumbo Jumbo*: "So this is what we want: to sabotage history. They won't know whether we're serious or whether we are writing fiction. They made their own fiction, just like we make our own. But they can't tell whether our fictions are the real thing or whether they're merely fictional. Always keep them guessing. That'll bug them, probably drive them up the walls."[37] In this statement we see, first of all, the oppositional character of Reed's writing. The use of "we" as opposed to "them" allows him to include his work within a general struggle in which the third-person plural describes agents of the historical establishment, whereas the "we" unites oppositional intellectuals like Reed himself. The passage also establishes Reed's highly subjective epistemology, according to which all history is just a form of fiction, a cultural construction where no clear distinction between reality and pure fiction can truly be made. Moreover, Reed seems to be particularly interested in blurring such a distinction as much as possible and mixing the discursive realms of history and fiction. To this end, he seeks to present a historical countervision, but without completely abandoning some of the formal procedures of history writing. In fact, the narrative of *Mumbo Jumbo* combines even the most extravagant fantasies with traditional forms of historiographic documentation. The novel includes an extensive bibliography in which Reed acknowledges his sources, frequent footnotes that expand the information of the main text or support his theses with new documentary references, as well as pictures, headlines, newspaper clippings, and reports that illustrate and confirm the novel's narrative body. In *Mumbo Jumbo*, Reed utilizes the documentary methods of historiography to protest against those versions of reality that are traditionally presented as "true."

Three temporal levels are used to articulate the historical discourse in *Mumbo Jumbo*: the narrative present, which—with the exception of the epilogue—is set in the United States during the 1920s; the present of the novel's creation (1969–1971); and the genealogy of these two presents that dates back to ancient Egypt. The backward and forward movement among these three levels allows Reed to exemplify his necromantic concept of history. In a self-interview, Reed uses this concept to explain the origin of *Mumbo Jumbo*: "I wanted to write about a time like the present or to use the past to prophesy about the future—a process our ancestors called necromancy."[38] The following section examines the narrative past, present, and future of the novel, focusing on the first two, which correspond to the mythical and historical levels explicitly commented upon in the diegesis (the origin of African-American culture and the renaissance of that culture in the twenties).

THE BLACK ROOTS OF WESTERN CIVILIZATION: A STOLEN LEGACY

The mythical and historical core of *Mumbo Jumbo* is found in chapter 52, in the form of PaPa LaBas's long speech about the origin of civilization (what critics refer to as "the Egyptian legend"). In this episode LaBas presents the history of religion and culture from a black point of view. Although allusions to key moments in history appear throughout the work, and although myths and rituals of African-American folklore play a crucial role in the novel's complex intertextual framework, it is only through PaPa LaBas's digression that many of these allusions and intertexts are satisfactorily explained. In the longest chapter in *Mumbo Jumbo*, PaPa LaBas seeks to clarify the novel's central mystery: the origin and meaning of Jes Grew and its Text, that is, the origin and meaning of African-American spirituality and culture. LaBas reaches back to predynastic Egypt, the period in which the framework for the novel's mythical and historical dynamics is established. The importance of this episode requires detailed commentary. The following analysis corresponds to the two parts into which LaBas's narrative is divided: 1) the legend of Osiris regarding the black origin of Western culture, and 2) the appropriation of Osiris's mysteries by Classic and Judeo-Christian civilizations. After a brief summary of LaBas's account, Reed's use of myth and history is examined. The analysis of the documentary sources considers both the novel's recognized sources and other historical perspectives that confirm or refute Reed's view.

The Legend of Osiris

In LaBas's version of the myth, Osiris was a black prince who was interested more in his intellectual education than in political affairs. After studying agriculture in Nysa (Arabia Felix), he traveled to Ethiopia and Sudan in order to absorb the wisdom of black Africa. There he discovered the importance that dance and songs played in the fertility rites that accompanied the agricultural cycles. His love for nature was so great that he was popularly associated with the myths of creation. In some of these myths he was the son of the sky (Nut) and the earth (Geb). In his human form, LaBas's Osiris is portrayed as a cultural hero, under whose rule the arts flourished, agriculture developed, and cannibalism was forbidden. Osiris himself was such an accomplished dancer that he was known as "the man who did dances that caught on" (162).

The peace and prosperity that Egypt enjoyed during the reign of Osiris were disturbed by the first outbreaks of Jes Grew. According to an artist named Thoth, this epidemic of frantic and uncontrolled dance was due to the absence of a Text that could feed the spirits, which is why Osiris devoted all his energies to teaching Thoth the wisdom he had learned about dance. Thoth transcribed Osiris's teachings in a book of litanies to which personal variations could be added. Although this work brought peace again to Egypt, the rest of mankind still suffered in ignorance. Moved by this universal suffering, Osiris traveled around the world along with Thoth and Dionysus, spreading his message of cultural peace and brotherhood. In his travels, he visited West Africa and then headed to the Americas, where he met the Navaho Indians, as well as the Olmecs, the Aztecs, and the Incas. Meanwhile, in Egypt, Osiris's brother Set spread the rumor that Osiris was traveling around the world drinking and fornicating.

When Osiris returned to Egypt, Set challenged him to prove himself as a true symbol of fertility by being buried and then reborn in the waters of the Nile, thus justifying his title of "human seed." Osiris was locked up in an coffer and thrown into the Nile, but that night Set's lackeys disinterred Osiris and dismembered him into fourteen parts. After his brother's death, Set began the persecution of Osiris's followers. Thoth went into exile and gave his sacred book to Isis, Osiris's sister and wife. Like Thoth, all those who knew of Osiris's mysteries were forced to flee the country and settle in other places, like Ife (Nigeria) and Greece (as was Dionysus's case). But soon after news of Osiris's death was made public, rumors spread that he had been seen in many places—in fact, in all those places where his mutilated limbs were found—thus validating his role as the "human seed."

Set established a military regime that glorified death and despised the arts and life. From his residence in Heliopolis, he created a monotheistic religion based on the worship of Aton (the solar disc). With the help of a group of legislators, Set manipulated the existing historical documents so that he himself was portrayed as the hero and Osiris as the villain. However, his reforms were not popular. On the contrary, Egyptians returned to the cult of Isis and Osiris, but without the Book of Thoth, the magical practices did not have the desired effects.

Reed's reconstruction of Osiris's mythical narrative essentially coincides with the two canonical versions by Plutarch and Diodorus compiled by Egyptologist Wallis Budge in *Osiris and the Egyptian Resurrection*.[39] Osiris's intellectual upbringing in Nysa is mentioned by Diodorus. Both Plutarch and Diodorus point out his mythical origin as the son of Geb and Nut and allude to his characterization as a cultural hero. In his human form (as king of Egypt), these two historians depict Osiris as the great reformer of customs, and the creator of agriculture, law, and religious rituals. His penchant for music is commented on in greater detail by Plutarch, who mentions his use of hymns, songs, music, and dance in his teachings. In Diodorus's account, Thoth receives more attention and is sometimes described as having some of the attributes of Osiris himself. In this version, Thoth was the other great cultural hero in the Egyptian pantheon. In addition to being Osiris's scribe and one of his favorite disciples (because of his talent and inventiveness), Thoth was considered the creator of language, literature, religious ceremonies, and sciences such as astronomy.

Osiris's journeys are also mentioned by both historians. In the two accounts he traveled to other countries and continents with the intention of divulging his cultural reforms. Before departing, he left the government in the hands of his wife Isis, who, as in the novel, was harassed by the ambitious Typhon (Set among the Greeks). As far as Osiris's itinerary is concerned, Diodorus mentions Ethiopia, Arabia, India, and Europe.[40]

One of the most surprising components of Reed's reconstruction of ancient Egypt is his reliance on the works of Budge, one of the most racist, and certainly not the most reliable of Egyptologists.[41] Although Budge's impact on the field of popular Egyptology is unquestionable, his work presents a cultural worldview that has nothing to do with Reed's (it is actually its antithesis). Due to what he considers an obvious case of racial inferiority, Budge asserts that African civilizations have always been at a much lower developmental stage than those of the Western world. In *The Gods of the Egyptians* (1904), for instance, he establishes an insurmountable distance between the spectacular achievements of Greek civilization and the "linguistic limitations" of any African culture:

> The Egyptians, being fundamentally an African people, possessed all the virtues and vices which characterized the North African races generally, and it is not to be held for a moment that any African people could become metaphysicians in the modern sense of the word. In the first place, no African language is suitable for giving expression to theological and philosophical speculations, and even an Egyptian priest of the highest intellectual attainments would have been unable to render a treatise of Aristotle into language which his brother priests, without teaching, could understand. The mere construction of the language would make such a thing an impossibility, to say nothing of the ideas of the great Greek philosopher, which belong to a domain of thought and culture wholly foreign to the Egyptian.[42]

Bernal quotes two other examples of Budge's works in which the British Egyptologist insists on the impossibility of comparing the religious ideas of a "half-civilized African people with those of such cultivated nations as the Greeks and Romans."[43] These opinions must be considered in light of the British occupation of Egypt, of which Budge was a fervent supporter. Nevertheless, it is surprising that Reed makes use of this historian's account instead of others more akin to his own reconstruction of the Osiris myth.

Some elements in the novel's legend, however, depart from the canonical versions of Osiris's deeds collected by Budge. The most striking aspect of Reed's story is its satirical and irreverent tone, which De Filippo has called its "hip style."[44] Reed makes use of his characteristic creative anachronisms. The narrator (apparently LaBas) elaborates a pastiche in which several mythological versions are intertwined with contemporary popular culture, and are expressed in a type of language that seems more appropriate for street use than for historical or religious treatises dealing with these topics.

Aside from this obvious difference between the style of Reed's narrative and the classical accounts of the myth, there also exist important divergences in content. For example, in Reed's version, Osiris's travel becomes a musical tour around Africa and the Americas in which Dionysus takes part as the choral director. In these voyages Reed introduces civilizations that flourished during different periods of history, as well as fantastic elements, such as the landing of spaceships in Teotihuacan, which one would expect to find in a science-fiction story rather than in a historical novel.

Some of the singularities in Reed's account can be explained in the context of the global view of culture and myth that *Mumbo Jumbo* conveys. Three of the most significant examples are those in which he deviates from the canonical versions, namely: Osiris's death and dismemberment as a metaphor of the African diaspora; the view of a Negroid Egypt in which art and wisdom belong exclusively to black Africa; and the depiction of Osiris's Egypt as a cultural utopia, which will also later materialize in the form of the Yoruba religion, Haitian voodoo, and North American hoodoo.

Neither of the canonical versions of Osiris's myth present the hero-god's death and symbolic resurrection in Reed's terms. In Plutarch's narrative Osiris was deceived by Typhon/Set, who crafted a beautiful casket that exactly fit Osiris. In a banquet honoring his brother, before seventy-two conspirators, Set promised the casket to the one person who would fit into it. One after the other each guest tried the casket, but it was only Osiris, of course, who fit exactly. Immediately Set and his accomplices closed the lid, sealed it, and threw it into the Nile, hoping that it would reach the river's mouth and be lost forever at sea. But this did not happen as planned, and it was washed ashore near the city of Byblos in Phoenicia. In that spot, a large tamarisk tree grew and enclosed the casket inside its trunk. Many years later, Isis, who had been searching for her husband, finally found the casket containing his body. After some adventures in which she had to demonstrate her great magical powers, she recovered her husband's body and returned it to Egypt, where she hoped to bring it back to life. However, at one point when the casket was left unattended, Set discovered Osiris's body, cut it into fourteen pieces, and scattered them all over Egypt. Isis and her sister Nephtys then searched until they found all the pieces and reconstructed their brother's body, which thereafter was used in commemorative festivals.[45]

Although Reed's account apparently follows Plutarch's, it incorporates substantial variations. Significantly, Reed completely ignores Set's mythical cleverness. Almost all other versions of the legend depict Set as an ingenious villain, a role similar to Tezcatlipoca's in the Nahua myth of Quetzalcoatl's fall (in both cases a trickster deceives the community's cultural leader). However, Reed's Set exemplifies the cruel and intolerant ruler who seeks to impose a monolithic worldview over a multifaceted reality. (He represents a recurrent character in many of his works.) Above all, Set is Osiris's antithesis. While Osiris is imaginative and emotional, Set is realistic and cold. Cleverness and ingenuity are virtues that Reed obviously reserves for his favorite cultural heroes, such as Osiris, Thoth, and LaBas. In all Reed's novels, the personality of the trickster (which will be examined in the section on fictions of origin) is inseparable from that of the subversive artist who is eternally opposed to power.

The most important aspect of Reed's interpretation of the myth of Osiris's dismemberment is its metaphorical value. As Fox has pointed out, the dismembering and scattering of the god's limbs symbolizes the diaspora of the Africans, who were forcefully uprooted, separated from their own people, and dispersed to foreign lands where they would rarely see other members of their communities.[46] As a consequence of the superimposition of metaphors, three interrelated levels can be distinguished throughout this episode of *Mumbo Jumbo*: Osiris's myth, LaBas's search, and Reed's aesthetics. Isis's search for Osiris's limbs is also suggestive of Reed's search for the fragments of African-American culture, a search that LaBas, in turn, dramatizes at a diegetic level. LaBas searches for the so-called Text, which is undoubtedly something more than the Book of Thoth. At the same time, he tries to solve a mystery, which is also something more than just an epidemic of dancing. In *Mumbo Jumbo* the Text is physically destroyed after having been divided into fourteen sections, and, as we have seen, in the canonical version of the myth Osiris dies after having been dismembered into an identical number of parts. In both cases there exists a hope of regeneration. Such a regeneration is manifested through the African-American cultural renaissances that have taken place in the twentieth century. The first of these cultural awakenings occurred during the twenties (the Harlem Renaissance) and coincides with the narrative present of *Mumbo Jumbo*; the other happened during the sixties (the culminating moment in the movement of affirmation of black culture) and is contemporary to the present of the novel's writing. The richness of *Mumbo Jumbo* resides precisely in this complex interrelationship between the literal and the metaphorical, the diegetic and the extradiegetic, the legendary and the historical.

The affirmation of black cultural power and its impact on Western civilization does not limit itself to modern times, however. In Reed's work, the importance of the black world in Antiquity goes beyond the figurative language of the metaphor; it receives its most exhaustive treatment in the Egyptian legend. Although this is clear enough in the legend itself, the Doubleday edition of *Mumbo Jumbo* (1972) includes several quotations, pictured in the form of a spiral, which introduce LaBas's story and advance important aspects of its content. The first of these quotations (Godfrey Higgins's *Anacalypsis*) categorically states: "Osiris and his Bull were black; all the Gods and Goddesses of Greece were black, at least this was the case with Jupiter, Bacchus, Hercules, Apollo, Ammon. The Goddesses Venus, Isis, Hecate, Diana, Juno, Metis, Ceres, Cybele are black."[47] Aside from the reservations that contemporary historians may have towards Higgins's odd work, it should be noted that the fragment quoted by Reed is taken from a context that contradicts his own cultural view. In *Anacalypsis* the Egyptian and Greco-Roman gods are black, as is Christ himself, as well as Buddha and Krishna.[48] Reed omits all references to the supposed blackness of Christ in order to maintain his view of history as the eternal combat between the liberating power of African religions and the repressive nature of Judeo-Christian culture.

The rest of the quotations are similar in nature to Higgins's. They develop the idea of a mostly Negroid Egypt where the highest manifestations of culture and knowledge come from Ethiopia and Sudan. If we add all this to the importance given to Egyptian civilization in the formation of classical Antiquity, we have established the basis for an Afrocentric perspective in cultural history.

Although the details of this history are usually the result of Reed's manipulation, the general thesis does not lack supporters both in and outside of academia. Indeed, the last decades have witnessed the emergence of Afrocentrism in the interpretation of history. What may seem preposterous in Reed's satirical vision is the subject of serious argument by some contemporary scholars. One of the latest works within this orientation (and one of the first receiving extensive academic attention) is Martin Bernal's essay *Black Athena* (1989). Using ample documentary evidence, Bernal discusses Egyptian and Phoenician cultural influences on Antiquity.[49] These influences would manifest themselves in religion and all forms of cultural expression.[50] The impact of Christianity and other Asian religions and cults was noticeable in the Mediterranean region only after the decline of Egyptian religion in the second century. Even after the emergence of Christianity as the dominant religion in the West, the influence Egypt had on the configuration of Classical Antiquity did not disappear. Although they maintained the superiority of the biblical tradition, the church fathers continued to accept Egypt's civilizing role. According to Bernal, throughout the entire Middle Ages, Hermes Trismegistus ("the rationalized version of Thoth") was still considered the founder of nonbiblical or gentile culture.[51]

The hermetic tradition reemerged during the Renaissance as a consequence of the Neoplatonic movement led by Marsilio Ficino. The different forms of masonry (speculative and radical), which flourished during the eighteenth century and used Egyptian symbolism extensively in their rites, are said to belong to this tradition. The exclusion of the Egyptian and Western Semitic component in Western civilization, in Bernal's view, is related to the wave of ethnocentrism and racism that dominated the Romantic movement at the end of the eighteenth century. The paradigm of racial purity began to be applied to all areas of the humanities, and especially to history. In order for a civilization to enjoy its creative splendor, the purity of its race was a necessary condition. With this presupposition it was difficult to tolerate the concept of a Greece whose origins consisted of a hybrid of European, African, and Semitic cultures. Ignoring Egypt and Phoenicia in the new Western historical constructions would have been the result of a series of philosophical, political, and socioeconomic circumstances that occurred at the end of the eighteenth and the beginning of nineteenth centuries. Among others, Bernal mentions the displacement of interest from Greece and Rome toward ancient India as a result of discoveries regarding Sanskrit; the attacks launched by Christianity against the threat of Egyptian "wisdom"; the development of theories of racial superiority that attempted to justify the expansion of the imperialist powers; and the development of an Aryan model under the aegis of positivism.

Black Athena is not an isolated treatise. In his essay Bernal includes a brief review of all the works that have laid the foundation for his thesis. He emphasizes the pioneering work of popular historians such as George G. M. James, whose *Stolen Legacy* (1954), although lacking the formal and theoretical requirements of contemporary academic history, opened a path for the destruction of the myth of the cultural inferiority of the black world. Other more recent authors, such as Cheikh Anta Diop, Ben Jochannan, and Chancellor Williams, have undertaken the task of supporting this Afrocentric view of history from an equally radical and "mythic" point of view.[52] While James studies the relationship of Greece to Egypt, Diop (1974), for example, focuses on that of black Africa to

Egypt. Another group of scholars led by Ivan Van Sertima (1976) has even expanded the area of influence of black Africa to the pre-Columbian Americas.[53] As a consequence, a remapping of the areas of influence has been taking place in the field of cultural history. The most positive outcome of this debate is probably the increasing tendency to consider cultural evolution as the result of an endless process of intermingling and exchange in which no civilization or race has the monopoly of truth or genius.

What is Reed's position in this debate? Obviously, we cannot expect the goals and ambitions of academic history from a work like *Mumbo Jumbo*. Reed's novel is, above all, a fictional text that rejects the restrictions of any genre, beginning with the traditional restrictions of the novel itself. The function of LaBas's Egyptian legend is significant in relation to the rest of *Mumbo Jumbo*, but it is also provocative in relation to the conventional versions of history and religion. This defiant—and sometimes offensive—attitude regarding the dominant cultural myths leads Reed's characters to sympathize with the most radical views of Afrocentrism. Hence the opening quotations in chapter 52 and the intensity with which LaBas's account insists on the Negroid character of all that is good in Egyptian civilization and, especially, of that which has most influenced the creation of Classicism. However, the radical point of departure of this episode does not stop Reed from using historians like Budge (who, as noted, represents the opposite of an Afrocentric perspective in history) or even more questionable sources, such as H. P. Blavatsky or Aleister Crowley. In this sense, *Mumbo Jumbo* aligns itself with the rest of those postmodern historical novels that mock the scientific and objective pretensions of historiography and favor the supernatural and esoteric interpretations of the past.

In his process of selecting and manipulating documentary data, Reed depicts Osiris's Egypt as the materialization of the cultural utopia he pursues in all his works. As noted, Plutarch's and Diodorus's canonical views depict Osiris and Thoth as cultural heroes. LaBas takes this view of the myth to the extreme. Reed's Osiris was a black prince of divine origin who devoted his life to learning, social reforms, and securing the welfare of his people. In all facets of his creative spirit, art and especially music played a crucial role. The agricultural mysteries consisted of the theatrical and musical representation of the agrarian cycles; LaBas calls them "a theater of fecundation generation and proliferation" (161). Religion also manifested itself through ritual forms characterized by flexibility, syncretism, and openness. The compilation of litanies in the sacred Book of Thoth, for example, is described in terms that evoke the terminology of a jazz musical performance. Like jazz, Thoth's work did not respond to fixed patterns that must be faithfully repeated. The Book of Thoth, which comprises Osiris's teachings, was not a rigid code of rules to be followed by adherents, but "a Book of Litanies to which people in places like Abydos in Upper Egypt could add their own variations" (164).

Regarding the realm of social organization, Osiris's policy was directed toward the economic and cultural welfare of Egypt and to peaceful coexistence with other peoples. Even Osiris's presence in foreign nations must be understood as a cultural mission, rather than as an expansionist adventure. Among Osiris's preferred traveling companions, PaPa LaBas mentions Thoth and Dionysus, who are two artists in his version of the myth.

The utopian vision Reed presents is that of a universe in which there was no conflict between the spheres of art and power. However, his cultural paradise was subverted by the manipulative action of Set, who represents the antithesis of Osiris's values. Set is described as the archetype of the ambitious, intolerant, monotheistic, dogmatic, militaristic, anti-intellectual, and imperialist man of power. His violent enthronement introduced a schism between art and political power. As in Fuentes's vision of the myth of Quetzalcoatl, in *Mumbo Jumbo* Osiris's narrative is the narrative of a fall: the fall of art as the structuring element of society.[54] This nostalgia for a lost cultural paradise is evident in LaBas's commentary: "In Egypt at the time of Osiris every man was an artist and every artist a priest: it wasn't until later that Art became attached to the State to do what it pleased" (164). Set's enthronement inaugurated, therefore, a world view in which the community's life was no longer organized by art, but instead by institutional power.[55]

The Appropriation of the Myths of Blackness

In the second part of his long digression, LaBas comments ironically on the successive plunders of black culture throughout history and on the fact that both Greco-Roman and Judeo-Christian civilizations have used symbols and myths of blackness in the configuration of their world views. LaBas reinvents the story of Moses as that of a new Set, an ambitious initiate into Egyptian mysteries who obtained wisdom by means of force and deceit. The last segment of the legend discusses the origins of Classical and Christian cultures as a result of this same dynamic of appropriation and piracy of black cultural myths.

Several centuries after Set's and Amenhotep IV's unsuccessful monotheistic rules, Moses restored worship of the solar disc in a unique way. An initiate of Osiris's religion, Moses studied music and the magical arts under a black hoodoo musician named Jethro, and, through a series of tricks eventually appropriated the musician's wisdom. It was in fact Jethro who had told Moses about the existence of the Book of Thoth in the Temple of Isis at Koptos, warning that the book was guarded by an immortal serpent. Having retired to the desert in order to meditate and find a safe way to seize the Text, Moses was visited by the spirit of Set, who offered him the answer with the condition that he restore Atonism in Egypt. However, since the Text was obtained under the wrong phase of the moon, Moses only had access to a deformed version of the mysteries.

Once in possession of the sacred Text, Moses tried to exploit its wisdom. He organized a large concert in which he performed some of Jethro's musical pieces contained in the Book of Thoth. The concert, however, ended in a riot. Distorted by having being obtained under the wrong conditions, the Text's litanies had disastrous magical effects that provoked the uprising of the people of Egypt. As revenge for these revolts, Moses caused a great plague (an atomic explosion, in LaBas's anachronistic version) and went into exile with his followers. Many years later, upon returning home after a long period of meditation, he discovered his followers dancing and worshipping a bull (one of the most common images of Osiris). In order to avoid a reemergence of Osiris's religion, he hid the Book of Thoth in a tabernacle where it was to remain forgotten for centuries, becoming one of Moses's lost books.

Meanwhile, during his Greek exile Dionysus had taught the art of Osiris, and it survived in the form of mysteries until the time of Constantine. During this entire time, the Greeks dedicated temples to Osiris and incorporated many of the mysteries and symbols of ancient Egypt into their civilization. A fourth-century revival of monotheism, which was a result of the pact between the Roman state and Christianity, led to a renewed persecution of Osiris's followers. The cult of Isis, for example, survived under the guise of worship of the Virgin Mary, and many of Osiris's attributes were transferred to the figure of Christ, who was, nevertheless, an impostor in LaBas's eyes.

The Book of Thoth did not reemerge until 1118, the year in which the Knights Templar built their headquarters over the Temple of Solomon—which, according to the legend, had been built over Moses's tabernacle. The Templars' librarian, Von Vampton, came upon the Book of Thoth by chance and frantically undertook its translation. However, he was only able to decipher a small part of it, the portion which made up the so-called Rule of the Temple. Practicing some of the Text's rituals without the appropriate training brought doom to the Templars. In 1307 Philip IV of France, aided by Pope Clement, began the persecution, imprisonment and, in many cases, execution of the Order's knights. Accused of practicing sacrilegious rites, which included the worship of the black god Baphomet, the leaders of the Templars were burnt alive, but Von Vampton escaped death. According to LaBas's account, a corrupted variation of the Templars' rites continued under the form of freemasonry.

This second part of LaBas's narrative follows the same pattern as the story of Osiris. While the latter serves to establish the blackness and originality of Egyptian culture, LaBas now insists on its impact on the Classical world and Judeo-Christian civilization. In his atypical representation of Moses and Jethro as magicians, Reed deviates from Western interpretations and follows, instead, the image that African-American folklore and Zora Neale Hurston have given of both.[56] In *Mules and Men* (1935) and in her novel *Moses, Man of the Mountain* (1939), Hurston rewrites some of the most popular versions of the story of Moses. In a folktale from New Orleans, included in *Mules and Men*, Moses gains his knowledge of magic from Jethro, who is described as a great hoodoo man from Ethiopia. This same popular story then tells how Solomon obtains wealth and wisdom thanks to the Queen of Sheba, another native of Ethiopia "with power unequal to man."[57] Both anecdotes repeat a theme that is also characteristic of *Mumbo Jumbo*: The key players in Judeo-Christian culture have acquired their greatness from black Africa.

This thesis recurs in *Moses*, Hurston's most ambitious book.[58] As Reed does in *Mumbo Jumbo*, Hurston combines allegory with the picaresque tradition.[59] Similar to LaBas in his Egyptian legend, Hurston skillfully mixes humor, stories of conjure, folktales, and African legends. In her novel Hurston brings to light a tradition of Mosaic narratives that existed throughout Africa and that came to the New World as a result of the African diaspora.[60] As Hemenway points out, "Hurston attempts nothing less than to kidnap Moses from Judeo-Christian tradition, claiming that his true birthright is African and that his true constituency is African American."[61] Many of the more significant details in Hurston's novel lay the foundations for LaBas's story. In *Moses*, for example, the protagonist is also a conjurer who receives knowledge through Jethro's teachings, and he also acquires the infinite wisdom contained in the Book of Thoth after traveling to Koptos.[62]

The language and tone of Hurston's novel established a clear precedent for Reed's style, as well. What first attracts our attention in *Moses* is the "strange" combination of the comic and the sacred, something that is common in African-American folklore, and unthinkable from the stern Judeo-Christian mindset. Like Reed, Hurston sought to demystify the figure of Moses and the biblical tradition in general. To do so she resorted to the radical humanization of her protagonist.[63] It is surprising that critics have not perceived an influence as clear as Hurston's in Reed's work.[64] Like Reed, Hurston was interested in voodoo-hoodoo as an essential sign of black culture. Like Reed, "Hurston established her fascination with rewriting the sacred myths of the Judeo-Christian tradition in African-American terms and idioms."[65] Even in terms of reception, their works have shared a similar destiny. Both have been and still are the target of many black social-realist critics, who consider their works lacking both political strength and social consciousness.[66] Both have responded to these attacks in similar ways, advocating the freedom of black artists to create without submitting themselves to the prescriptive codes of a narrow aesthetics, be they black or white.

The intertextual echoes of Reed's myth of Moses conform to his concept of literature as a critical rewriting of earlier models. Thus, Reed rewrites Hurston, who rewrites African-American folklore, which, in turn, rewrites both Judeo-Christian tradition and legends of African origin. It is this process of rewriting that serves to explain the difference between the Hurston and Reed versions of the myth. While Hurston compiles African-American folktales with anthropological scrupulousness, Reed creates a new myth in which the protagonists of Judeo-Christian culture have systematically plundered the symbols and mythologies of black civilizations. As for the image of Moses that the two authors present in their novels, Hurston focuses on his status as both a hoodoo man and a charismatic leader. Following a tendency common to black folklore, she also depicts Moses as "the great father of magic scattered over Africa and Asia."[67] Reed, instead, seems to take pleasure in denigrating Moses. As a result, he completely denies the Judeo-Christian component in African-American folklore and questions the power aspect of this character.[68] In LaBas's legend Moses, who is fueled by personal ambition, becomes the clumsy apprentice of a sorcerer. In Reed's historical scheme, Moses is a member of a cultural genealogy that goes from Set to the U.S. political and financial oligarchy, and includes Akhenaton, Christ, the Apostles, Constantine, and the Knights Templar.

In his description of the origin and history of the Templars, Reed closely follows David Annan's account in *Secret Societies* (1967), a work he mentions in the "Partial Bibliography" to *Mumbo Jumbo*.[69] Like Annan, Reed highlights the eastern origins of the Order (Hugues de Payens, the founder of the Templars, modeled his organization on the Assassins, a secret society that originated in eleventh-century Persia). In the same vein, Reed exposes the economic power reached by the Order in the Middle Ages, a power that let the Templars become the premier bankers first of the East and then of most European monarchies. The fall of the Templars very likely occurred as a consequence of their political and economic conflicts with the French monarchy. King Philip IV of France, who had frequently borrowed money and favors from the Templars, viewed their power and independence with suspicion. When the Great Master of the Order, Jacques de Molay, refused Philip's plans to amalgamate the Templars with the rival Hospitalers under the leadership of a prince of France, Philip denounced the Order to the Inquisition on a charge of heresy. Under torture, its members confessed to having been involved in heretical practices. However, these charges, based only on the evidence of forced confessions, have been dismantled by contemporary historiography, which sees in them only Philip's excuse to end the power of a rich military religious Order.[70]

As on many other occasions, Reed once more exploits the most eccentric aspects of the legend; hence, his strange grouping of economic and esoteric interpretations in the reconstruction of the Order's history. For example, Von Vampton's secret activities in his New York apartment suggest blasphemous rites honoring Baphomet, rites which political and religious authorities attributed to the Templars. On the other hand, the Order's decadence is directly explained as a result of their misuse of the sacred Book of Thoth. In his description of legends about the Order, Reed simultaneously uses contradictory versions of the events. His aim is clearly to counter both the official versions of history and those sanctioned by Christian theology and dogma. By insinuating the economic and political value of the persecution, Reed attacks the machinations of the political and religious powers of the time. By suggesting the existence of sacrilegious rites among the Templars, he underlines the survival (although distorted) of pagan mysteries within Christianity as well as the ultimate inefficiency of hegemonic power to impose a dogmatic worldview based on repression and terror.

La Bas's digression plays a crucial role in both *Mumbo Jumbo* and Reed's global work. Through this seemingly fantastic account,

LaBas connects dispersed elements from different traditions and inscribes them into a new mythical pattern. This original construction adopts the symbols and images that originated in Western, African, and African-American cultures. Reed's final synthesis aims at providing an alternative world history in which blacks play the role of the protagonist. At first sight, the satirical tone of the legend, like that of *Mumbo Jumbo* in general, and the exaggerations about the canonical myths of Western civilization may give the impression that LaBas's story is a foolish fancy. However, apart from the fantastic component that characterizes this novel, Reed tends to synthesize already existing mythical and historical motifs and to depend on forms of documentary validation that are characteristic of historiographic discourse.

In the Egyptian legend, Reed explores a great dark area of the historical record, an area that extends from a pre-Classical period to our present century. He also attempts to validate his own views by appealing to the design and experience of a supernatural past. After a detailed analysis, LaBas's version is less extravagant than it first appears. Reed presents a mythical countersystem that is original and simultaneously rooted in several traditions. In order to substantiate it, he resorts to a heterogeneous stock of sources, including classic works of popular Egyptology, theosophical reconstructions of Antiquity, the most recent Afrocentric theories, the oral tales of African-American folklore, and the expressive forms of popular speech and culture. The result is an amalgamating construction that is as preposterous or as factual as the received versions of the past; but it is one that allows Reed to explain the novel's two main temporal levels: the narrative present (the 1920s) and the present in which *Mumbo Jumbo* was being written (the 1960s and 1970s).

THE ROARING 1920S: BETWEEN POLITICAL CONSPIRACY AND CULTURAL RENAISSANCE

From its beginning, *Mumbo Jumbo* informs the reader about the importance of the 1920s in the formation of modern North America (20). The mythical 1920s are, above all, an age of contrast in which the dominant tendencies of U.S. history are dramatized. The fear and insecurity that characterize both the beginning and the end of the period contrast sharply with the image of frivolity that this decade usually evokes. The U.S. 1920s are also the Harding era, a time dominated by political corruption and an array of scandals. Finally, the twenties were also the Jazz Age, the period that gave birth to the first truly African-American cultural movement: the Harlem Renaissance. All these facets are contemplated with great detail in *Mumbo Jumbo*. However, as also occurs with the rest of the novel's historical motifs, Reed's concern for the past is not merely archaeological or exotic. Rather, he is interested in the past insofar as it can explain the present in which the novel is being written. In the analysis of the novel's narrative present, I shall first examine the conspiratorial context re-created by Reed (the Harding administration), and then the treatment of the African-American cultural revival (the Harlem Renaissance).

The Harding Administration

In *Mumbo Jumbo* President William G. Harding comes to power as a result of the influence of the scheming Harry Daugherty, who is, according to Reed's conspiracy theory, a member of the Wallflower Order. The Order's leaders see in Harding the ideal candidate to stop the Jes Grew epidemic: He is the typical self-made man, with roots in rural North America; he has a good relationship with the press (he himself was a newspaper editor); he is not an intellectual light, but is endowed with personal charm. The portrayal of Harding, based on popular history, presents the image of an incompetent politician with an extroverted, naive, and shallow personality. In short, he is a perfect candidate for the manipulations of the Wallflower Order. In his electoral campaign he promises to end the epidemic, but soon shows symptoms of being infected himself.

To begin with, an uncontrollable explosion of rumors, supported by documents and newspaper releases, suggests the candidate's black ancestry. The narrator alludes to a book written by William Eastbrook and based on interviews conducted with Harding's neighbors in Marion, Ohio, who declared that they had never treated Harding's father as a white man. A second book of the same nature, *Warren Harding, President of the United States*, is kept only in the Rare Book Room of the New York Public Library. All other copies of the book, and even the plates, were secretly destroyed (in this case, by Woodrow Wilson's personal order), as were the 250,000 copies of a third work that asserted Harding's "Negro blood."

But there are other reasons why Harding falls into disgrace in the Atonists' eyes. He has been seen in Harlem with Jes Grew carriers and, worse than that, he has registered his opposition to the U.S. invasion and occupation of Haiti. At a public gathering to collect money for antilynching campaigns, Harding has made public remarks against the U.S. secret war in the Caribbean country. The details about this war are given through a dialogue between Benoit Battraville, the leader of the Haitian rebels, and LaBas (chapter 42). The novel mentions how since July 28, 1915, when U.S. marines invaded the island and subdued the population by force, Haiti has been under a bloody occupation. The invasion was carried out without any decree by the U.S. Congress or any representative institution, and at this point the North American people did not yet know about it. It was only through a news leak that news of the invasion and the events that followed came to light. In *Mumbo Jumbo*, the secret operation in Haiti is actually a new emergence of the crusade against heresy that has been led by the Atonists since the times of Set. It is an economic as well as a religious and cultural war and its most immediate goal is the destruction of voodoo beliefs in the Caribbean. The war is thus connected with the Atonists' operative to stop Jes Grew in the United States, since the epidemic feeds on the same kind of spirituality as that of voodoo.

Finally, the Wallflower Order is alarmed by Harding's ambiguous public statements. For example, when he affirms that "the Negro should be the Negro and not an imitation White man," Atonists believe that he is giving a code to black activists. The leaders of the Order realize that Harding is no longer useful for their ends and decide to eliminate him. But instead of using a psychopath (as it seems they had done with President Garfield), they choose to poison him. Chapter 46, which deals with Harding, ends with the Order's hierophant ordering Harry Daugherty to assassinate the president.

After unsuccessfully attempting to warn Harding about the plot, Jesse W. Smith, his personal friend, is murdered. Harding's own execution is gradually accomplished during a tour throughout the United States that will later be known to historians as "Harding's mysterious journey West" (147). As soon as he boards the train, he slowly becomes poisoned, and by the time he arrives in California on July 29, he is showing alarming symptoms of decay. In the San Francisco's Palace Hotel, the president dies.

The fictional account of the history of the Harding administration has two recognized sources: Mark Sullivan's sensationalist history *Our Times* (1935) and Robert Murray's meticulous historical essay *The Harding Era* (1969).[71] From the perspective of academic historiography, the greatest flaw of Sullivan's work originates in the excessive emphasis placed on biographical anecdotes and unfounded rumors. Those rumors, whose origin and veracity are difficult to es tablish, overshadow political and economic events and interpretations. Moreover, because Sullivan was never allowed to consult the Harding papers, he perpetuated trite myths about the period. Leaving these precautions aside, *Our Times* is interesting as an anthology of rumors about an age in which scandals made the elucidation of historical truth particularly difficult. Of a more rigorous orientation, Murray's *The Harding Era* combines biographical information with a study of political problems in the Harding administration. Murray's work falls under academic historiography, which can be identified by its abundant documentation, the detailed revision of relevant previous works, and the thorough verification and evaluation of sources.

As with the rest of the novel's historical episodes, the history of the Harding administration is reconstructed on the basis of a documentary collage in which the darkest anecdotes and the most spectacular events are clearly favored. In Reed's rewriting of the Harding era, four topics receive preferential treatment: the rumors about Harding's "Negro blood," his timid concessions to the civil rights movement, the relationship between the United States and Haiti, and the president's death under mysterious circumstances. In his analysis of the most hazy biographical aspects (Harding's ancestry and death), Reed favors the more sensationalist versions of history, such as Sullivan's; however, he resorts to Murray's work for a treatment of Harding's domestic and foreign politics.

The rumors about the Negro blood of candidate William G. Harding began to spread as the presidential election of November 1920 approached. In reality, as Randolph C. Downes points out, this charge against him was not new but had actually emerged in most of the campaigns in which he had run.[72] Furthermore, rumors about the ancestry of Harding's family had been circulating for almost one hundred years. According to Murray, the origin of the story dates back to the time in which the Hardings emigrated from Pennsylvania to Marion, Ohio. For a brief period of time they lived in the same area as several black families, with whom they were on good terms. Many years later, the political enemies of Harding's father magnified and distorted the facts to the extent of talking about the family's black origins.[73] The first documentary evidence of these charges originated in an editorial in the Marion Republican newspaper *Independent* (May 20, 1887), at the time that Harding Jr. was the young editor of the rival Republican Marion *Star*. Although the editors of the *Independent* publicly retracted the charges, the Democratic *Mirror* resuscitated the rumors and began the spiral of defamation that did not abandon Harding until his death.[74]

The climactic moment of these charges occurred during Harding's presidential campaign. Circulars and posters signed by "Prof. William E. Chancellor of Wooster University, Wooster, Ohio" suddenly began to circulate with the financial help of several Democrats. One of them, dated October 18, 1920, was addressed "To the Men and Women of America, AN OPEN LETTER." In it Chancellor purported to save the country from a "Negro president" and his "pro-Negro ideas." According to the letter, his charge about the black origins of the Republican candidate was founded on four principal criteria: 1) a genealogical tree in which more than two-thirds of Harding's ancestors were "colored;" 2) notarized affidavits he had collected from the Hardings' neighbors in Marion; 3) the scientific authority he claimed for himself as a trained ethnologist; and 4) his own previous experience as superintendent of Washington, D.C., schools, which gave him the opportunity to deal with the largest black population of any U.S. city. Of these four doubtful criteria, only the last (the most irrelevant) seems to have been true. The alleged Harding genealogical tree was completely false.[75] Sullivan shows portraits of the family that contradict Chancellor's slander. He also comments ironically that, according to modern genetics, if the genealogical tree had been true and there had been so much black blood in the family, many of its members would have been completely black.[76] As for the affidavits, they consisted of four accounts full of phrases such as "it has been told," "it was the accepted belief that," "it has been repeatedly reported that," "the Harding family has never, to my knowledge, denied that."[77] As far as Chancellor's competence as an ethnologist is concerned, there is only evidence to the contrary.[78] The simple fact is that rumors snowballed, and the posters, circulars, genealogies, and open letters supporting or rejecting the accusations spread throughout the country. In *Our Times* Sullivan reproduces Chancellor's open letter "To the Men and Women of America."[79] Reed, in turn, inserts Sullivan's reproduction in *Mumbo Jumbo* (Doubleday edition), embellishing it with a collage on which, along with Harding's image, there is the picture of one of his supposed black ancestors.

Behind these escalating rumors was a desperate campaign enacted by members of the Democratic Party at a moment when Harding's election to the presidency seemed unavoidable. Chancellor, himself an ardent Democrat, represented an attitude common among many conservatives, who saw in Harding's election a threat to the system of racial discrimination.[80] All evidence points, therefore, to a campaign of political defamation aimed at discrediting Harding on the eve of the election. Among the main instigators were those who supported discrimination and wanted to present Harding's nomination as a plot to implement black domination throughout the country. This dirty war was disseminated and magnified by the press. Unfortunately, Harding's public statements, few and indiscreet—as Reed presents them in the novel—failed to dissipate the rumors, and instead helped to feed them.[81] In the face of these facts, we might wonder why Reed justifies the rumors about the president's "Negro blood." In his fictionalized account, Reed uses a letter and book written by Chancellor, a paranoid racist, as the only evidence of Harding's black ancestry. Although from an ideological point of view Chancellor and Reed are diametrically opposed, their views share an important outlook: They both see Harding's coming to power as the possibility for expansion of the black presence in U.S. society. However, what Chancellor contemplated with apprehension, Reed sees with hope.

Black votes were key in Harding's election as president. Since the end of the Civil War, the black population had begun to leave the Southern states en masse. This migratory movement increased during the first two decades of this century, resulting in large concentrations of African Americans in the industrialized Northern cities. Their increasing political power was channeled by activist organizations such as the National Association for the Advancement of Colored People (NAACP). In the past, Republicans had secured the black vote, regardless of their candidates' agendas. Now, aware of their decisive role in elections, African Americans began to put pressure on the party's leaders to adopt measures against discrimination and to seek better relations with black countries. At the Republican convention in Chicago (June 1920), the five black representatives submitted a reform proposal centered around three major points: 1) the adoption of legislative and law-enforcement measures to secure the right of all Southern blacks to vote; 2) the legal abolition of discrimination and segregation in all states; and 3) the suspension of imperialist aggression abroad (that is, the United States should secure democracy at home before trying to defend it in other countries). None of these points was completely accepted, but a petition for an antilynching law was approved. This small but important concession, along with veiled promises of the withdrawal of U.S. marines from Haiti, made the Republican platform more appealing to blacks than the Democratic one.

Throughout the electoral campaign Harding's attitude toward the civil rights movement was, as Downes points out, ambiguous. It depended on where and under which circumstances his speeches were given.[82] For example, in the North he supported black rights without giving details. His agreement with the NAACP on a moderate program secured African-American votes without making too many concessions. In the South, however, he softened his progressive rhetoric with regard to racial relations and was specific in his defense of the continuity of segregation. In any case, once Harding was elected in November 1920, he tried to set a moderate reform program for the improvement of race relations in motion. However, most of his attempts were frustrated by Congress and the lobbies. As Murray points out, Harding's proposals for an interracial commission, an antilynching law, the withdrawal of troops from Haiti, and the end of discrimination in education were all turned down by the House of Representatives, the Senate, the State Department, and the local authorities, respectively.

Especially important to the analysis of Reed's novel is Harding's foreign policy in the Caribbean. Harding's arrival at the White House temporarily interrupted the escalation of U.S. interventionism in that area, which had reached its height during the preceding administrations of Roosevelt, Taft, and Wilson. Throughout the novel, news headlines refer to the invasion of Haiti by U.S. marines. *Mumbo Jumbo* also alludes to Harding's opposition to the occupation (one reason why the plot for his assassination is initiated) and to the initial attempt to conceal the military operation.

The importance of Haiti in Reed's novel is manifested on many levels: It is the first black nation to obtain its independence, and it is also a link between Africa and America; but, above all, it is the cradle of voodoo, which forms the spiritual and aesthetic foundations for Reed's multicultural utopia. In his description of the cultural reality of this small country Reed uses terms that are similar to those employed in his characterization of Osiris's Egypt: "Haiti is a nation of artists. Artist societies are everywhere."[83] Thus, Haiti is more than a country. It is a symbol especially dear to African Americans and essential for Reed's worldview. Haiti's conflict in *Mumbo Jumbo* dramatizes the eternal struggle between Atonism (exemplified by the twentieth-century political and cultural systems in the United States) and the alternative, syncretic worldview represented by voodoo.

Most details about the occupation are relayed through the dialogue between the Haitian leader Benoit Battraville and PaPa LaBas in chapter 42. Generally speaking, Battraville's description of the occupation conforms with documented historical reality: invasion of the island by U.S. marines on July 28, 1915; bloody repression of all forms of political opposition; creation of a guerrilla army commanded by Charlemagne Peralte and Battraville himself;

renaissance of cultural nationalism among the Haitians; support of the NAACP and, especially, of James Weldon Johnson for the rebels; manipulation of events by the U.S. press; and Harding's opposition to the invasion. The basic framework of the story responds, therefore, to the commonly accepted versions of the case. Even some of the most puzzling aspects, such as the role of voodoo as a unifying force among the rebels, can be easily documented.[84]

But it is through differences rather than similarities that we can discover the free use of documentation that characterizes Reed's work. First of all, U.S. military action was not an isolated case in the Caribbean. Indeed, the direct intervention of the U.S. army in the countries of this area was the norm during the administrations of Roosevelt, Taft, and Wilson.[85] Most of these actions were not as secret as Reed portrays them, nor were they carried out without authorization of U.S. representative institutions. The military action against Haiti, for example, was commanded by the executive power and sanctioned by the U.S. Senate on February 28, 1916.[86] While it is true that the press gave a distorted image of the occupation (a normal tendency in U.S. news coverage of international politics), there were many examples of voices that protested the intervention.[87] The reasons for the invasion also differ from the existing historiography about the event. According to Reed, the occupation was part of a religious and cultural war that dates back to the very origins of civilization (136). While it is commonly accepted that part of the repression by the occupation forces was aimed at all forms of Haitian cultural nationalism, to transform such an obvious case of economic imperialism into a new version of the Crusades corresponds to the same hyperbolic and caricaturing tendency that characterizes Reed's view of history. The United States invaded Haiti in an attempt to consolidate its political and economic presence in the Caribbean. After negotiations failed to obtain a trade monopoly there, and after all the political turbulence caused by the mass slaughter of political prisoners, U.S. authorities adopted the same military strategy employed in the rest of the area (the Dominican Republic, Cuba, Guatemala, Honduras, Panama, and Nicaragua):[88] As a result of the occupation, Haiti became another "client" government of the United States, and, from that point on, the majority of its national income was destined to paying off its debt to the invading power.[89] When in 1922 the *Banque Nationale de la République d'Haïti*—which until then depended on *L'Union Parisienne*—was integrated into the National City Bank, French financial control in Haiti officially ended, and U.S. economic control over the region was confirmed.[90]

While Reed is partially faithful to the academic versions of Haiti's occupation, in his description of Harding's death he returns to the rumors that the yellow press spread. Instead of a heart attack causing his death (the official diagnosis), the president is poisoned. In his search for documentary support for his conspiratorial view of the United States in the 1920s, Reed again resorts to Sullivan's eccentric theories. Sullivan tells how immediately after Harding's death and the subsequent discovery of many economic scandals, an unparalleled series of rumors began to circulate.[91] These rumors concerned various subjects, including the president's numerous affairs, his illegitimate daughter, manipulations by Mrs. Harding and Harry Daugherty, but, especially, his mysterious death. Some talked about suicide, others about assassination. Gaston B. Means, a consummate liar,[92] published *The Strange Death of the President*, where he imagined that Mrs. Harding had poisoned her own husband.[93] Other works, such as Samuel Hopkins Adams's novel *Revelry*, suggested suicide. As in the case of the Negro ancestry story, rumors about Harding's suicide or murder were so pervasive that they invaded the historiographic field. Sullivan mentions several historians and "middlebrow" journalists who play down the mysterious character of Harding's death: James Truslow Adams, (*The March of Democracy*), J. Hampden Jackson (*The Post War World*), and Frederick Lewis Allen (*Only Yesterday*). Yet none of them provides any substantial evidence that he was murdered or comitted suicide.[94]

Reed's vision of Harding and his presidential term is based, in short, on very diverse sources. In some cases the novel presents a decidedly paradoxical synthesis: Reed adopts the most daring theories about Harding's private life and naive personality from popular history; he frequently goes even further by creating new plots that overshadow those proposed in the documented sources he cites; on other occasions, he magnifies an obscure source; sometimes he tries to justify his conspiratorial view of history by referring to nonexistent works or by misquoting a historian. From this final conglomeration emerges the story of a secret society that initially used Harding for its conspiratorial purposes but then decided to eliminate him (as it had done before with other presidents). The deciding factors in Harding's tragic fate are, according to the novel, his intention to withdraw troops from Haiti, his Negro blood and behavior, and his support for some aspects of the civil rights movement.

However, as is also the case with other historical motifs in *Mumbo Jumbo*, we must go beyond the novel's literal level. Many of the details of Harding's portrayal have metaphorical value. If

Reed makes Harding an African American, for example, it is not because of a naive essentialism aimed at making blacks into relevant political figures. Harding behaves black in *Mumbo Jumbo*, because, during the years of his administration, U.S. society had somehow begun to "go black," by adopting the expressive forms and behavior of African Americans.[95] The Roaring 1920s represent the first time in which black culture exceeded the limits of the African American community and influenced the habits and behavior of U.S. society at large.

The Harlem Renaissance

Harding's administration coincided with the Jazz Age, an era in which Harlem became the capital of African-American culture as well as a vital center of artistic life and entertainment. Several factors—demographic, economic, and cultural—interacted to influence the emergence and development of this renaissance. In the first place, as a result of economic problems and the general racism in the South, black families began a massive migration to Northern cities (mostly East St. Louis, Chicago, Washington, and New York). This movement was particularly strong during the First World War, when the number of black farmers relocating to urban centers was close to 250,000.[96] The number of people resettling in the New York neighborhood of Harlem was particularly high, and a prosperous black community began to flourish there. The job opportunities and the neighborhood's intense cultural life began to attract African-American intellectuals, who made Harlem their temporary or permanent home. James Weldon Johnson came from Florida and W. E. B. Du Bois from Atlanta, while Claude McKay and many other writers moved from the West Indies.

At that time New York was the economic and cultural center of the United States.[97] Living in New York offered many advantages for any writer, musician, or painter. In addition to the city's explosion of creativity, artists could benefit from direct contact with publishers, producers, and art dealers. The cultural atmosphere of the twenties was also especially accepting of artistic expressions that reflected the transformation of values produced by the urbanization of North America. Theodore Dreiser's and Sinclair Lewis's novels, as well as John Dos Passos's first modernist experiments criticized both the evils of industrialization and uncontrolled urban growth. The emergence of autochthonous forms of expression that voiced similar preoccupations within the black community was, in general, welcomed with interest. In fact, it was from this trend that the figure of the white patron appeared. The patron's role was to help black artists come into contact with the great mediators of the cultural establishment. Almost all forms of African-American art and entertainment were influenced either positively or negatively by this system of white patronage.

The increasing political mobilization of U.S. blacks also affected the birth of this cultural phenomenon. Led by the NAACP since 1910, the civil rights movement had achieved one of its peak moments. Its activists' condemnation of racism as well as their claims to equality and their massive mobilizations created a climate of responsibility and confidence within the black community. What had previously been mostly individual, occasional, and sometimes violent manifestations of nonconformism, became integrated into a platform of organized activism that had a great influence on the political life of the nation as a whole.

The politics of docile integration supported by Booker T. Washington, which had been so popular thus far, became the target of attacks launched by two very different leaders, W. E. B. Du Bois (one of the founders of the NAACP) and Marcus Garvey (the creator of the Universal Improvement Association). Although separated by insurmountable differences, both Du Bois and Garvey stood out for their militant pan-Africanism. In Du Bois's case, such tendencies were exemplified by the organization of several pan-African congresses (the first of which met in Paris in 1919) in an attempt to tighten the relations between U.S. blacks and their African counterparts. Garvey, on the other hand, championed a black separatist back-to-Africa group. Apart from their differences, both men helped to lay the foundation for the explosion of ethnic pride that characterized the cultural aspect of the Harlem Renaissance.

Although Harlem was not the only place where black culture flourished in the twenties, it was, without question, its cultural center and the symbol of the African-American city par excellence. Its great protagonists spared no superlatives in describing the Harlem of the mid-twenties. For James Weldon Johnson it was "the recognized Negro capital," "the Mecca for the sightseer, the pleasure seeker, the curious, the adventurous, the enterprising, the ambitious, and the talented of the world." In Langston Hughes's view, Harlem was "a great magnet for the Negro intellectual," "erotic, colorful and sensuous, a place where life wakes up at night." Duke Ellington assures that one could find "the world's most glamorous atmosphere" there, and Alain Locke even affirms that "it is—or promises to be—a race capital."[98]

In *Mumbo Jumbo* Reed re-creates this glamorous atmosphere.

Through fictional and historical characters, he discusses some of the most distinguishing aspects of the Harlem Renaissance. He either sets most of the action in Harlem or has Harlem-based characters play a crucial part in the novel, while mentioning some of its most famous places of amusement. The Cotton Club and the Plantation Club (Plantation House in *Mumbo Jumbo*) play a role that goes beyond their exotic settings. As noted, the Text is discovered in the center of the Cotton Club, the most opulent of those clubs born during the Jazz Age. In the same fashion, the novel reproduces a club program, and one its stars, Cab Calloway, is frequently mentioned as embodying the spirit of Jes Grew. Like the historical Plantation Club, Plantation House is located outside Harlem, near the Broadway theaters and, like its real-life counterpart, includes among its customers members of the upper class. With its minstrels and degraded versions of black dances, Plantation House represents the corruption of those forms originally produced in Harlem.

The *Mumbo Jumbo* Kathedral, the center of Harlem intellectual activity, is located on 136th Street, where A'Leilia Walker's historical mansion once stood. In fact, one of the Kathedral's rooms, or "chapels," is called the Dark Tower, which was how people referred to A'Leilia Walker's house, the meeting place of Harlem's African-American intelligentsia.[99] As noted, Villa Lewaro, Madame C. J. Walker's elaborate mansion at Irvington-on-the-Hudson, also appears in the novel as a social and cultural meeting place. In addition to these exclusive salons, *Mumbo Jumbo* also refers to popular places of entertainment open to African Americans such as the rent parties, fund-raising gatherings that enabled some blacks to pay their rents in the Harlem of the 1920s.[100]

The cultural magazines of the time are represented by references to *Fire*, the ephemeral publication on which the most prominent representatives of the movement collaborated, and whose first and only issue was edited by Langston Hughes, Zora Neale Hurston, and Wallace Thurman. Although given fictional titles, other publications that appear in *Mumbo Jumbo* allude to some of the Harlem Renaissance's most popular magazines, such as *Messenger*, *Crisis*, and *Opportunity*. These periodicals, open to the collaboration of young black intellectuals, encouraged creativity by sponsoring literary prizes and, at the same time, exercised a militant political activism in favor of civil rights.

Many of the historical protagonists of this "new Negro awakening" are mentioned outright. Among those political personalities who at the turn of the century helped set the foundations for the movement, the novel discusses the role played by Booker T. Washington, W. E. B. Du Bois, and Marcus Garvey. James Weldon Johnson's contemporaneous work is also mentioned (especially his articles about Haiti), as are those by creative writers such as Langston Hughes, Claude McKay, and Countee Cullen. Cullen himself appears as "the Queen of Ubangi" in the scene that takes place in Villa Lewaro, and some features of his works are commented on by the fictional character Nathan Brown.[101] The novel begins with a quotation by Zora Neale Hurston and the epilogue ends with another by Arna Bontemps, two of the greatest protagonists and theoreticians of the movement. African-American music also plays a leading role in *Mumbo Jumbo*. The Jes Grew epidemic is, most of all, an epidemic of black music and dance. When, on several occasions (6, 17, 34, 189, 211), the novel mentions a first breakout of the epidemic in 1890, Reed is referring to the first ragtime compositions, which were produced at that time and had an extraordinary impact on U.S. popular culture.[102] Scott Joplin, the creator of ragtime, is consistently mentioned as a predecessor of later musical developments. The very chronology of the African-American cultural renaissance is intensively related to different types of black music. Thus, when the novel refers to the importance of 1920 as the threshold of a new era, it explains that this was the year in which Charlie Parker, the great saxophonist who revolutionized jazz, was born. Even the itinerary of the epidemic (from New Orleans to Chicago and New York) corresponds to the geographic progression of jazz forms.[103]

Besides the great number of explicit references to writers and musicians, Reed's novel also reflects on the "Negro awakening," imaginatively re-creating some of the attitudes and situations that shaped the movement. In a certain sense, *Mumbo Jumbo* is Reed's novelistic homage to the Harlem Renaissance. Unlike the social realists, who criticized the movement's lack of political commitment, Reed has always eulogized the cultural activities of Harlem in the twenties: "one of the classiest, noblest, artiest, brightest, most terrifically spiflicated, smartest, shook-up and elegant moments of our Century."[104]

However, Reed's celebration of the awakening is not unquestioning; his homage is a critical one. *Mumbo Jumbo* is particularly aggressive in its treatment of the role played by the supposedly unselfish and altruistic white patrons. Almost all critics have seen a clear allusion to the historical Carl Van Vechten in the character of Hinckle Von Vampton. Van Vechten was one of the intellectuals who popularized the black cultural renaissance among a white audience. As part of the crusade against Jes Grew, Von Vampton invents a "Talking Android," a figure from the black community whose purpose is to undermine its cultural foundations from within. Reed's use of this character allows him both to criticize those among the white intelligentsia who profited from the exploitation of black artists, and to censor manipulation by the cultural industry, which only follows the dictates of the market. In opposition to this form of intellectual exploitation, Reed proposes the creation of an independent cultural industry under the control of the artists themselves.

We must keep in mind, however, that Von Vampton is a fictional character, who is not intended to literally reflect Van Vechten's activities in Harlem. The place of this historical personality in the movement is one of those dark and controversial areas that Reed purports to expose. Most of the protagonists of the renaissance (especially Hughes and Johnson) refer favorably to the role played by Van Vechten in the popularization of Harlem in the 1920s.[105] On the other hand, many of those who criticized Van Vechten's work and activities, like Du Bois, were critical of the writers and artists of the Harlem Renaissance as well. Reed's intention here is rather to use characters, situations, and attitudes with historical echoes to justify his vision of black culture that has been permanently plundered by Judeo-Christian culture. From this point of view, he uses the role played by white patrons of the arts to launch a severe critique against the cultural imperialism exercised by the economic and intellectual establishments.

In the novel, as in history, the African-American cultural renaissance ends with the onset of the Great Depression. Reed's originality lies in his inversion of the cause and effect relationship. Many of the canonical works about the Harlem Renaissance point to its decline as the result of the economic depression that the United States suffered in the late 1920s.[106] However, in *Mumbo Jumbo* the Great Depression is only one more scheme of the Wallflower Order. According to the version presented in chapter 50, the collapse of U.S. financial networks is part of a plot machinated by "the Sphinx," the name by which the highest leader of the Order, Walter Mellon, is known.[107] The bizarre reason given in the novel refers to Mellon's plan to avoid a new outbreak of Jes Grew (another Negro Awakening) by creating a depression of cataclysmic effects. The episode serves to underline the value Reed gives the renaissance, the first time in which African-American culture exercised a lasting influence on the rest of North American society. The Harlem Renaissance put black arts at the forefront of the U.S. cultural scene and prepared the path for later movements.

Both culturally and politically, Reed's interest in the twenties has to be understood in relation to his necromantic concept of history. By conjuring up the past he interprets the present and predicts the future. Apart from obvious differences in the personalities of their presidents—in politics and in culture—the Harding era is, at least in Reed's reconstruction, suspiciously similar to the present in which *Mumbo Jumbo* was written (1969–1971), that is, to the Nixon era. Moreover, in some details the historical vision offered by Reed's novel seems to predict some of the events that occurred immediately after it was published. Reed himself has suggested these similarities in several interviews.[108] During their presidential terms, both Harding and Nixon had to face a postbellum economic crisis (after WWI and Vietnam, respectively); U.S. society seemed infected by an epidemic of African-American music and dance (jazz in the twenties and its derivations in the sixties and seventies); Egypt captured international attention (intensive archeological excavations and war against Israel); the government was involved in plots and scandals (the conspiracy of the Ohio gang and Watergate); the destruction of documents was ordered to avoid having the scandal publicized; the president was surrounded by amateur, incompetent burglars. As a corollary to this network of coincidences and schemes, the first edition of *Mumbo Jumbo* included a photograph of the Watergate conspirators one year before the conspiracy was made public.[109]

Besides all these coincidences in the political sphere, both periods are characterized by an unprecedented revival of African-American culture. This is the reason why Reed makes the Jes Grew epidemic reappear in the 1960s, "the decade that screamed," and a period that was also referred to as the New Black Renaissance.[110] Rooted in the black activism of the sixties, the first attempts at codifying a truly African-American aesthetics began to take place. Such attempts resulted in both the social-realist poetics of academic intellectuals—such as Addison Gayle, Jr., Houston Baker, Jr., and Amiri Baraka—and Reed's first avant-garde experiments. Through a temporal superimposition, Reed projects the aesthetic debate of the late sixties onto the twenties. As Gates points out, "*Mumbo Jumbo* is a thematic allegory of the Black Arts Movement of the 1960s rendered through causal connections with the Harlem Renaissance of the 1920s."[111]

From a referential point of view, the amalgamation of fact and fiction is the most striking feature in *Mumbo Jumbo*. In the relationship that the novel maintains with its historical referent three basic possibilities can be easily identified: 1) references with empirical evidence—from the influence of Egyptian culture on Western civilization to numerous details about the 1920s, such as the turbulence of the period, the invasion of Haiti by U.S. troops, the financial scandals of the Harding Administration, the Harlem cultural renaissance, and even the tensions between white and black Masonic chapters; 2) references with an unreliable documentary base—the original blackness of all the great myths of civilization, heretical practices of the Templars, Harding's alleged Negro ancestry and possible murder, and much of Reed's conspiratorial view; 3) references with no supporting evidence at all—atomic explosions in Ancient Egypt, the landing of spaceships in precolonial Mexico, the simultaneous chronology of civilizations that are very far from each other in time, the Great Depression of 1929 as a plot against African Americans, and a long list of completely apocryphal characters and situations. These three possibilities broadly correspond to three narrative modes that are usually found separately: historiography, historical journalism (or popular history), and fiction.

Reed's combination—and intentional confusion—of these three referential levels gives way to a new mythical and historical countersystem in which the black world (and especially the black artist) plays a leading role. Reed inverts the terms of the Western academic establishment and presents a worldview that is ultimately as valid or preposterous as the dominant Eurocentric perspective. In *Mumbo Jumbo* Reed also establishes the coordinates that allow one to understand his later work. The basic dynamics of his countersystem respond to a "necromantic" view of history in which the writer-shaman revives the past in order to understand the present and predict the future.

Structural Levels of Reflection

All of Reed's novels contain an important metafictional component that shares the referential spectrum with historiographic reflection. In *Mumbo Jumbo* the richness of the metafictional component is so extraordinary that it seems impossible to systematize the totality of its self-referential techniques. Most of the possibilities examined by Dällenbach, Bal, and Ricardou are present in the text: specular metaphors, intertextual summaries, allegories of the acts of reading and writing, representations of the aesthetic code through analogical images, and the use of mythological emblems or narratives that reveal the originating reality of the text. This section examines some of these possibilities according to Dällenbach's four structural levels of reflection: the utterance, the enunciation, the code, and the transcendental origin.

Reflections of the Utterance

The most evident examples of this modality in *Mumbo Jumbo* can be found in the opening chapter, the episode known as the "Egyptian legend," and in the epilogue. All three cases provide a summary of motifs, characters, symbols, and other key elements central to understanding the different levels of meaning in the novel. While in the former example the summary works as a prolepsis (advancing information), in the latter two it functions as a synopsis of previously explained data.

In *Mumbo Jumbo*'s first chapter, the function of this proleptic summary is very similar to that of a news flash or a film preview. A collage of motifs and situations that condense the global meaning of the work is presented in advance. Above all, chapter 1 establishes the origin and nature of Jes Grew. The epidemic breaks out in New Orleans, which is presented as the multicultural city par excellence. The mention of New Orleans allows Reed to introduce information about voodoo/hoodoo, such as the symptoms of possession by a *loa* and the figure of the nineteenth-century hoodoo Queen Marie Laveau.

In its description of the nature and effects of the epidemic, this introductory chapter also creates the dynamics of cultural conflict that dominate the historical view in *Mumbo Jumbo*. Reed's counter-system reproduces the eternal combat between Eros and Thanatos, a combat in which Africa and Afro-America are on life's side, while the Judeo-Christian world is on the side of death.[112] Jes Grew, with its roots in Africa and Haiti and its frequent identification with the spirit of voodoo, is therefore a threat to the values of Western culture, not because of its destructive potential, but rather for its enlivening energy. In fact, Jes Grew is not a plague, but an anti-plague. Instead of weakening the body, it gives it spirit. As the novel later explains, Jes Grew is like a discharge of vital energy that is released through spontaneous music and dance, something that, according to Reed, is radically opposed to the somber frame of mind of Western culture (the culture of guilt and suffering in *Mumbo Jumbo*).

Other motifs advanced in this prologue include the condition of the epidemic itself searching for its Text, which will later be interpreted as the search for a new aesthetic that would account for the new forms of African-American culture; Jes Grew's most immediate outbreak, which took place in 1890 (the era of ragtime), but vanished because of the absence of a text (a truly black aesthetics); its politically transgressive character (it incites the slave against his master); its openness ("it knows no class no race no consciousness") and its spontaneity ("it is self-propagating and you can never tell when it will hit"); and, finally, the role of the Wallflower Order in the fight against the epidemic.

In the mythological and historical digression of chapter 52, LaBas solves some of the novel's enigmas. In the recognition scene in the library at Villa Lewaro, Reed resorts to the above-mentioned four levels of reflection. As a reflection of the utterance, the episode works as a summary and as an explanation of the novel's events. On the one hand, it repeats and condenses some of the events regarding the history of the Text; on the other, it solves some of the many mysteries posed by the novel. The reader is now able to understand the identity of Von Vampton and his complex and tense relationship with the Wallflower Order, the meaning of the cryptic message that LaBas finds with Abdul's lifeless body, and numerous details related to the identities and actions of the main characters. More importantly, however, the legend also explains the mysterious origins of Jes Grew and the Text. To further his explanation, LaBas goes back to the origin of writing itself and creates a countervision which dramatizes the conflict that, in his view, rules history: the struggle between the creative power of imagination (represented by African and African-American cultures and personified by Osiris, Thoth, Jethro, and LaBas) and the monolithic forms of power (represented by the Judeo-Christian civilization and personified by Set, Moses, Von Vampton, and the members of the Wallflower Order). The network of connections that makes up the legend incorporates the novel's characters and situations with a mythical design.

The spiral of quotations that opens chapter 52 in the Doubleday edition further adds to the complexity of the passage. As noted, in that edition Reed includes a series of quotations in which several critics, novelists, and historians assert the black roots of civilization. This series is formally organized as a chain spiraling around a photograph that represents a highly reflexive scene. In the photograph three black marines are taking a picture of a sculpture of three African warriors in a museum gallery whose only other occupant is a white man who detachedly observes the scene from a distance. In terms of both form and content, the quotation is a clear example of fictional *mise en abyme*, since it announces the leitmotif of LaBas's digression: the black origins of civilization and its plunder by the Judeo-Christian world. Godfrey Higgins's quotation claims the blackness of all the deities of the Egyptian and Classical pantheons; Hurston's suggests the extension of Mosaic legends throughout the entire black world; Louis Marss's establishes a relationship between ancient Greek rituals and Haitian voodoo ceremonies; Aleister Crowley insists on the blackness of Osiris; Sir E. A. Wallis Budge comments on the value of dance as a form of worship in African religions and refers to Osiris as the patron of dance and music; and Reed speculates about Christianity's traditional aversion to dance. The spiral ends with one of Carl Jung's statements about the Osiris myth as a clear precedent for the Christian legend of Salvation.

If we compare the content of these quotations with that of the Egyptian legend, it is apparent that, as happens in the novel's opening chapter, we are dealing with a proleptic reflection of the utterance, since it advances the content of the narrative that immediately follows. Even on the formal level the quotations as well as the collage of quotations and photograph play a proleptic role. The image of the spiral represents a clear invitation to the reader to plunge into the depths of a matter, in this case, the depths of myth and history. LaBas traces the origin of the novel's mysteries into the deepest past, into that nebulous region where the historical record fails to reach and one must trust myth. The thematic content and disposition of the collage are highly significant. On the visual level, the novel insists on comparing a remote past where the black world was dominant with a present where the images and symbols of that origin have been kidnapped by what Reed calls Art Detention Centers (Western museums that feed on the looting of Third World cultures). The ultimate effect of the collage is that of a serial duplication between its multiple framing and framed components. The sculptures partially reflect the spirit of the characters who are trying to capture them with their cameras, while the photographic motif as a whole visualizes the contents of the quotations that frame it. The series of quotations, in turn, summarizes (and thereby reflects) the content of LaBas's digression, which works as a synthesis or expression of the content and motifs of *Mumbo Jumbo*.

The effect of this vertiginous specular structure is close to what Dällenbach calls infinite duplication, in which the reflecting and reflected elements multiply each other *ad infinitum*, like images in two mirrors placed across from each other. The only difference stems from the fact that in this particular example the reflection is limited by two poles: the sculpture and the novel we are reading; hence my use of the phrase multiple or serial duplication, instead of adopting the simple or infinite kinds of duplication proposed by Dällenbach. In each degree of reflection (sculptures, the photograph, spiraling quotations, the Egyptian legend, and the novel), the original is compared to the contemporary situation in which power relations have been reversed. The condition of closure of the sculpture (held in a museum) speaks of an antithetical reality in which the once-powerful black myths are under the controlling watch of the plunderers.

The episode, therefore, goes well beyond a mere summary or the quotation of content (features that Dällenbach assigns to the fictional *mise en abyme*). As discussed in the section on historiography, LaBas goes back to the origin of Jes Grew, which is equivalent to the origins of civilization. The resolution of the mystery of the Text also compels him to track the origins not only of the Book of Thoth but also of writing itself. The transcendental character of LaBas's search and his attempt to discover the reality in which the novel originates also make the legend a prime example of Dällenbach's fourth level of reflection, the fiction of origin, which will be discussed at the end of this section on metafiction.

The last example of fictional *mise en abyme* occurs, appropriately, at the very end of the novel. In the epilogue, the hundred-year-old LaBas gives a lecture about Jes Grew before an audience of young students. The time of the action is indeterminate, although there are indications that suggest the period when *Mumbo Jumbo* was being written, that is, the end of the 1960s or beginning of the 1970s. In his lecture LaBas haphazardly recapitulates some of the novel's leitmotifs, especially those that are presented in the introductory chapter. What at the beginning seemed to be a series of eccentric ideas gains new meaning as the reader nears the end. In spite of the disorganized nature of LaBas's discourse (supposedly an old man's ramblings), the reader finally understands the full meaning of the epidemic and the search for the Text. In these final moments Jes Grew is identified with 1) the transformation of U.S. society as a result of the influence of African-American culture (209); 2) the spirit of jazz, blues, and ragtime (211, 214); 3) the Harlem Renaissance (217); and 4) the forms of popular speech (214).

After the avalanche of characters (both fictional and historical) and situations that populate *Mumbo Jumbo*, the epilogue serves to resolve those uncertainties that may still exist for some readers. Among other topics, the epilogue explains Freud's strange reaction when he visited the United States by viewing it in the light of Jung's essay "Your Negroid and Indian Behaviour." The vision so terrifying to Freud ("The Black Tide of Mud"), which made him declare America "a big mistake," originated, according to LaBas, in the infection of North American society by some forms of black behavior. What Freud saw with apprehension, LaBas contemplates with satisfaction. In his final speech, LaBas proposes the recuperation of the signs of African American cultural identity which, in his opinion, must be found in autochthonous traditions (Egyptian mythology, the Yoruba religion, and Haitian voodoo), and not in systems imported from Europe, such as Marxism or psychoanalysis.

The illustrations included in the epilogue (Atheneum edition) also fulfill this summarizing and explanatory function. The first two show the peripheral role assigned to blacks in North American history. They are two nineteenth-century engravings in which whites are in the center, while blacks remain in the background, silent witnesses to acts of violence. The other two pictures (a caricature of the forced Christian evangelization of the Americas and an engraving picturing a Mardi Gras parade) represent two conflicting forces that Reed sees behind all historical events: the repressive power of Christianity and the popular culture of laughter that Reed associates with the African-American tradition.

Reflections of the Enunciation

Through the textual mirroring of the enunciation, *Mumbo Jumbo* makes its process of production and reception present at the level of the diegesis. As in other postmodern works, Reed's novel repeatedly allegorizes the acts of writing and reading and, as also happens in other postmodern fictions, both acts are represented in similar terms.[113] All writing implies a reading, since the writer must first be able to read a reality that is conceived in textual terms and to configure his or her own writing on the model of previous texts. Similarly, the act of reading implies a re-creation, a rewriting, of the reality contained in the text, and this is either accomplished or not accomplished according to the reader's cultural capacity and to his or her own past experiences.

In *Mumbo Jumbo* Reed is seeking artistic forms that allow him to create in freedom. In many of his essays and interviews, he has expressed his rejection of those narrow codes imposed by a unilateral reading of reality—hence his frequent confrontation with the new black aesthetic critics. This search is frequently revealed on the level of the diegesis. Throughout the novel, the characters search for the Text (the aesthetics) that will consolidate the creative impulses contained in the source of energy that is Jes Grew. But *Mumbo Jumbo* goes even further than this simple authorial duplication, projecting the search onto the epidemic itself: "Jes Grew is seeking its words. Its text. For what good is a liturgy without a text?" (6). The novel traces this for a form of expression that will voice the creative tendencies within African-American culture without deforming its original nature.

Behind all these pursuits is something few critics have openly declared: the narcissistic self-representation of *Mumbo Jumbo*.[114] While on a literal level the book that Reed, PaPa LaBas, and Jes Grew are searching for is the Egyptian Book of Thoth, on a figurative level such a search is often identified with the pursuit of a new voice for African-American culture. On this figurative level, the book that is sought in *Mumbo Jumbo* is, in a certain sense, Reed's own novel. In no manner does the text openly admit this possibility; it only insinuates it. An explicit declaration in that sense would have been regarded as an act of arrogance, equal to saying that Reed has succeeded where the entire African American tradition (the Harlem Renaissance included) had previously failed. On the other hand, the sustained identifications between text and subtext that are characteristic of traditional allegorical readings are never totally satisfied in postmodern texts like *Mumbo Jumbo*. As McHale has suggested, postmodern novels invite allegorical readings but resist satisfying such a drive.[115] Their characteristic longing for openness and indeterminacy makes them avoid a compromise with this kind of reading. These precautions aside, it is beyond doubt that the accumulation of metatextual metaphors directs the reader's attention to the existence of a figurative subtext (the metaphorical frame of reference) in which Reed dramatizes the processes of writing and reading *Mumbo Jumbo*. Of course, the concept of the Text goes beyond the textual object that is *Mumbo Jumbo*. The search for the Text is not simply the search for the novel in which this search is inscribed, but also the search for the aesthetics engendering the novel. Behind the continuous allusions to the Text, therefore, we must understand the amalgamating aesthetics and the open cultural program in which the novel is rooted and on which it feeds. The result of this search is *Mumbo Jumbo*, not as a closed project, but as a starting point for new textual developments. The following discusses some elements of the novel that consider this figurative reading of *Mumbo Jumbo* to be a manifestation of the textual utopia that author, narrator, and characters seek in its pages. In the reconstruction of the dominant points of Reed's aesthetics we must inevitably invade the realm of the *mise en abyme* of the code.

Mumbo Jumbo holds a central position in Reed's literary career, because in it he constructs the countersystem in which his later works are rooted. Novels such as *The Last Days of Louisiana Red*, *Flight to Canada*, *The Terrible Twos*, *Reckless Eyeballing*, *The Terrible Threes*, and *Japanese by Spring* would be difficult to understand without the aesthetic, mythical, and historiographic apparatus that is articulated in *Mumbo Jumbo*. In those works that follow what is undoubtedly his masterpiece, Reed has devoted himself to developing tendencies that are already contained in *Mumbo Jumbo*, sometimes brilliantly (*Flight to Canada*), but sometimes poorly (*Reckless Eyeballing*). Although the individual evaluation of each of these novels has varied according to the aesthetic viewpoint and ideological orientation of the critic, *Mumbo Jumbo* is without question the required point of reference for each of them, probably because it is the only novel in which Reed systematizes his aesthetic and historiographic views from a black perspective. In this sense, *Mumbo Jumbo* fulfills within its pages the function assigned to the Text that is sought by characters and Jes Grew: It is the work that purports to give a written form to those energies that underlie African-American culture.

The similarity between the Text and Reed's novel is further clarified if we carefully examine the form in which the narrative itself directly or indirectly describes that "litany" sought by Jes Grew. The Egyptian Book of Thoth is the first manifestation of the Text. In his long speech at Villa Lewaro, LaBas provides the only description of this work when he refers to it as "a Book of Litanies to which people in places like Abydos in Upper Egypt could add their own variations" (154). In this way he establishes the openness and flexibility of the Text, an element that corresponds to the equally open and flexible code that Reed is seeking for his work and that he describes in his poem "The Neo-HooDoo Aesthetic."[116] At other times during his speech, LaBas declares that the Text contains Osiris's teachings, which are carried out through music and dance. From LaBas's commentaries also follows that its reading requires special training and that without this training its use may have disastrous effects (as in the cases of Moses and Von Vampton). The taxing interpretative demands of a novel like *Mumbo Jumbo* are also obvious. The density of its intertextual web, the extension of its encyclopedic breadth, the complexity of its entangled allegorical plots, and the parodic nature of its multiple levels of reading make *Mumbo Jumbo* a work that is particularly susceptible to misreadings. The narrative gives an explicit solution to some of its most important mysteries, but others remain obscure and will only be resolved by a competent and willing reader. Reading *Mumbo Jumbo* requires frequent encyclopedic consultations, at least if one wants to understand a good portion of its manifold levels of meaning. The idea of a complicated work that requires an equally intricate aesthetics emerges from other veiled allusions to the nature of the Text. In the epilogue that closes *Mumbo Jumbo* LaBas insists on the need of Jes Grew to find its Text: "If it could not find its Text it would be mistaken for entertainment" (211). The same confusion may occur, and in fact has occurred, if one approaches any of Reed's novels and ignores the theoretical keys contained in *Mumbo Jumbo* and the Neo-HooDoo aesthetics in which they are rooted.[117]

The association between the Text and the figures of LaBas and Reed himself is strengthened through continuous allusions to the Work, a word used in the novel to refer to the ritual practices of the voodoo/hoodoo (28). The different stages in the cultural manifestations of voodoo are, in fact, explicitly commented on in the novel. PaPa LaBas distinguishes, for example, between "the Old Work" (Haitian voodoo) and "the popular manifestations of the Work" (the Neo-IIooDooism to which Reed himself subscribes in his work and which consists of a synthesis of Haitian voodoo, its distinctive practice in the United States, and the forms of U.S. popular culture) (138–39). Furthermore, both LaBas and his collaborators are part of an organization whose headquarters are significantly named "*Mumbo Jumbo* Kathedral," a title which is clearly a new metafictional acknowledgment of their relation to the fictional universe of the novel.

Many of the paradoxes regarding the meaning of the text and its allegorical dimension reemerge in the most important episode of the novel: PaPa LaBas's speech (the Egyptian legend) at Villa Lewaro. After this long speech covering more than thirty pages, LaBas is challenged by the audience to prove that the Book is real. The passage has important implications for an allegorical reading of the novel: "T Malice goes out to the car and returns with a huge gleaming box covered with snakes and scorpions shaped of sparkling gems. The ladies intake their breath at such a gorgeous display. On the top can be seen the Knights Templar seal; 2 Knights riding Beaseauh, the Templars' piebald horse. T Malice places the box down in the center of the floor and removes the 1st box, an iron box, and the 2nd box, which is bronze and shines so that they have to turn the ceiling lights down. And within this box is a sycamore box and under the sycamore, ebony, and under this ivory, then silver and finally gold and then . . . empty!!" (196)

On a literal level, the disappearance of the Text is explained later in the novel. LaBas receives a letter from Abdul, who confesses to having burned the Book of Thoth because he considered it immoral. An allegorical reading of the passage, however, allows several interpretations without completely favoring any of them. Gates, for example, provides a suggestive reading of the episode, which he considers to be the most humorous anticlimax of all African-American fiction.[118] From his point of view, the ultimate absence of the Text suggests its radical indeterminacy. According to Gates, *Mumbo Jumbo* is, above all, a novel about ambiguity and plurality in the act of interpretation. In opposition to the uniformity defended by the Atonist Path and the Wallflower Order, Reed proposes the irreducible heterogeneity of every work of art and, therefore, the need for an aesthetics that respects it. Gates supports this reading of the novel with an impressive theoretical corpus that combines poststructuralist analysis with the African and African-American cultural traditions.

The ambiguous and indeterminate condition of the novel allows other possible interpretations in which reflexive images, again, play an important role. The sequence of the boxes that supposedly contained the Text clearly reproduces a common disposition in *Mumbo Jumbo*, where stories within stories mirror the structural pattern of the novel. Chapter 52, which precedes this episode, is an example of this Chinese-box organization. Both this passage and the other story-within-the-story episodes reproduce the most characteristic disposition of the *mise en abyme*. As noted earlier, André Gide created this concept on the basis of those coats of arms in which one quadrant reduplicates in miniature the structure of the entire coat of arms. The episode at Villa Lewaro represents, from this point of view, a new reflection on the reflexive structure of the novel itself. The act of interpretation itself is allegorized in the opening of the boxes within boxes that occurs after LaBas's digression. Reading a novel like *Mumbo Jumbo* requires a work of progressive probing in which a final meaning will never be established. The best we can do with a work like this is to come to provisional conclusions. A definitive reading or interpretation would invalidate the flexibility and openness for which *Mumbo Jumbo* strives at all times.

If the box-opening episode functions as an anticlimax, this is so not only because it undermines the closure that characterizes the recognition scene in traditional detective novels, but also because it deconstructs the essentialism that underlies the Egyptian legend. Indeed, LaBas's digression seeks to invert the canonical versions of history in which the black world occupies a peripheral and marginal role. In his version it is the white world that occupies such a place, while the black one becomes the instigator of all great advances of civilization: the invention of agriculture, religion, music, dance, writing, and law. LaBas's story is a history turned upside down, but it is one that, in terms of its general guidelines, may be supported with the same kind of validating evidences as those of canonical Western history.[119] The margin of credibility that the events of the Egyptian legend rightly deserve or the extent to which Reed is willing to credit the anecdotes that make up *Mumbo Jumbo* is an element that the novel resists explaining. What follows from this and from Reed's other novels is a multicultural frame of mind in which the inverted Manichaeism of the legend is hardly suitable. In light of these reflections, the box-opening scene acquires a new meaning. With the Text, LaBas seeks to confirm his alternative history. The Book of Thoth, according to him, would be the great Book of origin that could explain all historical events that still remain mysteries. But the box that was supposed to contain it is empty, and it is empty for the simple reason that such a Text is a fantasy. In this way, the novel finally refuses to validate the essentialism and racial chauvinism that too often follow LaBas's myth of the origin of blackness.

However, the anticlimax of the empty-box scene does not imply the end of the search in which author, characters, and reader are involved. The final message of *Mumbo Jumbo* is that the Text exists, but not as a mere inversion of the inherited views of history and culture. It exists only as a composite, a plurality of texts distinguished by their openness and dynamism. This great Text (with a capital "T") is ultimately Reed's aesthetic utopia, a desirable end that can be glimpsed but never fully grasped, since its concretization, its actualization, would belie its provisional and dynamic nature. At the end of the novel, when he receives the letter in which Abdul confesses to having destroyed the Book, LaBas performs an act of faith regarding the Text that recalls the declarations of faith in the cultural utopias that recur in Fuentes's *Terra Nostra*: "We will make our own future Text. A future generation of young artists will accomplish this" (204). LaBas pronounces these words in the 1920s. The future generation he talks about could very well be Reed's. The Text, or at least one of its plural manifestations, could very well be *Mumbo Jumbo*. The question, however, remains unanswered.

Reflections of the Code

The two previous sections have discussed some of the reflexive images that make up the aesthetic code of *Mumbo Jumbo*. The prologue (chapter 1), the epilogue, and LaBas's speech are three moments in which *Mumbo Jumbo* examines its own poetics with a greater intensity. All three indicate the search for a code characterized by openness, flexibility, syncretism, and a call for an active reader. However, in *Mumbo Jumbo* many of the features of this code are also defined through negation, hence the importance of cultural oppositions in the novel. Neo-HooDooism opposes the closure, rigidity, monolithic proportions, and reader passivity that, according to Reed, characterize the cultural forms of the Western world. Reed's textual utopia does not consist of a particular text, but rather of a composite one, a plural work that, like jazz music, must be open to endless variations in its performance.

The cultural conflict reaches beyond these three episodes, is repeated throughout the novel, and is often seen in specular metaphors. In the passage that describes LaBas's visit to Abdul's headquarters (chapter 26), Reed reflects on his own theory of satire. Through LaBas's consciousness, the narrator inverts some Western stereotypes about Africa. The sculptures on Abdul's desk represent scenes of colonial Africa. In the narrator's description the whites are depicted as having ridiculous attitudes and simian poses, in an ironic reversal of the racist images that pervade Western culture: "The subjects are represented giving bribes, drinking gin, leading manacled slaves, wearing curious, outlandish hats and holding umbrellas. Their chalk-faces appear silly, ridiculous. Outstanding in the collection is the figure of a monkey-like Portuguese explorer, carved by an Angolan. He is obviously juiced and is sitting on a barrel. What side-splitting, bellyaching, satirical ways these ancient craftsmen brought to their art!" (96).

The episode is significant inasmuch as it reflects one of the principal tendencies in Reed's writing, which is to inscribe attacks against African American culture into the novel itself, but in a dynamic of inversion in which the attacker becomes the attacked: "They had been removed to Europe by the slavers, traders and sailors who had taken gunpowder and uniforms to Africa. They did not realize that the joke was on them" (97). This mechanism of inversion expands in relationship to the oppositional characteristics that Reed attributes to forms of African origin. Although Africa was politically and economically subjugated, its culture and cultural influences kept their heterogeneity and syncretism, two qualities that Reed sees as radically opposed to the monolithic forms of Western art. As Gates points out, in some cases regarding the slave trade this colonial situation created the basis for a dynamic exchange between previously isolated black African cultures.[120] In this way the colonizers would have indirectly contributed to the development of a syncretism that threatened their own ideological assumptions.

The statues the narrator describes primarily serve as a starting point for a discussion regarding the genius and inventiveness of the African satire, which he compares to the lack of humor and endemic seriousness of Judeo-Christian culture. Unlike certain African *loas* (*orishas*) or representations of Buddha, the images of Christ are always somber: "Nowhere is there an account or portrait of Christ laughing. Like the Marxists who secularized his doctrine, he is always stern, serious and as gloomy as a prison guard" (97). Christianity's dark worldview is of singular importance in *Mumbo Jumbo* for what Reed considers its harmful impact on the African-American population. According to Reed, for centuries Christianity has aimed at converting the hedonistic and vibrant Africans into stern, cynical, and lifeless beings, and their intellectuals into writers of serious and turgid works. "They'd really fallen in love with tragedy" (97), the narrator declares. As a result of this morbid penchant for tragedy, African-American art of Christian or Marxist inspiration has produced works about enraged and bitter characters, works in which humor and the pursuit of pleasure, which characterize African cultures, are absent.

Another way in which the novel defines and predicts its own code is through dialogue with its possible critics. In fact, the aesthetic debates, characteristic of the *mise en abyme* of the code, occupy a central position in the novel as a whole. Through episodes such as Von Vampton's dialogues with candidates for Talking Android, the conflict between Set and Osiris in the Egyptian legend, the commentaries of a contemporary editor about Abdul's translation of the Book of Thoth, and the argument between a Marxist critic and LaBas, Reed injects into *Mumbo Jumbo* a debate that had been taking place since the publication of his first novel. In this sense, critical attitudes toward Reed have proven contradictory. Both black nationalists and Marxist critics reject his work for its tendency to evade social problems and its absence of moral values.[121] White critics specializing in popular culture accuse him of "verbal gymnastics" and pretentious avant-gardism.[122] Others consider his work trivial and merely entertaining.[123] Fervent supporters of the Great Works of Western tradition see in *Mumbo Jumbo* a work lacking the universality that any masterpiece should seek.[124] Black nationalist critics accuse him of trying to please a white audience, while ignoring topics of real interest to the black community.

The anticipation of these possible criticisms is accomplished mainly through episodes about the Talking Android. The Talking

Android is part of Von Vampton's plot to end the influence and increasing prestige of black culture in U.S. society. The plan is organized around the manipulation of a black intellectual in order to discredit the spirit of Jes Grew (the spirit of African-American culture): "He will tell it that it is derivative. He will accuse it of verbal gymnastics, of pandering to White readers" (69). The charges Von Vampton wishes to see expressed through his Talking Android correspond to some of the critiques Reed's first two novels received and therefore predict the critical reception of *Mumbo Jumbo*. Many reviews of *Pallbearers*, *Radio*, and *Mumbo Jumbo*, whether positive or negative, tended to consider Reed within the tradition of the U.S. white novel. By pointing out Reed's debt to modern white writers, some critics directly or indirectly suggested that his work was derivative of Western culture. In a review of his first novel, Lawrence Lipton compared Reed to Norman Mailer. Toni Cade compared him to George Orwell, Kurt Vonnegut, Anthony Burgess, and Ray Bradbury. Kenneth Kinnamon affirmed his debt to William Burroughs, John Barth, Joseph Heller, and Terry Southern. Bob H. Singer saw in *Radio* the same influences as Kinnamon, to which he added those of Donald Barthelme and Allen Ginsberg. Edward M. White considered Reed's antirealism a legacy of John Hawkes's style. Roger Whitlow suggested the influence of the tradition of the absurd developed by Mailer, Salinger, and Heller. Roland E. Bush attributed Reed's declarations about the impact of the mass media on his work to the direct influence of Marshall McLuhan. Finally, John Alfred Avant considered *Mumbo Jumbo* as "a loose pop-version of Thomas Mann."[125]

Reed's disagreement with a wide sector of the critical establishment can be explained in light of the aesthetic project that he undertakes in *Mumbo Jumbo*. Reed is always looking for the most flexible forms possible, something that does not suit most critics' tendencies to pigeonhole new authors. His attention to West African religions and voodoo is not due solely to genealogical interest, but is the result of his penchant for syncretic cultural forms. The lack of understanding on the part of many readers may be attributed more to intellectual laziness than to the author's self-gratifying puns or a gratuitous hermeticism. *Mumbo Jumbo* is without question a difficult work, since it demands a certain familiarity with the numerous intertexts that form it, but in no way can many of the above-mentioned charges be justified on the basis of the text itself. The novel responds to accusations of derivation by presenting a whole new mythical countersystem based on the blending of Western popular culture with African and African-American traditions.

It reacts to those of triviality by providing one of the most ambitious literary and historical projects in postmodern fiction. To reproaches of pretentiousness, it presents the use of a caustic humor that undermines any act of intellectual arrogance. To those of evasion, it reacts by discussing—within the work itself—the historical and social context that engendered it.

Mumbo Jumbo contains in its pages text and metatext, novel and commentary. It foretells the critics' responses and, through literary debate with them, discloses the aesthetic code in which Reed's worldview is rooted. As a consequence of the inscription of criticism within the text, Reed seeks to neutralize some of the positions that are most radically opposed to his cultural project and to invert many of the cultural stereotypes that Western readers have come to accept as normal.

Fictions of Origin

As discussed in the previous chapters, the fourth level of reflection proposed by Dällenbach is identified with the transcendental *mise en abyme*, or "fiction of origin." With this phrase Dällenbach refers to those metaphors (frequently mythological) that reflect a reality that simultaneously generates, motivates, institutes, and unifies the text.[126] In most cases the fiction of origin poses a philosophical problem about the mechanisms of representation. *Mumbo Jumbo* is, as Gates rightly points out, a text that reflects upon other texts, but also one that primarily reflects upon itself.[127] In this reflection both the origin of the novel itself and the origin of African-American culture play a dominant role, a preoccupation that results in an impressive arsenal of reflexive metaphors and mythological motifs. In particular, Reed frequently refers to Egyptian, Yoruba, and voodoo religious systems. This section will discuss two elements that are associated with these mythical systems and are used to present fictions of origins: the legend regarding the invention of writing and the character of PaPa LaBas as a re-creation of the African and African-American trickster.

The synthesis of the three above-mentioned religions and their correspondence with the historical and fictional situation presented in *Mumbo Jumbo* are reached in the much-quoted Egyptian legend. LaBas dates the invention of writing back to the time of Osiris. After the first outbreaks of Jes Grew, an artist named Thoth suggests to Osiris that a sacred book of litanies be written to benefit from the creative energy of the epidemic. Thoth begins to transcribe the dances and teachings of Osiris into a book that he leaves open to new variations. In Reed's version, the myth of Thoth describes a dynamic of writing and interpretation that conforms substantially to postmodern theories of reading. Both Osiris and Thoth re-create the figure of a composite creative identity that comprises the entire process of elaboration and reception of a literary work of art. Thoth is portrayed as a scribe who gives written expression to Osiris's teachings, which are communicated mostly through dance. These teachings are not revealed to him directly, and the Book's transcription thus requires a process of interpretation. Osiris executes dances that symbolically encode the mysteries that Thoth can interpret and translate them into written code. This interpretation is, in turn, made available to Osiris's priests, who will then be able to produce new interpretations and ultimately profit from Jes Grew.

The form in which Reed rewrites the myth of Thoth lays the foundation for the creation of the literary ideal that becomes a point of reference in all of his work. According to Reed, the Book of Thoth is a collective work in which there is not a definite original source. Osiris himself, who might seem to be such a source, is only a mediator, since he had learned the sacred dances in his travels through black Africa. Furthermore, Thoth's transcription is not definitive, but open to infinite variations. Reed presents at the beginning of the Egyptian legend the first written manifestations of a wisdom whose ultimate origin is lost in the labyrinths of oral lore. In this way the myth of Thoth allows Reed to establish the first of the multiple manifestations of the Text everyone seems to be seeking in *Mumbo Jumbo*.

As happens with so many of the other mythological motifs used by Reed in his novels, this apparent fantasy is based on hermetic and historiographic traditions. In Egyptian literature there exists a whole tradition about Thoth's secret knowledge that Reed incorporates into his version of the myth. Several texts also allude to the identification of Thoth with Hermes Trismegistus,[128] while others refer to transcriptions of Thoth's teachings that the Egyptians kept in their sanctuaries. Even the name "hermeticism" comes from Hermes, whose first manifestation is associated with Thoth himself.

On the other hand, Reed's subscription of Thoth to the domain of cultural heroes originates in a widespread tendency among Egyptologists. Contemporary specialists are inclined to attribute some features formerly used to characterize Osiris as a cultural hero to Thoth. Bleeker, for example, considers this mythical figure the founder of culture for having given humankind the spoken word, for introducing the art of writing, and for creating law, religious ritual, and medicine. In the Classical tradition Thoth becomes

Hermes, the archetypal mediator—the same function Yoruba religion assigns to Esu and voodoo gives to Papa Legba (Papa Labas). Thoth is the conciliator between the opposing pairs (Horus and Set, for example) and a mediator in the afterworld, enjoying a decisive power in the trials of the dead. But Thoth's most important function within Reed's worldview is that of the writer as shaman. Thoth is the patron of scribes and supervisor of the "House of Life," a center of wisdom associated with the production of sacred books and the training of writers.[129] In one version of the myth, Thoth gives Isis and Nephtys the prayers required to reconstruct Osiris's mutilated body. In this sense, two important roles meet in Thoth's representation: on the one hand, the great magician, both priest and physician, with the power to transform reality supernaturally; on the other, the founder of written language, who compiles the formulas that are able to put such transformations into effect through words.

Another mythical referent with similar characteristics connecting LaBas with the creation of culture and the myths of origin is that of the different transformations of the African-American trickster. Common in the cultures of Africa and the Americas, tricksters are mythical figures who stand out for their wit, ingenuity, and ability to deceive. They are also frequently depicted as cultural heroes.[130] According to Pelton, by presenting everything that is anomalous, these irreverent figures undermine univocal views of reality.[131] Their characterization tends to emphasize the absurd, the scatological, and the corporal in representations that are dominated by what Pelton calls a "polymorphous perversity." But, unlike other tricksters, those in the African tradition maintain direct contact with everyday experience. They act as mediators who bring the sacred with the worldly into contact. Finally, and most especially, tricksters are characterized by their transforming value. Hence the importance of their presence, be it either literal or figurative, in *Mumbo Jumbo*.

Legba (pronounced *Labas* in Haiti) is the trickster deity par excellence. In West African and American cultures different variants of this trickster god have developed. This sardonic deity, who appeared for the first time in the Yoruba pantheon under the name of Esu-Elegbara, was invested with new attributes among the Fon of Dahomey, and passed to the New World under the forms of Exú (Brazil), Echu Elegua (Cuba), Papa Legba (Haiti), and Papa La Bas (United Sates). Most of the qualities that Gates observes among these trickster variants are likewise present in *Mumbo Jumbo*: individuality, satire, parody, irony, magic, indeterminacy, openness, ambiguity, sexuality, chance, and rupture.[132] In all instances Legba plays a mediating role by communicating the gods' will to men and transmitting men's pleas to the gods. He is spatially represented on the threshold, since he communicates with and between the worlds of the visible and invisible, the profane and the sacred.[133] Among all the qualities assigned to Legba, two seem to have had an impact on LaBas's characterization and on the construction of the allegorical structure of *Mumbo Jumbo*: his role as interpreter and his relation to the myths of origins. The Yoruba and Fon religions share a dynamic system of interpretation in which Legba is represented as the divine reader who interprets the book of destiny.[134] The creative potential of this figure is underscored by depicting him as carrying a calabash, where he keeps the *ase* (the energy with which Olodumare created the universe). He is also related to the Yoruba myths of creation, where Esu-Elegbara appears as one of the primal agents.

The fictional character, PaPa LaBas, exemplifies most of the features that Gates identifies in Legba. Reed uses his protagonist as a speaker for his Neo-HooDoo aesthetics. Thus, the tendencies that characterize all members of the *Mumbo Jumbo* Kathedral are the same as those assigned to the aesthetic of the novel. The aesthetic code that Reed expresses through LaBas prioritizes the creative individuality of the artist, the use of humorous forms with a parodic intention, a nonempirical but intuitive epistemology, openness to new variants and future metamorphoses, and a hedonistic and sensual concept of life. Both his ethics and his aesthetics are solidly based on Yoruba and voodoo traditions, which, in Reed's view, lack a hierarchical and repressive system, and in which, as seen, Legba plays an important role.

For Reed, the appeal of this mythical figure is doubtless multiple. In addition to the above-mentioned characteristics, Legba is a paradigm of syncretism. In his circulation throughout Africa and the Americas Legba has absorbed elements of all the cultures he has visited. The transformations he has undergone as a consequence of his adaptation to new cultural habitats also make him a symbol especially dear to African Americans. As Deren and Cosentino suggest, in his metamorphoses he embodies the African diaspora, aged by years of suffering but enriched by the experience.[135]

Like the mythical Legba, LaBas is the archetypal interpreter linked to the myths of origins. This character is portrayed in the novel as a reader who seeks to decipher the identity of African-American culture. As Gates has rightly suggested, "PaPa LaBas is the figure of the critic, in search of the text, decoding its telltale signs in the process."[136] The entire novel describes this search (and learning process), where knowledge is gained through the textual experiences of its characters. The possibility of a definitive Text that could account for the origin of all types of blackness is finally presented as an implausible literary utopia, but one which may be partially attained through multiple and heterogeneous texts. Throughout its pages, *Mumbo Jumbo* favors a dynamic and perfomative conception of the aesthetic object. The literary work is not, in Reed's aesthetic proposal, a closed object of worship, but rather an amalgamating artifact that is enriched through its contact with new cultures and traditions.

CONCLUSION

In *Mumbo Jumbo*, Reed lays the foundation for the historical and aesthetic worldview that he will develop throughout the rest of his career. Stemming from a heterogeneous collection of cultural systems, he constructs a whole new mythology that seeks to undermine some of the dominant assumptions regarding the role of blacks in history. The novel's goals must ultimately be understood in light of this oppositional nature. Rather than attempting to impose a new cultural system, Reed focuses on the relentless critique of prevailing views. Byerman synthesizes Reed's oppositional drive when he states that "the test for the power of his art is his ability to expose and negate, not to assert and control" (221). In his negation of the dominant forms, Reed targets the conventions of traditional historical and fictional discourses. Like other postmodern historical novels, *Mumbo Jumbo* articulates historical reflection and metafictional experimentation without encountering a contradiction between the two. On the contrary, reflexive metaphors are used to clarify historical motifs, and historical motifs are used to exemplify the novel's inner workings. Reed's use of both history and fiction is ultimately aimed at directing the reader's attention to the textual nature of the received versions of the past.

From a historiographic point of view, Reed's novel seeks to displace the prevailing notions of history. *Mumbo Jumbo* was originally conceived as a response to those who denied the existence of a unique African-American cultural tradition and accused black artists of being derivative. In this novel, Reed undertakes the task of reconstructing the origin and history of that tradition. To that end, he re-creates a past in which documented and apocryphal characters and events coexist, the result being a hybrid that inverts stereotypes about African-American cultural inferiority. In Reed's version, the cradle of civilization is located in the black world, which has been immemorially plundered and exploited by the West. Although Reed frequently resorts to apocryphal data, he also supports his version with others that are empirically demonstrable. His intention is to make the boundaries between fact and fiction problematic so as to question the legitimacy of those discourses that have been used to validate the dominant ideology.

Regarding its metafictional aspect, the novel's radical reflexiveness stems from its main allegorical structure. This structure depicts a novel (*Mumbo Jumbo*) in which an archetypal reader (LaBas) seeks a book, produced by an archetypal writer (Thoth), which inaugurates literature, and which, all seems to suggest, is a book with the same characteristics as *Mumbo Jumbo*. The result of this self-begetting plot is a most complex reflexive figure: the endless spiral that originates in what Dällenbach calls aporetic duplication ("a sequence that is supposed to enclose the work that encloses it"). As a consequence of this mechanism of paradoxical duplication, *Mumbo Jumbo* spotlights the textual nature of its whole referential universe, including the historical referent itself. Both the novel's starting point (supposedly the Book of Thoth) and its end (*Mumbo Jumbo*) underscore the textual nature of all cultural constructions, be they historical or fictional.

This revisionist concept of history and fiction is integrated into a cultural project that Reed calls Neo-HooDooism. Built on the contributions of West African cultures, Haitian and North American voodoo/hoodoo, and some forms of U.S. popular culture, this project seeks to update the artistic expressions of African-American culture. Unlike other worldviews, Neo-HooDooism resists restrictive encodings. Reed thus avoids open definitions of the term and prefers, instead, to demonstrate it through the works of many modern artists. From these examples and their manifestations in *Mumbo Jumbo*, we can identify a series of tendencies that constitute Neo-HooDooism, including: 1) formal and ideological syncretism, which results in the use of interdisciplinary collage and the amalgamation of different cultural systems; 2) openness on all possible levels, which leads to a conception of history and literature as discourses that are susceptible to new interpretations; 3) subjectivity, intuition, mystery, and emotion, as opposed to the rational and logical patterns of Western thought; 4) improvisation and expressive freedom, both of which reject the value of preestablished codes and seek, instead, endless variations; 5) participation, which considers art as a communal experience and not as the privilege of an intellectual elite; and 6) a hedonist worldview, according to which the most important value is to enjoy the pleasures of life intensely. All these characteristics form a historical-aesthetic countersystem that seeks to rewrite historical and literary traditions in order to demystify the dominant forms of representation.

4

Between Political Commitment and Epistemological Skepticism: Julio Cortázar and E. L. Doctorow

In an attempt to clarify the distinctiveness and ambivalence of New World historiographic metafiction, the previous chapters have examined the problematic articulation of history and reflexivity in the encyclopedic works of Fuentes and Reed. Novels such as *Terra Nostra* and *Mumbo Jumbo* are vast literary projects that seek to rewrite Western history and mythology from the point of view of the Spanish-American and African-American periphery. More modest in scope, Julio Cortázar and E. L. Doctorow deal with another paradox that is also central to postmodern aesthetics in the Americas: how to create a literature of opposition within an increasingly relativistic context. In many of their works (the majority in Doctorow's case and the later productions in Cortázar's), these two authors reflect on the intellectual's ideological commitment within a climate of political change and philosophical skepticism. Although coming from different historical and literary traditions, Cortázar and Doctorow coincide in their analysis and diagnosis of similar problems and their possible solutions. Both authors seek a compromise between aesthetically and politically committed narrative forms which may provide an alternative to the extreme contingency of contemporary thought. On the one hand, they eschew the usual tendency of political literature toward realism; on the other, they try to avoid the narcissism that characterizes many of the antirealist currents in contemporary fiction.

There are two theoretical points of reference that allow us to understand the work of both writers within postmodern thought: the metahistorians' revision of historical production and the debate regarding the possibility of an aesthetic alternative to global hegemonic culture. Of all the revisionist philosophers of history, Hayden White has exerted the greatest influence—at least among

194

literary critics—because of his tropological approach to historiography. Throughout his essays, White dismantles the empirical pretensions of traditional history and shows the formal similarities between the discourse of history and that of fiction. His object of study is principally "the status of the historical narrative, considered purely as a verbal artifact."[1] By means of a minute analysis of the strategies of emplotment and figuration in historical narrative, White attempts to reveal the inevitable ideological mediations in the writing of history.

Similarly, Cortázar and Doctorow often reflect upon narrative theory. Occasionally, the superimposition of the historical and fictional levels shapes the structural pattern of their works. They tend to present official history as a mere simulacrum, a cultural artifice created on the basis of social needs and political pressures. Confronted by these monolithic visions of reality, they propose an alternative epistemology characterized by the plurality and flexibility of their discursive forms. Although they never deny the existence of the past—indeed, they obsessively reflect upon it—Cortázar and Doctorow suggest that our access to that past can only be channeled through other texts, which are by their very nature incomplete and limited. Within their consideration of the essentially narrative character of both historical and novelistic works, both writers mirror on the level of fiction the postulates developed by the metahistorians in the philosophy of history.

Historical relativism as posed in the works of Cortázar and Doctorow implies not a renunciation of representation, but a radical problematization of its practices. Unlike the exclusively self-reflexive experiments of many novels of the 1960s, their political metafictions refocus literary self-consciousness back onto the historical world. Opposed to the critical pessimism of many postmodern thinkers, Cortázar and Doctorow integrate historical revisionism into a program of social transformation. For them, epistemological skepticism and self-consciousness are two essential components in a program that seeks to transform the existing modes of representation in both history and fiction.

In their desire to democratize access to the past, Cortázar and Doctorow construct a flexible and open narrative that requires the active participation of the reader both in the process of textual reconstruction, and through his or her moral commitment to the message of change these works propose. This effort to unveil the inherent contradictions present within hegemonic cultural practices and simultaneously to place them at the service of a radical political agenda may be seen as a response to the cultural impasse of postmodernism, as theorized by leftist critics such as Fredric Jameson. Jameson's apocalyptic analysis of postmodern society, in which images and simulacra have displaced reality itself, questions the possibility of an effective oppositional alternative to the capacity of the system to co-opt all kinds of insurgency.[2] In this chapter, Doctorow's and Cortázar's novels are analyzed as conclusive examples of such a possibility.

Julio Cortázar

History and Self-reflexivity in the Writings of Julio Cortázar

While Fuentes and Reed show an early concern for the political and historical reality of their own countries, historical consciousness only emerges in Cortázar's fiction after a long period of development. The focus of his early work is on pure literature rather than on the sociohistorical phenomena explored by postmodern writers. Whenever historical motifs are present, they are only obliquely treated or employed to consolidate an aestheticist worldview in the line of international modernism. Even in those cases where Cortázar's works anticipate the historical vision of his late productions, this vision is presented only as secondary, without being clearly integrated into the work's core.

As in the best metafictions, Cortázar's first short stories are self-referential explorations that seek to unmask the production of reality. They reveal that what we regularly accept as reality is a construct manufactured and sanctioned by social convention. Sometimes this familiar order, where everything seems perfectly normal, begins to break apart, leaving in the interstices the access to an alternative utopian vision. As Jaime Alazraki has pointed out, all of Cortázar's works are marked by the search for a "second reality," an authentic and unexplored dimension that hides behind our everyday lives and that only can be briefly glimpsed through epiphanic moments.[3] In the tradition of surrealism, this idea of an alternative order stresses the incompatibility between the domains of reason and imagination, reality and fiction, everyday life and utopia.[4] Although it eventually takes on different shades of meaning, Cortázar's search for other dimensions of the real was first manifested in the artist's introspective withdrawal in search of unknown facets of himself. His first productions are, therefore, deeply reflexive but, at the same time, alien to the historical preoccupations that characterize postmodern fiction.

This lack of interest in historical issues is noticeable in his mythological play *Los reyes* (1949) and his first novel, *Los premios* (1960). Although these works are infused with a political dimension, aesthetics and politics are not successfully integrated into a final whole. On the contrary, they are presented as in tension but with no evidence of an ultimate resolution. In *Los reyes* the mythological plot (the famous struggle between Theseus and the Minotaur) hides an allegorical subtext with political echoes. Through an ironic inversion of the Greek model, the hero of Cortázar's version is not Theseus but the Minotaur, who embodies the archetypal artist. In this early work Cortázar depicts a motif that recurs in all of the authors under consideration: the figure of the artist, and especially the writer, as a cultural hero eternally opposed to the abuses of political power.[5] In *Los reyes* Cortázar defends the right to preserve his own space. The artist embodied by the Minotaur seeks, above all, to secure his ivory tower in the face of social pressures. The confrontation with institutional power does not stem from any revolutionary impulse of historical projection, but it is rather the result of what the artist perceives as the abuses of the public sphere. An incipient interest in the subjectivity of the Other can be perceived in stories such as "El perseguidor" (*Las armas secretas*, 1959), where an intense existentialist concern coexists with formal experimentation. As Cortázar himself has acknowledged, "El perseguidor" represents his first approach to human suffering, his first movement beyond the neo-fantastic plots of his short story collection *Bestiario*.[6] It is also in this story that Cortázar's characters are portrayed with psychological complexity and depth for the first time.[7] Using the dual perspective of its two main characters, the tormented jazz saxophonist Johnny Carter and his biographer Bruno, the story reflects on some of Cortázar's recurrent topics: the confrontation between magical thought and empirical reason, the exploration through art of a truer dimension of reality, and the manipulative potential of history and biography. To the existential pursuit of the rationally-oriented writer Bruno, he adds that of the visionary musician Johnny; these two modes of perception are, in their turn, used by Cortázar to meditate about his own artistic evolution. In "El perseguidor," Cortázar accomplishes an expansion of subjectivism, as a first step toward the social openness that characterizes his late productions.

This line of existential and metafictional probing has its continuation in his first novel, *Los premios*, where the sociological portrayal of Argentine society, pre-Columbian cosmogonies, and poetic self-reflections intermingle. Cortázar examines here—as he did in *Los reyes*—the conflictive relationship between intellectuals and Argentine society, but from a different perspective. Whereas an opposition between history and individual freedom was set up in *Los reyes*, a harmony between individual and collective destinies begins to be glimpsed in *Los premios*. Indeed, through the characters of Medrano and Persio, Cortázar expresses a veiled critique of his own previous ideology. The relationship between Medrano and the other passengers of the *Malcolm* suggest a progressive discovery of the lower classes, absent in Cortázar's first works. On the other hand, Persio's monologues—a mixture of metaphysical digression, poetic epiphany, and metafictional commentary—serve to communicate a poetic intimation of Latin American destiny.

Although some of these concerns—especially those of an existential nature—came of age in *Rayuela* (1963), the historical component is still practically absent in Cortázar's greatest novel. As Cortázar himself has recognized: "In the days of *Rayuela* I was in no distress because I was living on the edges of history and was only interested in ontology, in a timeless anthropological search."[8] In *Rayuela*, Cortázar takes his metafictional experiments to their utmost limits. Through the so-called "*capítulos prescindibles*" (expendable chapters) the novel provides its own metatext, which comments and theorizes about itself, about the author's short fiction, as well as about literary creation in general.[9] Among other subjects, *Rayuela* investigates all aspects of the production and reception of fiction. Both acts—writing and reading—are viewed as complementary. In Cortázar's aesthetics of the open work, the text is presented as an effective potential that awaits actualization through the act of reading. Thus, the novel favors an active reader (Cortázar calls him accomplice and copartner) who must force his way through the entangled text.

Cortázar's theory of reading, which achieves its fullest explanation in the expendable chapters, can be understood within the fiery antirealism of the novel. For Cortázar, realism is the artistic expression of bourgeois ideology. Through it, the established bourgeois order masks its contradictions and fosters an illusion of normality. What is unnatural, contradictory, or simply false, becomes, in this way, socially acceptable. It is precisely this pathology that Cortázar opposes, but his rebellion is posed in individual, intuitive, and existential terms. As a result, it lacks the program of a total and social revolution.

The great shift in Cortázar's political consciousness occurred after his personal contact with the Cuban revolution. As he constantly declared in autobiographical essays and interviews, his visit to Cuba in 1962 changed the direction of his career. In Cuba, Cortázar saw the collective struggle of people to achieve the radical transformation of experience that his characters were blindly seeking. In his interview with Omar Prego, Cortázar confessed that before this visit he had indeed held a political stance, but only on a private level.[10] The Cuban revolution had a cathartic effect on him. He wrote, "The Cuban revolution woke me up to the reality of Latin America: it was then that I progressed from a merely intellectual indignation to telling myself: 'Something has to be done.' "[11]

Cortázar's enthusiasm for this historical event is manifested in "Reunión" (1964). This short story is an early homage to the makers of the revolution and, especially, to the figures of Ernesto "Che" Guevara and Fidel Castro. In this story, Cortázar uses a pattern of juxtaposition that recalls the one employed in *Los premios*. The linear and realistic account of the events—in this case, "Che" Guevara's landing in Cuba in November 1956, his first confrontations with Batista's army, and his final encounter with Castro—alternates with epiphanic moments in which the narrative yields to poetic digression. As a consequence, the narrative adopts a pendular movement between extreme objectivity and subjectivity, without achieving a satisfactory final synthesis. It is not until his later collections *Queremos tanto a Glenda* and *Deshoras* that we witness richer resolutions.

A continuous progression in relation to his previous work is, however, noticeable. While *Los premios* presents only a confusing poetic vision of a continent's destiny, "Reunión" comments upon a specific moment in the political history of Latin America. One of the weakest aspects of the story is probably the disproportionate idealization of the revolutionary heroes. Cortázar's mystification of revolution in "Reunión" does not conform to the conflicting views that characterize historiographic metafiction. Although the story resists the superficiality and formal simplicity of socialist realism, it focuses on the great figures of recent history, who appear surrounded by a supernatural aura. This overidealization of a historical event is an element that will never occur again in Cortázar's fiction. Even in his more political stories, the protagonists tend to be ordinary people: the nameless artists of a Nicaraguan community ("Apocalipsis de Solentiname"); the victims of political repression ("Segunda vez"); or the students of an Argentinean school under military rule ("Escuela de noche"). The perspective in Cortázar's fiction also tends to progress toward increasingly problematic positions, such as in "Segunda vez," where we perceive the terrible reality of military repression from the point of view of one of its executioners.

Although "Reunión" is Cortázar's first experiment in political fiction, it does not imply a radical shift in his *oeuvre*. In fact, most of Cortázar's works followed the avant-garde tendencies and ahistorical orientation of his previous production.[12] The novelty of "Reunión" rests on the addition of a new subject that coexists with the ones with which he had experimented before. This new political flavor of Cortázar's fiction was not well received by critics. On the one hand, the supporters of aestheticism in literature disapproved of Cortázar's incursions into political issues. On the other hand, the most sectarian of the leftists criticized him for the obscurity of his work and for not being militant enough.[13]

The polemic of those years is recorded in several essays. In "Casilla del Camaleón" (1967) and "Carta abierta a Roberto Fernández Retamar" (1967), Cortázar affirms the artist's right to create in a free manner. In "Casilla," Cortázar reflects upon the chameleonlike condition of the writer who, although opposed to social injustice, does not need to display the colors of his political commitment.[14] As he will do throughout the rest of his life, Cortázar rejects philosophical and political dogmatism and vindicates the positive value of contradiction. In his open letter to the Cuban intellectual Fernández Retamar, he elaborates on these topics.[15] Although he reasserts his commitment to the ideals of the Cuban revolution, Cortázar underscores his desire to break away from the realistic patterns proposed by other Latin American intellectuals. Furthermore, he even suggests that the narrow nationalism supported by the most intolerant leftists finally reaches a xenophobic dimension, which works against the national interests it purports to defend.

The most extensive development of these ideas is provided by two other groups of documents: the articles in response to Oscar Collazos published in the Uruguayan journal *Marcha* (1969) and the collection of essays *Viaje alrededor de una mesa* (1970). A supporter of socialist realism, Collazos had launched direct attacks against both Cortázar's public statements in support of writers' political independence and against the artistic practices of most Latin American "boom" writers. In a scathing reply, Cortázar declared that a revolutionary literature cannot merely limit itself to the complacent praise of socialism, but it should also seek a revolution of forms, something that is not frequent among "revolutionary" artists. As for Cortázar's commentaries in *Viaje alrededor de una mesa*, they originate in a roundtable discussion that took place in Paris in 1970. On that occasion several writers and critics met to discuss the problems of creation and political commitment in Latin America. In *Viaje*, Cortázar insists on the necessity of distinguishing between form and content. Too often, revolutionary writers tend to forget formal innovation, which is the mark of all good art. As in other essays, Cortázar proposes the creation of a new aesthetics with the power to counter the fossilization of language and literature. But he is more categorical in his refusal to accept a functional point of view as the exclusive standard in criticism. Although he does not deny the transforming power of all works, he is radically opposed to *contenidismo* (the dominance of content over form), which tends to present a narrow and simplistic vision of reality. Above all, Cortázar emphasizes the need to leave the last word about the future of art to artists and not to governments.

Although this controversy was to accompany Cortázar for the rest of his life, it became particularly intense during the 1970s, as dramatized in his novel *Libro de Manuel* (1973). After having tested the waters in "Reunión," his real entrance into the genre of political fiction occurs in his fourth and last novel. Indeed, *Libro de Manuel* is Cortázar's reflection about the new orientation that his work began to adopt as a result of new developments in Latin American politics. In *Libro de Manuel*, the Argentinean writer seeks a solution to the dilemma of how to write innovatively within an increasingly revolutionary context. The world of politics, which had been manifested through essays and a few poems up to that point, then began to occupy a prominent role in his fiction. In the prologue itself, Cortázar recognizes this "long process of convergence" between the political subjects of many of his essays and the fantastic bent of his fiction: "Si durante años he escrito textos vinculados con problemas latinoamericanos, a la vez que novelas y relatos en que esos problemas estaban ausentes o sólo asomaban tangencialmente, hoy y aquí las aguas se han juntado" (7). *Libro de Manuel*, he also suggests, is mainly a recapitulation of his ideas about the role of the intellectual in a political arena.

This articulation of a reflexive discourse and a problematic view of history can also be found in the short-story collection that follows *Libro de Manuel. Alguien que anda por ahí* (1977) contains two stories that appropriately illustrate this new perspective in Cortázar's short fiction: "Apocalipsis de Solentiname" and "Segunda vez." In "Apocalipsis" Cortázar portrays Fascist violence in Latin America and the need for action by intellectuals in order to prevent it. This story is particularly important because of both its pan-American vision and its critical utopianism. Images of Edenic innocence and extensive political violence are simultaneously conjured

up in "Apocalipsis" to present and problematize the old notion of
the Americas as a land of possibilities, a ground where projects of
transformation are continuously tested and subverted. The anonymous "primitive" paintings of the Catholic peasant commune of
Nuestra Señora de Solentiname—the nucleus of the Nicaraguan
cultural revolution—are suddenly transformed into scenes of torture and murder in Guatemala, El Salvador, Argentina, Bolivia,
Chile, Santo Domingo, Paraguay, Brazil, and Colombia. In "Apocalipsis" Cortázar speaks of the achievements of popular art and
the promises of revolution, as well as of the need to preserve them
from destruction. On a deeper level, the story also suggests the extent of Cortázar's growing commitment to Latin American politics.
The fact that the autobiographical narrator is able to perceive the
historical reality through the frame of popular art marks a new step
in the expansion of Cortázar's concept of culture.

Another story in the same collection, "Segunda vez," represents
one of his first denunciations of Argentinean military rule. Along
with later stories, such as "Recortes de prensa," "Graffiti," "Pesa-
dilla," "Satarsa," and "Escuela de noche," "Segunda vez" protests
against the evils of state terrorism. All these stories were produced
under the influence of the "Dirty War," the name given to the darkest period in Argentinean modern history: the series of dictatorships
that began with the coup of March 1976 and ended with the restora-
tion of democracy in October 1983. Under the military regimes of
Viola, Videla, and Galtieri, thousands of citizens were imprisoned,
tortured, and murdered. With the excuse of fighting subversion, the
government exercised the most brutal repression ever known in the
history of Argentina. The possibility that those crimes were legally
condoned and collectively forgotten moved different sectors of society to undertake a campaign to ensure that these crimes be investigated and the guilty parties be punished. Intellectuals played a
crucial role in this campaign; the president of one of the commis-
sions in charge of the investigation was actually a novelist, Ernesto
Sábato.[16] Cortázar's work during the seventies and eighties (until
his death in 1984) reflects the urgent need that writers felt to leave
their testimony.

Covering a period of six years (1977–1983), all of these stories
present Cortázar's craft of fiction at its highest level. In these disturbing works metafiction and historical consciousness are brilliantly articulated to convey the horror of living in a police state.
Their nightmarish quality does not simply stem from the portrayal
of violent events, but rather from the atmosphere the author creates
through narrative technique. As Cortázar himself admitted in an in-

terview, "horror increases because it becomes a kind of all-embracing latency, something in the air."[17] It is difficult to point to simple causes and responsibilities in these allegorical reconstructions of Argentine society during the Dirty War. Here the author avoids the temptations of propaganda or sentimentalism in order to offer instead a feverish portrayal of a humanity deformed by extreme cruelty and oppression. Cortázar compares the atmosphere achieved in his stories to the effect produced by anti-utopias, such as those depicted in Kafka's *The Trial* and Orwell's *1984*.

These stories are historiographic metafictions inasmuch as they bring together formal self-consciousness and historical meditation. In all of them the inner withdrawal that characterizes Cortázar's early productions coexists with a centrifugal movement, through which narrative expands toward its contextual referents. But, unlike traditional historical fiction, Cortázar's stories narrate historical events from highly subjective and questionable perspectives, which makes the reader probe into a reality that is never fully described. The historical materials of these fictions are not the great names that make up the official record; instead they originate in the everyday lives of ordinary people: the victims and executioners who dwell on the edges of history. The crimes of the "Dirty War" provide a fertile ground for postmodern historical fiction. If postmodernism feeds on the exploration of the dark areas of the historical record, Argentinean history offers a lamentable record in this sense. Repression under the military regime was based on the systematic elimination of all opposition, a state-organized repression that remained unpunished in most cases.[18] Cortázar constantly suggests in his fiction and essays that reality imitates fiction. In this case, we face a materialization of the worst anti-utopian nightmares: the systematic repression of opposition and the dissolution of collective memory.

Given this historical situation, it is not surprising that Cortázar increased his production of political essays in his final years. Without abandoning playful experimentation—as in *Los autonautas de la cosmopista* (1983) and *Salvo el crepúsculo* (1984)—Cortázar became progressively involved in two major areas of political activism: investigation and punishment of all the crimes of the "Dirty War" and support for the threatened Sandinista revolution. His collections of essays *Nicaragua: tan violentamente dulce* (1983) and *Argentina: años de alambradas culturales* (1984) reflect Cortázar's growing political concerns. In these essays he revises some basic concepts of his work, such as the notions of culture, reality, and history.

While in Cortázar's early works culture is limited to the forms of high art and literature—from Romanticism to surrealism and existentialism—in his later essays he proposes a more democratic and comprehensive concept of the cultural enterprise: "We must overcome the old notion of culture as personal property and attempt the impossible to transform it into real property, into a part of the community that is offered, given, taken, exchanged, and modified."[19] In opposition to the bias of many intellectuals against popular and mass culture, Cortázar advocates their reappropriation with revolutionary aims. Media such as the cinema, video, television, and comic strips are powerful vehicles of communication that can be successfully used in counterhegemonic practices, outside the control of the culture industry.

The evolution of Cortázar's aesthetics points to a blurring of the borderline between academic and popular culture. Furthermore, there is a new tendency to privilege a vision of culture as the manifestation of collective identity: "What we call culture is nothing but the presence and exercise of our identity in all its power."[20] This same idea achieves its fullest articulation in Cortázar's essays about Nicaragua. Cortázar remained, until his death, an enthusiastic and active supporter of the changes experienced by Nicaragua after the revolution of 1979. One of the reasons for such unconditional support was the specific cultural politics undertaken by the Sandinistas. As he declared in his "Discurso de recepción de la Orden Rubén Darío," the Sandinistas "have expanded the concept of culture right from the start, have removed that elegant varnish that it has in Western Europe, have pushed the word *culture* into the streets."[21] Cortázar supported the Nicaraguan revolution because it not only sought to change the political order and economic dependency of the country, but it was also part of an integral cultural revolution that would eventually lead to the creation of a New Man and a new humanity. Moreover, the revolution was led by intellectuals, such as the novelist Sergio Ramírez and the poet Ernesto Cardenal. Unlike the scientific materialism adopted by other revolutions, the ideology of the Sandinistas was based on an eclectic synthesis of various traditions, ranging from anarchist communism and the New Marxism of the Cuban revolution to freemasonry and the Christian Theology of Liberation.[22] The Nicaragua Cortázar portrays in his essays is very similar to the cultural utopias recreated by Fuentes in *Terra Nostra* and Reed in *Mumbo Jumbo*. In all three cases, they are utopian societies in which culture and power, art and public institutions coexist in harmony.[23]

This new concept of culture has to be understood within the context of equally drastic changes in Cortázar's historical vision. While in his early works history is presented as a threat to the artist's private domain, in his later writings it achieves a utopian and socializing expression. In his book about Nicaragua, for example, history implies a possibility of collective betterment, a vision of future and hope. The public sphere stops being only a source of nightmares and provides, instead, lessons from which the artist can benefit. The "true" reality Cortázar's characters desperately seek is no longer a mystification of the artist's subjectivity, an escape from the *"horror cotidiano"* in which he or she lives, but an ideal—and possible—synthesis between art and history.[24]

Cortázar's literary career shows, in short, an evolution from the aestheticism and individualism of the historical avant-garde to a final engagement with the historical and political reality of Latin America. Although metafictional or/and historical elements recur in many of his works, he only began to write historical fictions and essays regularly after his firsthand discovery of revolutionary Cuba. In *Libro de Manuel* Cortázar reflects on this shift in both his life and his work. Apart from the minor formal inconsistencies pointed to by critics and by Cortázar himself, *Libro de Manuel* is a crucial part of Cortázar's oeuvre. Without this work it would be difficult to understand his political and literary evolution. The following section discusses one of the most striking aspects of the novel in relation to historiographic metafiction: its use of a fragmentary discourse to communicate a panoramic view of Latin America in the early 1970s.

Political Collage and Montage in *Libro de Manuel*

Cortázar regularly employed narrative fragmentation and juxtaposition in many of his works. In book-collages such as *La vuelta al día en ochenta mundos* (1967) and *Último Round* (1969), he combines different visual objects (drawings, pictures, and graphs) with various literary genres (poetry, essay, and short-fiction). The result is a melange of artistic and literary forms that challenges the notion of the text as a rigid artifact. This combination of the visual and the verbal is also apparent in works as unclassifiable as his illustrated collection of poems *Salvo el crepúsculo* (1984); the visionary *Prosa del observatorio* (1972), which merges mysticism, science, architecture, and photography into a flowing poetic prose; and the art "anthology" *Territorios* (1978), in which the narrative texts maintain an active dialogue with the works of several Latin American visual artists.

In addition to the amalgamation of distinct discourses, Cortázar's works tend to mirror techniques of film montage, in that they are organized into fragmented segments and narrated from multiple points of view. Some of his earliest stories are composed on the basis of interwoven levels that offer the reader various perspectives and suggest original syntheses.[25] The influence of cinematography can be seen on thematic and symbolic levels to the extent that Cortázar occasionally employs references to movies and film metaphors to mirror the inner workings of his own writing.

In *Libro de Manuel*, Cortázar freely uses the expressive possibilities of both collage and montage to convey his aesthetic and political vision. Even though most of these possibilities had already been mastered and refined by previous modernist writers, Cortázar imbues *Libro de Manuel* with a new sense of political immediacy that must be understood within the highly politicized context of Latin America during the 1970s. The plot of *Libro de Manuel* revolves around the activities of a revolutionary group of Latin American expatriates in Paris who carry out an intricate plan ("La Joda" ["The Screwery"]) to kidnap an international undercover agent. Throughout the novel, members of the group prepare a scrapbook of newspaper clippings to preserve the memories of their times for Manuel, the infant son of one of the revolutionaries. It becomes progressively clear that Manuel's scrapbook is in fact the novel we are reading, a novel in which the narrative alternates with various documentary materials. Aside from this journalistic collage, *Libro de Manuel* is organized into segments through which it becomes impossible to establish a stable narrative authority. The final impression is that of a series of fragments that, as in film montage, require final assembly by the viewer/reader.

The novel presents a similarly scattered vision of Latin American reality in the early 1970s in which well-known political events are interspersed with seemingly trivial news without the establishment of a definite hierarchy or even a rigorous chronological order. From these pages emerges a lesser-known version of history that favors discontinuity and fragmentation over organic and totalizing perspectives. Cortázar's manipulation of these forms seeks to underscore the importance of playfulness, to spotlight the mass media's preoccupation with the here-and-now, and to communicate a political message about the relationship between the Latin American intellectual and his or her historical reality. The following sections describe and discuss the two major forms that narrative heterogeneity and fragmentation take in *Libro de Manuel*: the insertion of newspaper clippings in the novel (paratextual collage); the division of the novel into a series of narrative segments and multiple perspectives left to be "assembled" by the reader (montage).

Collage

In *Libro de Manuel* the paratextual materials consist mostly of newspaper clippings that are contemporary to the period in which the novel was written. These paratexts can be organized into three major areas: 1) repression under Latin American military rule, 2) acts of armed resistance against that repression, and 3) eccentric news and advertisements. As the narrative voice of the prologue points out, the clippings were randomly incorporated as the novel was written (1969–1972). In an attempt to offer an almost day-to-day chronicle of events in Latin America during these years—"la historia de nuestros días" (7) ["the history of our own times"] (3). The only clippings that openly attempt to manipulate the reader's opinion are to be found at the novel's end, where Cortázar directs the reader's attention toward the international web of political repression and, more importantly, the role of the U.S. government within it. An analysis of their content reveals that, although the clippings do not refer directly to some of the most significant political events of these years, they do reflect the major trends of Latin American society during the late 1960s and early 1970s.

The novel's paratexts provide detailed information about human rights violations in Central America (55), Argentina (123; 122), Brazil (241; 244), the Soviet Union (350; 353), and Vietnam (370–77; 373–82). The portrayal of Latin American political life focuses on events that occurred under Argentine military rule, paradoxically known as the "Revolución argentina" (1966–1973). Among the events mentioned are General Onganía's coup d'état (107; 106), the imposition of military values on civil society (124; 123), the popular struggle and uprisings during this period (213, 304; 215,305), the increasingly high foreign debt (308; 309), the government's servility toward the United States (331; 333), waste in military spending (333; 335), and the torture and inhuman treatment of political prisoners (370–81; 373–84). Even those articles concerning Northern countries (France and the United Sates) are somehow related to the situation in Latin America, pointing to the fact that military repression initiated during Onganía's and Levingston's presidencies and further intensified during Videla's and Galtieri's regimes, utilized many of the techniques developed by the

French counterinsurgence in Algeria and the U.S. army in Vietnam.[26]

These international connections are dramatically revealed by the incorporation of impersonal statistics in the paratexts. By alluding to the participation of French security forces in the repression of Third World liberation movements, Cortázar seeks to destroy the image of France and other Western countries as the custodians of international peace and democracy. The novel's criticism of the repressive role of the United States goes even further in the final four articles, in which U.S. intelligence services and armed forces are depicted as being directly responsible for political repression, especially in Latin America and Southeast Asia. In the first of these clippings, U.S. interventionism in Latin America is established by means of a chart showing the increasing number of U.S. military assistants in the region. The following two paratexts are reproduced in parallel columns: on one side we are presented with testimonies given by political prisoners tortured in Argentine prisons; on the other, the confessions of U.S. soldiers who participated in torture sessions in Vietnam. The last clipping in the series is another chart, this one showing the number of Latin American military officers trained in the United States. The source for both charts is the U.S. Department of Defense. Although the conclusion makes no explicit accusations, its implications could not be clearer: The U.S. government finances political repression in Latin America and trains its executioners; the struggle against state terrorism goes hand in hand with the fight against U.S. imperialism.

In addressing this situation of generalized state terrorism, the novel justifies revolutionary violence. On both the textual and paratextual levels, *Libro de Manuel* contemplates the urban guerrilla movements' final moments of splendor, before their rapid decline. Many of the articles specifically cite the guerrilla activity in Argentina (152, 184–85, 303; 154, 186–87, 304), Uruguay (82, 217, 321; 80, 219, 322), Brazil (98, 202, 298; 96, 204, 299), Mexico (317; 318), and Bolivia (309; 310). In most cases, they describe kidnappings carried out by the extreme left. Such kidnappings were used as a means of attracting international attention and obtaining either the liberation of political prisoners or money to finance their activities.

The political strategies of these radical movements were initially based upon the principles of *foquismo*, the theory of guerrilla warfare generated during the Cuban revolution, refined by Ernesto "Che" Guevara, and popularized by the French philosopher Régis Debray. *Foquismo* was based on the assumption that the revolutionary process was a spontaneous and dynamic one. Therefore, in order for a revolution to occur, no certain, specific objective conditions must be met; rather the process itself will create them. *Foquismo* theory originally advocated the establishment of an operative base—a *foco*—in a remote region (preferably in the mountains) that would act as a stimulant and catalyst for mass revolution.[27] This idea began to lose credibility after "Che" Guevara's failed Bolivian expedition (1967), but nevertheless survived under different manifestations. In most cases, rural headquarters were replaced by urban centers, and in this way large cities became the operative hubs of activity for many guerrilla movements.[28] In South America *foquismo* theory was put into practice by several armed groups in Argentina, Uruguay, Venezuela, Bolivia, Colombia, and Perú during the 1960s and 1970s. Most of these urban guerrilla movements were crushed by police, the army, and paramilitary groups during the mid-1970s, as was the case in Argentina. In Venezuela and Uruguay, these armed organizations were integrated into the political mainstream as legal parties, while in Colombia and Perú they continued on the path of armed struggle.

In the years after 1972, Argentina's political panorama would rapidly and radically change, with guerrilla groups playing a comparatively insignificant role. In light of this fact, together with the novel's specific subject matter and its precise, pragmatic goals, it is not surprising that Cortázar tried to publish it as quickly as possible. *Libro de Manuel* was in press by the end of 1972, but its actual publication was delayed until the spring of 1973. It was finally released only a few days after the Peronist candidate Héctor Cámpora won the March elections. Cortázar's anxiety about the novel's publication can be understood in relation to the crucial political changes that were taking place during those years, including the possibility of a political normalization in Argentina, the increasing suppression of guerrilla warfare, and the announcement of the withdrawal of U.S. troops from Vietnam. Had Cortázar spent more time making stylistic changes and working out various inconsistencies, *Libro de Manuel* could have lost its impact, which was wholly dependent upon the timeliness of its release. A return to democracy in Argentina might have lessened the applicability of many issues raised by the novel. The dying urban guerrilla movement may have also lessened the impact of a novel whose plot centers around the activities of just such a group. Finally, regarding the issue of U.S. interventionism, the final phase in Cortázar's writing of *Libro de Manuel* coincides with the beginning of peace talks with the Vietcong. The withdrawal of troops from Vietnam could have been viewed as the first step toward a new era of moderation in U.S. expansionist policy.[29]

A final group of newspaper clippings consists of advertisements and stray news items. Among those included are articles about a sordid homosexual crime (320; 321); a boxing match narrated in an unintelligible language (265); a robbery committed by a sociology student (31; 26); the revolt and escape of young girls at a boarding school (108; 107); and a surrealistic advertisement of sleeping bags (318; 319).

What is the significance of Cortázar's apparently random inclusion of journalistic documents in *Libro de Manuel*? Why are advertisements and sports chronicles placed next to political news? As is characteristic of the collage technique, Cortázar refuses to artificially impose a comprehensive vision into which all these events might be integrated. Instead, he opts for an imperfect juxtaposition of what could be called "reality jolts." Unlike the decontextualization of collage in modernist painting, *Libro de Manuel* creates a recontextualization of its paratexts. Headlines preserve the original information, which in turn acquires new meanings within the novel's network of relationships.

Sometimes the paratexts comment on each other without any direct participation by the characters or the narrator. Such is the case in the above-mentioned clippings concerning U.S. military aid to Latin American countries. Whether isolated or preserved in their original context (for example, the U.S. Department of Defense reports), these clippings present a harsh statistical reality. However, because they are placed directly before and immediately after the confessions of tortured militants in Latin America and North American torturers in Vietnam, they acquire new meaning colored by the emotional import of these interviews. Similarly, guerrilla violence is not directly justified by a political speech, but rather through another clipping in which the widow of a Tupamaro guerrilla fighter explains the circumstances in which armed insurgence originates: "es importante darse cuenta de que la violencia-hambre, la violencia-miseria, la violencia-opresión, la violencia-subdesarrollo, la violencia-tortura, conducen a la violencia-secuestro, a la violencia-terrorismo, a la violencia-guerrilla" (323) ["it is very important to realize that hunger-violence, misery-violence, oppression-violence, underdevelopment-violence, torture-violence lead to kidnapping-violence, terrorism-violence, guerrilla-violence"] (324). As for the most surrealistic clippings, their random inclusion serves several different purposes: By means of them, Cortázar criticizes the alienating effects of advertising, cautions the reader about manipulation by the mass media, destroys the illusion of freedom of choice in a consumer society, and, perhaps more importantly, injects some comic relief into the novel's political debate.

In addition to the interaction among paratexts, we also need to consider the relationship between these and the text itself. The clippings are not aimlessly inserted into the novel, but rather maintain an active dialogue with the central narrative. Thus, members of the Joda translate the news from the French press, all the while commenting on its content in a tone that oscillates between irony and indignation. These commentaries tend to underscore the characteristic features of each clipping, while at the same time justifying their inclusion in terms of documentary relevance (as happens with the political chronicles and the human rights reports) or for their ludic value (as is the case of the advertisements and the more absurd articles).

But the true significance of the novel can be appreciated only by centering on its declared goal. Unlike Cortázar's previous works, *Libro de Manuel* is a novel with a straightforward and practical purpose. It is the result of an immediate historical reality and seeks to affect the very same context from which it arises. To that end, *Libro de Manuel* must first educate the reader in terms of a "reality" that is often manipulated by the mass media. The postscript added to the novel's prologue attacks what it calls the "masaje a escala mundial de los *mass media*" (9) ["the worldwide massage of the mass media"] (9). The indignation of the narrator (easily identifiable with Cortázar) results from the media's disproportionate coverage of the terrorist shootings at the 1972 Munich Olympic Games, and their virtual oversight of events simultaneously occurring in Trelew, Argentina.[30] International press agencies only cover the Third World when events there affect more powerful nations. Instead of informing, newspapers, radio, and television frequently make access to information even more difficult.[31] In Latin American countries, especially during the period when *Libro de Manuel* was published, this access was further hindered by censorship and, in many European countries and the United States, by the lack of interest in news of the developing world. When this information is finally offered, it is short-lived and goes practically unnoticed among the endless stream of news items.

In *Libro de Manuel*, Cortázar seeks to counter the transient nature of news. As Theo D'Haen points out, "when the documentary materials become part of a work of literature, they are estranged from their natural sphere and instead of possessing the ephemerality of a newspaper article—read today and forgotten tomorrow—

they are embedded into a work of art which is supposedly eternal and which demands a different and increased kind of attention from the reader. As a result, the horror of the events described is arrested and emphasized."[32] By including newspaper clippings in the text, Cortázar seeks, therefore, to utilize two different genres—journalism and the novel—for his own purposes. On one hand, he exploits the urgent sense of the "here and now" normally attributed to the press; on the other, he takes advantage of a different medium, that of novelistic discourse, to stress his political message.

The reader's political response to the novel is also activated through the paratextual emphasis on the conditions of injustice and repression suffered by the "Third World." By incorporating detailed descriptions of torture and human rights violations in Latin America and Vietnam, Cortázar seeks to incite the reader's reaction against these situations. Although *Libro de Manuel* does not offer specific solutions to the current state of affairs (nor does it claim to do so), it does establish the need for corrective action. Cortázar himself referred to the novel's power when he wrote that he was seeking to create "an unexpected boomerang" (22), that is, a reverberating effect on the very sociohistorical context from which the work sprang.

The critics' rejection of *Libro de Manuel* has repeatedly been based on the great contradiction it apparently contains: The novel questions the validity of mass media to convey truth (and even suggests that the media manufacture "reality"), while simultaneously utilizing its legitimizing influence.[33] This blatant paradox is not, however, unique to *Libro de Manuel*, nor does it invalidate its political message. Rather, Cortázar's use of the media must be understood in the context of postmodernism's confrontational stance in the face of hegemonic culture: "Today, there is no area of language exterior to bourgeois ideology: our language comes from it, returns to it, remains locked within it. The only possible answer is neither confrontation nor destruction but only theft: to fragment the old texts of culture, of science, of literature, and to disseminate and disguise the fragments in the same way that we disguise stolen merchandise."[34] Through the use and manipulation of documentation, postmodern historical fiction seeks to undermine the hegemonic values that documentation has traditionally served. Instead of endorsing a particular interpretation of reality, the documentary apparatus of these novels plays a problematizing role. On the one hand, it emphasizes the discursive—and therefore mediated—value of all representations. On the other, it denaturalizes the normalizing function of the document. This transgressive use of documentation suggests the need to adapt contemporary oppositional practices to a new literary and historiographic context, one in which the great master narratives yield to a fragmentary and eccentric view of reality.

Libro de Manuel constitutes an extreme case in which the components of political affirmation and communicative immediacy go well beyond those of most postmodern novels. This characteristic explains why the subjective epistemology that distinguishes historiographic metafiction, although always present, frequently loses prominence within the novel. One of the book's objectives is to protest a situation of injustice and to disseminate the political uprisings in Argentina in the 1960s and 1970s, a series of events that, too often, goes unnoticed. To that aim the author employs all available strategies in a critical manner, even those utilized by the media to overlook the situation. The journalistic paratexts are subject to the scrutinizing eyes of the book's characters and, ultimately, to the analytical observations of the reader. While traditional historiography and literary realism used empiricist documentation "to support linear theories of historical development,"[35] Cortázar uses it extensively to problematize the organic worldviews at both the historiographical and the literary levels.

The main problem Cortázar faced was how to preserve political immediacy without sacrificing the experimental and jocular character of his novel. In order to solve this dilemma he employed the fragmentation that characterizes collage. The document is presented in all its integrity within a certain context—the novel—that is both political and playful. Instead of serving principally as visual stimuli (as in modernist collage), the paratextual clippings preserve their documentary and informative value, while at the same time gaining new significance through their incorporation into the novel's syntagmatic axis. It is precisely this syntagmatic level of fragmentation that is analyzed in the following section.

Montage

Although utilizing some of the strategies of modernist collage, *Libro de Manuel* goes beyond the simultaneity and juxtaposition of the actual technique. The novel's educational and moral character demands incorporation of the paratextual "reality jolts" into a mobile and dynamic whole. The realization of a final synthesis—a distinguishing feature of film montage—is, however, problematic in this novel, as it is in all postmodern works. *Libro de Manuel* allegorizes the difficulty of achieving such a synthesis and suggests that the realm where it actually takes place is not located in the text, but rather in the consciousness of its future readers.

In *Libro de Manuel*, Cortázar employs fragmentation on two main levels: division into disjointed units and dispersion of the narrative voice. The novel is organized into a large number of narrative segments with little or no transition between them. On many occasions, the segments are left unfinished and/or consist of equally incomplete dialogues or narratives. On others, they begin in medias res, without informing the reader of the context in which they occur. Their sense of discontinuity is enhanced due to the fact that no clear narrative agency exists, but rather several voices follow—or are superimposed onto—one another, without any explanatory commentary or transition.[36] Two characters share the principal narrative role: *el que te dije* (the-one-I-told-you) and Andrés. The-one-I-told-you is the initial chronicler of the Joda.[37] Although occasionally interacting with the other characters, he is usually withdrawn from the main action, preoccupied by the recording of events in an endless series of notes that he will never be able to organize. A sharp criticism of the methodology and goals of conventional historiography emerges from the novel's portrayal of this character. Like the conservative historian, the-one-I-told-you tries to keep an objective record of the events with minimal ideological interference. To that end, he accumulates a chaotic pile of index cards and scraps of paper that he tries to organize according to the rules of causality and logical taxonomy: "¿Por qué esa manía de andar dividiendo las cosas como si fueran salames? Una tajada de Joda, otra de historia personal, me haces pensar en el que te dije con sus problemas organizativos, el pobre no entiende y quisiera entender, es una especie de Linneo o Ameghino de la Joda" (239) ["Why that mania for going around slicing things up as if they were a salami? One slice of Screwery, another of personal history, you remind me of the one that I told you with his organizational problems, the poor guy doesn't understand and would like to understand, he's a kind of Linnaeus or Ameghino of the Screwery"] (242). Through other characters and narrators the novel also mocks the neutrality the-one-I-told-you tries so hard to maintain: "Esta neutralidad lo había llevado desde un principio a ponerse como de perfil, operación siempre riesgosa en materia narrativa, y no digamos histórica, que es lo mismo" (11) ["That neutrality had led him from the beginning to hold himself as if in profile, an operation that is always risky in narrative matters—and let us not call it historical, which is the same thing"] (11).

The novel's ambiguous end implies either the death of the-one-I-told-you, or simply his inability to complete the narrative project. Consequently, Andrés is left to organize the notes in a more or less coherent way (11; 6), but he will only be able to do so after a violent break with his past. Only by means of his own personal acts of sexual and political transgression will Andrés emerge regenerated and willing to assume his narrative role. In fact, the novel suggests that radical transgression and political engagement are prerequisites to writing in postmodern society. However, Andrés does not completely rewrite the materials he inherits, and sometimes allows the story to be told from the perspective of the-one-I-told-you (25–28; 20–23), Ludmilla (236; 239), or Francine (289–90; 290–91). During these moments, Andrés assumes the simpler role of a regular character, and the absence of markers indicating the shift in perspective contributes to the novel's sense of fragmentation.[38]

What are the consequences of this entangled web of multifarious narratives and limited narrators? Above all, the novel professes to be a collective creation that questions all sources of knowledge. History in *Libro de Manuel* is really a group of stories, a multifaceted conglomerate that can only be approached from multiple points of view. The novel presents a chain of limited interpreters of fragmentary texts that resist closure, giving the impression of a polyphonic and heterogeneous discourse.

In addition to this aspect of multiple perspectivism, the influence of cinema is manifested through film metaphors that reveal the novel's mechanisms of production. The metafictional center of *Libro de Manuel*, its dominant *mise en abyme*, is Andrés's cinematic dream. By means of this obsessive metaphor, Cortázar figuratively presents a synthesis of his own aesthetic and political evolution, an explanation of the novel's inner workings, and a complete theory as to how the novel should be read. In his recurring dream, Andrés is in a motion-picture theater watching a Fritz Lang mystery film. In the room are two perpendicular screens. Although Andrés tries to watch the film from several locations, there is always something between him and the screens. While shifting seats, Andrés is beckoned by a waiter: Someone, a Cuban, wants to see him. As he enters the dark parlor where this mysterious character awaits him, "la escena se corta" (103) ["the scene is cut"] (100). When Andrés leaves the room, he feels transformed. Now he has a mission to carry out. His meeting with the Cuban appears to have changed his outlook. He feels as if he were acting simultaneously in and outside of the film. He is both the film and its spectator:

mientras volvía a la sala sentía el bloque total de todo eso que ahora estoy segmentando para poder explicarlo aunque sea en parte. Un poco como si sólo gracias a esa acción que debería cumplir pudiera llegar a saber lo que me dijo el cubano, una inversión de la causalidad completamente absurda como te das cuenta. Hay la mecánica del tríler pero yo voy a cumplirla y a gozarla al mismo tiempo, la novela policial que escribo y que vivo al mismo tiempo (103).

[while I was coming back to the theater I could feel the total weight of all this I'm breaking into segments now in order to explain it, even though it's only partial. A little as if only thanks to that act I was to fulfill could I come to know what the Cuban has told me, a completely absurd reversal of causality as you can see.[53] We have the workings of the thriller but I will fulfill it and enjoy it at the same time, the detective story I'm writing and living simultaneously] (101).

Andrés's dream clearly allegorizes his—and Cortázar's— "confuso y atormentado itinerario" (7) ["confused and tormented path"] (3), to which the novel's prologue alludes.[39] This effective metaphor portrays Andrés's ideological ambivalence at the beginning of the novel. The two screens suggest what initially seem to be two incompatible alternatives: the artist's engagement with art versus his or her engagement with history. Although details of the meeting with the mysterious stranger are never revealed, the encounter clearly refers to the impact of the Cuban revolution on Cortázar's artistic and public personae.

The Cuban's message is not revealed until the final pages of the novel. Up to that point, Andrés refers to the meeting as a gap in his memory, a black hole. When he finally decides to join the Joda— that is, to actively participate in the revolutionary struggle—the veil covering this incident is lifted and we discover that the message is summarized in an expression that alludes to Andrés's awakening to history, and to revolution:

se me vislumbra la antena y reconstruyo la secuencia, miro al hombre que me mira desde el sillón hamacándose despacito, veo mi sueño como soñándolo por fin de veras y tan sencillo, tan idiota, tan claro, tan evidente, era tan perfectamente previsible que esta noche y aquí yo me acordara de golpe que el sueño consistía nada mas que en eso, en el cubano que me miraba y me decía sólamente una palabra: *Despertáte* (356).

[I catch a glimpse of the antenna and reconstruct the sequence, I look at the man who looks at me from the chair slowly rocking, I see my dream as if I'm finally dreaming it and so simple, so idiotic, so clear, so obvious, it was so perfectly foreseeable that tonight and here I should re-

member all of a sudden that the dream was nothing more than that, that
the Cuban was looking at me and saying only two words to me: *Wake
up*] (359).

Aside from its obvious allegorical meaning, Andrés's dream has a
specular value, which permits the novel to comment upon all aspects of its internal structure (story line, theme, form, and structure). In this precise metaphor lie some of the most important clues
to understanding not only *Libro de Manuel*, but also Cortázar's political evolution.

Until this point we have examined the importance of this metaphor as it relates to the story line, its most obvious aspect, as well
as the one most frequently discussed by critics. But Andrés's dream
also mirrors the novel's aesthetic qualities, and, in relation to the
topic under discussion, it reflects the basic conflict between the
principles of postmodern collage and montage that dictate the structural pattern of *Libro de Manuel*. On the one hand, the dream dramatizes the tension between the will to preserve the diversity of
forms and ideas contained in the novel, and the search for a synthesis that could transcend them, thus making them politically effective. On the other hand, it suggests that this utopian synthesis can
only be achieved through critical reading.

Through this specular metaphor Cortázar re-creates and complements the theory of reading that he had developed prior to writing
Libro de Manuel. In previous fictional works and essays he had outlined a poetics that called for the active participation of the reader.
According to this poetics, the meaning of a work is never considered an essence but rather an act, the result of the interaction between the reader and the text. In several short stories, as well as in
Rayuela and the *Morellianas*, Cortázar condemns the codes of realism, which demand a passive and complacent attitude from readers.
Instead, he proposes a participatory aesthetics in which readers
must collaborate with the author in the production of meaning. By
projecting their consciousness onto the text, they are able to discover aspects of their inner world that they had hitherto ignored.
From this perspective, reading acquires a crucial cognitive value,
deepening our knowledge of the world and of ourselves.[40]

This formalist and psychological theory of reading, similar to
that proposed by reader-response critics during the 1970s, is complemented in *Libro de Manuel* by a unique focus on politics. The
novel's intention is aimed not only at the reader's self-awareness,
but also at his or her transformation into a militant reader, one able
to implement specific changes in his or her sociohistorical context.

From this point of view, it is not a simple coincidence that critics have drawn upon Bertolt Brecht's theories to explain the underlying aesthetic and political codes in *Libro de Manuel*.[41] Like Cortázar, Brecht was interested in communicating politically with his audience, without having to minimize his aesthetic aspirations. Brecht also based his literary theory on an admitted antirealism and was involved in a long-standing polemic with theoreticians of social realism. However, this antirealism did not imply a rejection of the mimetic principle in his works, but rather an investigation into its nature. Because both Cortázar and Brecht search for an art that is able to strip phenomena from the mark of normality, their works tend to defamiliarize everything we, the readers, accept noncritically as natural.

Among all the elements of Brecht's dramatic theory, his "alienation effect" plays perhaps the greatest role in understanding the "awakening" of Cortázar's protagonist. Although distancing and defamiliarizing techniques were not unusual in the literary tradition, Brecht developed a whole theory of drama around them, and applied them to serve political goals. According to Brecht, bourgeois ideology masks its own contradictions and limitations, thus creating a pathological sense of normality. In his view, art should liberate the spectator from the passiveness bred by the established patterns of thought. To that end, he proposed to undermine everything that we would conventionally consider as normal and acceptable.

The so-called alienation effect (*Verfremdunsgs-effekt*) relies on converting the familiar into the bizarre in order to understand its social and political functions, increasing the social consciousness of the viewer. As Brecht himself explained, "the A-effect consists in turning the object of which one is to be made aware, to which one's attention is to be drawn, from something ordinary, familiar, immediately accessible, into something peculiar, striking and unexpected" (143). Unlike Aristotelian theater, which is based on empathy (identification of spectators with characters) and catharsis (liberation of emotions through dramatic tension), Brechtian drama fosters the audience's critical detachment. The attention is not focused as much on the final result, as it is on the performing process itself. One of the ways to achieve this goal is through the use of metatheatrical techniques, some of which originate in the novelistic tradition. Brechtian epic drama often includes a prologue that anticipates the dramatic action and/or an epilogue that summarizes it. Scenes are frequently interrupted by characters who address the audience, or by the projection onto screens of headlines or legends

that comment on the drama. Other techniques are typically theatrical (such as the manipulation of lights and mobile stages) or borrowed from cinema and the other arts. All these devices serve to
remind the audience that what they are watching is not a slice of
life, but rather a dramatic production. The spectators are alienated
from what happens on stage, and therefore are able to judge the
facts with critical detachment and reflect on possible alternatives,
hence the emphasis Brecht placed on active viewer participation.

Although Andrés's position in the dream is that of one of Cortázar's archetypal readers, the scene is pervaded by the Brechtian
model of revolutionary art. Andrés's initial condition is that of a
passive spectator. There are two screens in the theater and he alter-
natively contemplates each without comprehending the action of
the Fritz Lang film being shown.[42] His situation at the beginning of
the dream is hardly different from that of the main characters in two
of Cortázar's most famous short stories: "Instrucciones para John
Howell" and "Continuidad de los parques." In "Instrucciones" a
spectator is invited to participate in the play (a simple melodrama)
he is watching, eventually exposing his personal life as he trans-
gresses his assigned role. In "Continuidad" a reader is fatally implicated in the events of the novel he is reading. However, that
which in the stories constitutes an attack on forms of realistic illu-
sionism and reader passivity, acquires, in *Libro de Manuel*, political
overtones. Cortázar's active spectator becomes here a militant activist, who is called upon to participate along with the author, narrators, and characters in the transformation of historical reality.

In *Libro de Manuel*, this call to political action is symbolically
expressed through the meeting with the Cuban. As the novel's end
reveals, the Cuban admonishes Andrés for his previous blindness
and inaction ("Despertáte" or "Wake up"). As a result of this meeting, Andrés undergoes a transformation, becoming aware of the
alienation he has experienced thus far and of the need for active
participation in the political reality in which he lives. From this moment on, he becomes conscious of a schism—"soy doble" ["I'm
double"]—which is also one of the steps in the Brechtian learning
process. In Brecht's epic drama the spectator's awareness of his or
her own alienation is followed by his or her critical involvement in
the action. Such involvement is characterized by a double impulse
of participation and withdrawal. In order to activate the spectator's
critical capacity, the work must make him or her continuously
aware of the play's own dramatic condition, its "artificiality." In
this way, the spectator is alienated from the action and is no longer
influenced by the illusionistic emotionalism essential to Aristote-

lian drama. In this phase of the dream, Andrés's schism is not presented as something exterior to his experiential realm, but rather as his self-awareness of living simultaneously as both participant and spectator ("alguien que fue al cine y alguien que está metido en un lío típicamente cinematográfico" (103) ["someone who went to the movies and someone caught up in a typical movie plot"] (101). It is precisely at this moment that the character begins to perceive the possibility of achieving a synthesis. Amidst the fragmentary perspective of collage and montage, an underlying whole begins to emerge: "mientras volvía a la sala sentía el bloque total de todo eso que ahora estoy segmentando para poder explicarlo aunque sea en parte" (103) ["while I was coming back to the theater I could feel the total weight of all this I'm breaking into segments now in order to explain it, even though it's only partial"] (101). The last phase in this process of learning refers to the revolutionary praxis beyond the text's limits, to the spectator's transformation into the creator of his/her own work: "Hay la mecánica del tríler pero yo voy a cumplirla y a gozarla al mismo tiempo, la novela policial que escribo y que vivo al mismo tiempo" (103) ["We have the workings of the thriller but I will fulfill it and enjoy it at the same time, the detective story I'm writing and living simultaneously"] (101).

As in the epic drama, *Libro de Manuel* depicts the process of learning that leads to sociohistorical engagement. The central metaphor of Andrés's dream points, therefore, to the transformation of the character from a passive consumer into an active agent of social change, made possible only after he becomes aware of his own alienation. In depicting this process, the novel utilizes a broad range of specular images that extend from initial fragmentation and total detachment toward a progressive involvement with the social body. Through Andrés's apprenticeship in both perception and social action, Cortázar again suggests an integration of literary and political activism. Andrés accepts the task of organizing the novel's narrative material only after embracing the human community, symbolized by his participation in the Joda. His involvement in political action is thus one of the prerequisites for the creation of *Libro de Manuel*. The final synthesis, however, is not in his hands, but in those of the critical reader, who will likewise have to respond to the novel's ethical and aesthetic demands.

The book's epilogue presents the penultimate step in the synthesis required from the reader. In a morgue, Lonstein, the novel's most eccentric character, washes the lifeless body of a revolutionary killed in the police raid that wipes out the Joda. In this last narrative segment, the realms of collage and montage intersect in order to reemphasize the ideological message behind *Libro de Manuel*. As the text itself suggests, this final scene is also the last entry in the scrapbook that the characters have made for Manuel.[43] By means of a metalepsis, the structural levels of the text (that of the characters) and the paratexts (that of the news collected by these characters) converge to form a single entity. In this way, the text seems to insinuate that the manual created for Manuel by the characters is in fact the novel we have just read, which is, in turn, part of Latin American reality, "ese inmenso libro que podemos escribir entre todos y para todos" ["that vast book that we can write among all and for all."][44]

The use of this metalepsis also implies a final connection between the techniques of collage and montage, as well as between aesthetic and political programs. The fragmentation that results from the use of both techniques leaves a trail of blank spaces, of kaleidoscopic arrangements that cannot be resolved within the physical limits of the text. Indeed, this last clipping of Manuel's manual is also the final frame of Cortázar's film/novel, whose assembly will be produced in the reader's consciousness. In a scene that evokes visions of the famous photograph of "Che" Guevara's dead body, *Libro de Manuel* reflects upon its leitmotifs for the last time. The narrator, probably Andrés, refers to the morgue as that place where "toda huella de historia" (386) ["all marks of history"] will be washed away (389). The scene portrayed in the epilogue summarizes the paradoxical concept of history that characterizes *Libro de Manuel* and postmodern historiographic metafiction, in general. Primarily, history continues to be the "permanent catastrophe" that Cortázar envisioned in most of his works. In response to the Hegelian view of history as an organic progress toward perfection, Cortázar presents us with a destructive process that leaves its traces on the individual. This view of history as oppressive and unjust calls for a discourse able, on the one hand, to counteract the erasure by time of memory and, on the other, to exercise a corrective function in the face of specific acts of repression and abuse. The fact that this rewriting of history stems from the encounter with Lonstein, the embodiment of playfulness in the novel, reinforces Cortázar's recurrently expressed view that a revolutionary work should not forget the spirit of play and experimentation that makes any work truly revolutionary. This search for a synthesis between revolutionary action and play, ethics and aesthetics, dominates Andrés's journey throughout the novel and pervades both the collage of newspaper clippings and the montage of disjointed narrative segments.

Cortázar's historical vision is paradoxical in its quest to attain a difficult synthesis between historical relativism and political affirmation, between antiorganicism and socialism. As a consequence of the equalization of the fictional segments and the documentary paratext, the truthfulness of the novel's political message must be questioned. At the end of the novel, Lonstein exclaims "van a pensar que lo inventamos" (386) ["they're going to think we made it all up"] (389). Indeed, *Libro de Manuel* is the result, among other things, of Cortázar's creative invention. However, what critics have seen as a blatant inconsistency, a dead end that hinders the interpretation of the novel is, in reality, one of its most redeeming factors. The work's historical relativism is part of the self-criticism that Cortázar deems necessary in both literature and politics. Acceptance of an organic and totalizing historical discourse would have been incompatible with the simultaneous processes of political condemnation and epistemological subjectivism that characterize this novel in particular, and postmodern fiction in general.

Through this paradoxical vision of the relationship between history and literature, the novel affirms the need for historical documentation, recognizes the sheer difficulty of recording a gruesome past before its traces are erased and forgotten, and simultaneously warns against the conversion of this record into a new dogma. This need has been and still remains particularly urgent in Argentina, where previous decades have witnessed one of the most spectacular attempts at institutionalizing national oblivion. The disappearance of thousands of citizens has been followed by the military's attempt to seal the historical archive by granting general amnesty for most crimes committed during the Dirty War. Cortázar's attempt to establish a corrective historiography is subject to the verbal limitations and ideological implications inherent in all historiographic works. The historian, the chronicler, and the novelist are always mediators between external reality and the textual realm. Their work is always influenced by both the rhetorical conventions of their discourse and their own ideology.[45] In this sense, Cortázar's novel is caught in the dilemma of all oppositional works in the postmodern era: How can we make political statements in a time of growing skepticism, and make them effectively? How can we reconstruct the past if the materials needed for such reconstruction are tinged with prejudices and ideology? The novel does not provide an explicit solution to these problems. It favors neither the denial of relativism and self-criticism nor the refusal of historicity and political commitment. It merely states the inevitability of these polarities, as well as the need for their future articulation. The collage of newspaper clippings and the montage of multiple perspectives contribute to the creation of a heterogeneous and kaleidoscopic space, whose resolution is projected onto a utopian future, the realm of the Messianic Manuel, *el hombre nuevo*, the ideal reader.

E. L. DOCTOROW

History and Self-reflexivity in the Writings of E. L. Doctorow

Literary critics have resorted to the most disparate labels to classify Doctorow's style. His works have been defined as realist and postmodern, traditionalist and avant-garde. Some even prefer the paradoxical term "postmodernist realism" when referring to his idiosyncratic style of writing.[46] An explanation for such disparity can be found in the multifaceted character of his fiction. Doctorow's novels employ different narrative techniques to cover some of the greatest (and darkest) moments in U.S. history. This critical remembrance of the American past coexists with an exploration of the process of history writing. The result is a prime illustration of historiographic metafiction.

Doctorow's first two novels, *Welcome to Hard Times* and *Big as Life*, explore the potential offered by two popular genres—westerns and science fiction, respectively—for scrutinizing U.S. mythology, history, and literature. In *Welcome to Hard Times*, Doctorow describes the emergence and destruction of a Western community at the beginning of the nineteenth century. By means of an allegorical plot in which characters represent various attitudes and archetypes of U.S. society, Doctorow questions the endless horizon of expectations created by the expansiveness of the frontier. Life in this symbolic community embodies the contradictions and destructiveness that Doctorow perceives at the very foundations of the U.S. socioeconomic system. It is in this context that Blue, the novel's narrator, assumes the role of both historian and fiction writer. He keeps a daily chronicle of events in his ledgers, where, on his deathbed, he writes the story of his life: the very novel we are reading. As will happen throughout his work, Doctorow problematizes the limits between the writing of fiction and the writing of history. Both are conceived of as narrative artifacts restrained by the narrator's subjective perceptions and limited mnemonic capacity.

Doctorow revives some of the themes of his first novel, transporting them into an imaginary future in the novel *Big as Life*. Power relations in the capitalist world are here criticized, especially as they relate to the manipulations of the historical archive. The protagonist, Wallace Creighton, is himsef a historian devoted to the interpretation of an elusive reality. Entrusted by the authorities to write the history of NYCRAD—a consortium of government, military, and religious agencies—Creighton discovers that his function is really to cover up the secret activities of an immense corporate state. As a historian, Doctorow's character attempts to capture a chaotic reality within the pages of his book but is defeated by an overwhelming amount of data. The predictable character of the events, the mechanical use of science-fiction conventions, and the implausible characterizations make *Big as Life* Doctorow's biggest failure, something that he himself has frequently acknowledged.[47]

After his problems with popular fiction, Doctorow's career headed in a new direction. In *The Book of Daniel* (1972), he demonstrated his will to break with the traditional narrative models of his earlier work. Narrative is dissolved in this novel into fragments and multiple voices that are ultimately articulated through the single voice of the protagonist. Doctorow introduces characters who evoke historical persona, and he frequently alludes to protagonists of U.S. political history. The major historical issues here examined are the Cold War and the emergence of New Left movements. The trial and execution of the Isaacsons—the Rosenbergs—in the early 1950s is reconstructed amid the ideological turmoil of the late 1960s by Daniel, one of their children. While writing his Ph.D. dissertation, Daniel seeks to explain the mystery surrounding his parents' trial. Daniel's book—both his dissertation and the novel we are reading—reaches beyond the character's biographical reconstruction and explores the limitations of language and memory in the representation of historical reality.

Ragtime, Doctorow's most popular novel to date, again explores the problematic borderline between fiction and history. Unlike *The Book of Daniel*, in which the main characters—though evocative of historical figures—are imaginary, *Ragtime* intertwines the real and the fictional in even more radically a manner. J. P. Morgan, Henry Ford, Stanford White, Sigmund Freud, Emma Goldman, Booker T. Washington, Evelyn Nesbit, and Harry Houdini play a crucial role in the development of the action and interact with other, entirely fictional, characters. Given the lack of a single protagonist or plot, the novel creates the impression of a choral work in which historical events appear to be filtered through a prism without the favoring of any particular one. The result is a spectacular overview of contemporary U.S. society in which some of its most honored myths are tested and revised.

By means of a methodical combination of apocryphal history and official records, *Ragtime* rewrites the U.S. past and its mythology. This singular combination allows the author to challenge the privileges and values that have been traditionally attributed to the great figures of U.S. history. Like Fuentes in his "Theater of Memory," Doctorow transforms the possible into the real. Thus he portrays the imaginary meeting of two African Americans (fictional Coalhouse Walker and historical Booker T. Washington) inside the Morgan Library, the symbolic center of a hegemonic power that has systematically excluded all marginal sectors of society. Morgan himself, one of corporate America's greatest financiers, is presented as a lunatic obsessed with reincarnation and his kinship with the dynasties of ancient Egypt. In presenting the eccentricity of one of the magnates of the time, Doctorow attempts, on the one hand, to destroy the aura of splendor with which these figures are endowed in the official record and, on the other, to invert the hierarchical system of traditional history. In *Ragtime*, the eccentric (Coalhouse, Tateh, and Houdini) is often portrayed as central, and the central (Morgan, Ford) at times becomes peripheral.

However, the greatest innovation of this novel is not thematic, but rather technical. It stems from the author's use of narrative distance. Doctorow has frequently explained how in this novel he sought a tone that was not as aseptic as that of traditional historiography nor as intimate as that of the autobiographical novel.[48] In *Ragtime*, the narrator's moral posturing is relayed from an ironic distance. Whereas *The Book of Daniel* itself dramatizes the search for an appropriate narrative voice, *Ragtime* demonstrates from the outset a detachment that will be sustained throughout the novel, generating a voice that is difficult to categorize. It creates the general impression of mischievous superficiality armed with large doses of irony, if not outright cynicism. This voice, which Doctorow himself has labeled "mock-historical pedantic," parodies the nostalgic historical style of mass culture.[49]

The structural elements of this novel—both rhythmic and thematic—appear as the narrative equivalent of ragtime music. As in ragtime, the novel provides "variations on themes provided by representative figures and events of the time."[50] It combines fact and fiction, nostalgia and antinostalgia, the private life of the powerful and the daily existence of the nameless. The metafictional component in *Ragtime* is revealed through these musical metaphors. However, unlike *The Book of Daniel*, self-reflexivity is present only in a very subtle manner. The narrator's constant appeals to the reader and self-referential digressions are absent in *Ragtime*. Self-consciousness in this novel is concealed behind a more linear narrative skeleton. This does not mean that *Ragtime* is less experimental, but it is certainly less attuned to the extreme discontinuity and radical perspectives of works such as *The Book of Daniel* or the novels by Fuentes, Reed, and Cortázar that we have discussed thus far.

Doctorow's next novel, *Loon Lake* (1981), implies a return to the experiments in perspectival mobility that he had initiated in his third novel.[51] Through constant changes in space, time, and voice, *Loon Lake* offers two autobiographical accounts with numerous parallels, albeit through different styles: Joe Paterson's picaresque and worldly story and Warren Penfield's poetic remembrances. To these two voices, the novel adds computer data that interrupts the action and comments on Joe's and Warren's stories. The mixture of styles and voices helps to confer upon the novel the polyphonic effect that Doctorow often pursues in his works. But if the polyphony of *Ragtime* is the result of articulating a set of voices within an organic whole, in *Loon Lake* narrative fragments resist integration into a coherent totality.

Loon Lake revises the myth of the American Dream, and especially the success story in the Horatio Alger vein.[52] Unlike the classic versions of this central myth of capitalism, success in Doctorow's novel is not achieved through the winners' industry and constancy, but is rather the result of their moral perversion. In order for social success to take place, characters must renounce their class origins and accept the promise of individual reward offered by their integration into the dominant value system.

Loon Lake initiates a tendency in Doctorow's career toward increasingly private concerns. In his later works the representation of the past revolves around the protagonists' subjective reconstruction of their individual experiences. *World's Fair* (1985), for example, clearly evokes the author's childhood memories. Like *Loon Lake*, *World's Fair* employs several voices (three members of the protagonist's family) that become integrated into the central organizing consciousness of Edgar, Doctorow's protagonist and alter ego. Although welcomed by critics, *World's Fair* lacks the political ambition and artifice of his best novels. It is a private story with autobiographical overtones in which most of the intellectual preoccupations of historiographic metafiction are no longer present.

All main characters in Doctorow's novels tend to become prototypes for the artist and the historian. They obsessively attempt to capture an elusive reality by means of language. However, this enterprise is undertaken differently in each text. His first three novels dramatize the impossibility of achieving a satisfactory representation of the past, be it individual or collective. This failure affects not only the subjective introspection of Blue in *Welcome to Hard Times* and Daniel in *The Book of Daniel*, but also the objectivistic reconstruction through which Creighton seeks an order out of the chaos of events in *Big as Life*. While in these early novels narrative revolves around the difficulty of the main character registering historical reality, in *Ragtime* and *Loon Lake* Doctorow offers two distinct mimetic alternatives to the elusive nature of history. By means of a montage of narrative sequences and multiple perspectives organized either within an organic (*Ragtime*) or discontinuous (*Loon Lake*) whole, Doctorow suggests that reality can only be correctly perceived and represented through a "multiplicity of witnesses," constituting what he himself has labeled a "democracy of perception."[53] By exploring equally the realms of political history and individual subjectivity, Doctorow offers a way out of the existing dilemma in the U.S. literary tradition: the division between a sociological literature of realistic style and the psychological narcissism of many contemporary novels.

In addition to his novelistic production, Doctorow has expressed his ideas about literature and politics in his nonfiction works. Essays such as "False Documents," "The State of Mind of the Union," and "Ultimate Discourse" have an almost programmatic value that makes them works of necessary analysis in understanding the aesthetic background of his novels. Among them, "False Documents" (1977) offers some of the most important keys to interpreting the totality of Doctorow's oeuvre, and serves as a useful tool in commenting on *The Book of Daniel* as historiographic metafiction.

"False Documents" examines the role of fiction and history in the writing of literature. Doctorow begins the essay by establishing the subjective value not only of fiction, but also of history. Both are discursive forms that construct rather than reflect reality. For Doctorow, "there is no history except as it is composed," an idea that coincides with the historiographic revisionism that characterizes the latest trends in the philosophy of history.[54] From this statement it follows that history is not an essence to be discovered, but a discursive construction that acquires shape solely in the act of writing.

According to Doctorow, contemporary language serves two antagonistic powers: the power of the dominant regime and the power of freedom, both of which have their literary correlative in the forms of nonfiction and fiction, respectively. Doctorow illustrates the power of the regime with an article from *The New York Times*.

The power of journalism stems from its supposed proximity to truth, and this is so because our industrial society openly favors empirical thought and science. In this manner, Doctorow understands our easy acceptance of the authority of facts, something that in literature corresponds to the premise of realism. Journalistic language is contemplated not as an imaginary construction, but rather as a property of the facts themselves. The power of freedom, on the contrary, refers to a nonverifiable ideal world. Fiction allows us access to the cognitive experience of a superior order because it is unlimited and projected onto a future of possibilities. While the language of the regime founds its power on what we supposedly are, the language of freedom has, for Doctorow, a vast utopian potential, as it expresses that which we may yet become.

These linguistic powers are at odds in contemporary culture. Literature uses both to its own ends. It confuses fact and fiction and in this way seeks to recuperate a lost original unity. Following Walter Benjamin's "The Story Teller," Doctorow believes in the possibility that in ancient times "the designative and evocative functions of language were one and the same."[55] The figure of the storyteller would embody the unity of both powers, for in the past the act of telling a story was in itself an assumption of truth. The storyteller thus exercised both a magical and political power, since literature was a unifying element: "Literature was as valuable as a club or a sharpened bone. It bound the present to the past, the visible with the invisible, and it helped to compose the community necessary for the continuing life of its members."[56]

The situation is quite different today, according to Doctorow. Literature is no longer a survival tool and the contemporary novelist is but a deformed version of the traditional storyteller. He or she works alone, isolated from a community that no longer benefits from his or her advice. Quoting Benjamin again, Doctorow presents *Don Quijote* as symptomatic of this new power relationship. In *Don Quijote*, Cervantes portrays a man deprived of reason by the obsessive and lonely act of reading novels. But Doctorow's interest in this work rests above all on the way the author of *Don Quijote* reasserts his authority over his work by withdrawing from the events and denying his authorship. As in other "false documents" of the time, Cervantes's novel was presented as true, even though it was known to be Cervantes's invention. Through this "mixing-up of the historic and the aesthetic, the real and the possibly real," these works seek to recuperate the state of initial wisdom to which Benjamin refers, "before fact and fiction became ontologically differentiated—that is, when it was possible for fiction to give counsel."[57] In finding themselves confined to their own isolated universe, novelists must divide themselves into creators and documentalists, tellers and listeners, and thus communicate collective wisdom in their own language, but cloaked in the mask of feigned objectivity.

However, the status of novelists is not the same in all parts of the world. In industrialized Western countries, the writers of fictions are, in the best of cases, a nuisance. In Western democracies they are given free pass because they are assumed to be inoffensive. This "writer-nuisance" is relegated to the field of culture, an "antiuniverse"—a world of imitations—in which he or she can only acquire, at best, shamanistic powers. According to Doctorow, novelists in countries like the United States are not taken seriously because their work only reaches powerless minorities. On the contrary, in socialist countries and in the Third World literature exercises political influence and writers are often imprisoned and persecuted because of their subversive power.

Like a compilation of quotes (Nietzsche, Croce, Carr, Becker, and Barthes), Doctorow's last remarks in "False Documents" pose some of the most common problems found in the contemporary philosophy of history. Here Doctorow questions the objective value of the historical fact and reveals its constructed nature; his style becomes sententious and the essay grows increasingly subjective.[58] Finally, he undermines the traditional distinction between fiction and nonfiction. In his opinion, "there is no fiction or nonfiction as we commonly understand the distinction: there is only narrative."[59]

"False Documents" expresses Doctorow's main concerns about literature and history. His arguments, however, present several contradictions. In the first place, he poses a conflict between two different powers (the power of the regime and the power of freedom), which manifest themselves in two conflicting languages (nonfiction and fiction). He then states that his dichotomy did not exist in the past, since the storyteller utilized the power of both languages. However, Doctorow projects this contemporary dualism onto the past by affirming that literature was the element that connected present and past and allowed social cohesion and community survival. If this dichotomy between the power of freedom (fiction) and the power of the regime (nonfiction) did not exist at the beginning, we cannot properly speak of literature or fiction when referring to the storyteller. We may, however, speak of a discursive form that would encompass elements of both fiction and nonfiction. Doctorow's paradoxical line of thought does not stop here. After thoroughly establishing his dualistic proposition, he undermines it at the end by concluding that there is only narrative. These contradictions have not been completely overlooked by critics. Harpham, for example, summarizes the most obvious ones in these terms: "Citing authorities, making distinctions, observing rules of evidence, the essay takes the objectivist position outside imaginative distortion to claim, first, that there are two kinds of power in language; second, that there are two kinds of language; third, that one of those kinds dominates and even constitutes the other; and, finally, that there is only one kind of language but that is neither the first nor the second."[60]

Doctorow's position is further complicated by his distortion of Benjamin's theses in "The Story Teller."[61] Doctorow quotes Benjamin to present a contrast between the power and social influence of medieval storytellers and the modern novelist, "an isolated individual who gives birth to his novel whole, himself uncounseled and without the ability to counsel others."[62] In order to further stress the growing powerlessness of the novel, Doctorow reproduces Benjamin's thoughts on *Don Quijote*, the first of the "false documents": "The first great novel, *Don Quixote*, teaches how the spiritual greatness, the boldness, the helpfulness, of one of the noblest of men, Don Quixote, are completely devoid of counsel and do not contain the slightest scintilla of wisdom."[63] Doctorow interrupts his line of argument here without clarifying the meaning of a quotation that could easily work against his thesis. The idea implied is that the novel is not opposed to but is itself a form of storytelling without the status and social responsibilities that storytelling once held in the past. The task of the contemporary novelist should be to recuperate this status and its corresponding responsibilities, by bringing the novel back into the social sphere.

Doctorow's application of "The Story Teller" is highly questionable. To begin with, Benjamin does not contemplate a continuity—or even the possibility of such continuity—between storytelling and the novel. In fact, he considers that the decline of storytelling begins with the emergence of the novel. Unlike other forms of fiction, the novel depends on the book, and was made possible only by the invention of printing: "What differentiates the novel from all other forms of prose literature—the fairy tale, the legend, even the novella—is that it neither comes from oral tradition nor goes into it. This distinguishes it from storytelling in particular."[64] According to Benjamin, all attempts to "implant instruction in the novel"—as Doctorow seeks to do—"have always amounted to a modification of the novel form."[65] Naturally, Doctorow is involved in a transformation of the novel's form, but the possibility of achieving such transformation following the guidelines of Benjamin's thesis is not very clear. If we accept Benjamin's assertion that the novel has been traditionally devoid of counsel and wisdom, how can it amount to a system of knowledge, as Doctorow claims? Would it not be easier to hold to traditional or new forms of storytelling? After all, Benjamin's essay is not about a modern novelist but about a nineteenth-century storyteller (Nikolai Leskov). These questions are left unanswered, and lead to new contradictions that make Doctorow's position even more problematic.

The conclusion of "False Documents" points to the discursive superiority of nonrealistic fiction when it is able to combine the realms of imagination and history. What Doctorow is really trying to do in his essay is legitimize his own literary project by using the same kind of language (nonfiction) and tools (empirical analysis) he is seeking to undermine. In order to accomplish this task, the dualistic vision behind his thesis is gradually intensified. Fiction here is a cognitive vehicle superior to politics, journalism, and science. According to this neo-Romantic view, novelists are imbued with the ability "to compose false documents more valid, more real, more truthful than the 'true' documents of the politicians or the journalists or the psychologists."[66] Doctorow's justification of his own approach to fiction and history is presented as a return to an original era, described in idealized terms. Through this imaginary past, he creates a utopian model in which the writer is a privileged agent of change and a source of wisdom, a model Doctorow would like see reborn in the future.

"False Documents" contains an idea that recurs in the writings of Fuentes, Reed, and, to a lesser extent, in those of Cortázar: the nostalgia for a lost world in which the artist exercises a decisive power over communal life, a power that in capitalist societies has been dramatically diminished.[67] Those critics who have pointed out these inconsistencies have tried to justify them by making the essay itself into an example of the theory it contains. For Harpham and Morris, "False Documents" is really a "false document," a fiction in which the first-person narrator should not be identified with Doctorow, but rather with a persona used to propound a series of conflicting arguments.[68] The consideration of the essay as a deconstructive "false document" is, however, unsatisfactory for a number of reasons. Why should Doctorow intentionally advance contradictory ideas in a poetic manifesto? What is the point of purposely formulating "false" arguments in an essay that seeks to establish the "presumption of truth" in the discourse of fiction?[69] Moreover, "false documents" is the term Doctorow uses to label nonrealistic novels, and certainly nobody would think of Doctorow's essay as a novel, no matter how imaginative it might be. If the first-person voice in this essay is not the author but his persona, it is certainly the same persona that reappears in all of his works and interviews.

The answer to these questions has to be found rather in the paradoxes and contradictions of postmodernism. Postmodern fiction proposes a counterpart to the dominant value system, not to replace it altogether (it is usually too inconsistent), but rather to unmask the arbitrariness of the values and hierarchies of empiricism that we have accepted as normal. Throughout Doctorow's essay a double line of argumentation may easily be perceived. On the one hand, fiction is depicted as a superior and preferable system of knowledge capable of undermining secular assumptions about scientism and truth. The same kind of evidence used to validate history and execrate fiction is used here by Doctorow for the opposite purpose. On the other hand, "False Documents" unveils the intimate connections among the forms of historical and fictional discourse. Like the works of postmodern historiographers, history and fiction are contemplated as narrative constructs, cultural artifacts that are subjective and provisional. Be it "false" or "true," Doctorow's essay is a valuable document in the understanding of his oeuvre in the light of postmodern theories of narrative.

ALLEGORIES OF HISTORY AND FICTION WRITING IN *THE BOOK OF DANIEL*

Following an old tradition of self-reflexivity in literature, the literal or figurative representation of the act of writing and reading has become a distinguishing feature of much contemporary fiction. For the postmodern historical novel, this aspect is extended to include the act of writing and interpreting history. Both fiction and history are conceived of as narrative artifacts, "both wish to provide a verbal image of 'reality.' "[70] Doctorow's works go a step further in their characterization of historiography as a form of fiction-making, a proposition that achieves its fullest development in *The Book of Daniel*.

The Book of Daniel describes the process of its own writing through its fictional author, Daniel. Among the stacks of Columbia's Butler Library, during the turmoil of the student revolts of 1967–1968, Daniel re-creates the story of his parents, the Isaacsons (clearly the Rosenbergs): two young lower-middle class communists condemned and executed for conspiring to steal and convey the secret of the atomic bomb to the Soviet Union. Although the book he is writing is apparently a history dissertation on the Cold War, it is also a memoir about his childhood, an anthropological treatise concerning power and violence, a psychological study of the personality of U.S. radicals, a meditation on the Old Left from the perspective of the New, and a journalistic report covering the anti-Vietnam War demonstrations and U.S. counterculture.[71] Above all, Doctorow's work seeks to present itself as a "false document," a crossing point for different discursive modes.[72]

What follows is an analysis of the representation of the act of history and fiction writing in *The Book of Daniel*, divided into two sections meant to cover the main provinces of historiographic metafiction: the public and referential realm of historiography, and the private and self-referential sphere of metafiction. The first analyzes Daniel's representation of two historical periods (the Cold War and the emergence of the New Left), the latter examines the reflexive techniques Doctorow uses to convey his theory of the novel as a system of knowledge.

Allegories of History

All of Doctorow's novels revolve around important sociopolitical moments in U.S. history. Historical motifs in *The Book of Daniel* encompass the four decades that extend from the Great Depression to the student uprisings of the late 1960s. The novel's ultimate goal is to meditate on the evolution of the U.S. Left and to examine its impact on the nation at large. According to Doctorow, the contemporary United States owes a debt to its radical past, as of yet insufficiently recognized.[73] The notes Daniel takes for his book deal principally with the hysteria of the Cold War period, at its apex during the Rosenberg case, as well as with the critical portrayal of the new countercultural radicalism embodied by Artie Sternlicht.

Following revisionist historian William Appleman Williams, Daniel portrays the Cold War not as an attempt to avoid a nuclear catastrophe, but as one more episode in the economic expansion of the United States.[74] U.S. government and corporations sought to secure international markets to maintain and expand the country's prosperity and in this way overcome the fear of a new economic depression. The formation of military blocs in Potsdam is described as the result of schemes plotted by the most reactionary sectors of U.S. diplomacy.[75] The Soviets had asked for help to reconstruct their country, completely devastated after World War II, but were offered instead "free hands" in their area of influence. In this way, the novel blames the uncompromising attitude of the Truman administration for the expansionist politics of the postwar USSR.

According to Daniel's analysis, anti-Soviet propaganda led to a methodical falsification of reality aimed at masquerading instances of sheer imperialism as humanitarian assistance. Thus, the Truman Doctrine, and especially the Marshall Plan, were two-faced: Although apparently dedicated to protecting "free" nations from communism, in reality they sought to give military assistance in exchange for economic favors. The reconstruction of Western Europe served to secure U.S. investments abroad (290). Daniel's arguments are again in Williams's Marxist line of analysis, which tends to stress the economic aspect of U.S. foreign policy and warns about the "firm conviction, even dogmatic belief, that America's domestic well-being depends upon such sustained, ever-increasing overseas economic expansion."[76]

Throughout his digressions on the Cold War, Daniel utilizes the conventions of analytic historiography. He establishes a hypothesis that is supported by evidence, compared data, and cited authorities.[77] Only at the end of this analysis is Daniel's voice finally heard. In the midst of a minute deconstruction of the official justification of anticommunist repression as a way to guarantee the existence of the so-called "free world," Daniel remarks: "A MESSAGE OF CONSOLATION TO GREEK BROTHERS IN THEIR PRISON CAMPS AND TO MY HAITIAN BROTHERS AND NICARAGUAN BROTHERS AND DOMINICAN BROTHERS AND SOUTH AFRICAN BROTHERS AND TO MY BROTHERS IN SOUTH VIETNAM, ALL IN THEIR PRISON CAMPS: YOU ARE IN THE FREE WORLD!" (289). Daniel is obviously alluding to the Truman Doctrine, by which the United States granted military and economic support to democratic nations. Nevertheless, Daniel's list of countries tellingly maintained, in spite of their repressive regimes, excellent relations with the United States.

These brief commentaries, the selection of documentary sources, and Daniel's own personal conclusion regarding the Cold War seek to undermine the political rhetoric used by both sides to justify their positions. By Daniel's account, the U.S. government is not the arbiter of international peace and democracy it purports to be, but is rather the agent responsible for the arms race and, indirectly, a contributor to political repression in the Eastern bloc. Likewise, Daniel depicts Soviet international politics as another form of imperialism that replicates the expansionist strategies of Western capitalism. The repressive technologies of both blocs are described in a similar manner. The eradication and manipulation of the past by methodical falsification of the archive, the humiliation of political activists by public admittance of "personal errors," the fostering of a general paranoia regarding an omnipresent foe, are only some of the strategies shared by U.S. and Soviet intelligence services during the Cold War period.[78] On both sides the threat of a foreign enemy served as a powerful weapon to repress all forms of dissent and challenge to authority.

To the seeming objectivity of the *grand récit* concerning the economic motivations of the Cold War, the novel adds the emotional microhistory of its victims. Through his novel/dissertation, Daniel seeks to examine the impact that "great politics" exerts on the individual—even on the physical level. To that effect, he abandons the stiffness of academic historiography and often adopts the private tone of the personal memoir and the psychological novel. The novel's shifts toward more subjective perspectives result in an increase in the number of poetic images. Unlike canonical historiography, where the author's voice remains hidden, Daniel's voice frequently emerges to interpret the facts or to establish a moral judgment.

Through an intimate portrayal of his parents, Daniel reconstructs the personality of the radical militants of the time. For the Isaacsons, politics is a means of recuperating their self-esteem, a justification of their present suffering and a promise of a better future. Educated during a period of economic hardship and personal sacrifice, they fight for the establishment of an ideal society in an indefinite future. Unlike Daniel's younger generation of radicals, his parents blindly believe in the insignificance of the individual in the face of the transcendental value of collective destiny. In spite of the obvious discrepancies in method and mentality, Daniel's portrayal of his parents does not lack a certain continuity. Paul's obsession with making everything connect, his pathological search for evidence which is always insufficient, serves as a precedent for Daniel's hermeneutic struggle. At the end of his life, Paul seeks in the writing of letters and memoirs a way of giving his complex reality coherence. But, like Daniel, he is unable to make the final connection.

Rochelle, on the other hand, represents the pragmatic current among the radical militancy, having entered the Communist Party not because of ideological sympathies but as a consequence of her poverty ("the politics of want" [40]). Unlike Paul, who believes in the honesty of certain U.S. institutions, Rochelle radically distrusts the system. It is precisely the intuitive nature of her ideas that strengthens her political commitment to the party: "She was truer to the idea, in her way she was the more committed radical" (49). Her eschatological interpretation of history is not very different from that of the Judeo-Christian tradition: "some purchase on the future against the terrible life of the present" (51). Like Paul, Rochelle begins to write in prison, her testimony becoming a new documentary source for Daniel.

From their dialogues we rediscover important historical moments and crucial figures of the U.S. radical past, especially as it relates to the history of the Communist Party of the United States (CPUSA). Paul and Rochelle first meet in the 1930s, when the CP was enjoying its highest popularity. It was a moment when Communist organizations around the world were making alliances with other progressive forces against the emergence of Fascism, giving rise to the so-called "Popular Front." Roosevelt's triumphant reelection in 1936 inaugurated a period of political reform ("a Second New Deal") in U.S. society. In fact, Roosevelt's campaign was the first occasion in which a U.S. Communist organization gave its support to a non-Marxist political candidate. The CP publications reflected this reorientation toward social-democratic positions. Periodicals such as the *New Masses*, the *Daily Worker*, and the *Communist* were influential among the liberal middle class who harbored leftist sympathies.[79]

The period of 1936–1939 also coincided with the apogee of the nativist current of the CP as represented by Earl Browder. Elected as a General Secretary in 1934, Browder connected the organization to the U.S. revolutionary and abolitionist traditions, conferring a genuinely American face upon it. His public appearances were often graced with portraits of Jefferson and Lincoln alongside those of Marx and Lenin, and in his speeches he tended to associate his political opponents with "Tories," "Know-Nothings," and confederate racists.[80] It was Browder himself who popularized the slogan mentioned in *The Book of Daniel*: "COMMUNISM IS THE TWENTI-ETH-CENTURY AMERICANISM" (236–37). Under Browder's direction the CP reached its zenith of influence upon U.S. society, expanding to include 100,000 members. His reform effort represented an alternative to the traditional dependency of the party on the Comintern, as well as an attempt to resolve the CP's lack of relationship to U.S. radical history.[81]

The Popular Front era ended worldwide with the German-Soviet pact of 1939. This event, along with a series of new Soviet measures, marked the party's return to Moscow's leadership and its loss of popularity in the United States. Until the German invasion of the USSR, World War II was not contemplated as a fight against Fascism and was treated by the CP as an imperialist affair. That attitude set the basis for the future image of the CP as a conspiratorial movement. The leadership of the CPUSA put an end to Browder's reforms in June 1945 with the election of Robert Thomson as the new general secretary and with the expulsion of Browder himself from the party in February 1946. The new policy of the CP was directed toward bolstering its relationship with Moscow, hence their total support for Soviet repressive politics both nationally (Stalin's purges) and internationally (the occupation of Eastern Europe).

Unlike other militants, the Isaacsons remain faithful to the CP's governing board. According to Robert Cottrell, Doctorow's novel is "the first extended portrayal, both critical and sympathetic, of the Communist who remained true to the party as it moved further and further outside the political pale."[82] Although the depiction of U.S. communists has precedents in literary history (Cottrell mentions Dos Passos's *USA* and Steinbeck's *In Dubious Battle*), these were limited to a period easy to idealize: the years of the Popular Front, before the Stalinist purges ruined the international reputation of Communist parties.

The historical climax of the novel takes place during the trial and execution of the Rosenbergs in the 1950s (1950–1953). In his book, Daniel criticizes the myopia of party members in their analysis of the consequences of the Cold War. While conversing with Paul, one of the Communist leaders suggests that in the long run the repressive politics of the Cold War were going to consolidate the CPUSA (106). Although this repression was used politically by other Communist parties (especially in the Soviet Union), it meant the total disintegration of the CP in the United States. The Rosenberg trial is thus contextually placed within the larger general strategy of the fight against communism in the nation and abroad. Three historical events of great importance occurred in 1949, laying the groundwork for the trial: the triumph of a Communist revolution in China over the nationalist forces supported by the United States, the invasion of South Korea by the communist North, and the successful explosion of a nuclear device by the Soviet Union. As these events took place, rumors about international espionage networks began to spread through the media, culminating in the Rosenberg case. In February 1950, the British physician Klaus Fusch, who was involved in atomic research for the Manhattan Project, confessed to having engaged in espionage for the Soviet Union since the early 1940s. In July of that year Julius Rosenberg was arrested for "conspiring to commit espionage," as was his wife, Ethel, shortly thereafter. However, the trial went beyond prosecuting an isolated case of espionage, and soon became a trial against political dissidence supported by political institutions in a period of panic and international instability. In his well-known essay "Afterthoughts on the Rosenbergs" Leslie Fiedler suggests the existence of two Rosenberg trials: the literal one in which the U.S. justice system tried a case of espionage; and a symbolic one quickly transformed into Cold War propaganda by both sides.[83] Communist movements portrayed the Rosenbergs as victims of capitalism, while at home, they were presented as a clear example of an international conspiracy against Western democracies.

Many details in the novel's plot were taken from the historical trial. For example, all the protagonists (the Isaacsons, the judge, the prosecutors, the main witnesses for the prosecution, and the defense) are Jewish. Judge Hirsch, like the historical Kaufman, also seeks a promotion through the case (Kaufman was in fact appointed to the Supreme Court shortly afterwards). As in the actual trial, the Isaacsons are accused, not of committing espionage, but of conspiring to commit it (in which case the testimony of a single accomplice is considered sufficient evidence). The irregularities of the legal process and the attitudes of the participants are substantially the same. Similar as well is the portrayal of the devoted, compassionate lawyer who defends the Isaacsons in court while looking after their children.

Doctorow's fictional version of the trial, however, introduces changes of varying magnitude. In *The Book of Daniel* Julius and Ethel Rosenberg become Paul and Rochelle Isaacson; their two sons, Michael and Robert, become Daniel and his sister Susan; the main witness for the prosecution is not a relative of the defendants (David Greenglass, Ethel's bother), but a family friend (Selig Mindish); the judge's name is not Kaufman, but Hirsch; the defender is not a leftist but a conservative lawyer; and the name of the adoptive parents is not Meeropol, but Lewin. While these are clearly minor changes, other elements of the novel deviate substantially from the historical trial. In the real case, Julius Rosenberg was not just the unskilled electrician Doctorow presents in his novel, but an engineer who had worked for the U.S. Army Signal Corps. Moreover, the decisive testimony against the Rosenbergs was not given by a dentist (as in *The Book of Daniel*), but by a machinist (Greenglass) who had been part of the ultrasecret Manhattan Project. These two significant changes from the professional status of two key players in the real drama to their mundane status in the "fiction" contribute in highlighting the injustice of the case, which is interpreted as a hoax resulting from the conspiratorial climate of the Cold War United States. Although the novel never openly declares the Isaacsons's innocent or guilty, Paul's connection with a powerful spy ring is presented by his son as a delirious fantasy. Even when contemplating the possibility of espionage, he suggests that such an eventuality could never have had the importance attributed to it by the FBI.[84]

The Rosenberg case holds a twofold appeal for Doctorow: its inherent ambiguity and its symbolic transcendence. First, it is an historical event of tremendous opacity that has provoked the most disparate reactions among historians and political analysts. From the moment the trial began until now, an endless stream of books and articles have been published on the topic. Although the media unanimously promulgated the official version at the very beginning, in August 1951 the *National Guardian* published a series of articles in which the legitimacy of the trial began to be questioned. Since then, whenever an essay has been declared definitive, it has immediately been refuted by another one from the opposite perspective. The polemic has not waned even though part of the FBI archives were released to the public. A recent essay—Ronald Radosh's and Joyce Milton's *The Rosenberg File: A Search for the Truth* (1983)—attempted to establish the guilt of Julius Rosenberg and was hailed by the media as the final word on the case; it quickly became the target of scathing attacks by academic historians who pointed out the inconsistencies of the main argument, the lack of proof, and the authors' manipulation of data.[85]

Examples from this interpretative corpus are incorporated into Daniel's book. In his notes, Daniel alludes to six books written on the case, two which support the verdict and the sentence, two which support the verdict but not the sentence, and two in which the legitimacy of the case is categorically denied. Moreover, Daniel incorporates and comments on the apocryphal works of Sidney P. Margolis and Max Krieger, which represent two antithetical positions. Margolis's *Spies on Trial* reproduces the perspective of ultraconservative historians: "For all the hysteria drummed up by the commies, their fellow travelers, and their dupes, the Isaacsons received a fair trial. . . . Who but the very ideologues committed to overthrowing our democratic way of life can dare claim in view of the defendants' use of every legal dodge available under due process, that justice was not done?" (277). The other fictional interpretation, Krieger's *The Isaacson Tragedy*, presents the point of view of leftist sympathizers: "History records with shame the persecution and infamous putting to death in the United States of America of two

American citizens, husband and wife, the father and mother of two young children, who were guilty of not so much as jaywalking, for their proudly held left-wing views" (277). This imaginary polemic allows Daniel to stress once again the determinant role played the prejudices of the historian. History can no longer be considered an objective retelling of the past, but rather a vehicle through which historians legitimize their own ideas and views. As Doctorow points out in "False Documents": "the most important trials in our history, those which reverberate in our lives and have most meaning for our future, are those in which the judgment is called into question: Scopes, Sacco and Vanzetti, the Rosenbergs. Facts are buried, exhumed, deposed, contradicted, recanted. . . . And the trial shimmers forever with just that perplexing ambiguity characteristic of a true novel."[86] It is this ambiguity that, in Doctorow's opinion, makes the novel an ideal discourse for exploring the past.

The hermeneutic method employed by Daniel in his reconstruction of the historical case is thus a reflection of the multiple perception championed by Doctorow in all of his works. On one level, he examines the sociohistorical forces behind the conflicts that overcome the Truman administration, the interior and foreign policy of the Soviet Union, the Communist Party of the United States, and U.S. society at large. On another level, he re-creates the psychology of the victims, their family and social relationships, their private motivations, their fears and hopes. On yet another level, the book discusses the symbolic dimensions of the case and their relationship to other similar events in U.S. history. The final result is a multilayered work in which each level allows for multiple viewpoints, thus contesting the possibility of a definitive historical truth.

The analysis of U.S. radicalism in the novel is not limited to the Old Left, but also encompasses the new forms of protest that emerged and crested in the late 1960s, the era during which Daniel is supposed to have written his. From among the numerous activist groups of the time (the civil rights movement, socialist leagues, student unions, the peace movement, woman's liberation, the gay rights movement), Daniel chooses to focus on the countercultural sector of the New Left, which stands in stark contrast to the Communist militancy. The pivotal character of the novel within this context is Artie Sternlicht, reminiscent of U.S. counterculture leader Jerry Rubin.[87]

Described by Norman Mailer as "the most militant, unpredictable, creative—therefore dangerous—hippie-oriented leader available to the New Left" (251), Rubin represents that current of U.S. radicalism that attracted the most publicity during this period. Although he initiated his political career as a leader of the free speech movement, he soon abandoned the strategies of the New Left in favor of a politics of cultural provocation. Together with Abbie Hoffman he founded the Youth International Party, known as the Yippies. Through their eccentric behavior and protest against the entire American value system, they managed to win the attention of the mass media. A few of their spectacular actions are described and commented on in *The Book of Daniel*: their barging into the Stock Exchange and subsequent scattering and burning of money on the floor (May 1967); the march on Washington (October 1967) to make the Pentagon levitate (172), and the preparations for a forthcoming concentration of New Left organizations (168), which probably refers to the Chicago "Festival of Life" in 1968, one of Rubin's last public acts.[88]

Doctorow's fictional Rubin—Sternlicht—embodies some of the most idiosyncratic features of the U.S. counterculture: anti-intellectualism, antibourgeois provocation, individualism, narcissism, fascination for images, and rejection of history. In opposition to the neo-Marxist rhetoric of the SDS (Students for a Democratic Society) and other New Left groups, Sternlicht proposes direct action: "And you should hear them spin out this shit: Participatory democracy. Co-option. Restructure. Counter-institutional. Man, those aren't words. Those are substitutes for being alive" (168). The discourse of Doctorow's character evokes the anti-Marxism of the historical Rubin, for whom ideology was a "brain disease."[89] Like Sternlicht, Rubin rejected strategies and championed improvisation: "Act first analyze later. Impulse—not theory—makes the great leaps forward."[90] This shared emphasis on direct action is what leads both Sternlicht and Rubin to make "Che" Guevara and Fidel Castro into role models: "Like in Cuba they find out what their revolution is by working it" (169). Sternlicht is referring here to the guerrilla theory known as *foquismo*, according to which working within the system was rejected as too slow a path to socialism. Rubin fostered the idea of a violent uprising during which revolutionary circumstances would be generated.[91] However, Daniel's portrayal of Sternlicht emphasizes some of the most blatant contradictions inherent to the counterculture movement. Unlike Latin American revolutions, Sternlicht's movement lacks a political program and is therefore unable to move beyond occasional outbursts of irrationality; moreover, its subjectivity is susceptible of being assimilated into the system.

The characteristic actions of the counterculture revolved around antibourgeois provocation and direct confrontations with security forces. Historical reality becomes in this way a stage for the revolutionary's unrestricted narcissism. In a world in which images have replaced experience, posturing overcomes ideas in importance. Sternlicht proposes destroying the prevailing system of domination with the same mechanisms used by the very same system to perpetuate itself: images ("We are gonna overthrow the United States with images" [172]). Indeed most of the counterculture's actions were aimed at gaining the attention of the media, especially television.[92] That is why Sternlicht/Rubin considers that an event does not become real until it appears on TV. "Commercials are learning units," affirms Sternlicht (172); "every revolutionary needs a color TV," suggested Rubin.[93] Rubin wanted to make the street into a stage for his "politics of display."[94] One of the chapters of his book *Do It!* was significantly titled "Revolution Is Theater-in-the-Streets."[95] In this same chapter Rubin attacks the Living Theater and other supporters of happenings in contemporary drama. For Rubin, life itself should become a kind of permanent happening disseminated by the media.

Since both Sternlicht's and Rubin's revolutions lack long-term goals, their emphasis is on action. Above all, they seek a violent transformation of both the dominant order and the individual consciousness, only free of the rationalism that characterized the Old Left: "A revolution is someone who makes the revolution . . . A revolution happens. It is a happening. It's a change on the earth. It's a new animal. A new consciousness! It's me! I am the Revolution" (168–69). A revolution without clear goals, with neither program nor strategy, is destined to turn into a succession of spontaneous and dispersed acts lacking continuity. As a result, brief moments of genius can be generated, but it would be naive to believe they could overturn a political system. What countercultural outbursts may do is provoke changes in a society's behavior and self-expression. Here lies the value that Doctorow, vis-à-vis Daniel, finds in this aspect of the New Left.

Daniel's meeting with Sternlicht allows Doctorow to present a new perspective on U.S. radicalism, one that differs dramatically from that of the Isaacsons, and presumably shows the limitations of the New Left. Daniel decides to visit this counterculture leader in an attempt to understand his sister's insanity and the position of the New Left in relation to his parents' execution. When Daniel arrives at Sternlicht's apartment in the Lower East Side, he finds a journalist and a photographer for the magazine *Cosmopolitan* already there. Sternlicht is clearly enjoying the attention. Both his gestures and impulsive statements are indistinguishable from his media performances. In fact, his concept of revolution is almost exclusively based on provocation through images, and lacks the social program of the Old Left. Rather than the individual sacrifice that the old radicalism required of its militants, Sternlicht defends the importance of the individual over society. Unlike the emphasis placed by old communist militants on long-term social analysis, the countercultural wing of the New Left acts on the basis of improvisation and seeks immediate results. In the face of the extreme seriousness of former radical activists, counterculture proposes the merciless satire of all elements of society.

In his portrayal of old and young radicals, Daniel exposes the failure and limitations of U.S. leftism. Both Paul Isaacson and Artie Sternlicht lack contact with and deep comprehension of U.S. reality. Both are equally unable to make a connection with the historical aspirations of the working class. The Isaacsons's servility to party leadership is presented as a denial of the individual personality. Sternlicht, for his part, lacks sensitivity toward all sectors of society, with the exception of the limited group of middle-class youths with whom he associates. Daniel's central criticism of both the Old and New Left is aimed at their deficient—because limited—historical vision. In his account, the Isaacsons' eschatological vision of history blurred their perception of the present in which they were living. Sternlicht's "presentism," on the contrary, prevents him from clearly recognizing where his revolution is heading and deprives his movement of a sustained continuity.

The walls of Sternlicht's apartment are covered with a collage consisting of very diverse materials that form a kind of palimpsest entitled "Everything That Came Before Is All the Same." From a formal point of view, Daniel's description of the collage evokes the book he himself is writing. Both works are built of heterogeneous materials; both are open-ended forms (like the novel, the collage is alluded to as a work in progress). The ideological message that stems from these two fragmented works is, however, substantially different, marking the distance between Daniel and the countercultural New Left. Although similar events are constinuously repeated throughout Daniel's book, they are never reduced to a homogenizing, valueless plane, as occurs in Sternlicht's collage. In reality his book is proof that things traditionally considered identical such as the Old and the New Left, are often quite dissimilar. While Sternlicht's collage is an aggressive rejection of history (very similar to Jameson's problematic concept of postmodern pastiche), Doctorow's novel uses the forms and techniques of collage to communicate a deep historical concern. Daniel in fact seeks a way out of the eternal return proposed by Sternlicht. Like Cortázar, Doctorow historicizes the forms of modernist collage and confers upon them a political signification.

Daniel's meeting with Sternlicht's group ends with the latter singing a famous old radical song—"Which Side Are You On?"—right to Daniel's face. Daniel's book in turn is itself an attempt to find a complex answer to that simplistic question. The historical vision that emerges from his notes presents an enigmatic reality that escapes the easy pigeonholing practiced by both the establishment and U.S. radicals. Throughout his book Daniel rejects dogmatic attitudes and suggests that there are more than two sides to any analysis, especially when those who write history have been directly affected by the events narrated. The problematization of our knowledge of the past in *The Book of Daniel* corresponds to the search for a consensus on historical truth that characterizes Doctorow's works: "So I suppose my view of history is a phenomenological one . . . since history can be composed, you see, then you want to have as many people active in the composition as possible. A kind of democracy of perception. Thousands of eyes, not just one. And since we're not only talking about history, but reality as well, then it seems to me a noble aspiration of a human community to endow itself with a multiplicity of witnesses."[96]

Allegories of Fiction

Doctorow in *The Book of Daniel* explores the possibility of a synthesis between the designative and evocative functions of language. The allegorical subplot of the novel is therefore not limited to the problematics of historical production, but addresses equally the problems underlying the writing of fiction. Furthermore, *The Book of Daniel* favors subjectivity and imagination—two elements associated with the self-conscious novel—over totalizing reconstructions of the past, which Doctorow links with empirical historiography and realistic literature. Both history and fiction are ultimately seen as verbal constructs that transform real or imaginary events into narrative facts.

Doctorow's novel describes Daniel's coming of age as an artist, which coincides with the development of the novel he himself is writing.[97] This process becomes evident in the text through a series of self-conscious commentaries. The narrator initially accepts his lack of command over his narrative materials—"the way to start may be," "how would I get this scene to record?" "how do I establish sympathy?" (6–8); but as the novel progresses, so does his authority. Nevertheless, the discontinuous vision remains, not to prove Daniel's lack of skill, but to maintain a fragmentary and essentially ambiguous discourse.

In order to understand the importance of fragmentation and perspectival mobility in *The Book of Daniel*, it is also necessary to recall the details of the "real" process of its composition. As Doctorow himself has reiterated, he began to write the work "as a standard, past tense, third person novel," chronologically scrupulous, but passionless and superficial.[98] After 150 pages, he gave up his original project and began to rewrite the novel "with a certain freedom and irresponsibility." His intention was "to find the voice of the book," which eventually belonged to Daniel.[99] Although Doctorow claims to have thrown out that first manuscript, in *The Book of Daniel* the omniscient third person is not excluded altogether but rather coexists in tension with the protagonist's first person voice. This combination of two different persons—third (the social and public) and first (the visionary and private)—reinforces the paradoxical interweaving of extreme objectivity and subjectivity in the novel. While on the one hand Daniel scrutinizes historical reality analytically—"The novel as a sequence of analysis" (341)—on other occasions, he applies it to his own experiences— "The novel as a private I" (327). The most obvious example of the tension between narrative voices occurs in the alternation between the all-encompassing vision of the historiographic segments (as in the case of the debate over the Cold War) and the self-consciousness that characterizes Daniel's digressions and editorial commentaries. On occasion, the two voices and perspectives are complementary; on others, they contradict each other.

The opening of the novel itself dramatizes the transition from realist to antirealist narrative. *The Book of Daniel* begins with a third-person narration of Daniel on his way to see his sister Susan, who has been confined to an asylum after an attempted suicide. The omniscient point of view is soon interrupted by a parenthetical explanation, which is in turn followed by a minute hyperrealistic description of the scene in which Daniel is writing his book in the reading room of Columbia University's Butler Library:

This is a Thinline felt tip marker, black. This is Composition Notebook 79C made in USA. by Long Island Paper Products, Inc. This is Daniel trying one of the dark coves of the Browsing Room. Books for browsing are on the shelves. I sit at a table with a floor lamp at my shoulder. Outside this paneled room with its book-lined alcoves is the Periodical Room. The Periodical Room is filled with newspapers on sticks, magazines from round the world, and the droppings of learned societies. Down the hall is the Main Reading Room and the entrance to the stacks. On the floors above are the special collections of the various school libraries including the Library School Library. Downstairs there is even a branch of the Public Library. I feel encouraged to go (4).

This form of extreme reflexivity, along with the sudden perspectival changes, deconstruct the authority of the narrative voice. Instead of presenting itself as a "natural" account written from a privileged position, Daniel reveals from the very beginning the fictional, and therefore artificial, nature of his book.

The novel's fierce antirealism also manifests itself through continuous obstacles to the reader's potential empathy. Whenever the narration becomes sentimental, Daniel's voice emerges again with remarks such as, "Let's see, what other kind of David Copperfield kind of crap" (117). At other times, Daniel makes explicit his abhorrence of realistic chronology and linearity—"What is more monstrous is sequence" (300). Commenting on the film *The Spy Who Came In from the Cold*, he uses the arguments of realism to undermine its epistemology. In response to the thesis that the novel should be a mirror of life, Daniel ironically remarks: "Life is never this well-plotted but the picture is meant to be appreciated for its realism" (318). His strongest contempt for realist forms of representation is provoked by their inability to reflect a universe that is for the most part chaotic and fluid. Doctorow has frequently expressed the need to abandon the assumptions of the nineteenth-century novel in order to create and/or evaluate contemporary fiction: "Beginning with Daniel, I gave up trying to write with the concern for transition characteristic of the nineteenth-century novel. Other writers may be able to, but I can't accept the conventions of realism any more."[100]

The resulting discontinuity is further emphasized by the variety of materials that are inserted in the novel without transition. Apart from its historiographic and fictional components, the novel incorporates letters, diaries, biblical episodes and interpretations, travelogues, interviews, notes to the reader, reminders to the author, legal documents, political tracts, dramatic episodes, and poetic confessions. The result is a literary collage in which there is, nevertheless, a certain sense of unity and sequence. As in *Libro de Manuel*, fragmentation does not always hinder a final reconstruction of the novel's chronology. Narrative present in *The Book of Daniel*, for example, spans from Memorial Day 1967 to April 1968.[101] The novel also makes use of intermittent flashbacks that permits the inclusion of Daniel's family memories dating as far back as the 1930s, when his parents first met. In spite of several intentional chronological errors and ambiguities, most of the events in the novel can easily be situated within this framework.[102] A series of temporal markers spread throughout the novel assist the reader in developing a final synthesis, which leads us to consider the discontinuity and multiple perspectives of Doctorow's narrative in the light of film montage. In several interviews, Doctorow himself has recognized the impact of visual media on his work: "Obviously, the rhythms of perception in me, as in most people who read today, have been transformed immensely by films and television."[103] He suggests that in its construction *The Book of Daniel* follows some of the patterns of cinema and television of its time: "the idea of discontinuity and black-outs and running changes of voice and character—it was that kind of running energy I was looking for."[104]

Transposed onto the verbal universe of the novel, the perspectival mobility of cinema can have an alienating effect, since it disrupts the reader's feelings of empathy with characters and events.[105] This same effect is also produced by the aggressive tone adopted at times by the narrator. In order to turn the reader into a collaborator, the narrator must first strip him or her of the traditional literary expectations of voyeurism, character-identification, and evasion through plot. Sometimes, the overwhelming need to block the reader's expectations makes this relationship especially turbulent, as in the scenes in which Daniel stimulates and then frustrates our morbid curiosity. In one such scene, Daniel, applying the same sadism that society had exercised upon his parents, brutalizes his wife. The culminating moment of Daniel's attack is omitted and instead, is replaced by his intruding address to the reader: "Do you believe it? Shall I continue? (. . .)" "Who are you anyway? Who told you you could read this? Is nothing sacred?" (74).[106] Daniel then compares the situation with a famous sadistic scene in Buñuel's film *Un chien andalou*. The result is in both cases the alienation of the reader/spectator who feels simultaneously attracted and repelled by what is presented before his or her eyes. Although we might secretly desire to witness the act, its very brutality makes it impossible empathize with the characters in both the film and the novel. A similar situation occurs at the end of the novel, when Daniel finally decides to narrate his parents' execution: "I suppose you think I can't do the electrocution. I know there is a you. There is always a you. YOU: I will show you that I can do the electrocution" (359). On the one hand, Daniel's self-conscious remarks make our identification with the characters and the situation difficult. On the other, we are implicated in the horror of the case when we are made aware of our attraction to its most sordid aspects.

This aggressive relationship between narrator and fictional reader is a very pervasive feature in the postmodern novel.[107] It responds to goals similar to those examined in Cortázar's *Libro de Manuel.* Daniel's narrative attacks are targeted against a specific kind of reader: "the monstrous reader who goes from one word to the next" (300), that is, the passive consumer of realist novels against whom both Cortázar and Doctorow rebel. The aesthetically and politically ambitious novels of these authors demand a critical attitude from the reader, a kind of activism that can overcome the narrative difficulties of the text while also transforming the historical circumstances of the represented world. In revealing the mechanisms of its writing and reading, the novel produces a defamiliarizing Brechtian effect that forces us to judge the events from a critical distance and ultimately modify the extratextual reality.

The allegorical subplot through which Doctorow conveys the close relationship between all the components of literary communication (author, work, and reader) is crucial in understanding the aesthetics and ideologies that coexist within postmodernism. In his essay "False Documents" (written shortly after *The Book of Daniel*), Doctorow likens the novel to a "printed circuit through which flows the force of a reader's own life," as in the ubiquitous and ambiguous electric metaphor that recurs throughout *The Book of Daniel.*[108] In its positive aspect, it represents the force readers can use to regenerate a circuit that lacks meaning in and of itself; negatively, it alludes to the destructive capacity that the system can exert over the individual.

Daniel's parents have, indeed, been executed in the electric chair, and their death, described near the end of the novel, is presaged by numerous allusions to electricity. Thus, Paul is seen by his party comrades as "tireless, full of electricity" (59). The relationship between Paul and Rochelle is described as an electric current (126). As soon as they are arrested by the FBI, Daniel tells us how "there was an electric charge of life just outside" (137). Their trial is portrayed as a drama—"Frying, a play in ten overt acts" (193)—in which Rochelle feels "the electricity of rage." Electric metaphors also envelop other family members. In the physical description of his senile grandmother, Daniel refers to her hair having "waves . . . like electric wire." Susan, mentally unstable, undergoes shock therapy until she becomes inert (151). Daniel's minute description of such therapy (251) evokes Paul and Rochelle's electrocution, while its effect on the human mind is boldly compared to that produced by Disneyland on its visitors—"a mindless thrill, like an electric shock" (355). For Doctorow, this consideration of electricity as neutral energy, potentially beneficial and/or malevolent, becomes an appropriate metaphor of power in both its constructive and destructive aspects: the power of freedom and the power of the regime. In both cases, power produces knowledge. The power of freedom that Daniel exercises as a novelist ultimately generates a form of knowledge that Doctorow considers superior to both social and empirical science. The power of the regime, in turn, finds its verbal materialization in scientific empiricism and literary realism, which represent the blind acceptance of data. The idea of a multivalent fluctuating power (repressive and productive) associated with knowledge recalls Michel Foucault's "political anatomy," by which the social subject is constituted by means of power relations. Power, in his view, is not a property but a strategy, a network whose threads extend everywhere.[109]

Used by the state, power frequently squashes individual freedom and inexorably undermines dissidence. Paul's convulsions during his electrocution lead Daniel to describe the scene as a "portrait of electric current, normally invisible, moving through a field of resistance" (362). The ironic use of this new electric metaphor ("a field of resistance") to refer to Paul's body insinuates the inability of the Old Left to present an effective opposition to the repressive logic of the regime. Resistance in electric terms is not a source of energy, but an element of the circuit that favors the transmission of energy. In order to make political resistance effective in the social circuit, Doctorow seems to propose a two-step strategy: the dismantling of the legitimating apparatus of the system, and the creation of alternative forms of power channeled through fictional discourse. The novel suggests that the radical spirit take apart the ideological framework of the regime and expose its deepest contradictions. As in Foucault's philosophy, the novelist must strip knowledge of its apparent objectivity and dispose of any illusion of empirical truth.[110]

Daniel's book is offered as a discursive catalyst for forces opposed to the regime. This oppositional power of fiction is confirmed by the continuous analogies Daniel establishes between writing and political radicalism. The narrator conceives of both activities as attempts to make experience conform to artificial patterns of interpretation (40, 43, 48, 51). While realism in the novel represents the uncritical acceptance of facts and is associated with a conservative ideology, antirealist writers such as Doctorow and his alter ego Daniel seek instead to explore new perspectives that lead to new meanings. This attitude is compared to that of radicals involved in a similar search for endless connections. However, Daniel draws a line between past radicalism and its future reincarnations. Unlike traditional radicals such as his parents, or new forms of counterculture represented by Sternlicht, Daniel proposes a way out of the cyclical pattern of radical thought through a self-conscious revisionist attitude. For Daniel, the radical ends up connecting everything, at which moment he or she ceases to be a radical, as he or she has closed a system of relationships that should have remained open: "With each cycle of radical thought there is a stage of genuine creative excitement during which the connections are made. The radical discovers the connections between available data and the root responsibility. Finally, he connects everything. At this point he begins to lose his following. It is not that he has incorrectly connected everything, it is that he has connected everything. Nothing is left outside the connections" (173). The book Daniel writes tries to escape this closure through self-consciousness and indeterminacy. By means of a self-questioning discourse, Daniel discloses both the reach and the limitations of his vision, which the reader will have to take into account when analyzing the novel's ideological conclusions. Daniel's connections are presented as provisional, susceptible to revision, and never as fixed dogma. In his attempt to create a flexible system of knowledge without favoring an exclusive cultural or philosophical position, Daniel concretizes Doctorow's utopian view of fiction: "It [fiction] is but an expression of the cultural, personal, and spiritual diversity of mankind. Fiction is a harbinger of a multipolar and multicultural world, where no single philosophy, no single belief, no single solution, can shunt aside the extreme wealth of mankind's cultural heritage."

As noted in the discussion of "False Documents," Doctorow's overidealization of fictional discourse is highly problematic. Like any other narrative form, fiction is the result of mediating subjectivities and, even if its author champions "a democracy of perception," the novel's final vision will be closely related to the specific subjectivity and ideology of those involved in its production. The Nietzschean notion of the Will to Power in the act of writing history, which Doctorow has at times endorsed, is perfectly applicable to the act of writing fictions.[111] Meaning is always prior to fact and therefore every narrative, whether historical or fictional, serves to legitimize previously held ideas. Even when seeking inclusive and flexible alternative forms, the author imposes certain limits on the work's openness and indeterminacy. Doctorow seems aware of this ambivalence in his work, since many of his novels dramatize the existing tension between total openness and the need for closure. In novels such as *Ragtime* and *Loon Lake* we discover only at the very end that their seeming polyphony (its multiplicity of perspectives and voices) is really the narrative strategy of single fictional authors (Little Boy and Joe Paterson, respectively). Daniel, the fictionalized author of *The Book of Daniel*, is the work's organizing consciousness. His constant intrusiveness is portrayed not only as a way of denaturalizing the inscribed discourses, but also as a form of unveiling the crucial role fictional speakers play in all narrative practices.

Daniel's self-consciousness in relation to the problems of textual closure is thematized by the book's conclusion. Instead of presenting a definitive denouement, Daniel offers "THREE ENDINGS" (363). Although this attitude has been frequently interpreted by critics as Doctorow's last gesture in favor of openness and the reader's freedom of choice, the chronological order in which these finales are presented and their content suggest a single ending organized into three segments. The fact that the three endings are in no way exclusive and are organized in sequence, opens the possibility that the third ending could be the conclusion of Daniel's book. This multiplicity also conveys a false sense of openness that is undermined at the metaphorical level of interpretation, since the three segments present metaphors for the act of closure in relation to Daniel's narrative personalities (the Daniel of childhood memories, the Daniel who chronicles the story of his family, and the Daniel who writes his doctoral dissertation).[112] Through these three endings, Daniel summarizes the paths he has explored, rules out some alternatives, and suggests a political release from his existential dilemma.

The first of these conclusive segments ("THE HOUSE") describes Daniel's return to his childhood home in the Bronx. A black family now lives there and, although he would like to visit, he leaves without wanting to interrupt the domestic routine of its new dwellers. Through this ending, Daniel refutes nostalgic visions of the past and proposes instead a historical perspective based on the acceptance of change. The second segment ("THE FUNERAL") describes the funerals of his parents in the 1950s and his sister in the 1960s. Within the context of these two funerals Daniel presents, on the one hand, a reconciliation with his individual past achieved by literary meditation, and, on the other, the need to find alternatives to the legacy of the old and new forms of the political Left in the United States. Any radical alternative has to stem from the needs and imperatives of today and, in order to be effective, it must learn from the past. The last of the three segments ("THE LI-BRARY") brings Daniel back to the same place where the novel began: Columbia's Butler Library, where he is finishing his book. This return to the novel's opening scene does not imply a mere circular return to the origin. A deep transformation has taken place within the protagonist. Though initially lost in the midst of self-referential digressions, he now opts for a moral compromise. Previously, his ideology did not extend beyond nihilism; now he leans toward radical action. Thus, instead of discussing, as planned, "some of the questions posed by this narrative" (367), Daniel decides to join the demonstrators who have occupied Columbia University to protest against racism and the Vietnam War.[113] This commitment is presented not as a burden but as a liberation: "Close the book, man, what's the matter with you, don't you know you're liberated?" (367). Though addressed to Daniel, these words may be applied equally to the reader, since the novel's writing and reading have been presented as simultaneous events all along. Both (writing and reading) are conceived of as instruments of liberation. The novel thus emerges as a "false document" that empowers the writer and reader to first interpret and then transform the historical realities in which they live.

CONCLUSION

The novels of Cortázar and Doctorow dramatize the process of textual production of history and fiction. Through fictional authors/editors, *Libro de Manuel* and *The Book of Daniel* reflect upon the limits and possibilities of representation in a time of growing epistemological skepticism. On the historiographic level, these novels focus on two of the most problematic phases in the sequence of historical representation: Cortázar depicts contemporary history at the moment of its formation; Doctorow explores the difficulty of reconstructing the private past in a public arena ruled by totalizing views of reality. Both writers' visions of history are particularly akin to what Walter Benjamin has described as the struggle between historical relativism and revolutionary commitment. Both Cortázar and Doctorow are aware of the obsolescence of organic visions of history in a culture dominated by fragmentation and simulacrum. Furthermore, both are also cognizant of the need to develop a "corrective" political culture with the ability to transform, if not the social system, at least the intellectual attitudes that guarantee its continuity. To that end, they resort to fiction as the multiple and amalgamating genre par excellence. By means of collages made of the most diverse discursive forms (newspaper clippings, letters, and diagrams in *Libro de Manuel*; historical documents, journalistic articles, and memoirs in *The Book of Daniel*), they open up the repertoire of both historical narrative and the novel. The collage technique in these texts is by no means the ahistorical pastiche Jameson writes about, but rather the result of historicizing modernist experiments with fragmentation. This emphasis on narrative discontinuity, along with a cinematic use of perspective, demands an active disposition on the part of the reader. In the political novels of Cortázar and Doctorow, reading is not only conceived of as a reconstruction of the aesthetic object (as was already the case in modernism), but rather as a means of actively engaging the projects of social transformation proposed by these authors.

The degree to which these works are politicized and the perspectives of change that may be gleaned from their pages, differ in accordance with the sociopolitical contexts in which they were produced. At the beginning of the 1970s, Latin America offered prospects for revolutionary change unparalleled in the rest of the Western hemisphere. The mood following the Cuban revolution and the spread of guerrilla warfare throughout the region led analysts and intellectuals to seek possible strategies for the radical transformation of the continent. Simultaneously, the proliferation of military dictatorships placed artists in a moral dilemma that forced them to take a more active role in public life. The situation was certainly different from that of the United States, where radicalism during the same period was limited to more local struggles, or to cultural projects that were more easily co-opted. The politics of U.S. novels of the time were directed more toward revising the character of newly emerging movements. In spite of these obvious contextual differences, Cortázar and Doctorow coincide in their reflection on radicalism in the Americas as well as in their protest against the forms of state terrorism practiced in Argentina and in the United States. In both cases, the authors seek to recuperate a radical past that has often been forgotten or ignored.

The radical political agenda shared by Cortázar and Doctorow is at times in conflict with their epistemological pluralism. What many critics have seen as a contradiction that neutralizes the political message of their works should be viewed, rather, as an attempt to escape the political quietism and self-defeating nihilism that often characterizes postmodern thought.[114] Stemming from the poststructuralist emphasis on the local, the private, and the contingent, many of these thinkers have opted for a mystifying criticism that rejects social responsibility. According to this perspective, opposition is futile, as all discourses are eventually betrayed by the coercive forms of power inherent to them. Cortázar and Doctorow put their faith, instead, in the existence of pockets of resistance that lie beyond the reach of hegemonic systems. In novels such as *Libro de Manuel* and *The Book of Daniel*, they stress the need to develop projects for public transformation that are able to turn self-reflection into a sort of politics of affirmation. Both are self-conscious and critical in their work, but clearly state the need and potential for change. In fact, they are self-conscious precisely because they conceive of change in terms of a cultural revolution based on revision and a positive reflexive skepticism. Moving away from the simplistic solutions of the Old Left, both writers propose revisionism not only in political but, above all, in discursive terms: "only if one is self-consciously aware that 'history' like 'fiction' is provisional, continually reconstructed and open-ended can one make responsible choices within it and achieve a measure of freedom."[115] By means of works such as *Libro de Manuel* and *The Book of Daniel*, Cortázar and Doctorow contribute to the creation of a "pedagogical political culture" that can effectively help us to position ourselves within the global system of postmodernism.

5

Toward a Pedagogical Political Culture: Historical Revisionism, Fiction, and Resistance in the Americas

As the present analysis suggests, the emphasis of historiographic metafiction is neither exclusively self-reflexive nor historiographic, ontological nor epistemological. Rather, it combines these polarities within its dual nature. On the one hand, the metafictional element tends to explore the constitutive mechanisms of fiction as well as of historical narration. On the other, the historiographic aspect is centered not only on the discussion of specific motifs from the past, but also on problems relating to its textualization and knowledge as well. The ontological and epistemological space are so intertwined that it is difficult to speak of an absolute predominance of either. Metafiction and historiography thus overlap; at times provoking tensions, but just as often promoting harmony. Contrary to Hutcheon's study, which sees these two tendencies as contradictory,[1] I have been proposing a multiple relationship that is paradoxical and tense, but simultaneously dialectical and unifying.

The characteristic duality of the works here analyzed is resistant to the traditional demarcation between form and content and, therefore, to exclusively formalist or historicist readings. This study has focused on the way in which self-referential narrative techniques interact with the novel's historical dimension, and, following an approach similar to that taken by the works themselves, attempted to contemplate the formal and historical-cultural focal points within a framework in which both perspectives become interrelated and complementary.

HISTORY UNDER SUSPICION

Historiographic metafiction, opposed to the vision of postmodernism as ahistorical and depolitized, relocates self-reflexive prac-

255

tices within the context of its own production. Rather than "ahistoricism," one would have to speak of a new concept of history increasingly distanced from the empiricist prejudices dominant in academic history since the nineteenth century. In order to compare and contextualize the individual historiographic analyses of the novels of Fuentes, Reed, Cortázar, and Doctorow, we will now examine: 1) the general historical vision that emanates from these works; 2) their use of myth and apocryphal history as supplements to the official historical register; 3) their use and manipulation of documentary sources; and 4) the tension that exists in these works between a totalizing, metanarrative impulse and the microhistorical narratives of those groups traditionally excluded from the official historical record.

Historical Vision

These authors invoke the past in order to better understand the present and determine a future. Fuentes, for example, utilizes Valerio Camillo's Theater of Memory to present not only the "true" past, but other possible alternatives as well. Reed, in a similar fashion, offers a necromantic vision of history, conjuring a hidden past, the knowledge of which would allow us to understand the present from a revolutionary perspective. Cortázar conceives of a collective book whose characters testify to the convulsive reality of Latin America. His intention is that Manuel, archetype of the "new man," carry out revolutionary changes within this reality. Finally, Doctorow transforms the book that one of his characters is writing into a discursive receptacle of multiple perspectives regarding a specific history (that of U.S. radicalism), heretofore systematically ignored.

One can deduce a similar dynamic from these various historical visions in which past, present, and future remain in constant dialogue. Historical time is thus seen, not as something inert, awaiting the archeological labor of the historian, but as an open spiral in which the past is summoned forth and rewritten—not simply repeated—as a means of exercising control over an uncertain future. These authors search for a historical consciousness capable of escaping the interminable and meaningless repetition of inevitable sequences. This dynamic conception of time explains the importance that these authors attribute to the future, and leads them to broaden the temporal framework of their works, freeing the historical novel from its traditional limits. Instead of thematically confining their novels to the remote past, they can now temporally manifest themselves in multiple forms that permit an intimate relationship with the present in which they are produced.

The contingency and subjectivity that dominate the historical vision of these authors do not however imply a depolitization or absence of ideology in their works. Although they indeed favor perspectivism and provisionality, their inclination toward epistemologically subjective positions does not impede them from proposing specific plans for aesthetic and political transformation. In fact, such projects, while generally vague, do to a great extent condition the historical design of their works. Fuentes's novel, for example, reclaims the power of literature to materialize those utopias that are permanently deferred in the Hispanic world. Reed subjects his historical vision to a demonstration of the creative potential of African-American culture and to the inversion of racial and cultural stereotypes. The historical design in Cortázar's work is the result of a utopian vision of socialism as the only viable alternative to the politics of Latin America in the early 1970s. As for Doctorow, his reconstruction of the history of North American radicalism attempts to examine new aesthetic and political perspectives in the wake of the revolutionary movements that took place in the United States at the end of the 1960s.

Myth and Apocryphal History

In their re-creation of the past, the historiographic metafictions studied here consistently reach beyond the limits of empirical historiography. In the aim of exploring the dark areas of the official register, these authors resort to alternative documentary sources, such as myth and apocryphal history. As Lévi-Strauss suggests, myth is never ahistorical, because it is by nature rooted in the real experiences of the community.[2] Such experiences materialize in different forms of oral narratives that, while inherently unstable, are nevertheless always rooted in reality. Myth may deform "the truth," but it never lies ex nihilo. Never invented, it is always constructed upon the ruins of previous narratives.[3] The task of the novelists we have studied is not dissimilar from that of the traditional narrator of mythical tales. The latter is not so much a creator as an organizer, a compiler, or, as Lévi Strauss himself says, a *bricoleur*.[4] Fuentes, Reed, Cortázar, and Doctorow emulate the role of the narrator of myths in their recasting and coupling of the most varied historiographic, fictional, mythical, and magical materials.

On the one hand, myth allows for the exploration through writing of a past dominated by oral tradition. It therefore functions as a supplement to history, since it allows us to accept a reality that escapes the historical register. Fiction, on the other hand, is free from the empiricist constrictions of historiography. This freedom enables it to reorganize our construction of the world and to present alternatives that—though eccentric—may still be feasible. In the case of *Terra Nostra*, Fuentes's use of indigenous oral traditions not only reconstructs Nahua cosmogony, but also explains the traumatic clash between two civilizations from the point of view of the vanquished. In a world in which only the conqueror's version has been told, Fuentes's quasimythical narrative aspires to give voice to the silenced communities. A similar use of myth can be found in Reed's work. In *Mumbo Jumbo*, the Egyptian, Yoruba, and voodoo/hoodoo mythologies serve to present an alternative vision of the relationship between the Judeo-Christian world and African-American culture. Like Fuentes, Reed presents the reader with the history of "the other side," often inverting the myths and stereotypes generated by the official register. Cortazar, in *Libro de Manuel*, dismantles some of the dominant ideological myths through a political collage/montage which exposes their legitimizing rhetorical forms. This identification of the novelist with the teller of myths is also examined in "False Documents," in which Doctorow exhorts contemporary novelists to recuperate the pedagogical power and communal dimension of traditional oral narratives.

Within the context of postmodernism this use of myth may seem incongruous, and indeed has been the target of critical attacks.[5] As Roland Barthes affirms in his study on contemporary mythology, myth confers historical intention and natural justification on its belief system, giving to the contingent the appearance of the eternal.[6] Barthes identifies this process precisely with that which guides and supports bourgeois ideology, a process that is supposedly one of the favorite targets of the postmodernist novel. In this sense, one might doubt the capacity of these writers to present a viable alternative to the dominant ideology, since in their condemnation they make use of the same mechanisms they attempt to undermine.[7] But it is precisely this appropriation of the forms of hegemonic representation that makes these works characteristic examples of postmodern culture. In addition to the effectiveness and coherence of their cultural models, these authors aspire to dismantle the dominant political and cultural logic "homeopathically" (that is, by utilizing the latter's intrinsic forms of expression). As indicated, the transformative value of the historiographic metafictions studied here rests primarily on their oppositional nature. Above all, these works propose to undermine and deconstruct, so that new projects of representation might be constructed on the ruins of the reigning systems. Historiographic metafiction thus appears to be involved in a process of remythologization of the Americas, as a first step in the collective transformation of its sociopolitical and cultural condition.

Documentary Sources

The aesthetic vision behind these works is revealed through their priviledged use of certain motifs and historical sources. In his or her rewriting of history, the postmodern author tends to prefer the more sensational, spectacular, and eccentric versions of myth and history. This is clearly the case of Fuentes and Reed, who conceive of history as a cultural war between radically confrontational groups: on the one hand, the authoritarian political and military power structure that has its aesthetic and historiographic correlative in realism; on the other, creative imaginary power, represented by the forces of pluralism and diversity, and materialized culturally through more flexible alternative representational systems. In their re-creation of the genealogy of this immemorial confrontation, Fuentes and Reed revert to the most disparate sources: canonical myths and their myriad alternative ramifications; official and heterodox chronicles; and academic and popular historiographic works, together with accepted and apocryphal versions of the same. Any material corroborating the author's vision and contributing to the effectiveness of the narration is quickly assimilated into the omnivorous repertory of these two novelists.

One tradition especially favored by both of these authors is that of magical and heterodox thought. In contrast with science, which deals with abstract concepts, magical thought deals directly with the immediate phenomena of experience, and is thus particularly appropriate for the intuitive countersystems of Fuentes and Reed.[8] In *Terra Nostra*, Fuentes recuperates this magical tradition and its esoteric developments with aesthetic and historiographic goals in mind. In fact, memory arts, cultivated by the hermetic doctrines of the Renaissance, form the central metaphor of the novel (the Theater of Memory of Valerio Camillo), and are seen as part of a long heterodox tradition. The novel reconstructs significant moments in the history of this tradition, centering itself on the heresies and millennial movements of the Middle Ages. It is therefore no coincidence that Reed should also direct his attention in *Mumbo Jumbo* toward the exploration of the history of heterodox thought that, despite having been silenced, periodically resurfaces and influences the cultural reality of the Americas.

While references to hermetic doctrines are practically nonexistent in the novels of Cortázar and Doctorow, there remains a clear preference for subjectivist and intuitive models of knowledge. In Cortázar's work, this preference manifests itself in the incorporation of surrealist elements. In place of the dominant rationalism of Western culture, Cortázar proposes unusual access routes to the profound nature of reality. This is why the central political message in *Libro de Manuel* is conveyed through dreams and intuitions, something uncommon in a political novel. In *False Documents*, Doctorow emphasizes the difference between an authoritarianism whose epistemology and aesthetics he associates with realism, and a liberating force that adopts the traditional narrative forms of the ancient storytellers.

These authors subject history—whether canonical or esoteric—to a process of simplification that corresponds to their respective cultural and aesthetic agendas. Fuentes, for example, attributes the uprising of the townships of Castile to a revolt of the bourgeoisie and lesser nobility aimed at modernizing Spain. Hence, he privileges a historical interpretation of the events (that of José Antonio Marvall) contrary to other theories also incorporated in *Terra Nostra* (the caste theory of Américo Castro, for example). Reed similarly makes indiscriminate use of progressive or reactionary, academic or popular documentary sources in order to communicate his vision of history as a war between antagonistic cultures. At times the simplification of history in both writers reaches such extremes of caricature that the reader is led to maintain a skeptical attitude regarding the narrated events.

This reductionism is markedly less exaggerated in Cortázar and Doctorow for the simple reason that their novels have much more precise historiographic ambitions. The interests of *Libro de Manuel* and *The Book of Daniel* lie not so much in the elaboration of some great alternative design, as in the analysis of the process through which certain phenomena are textualized. In addition, both novels explore specific historical motifs, such as the evolution of radicalism in the Americas and the role of the intellectual in relation to new revolutionary movements. Although the use of documentary sources is also adjusted to the particular interests of these authors, the precision of the referents allows for a greater degree of complexity in the treatment of their historiographic repertory.

Microhistories and Totalization

One of the central paradoxes discussed throughout the previous chapters has its origin in the ambivalence that these authors demonstrate at the moment of choosing between global historical visions and microhistories of specific phenomena. Faced with the chaos that dominates the contemporary reality of the Americas, they construct systems of order and symmetry within their works, while simultaneously revealing through them the arbitrary and provisional nature of these systems. These authors present the constructions of reality that regulate our daily experience in all their contingency, and thus question the legitimacy of the hegemonic cultural forms that we accept as natural.

The impulse toward totalization is present in all of these authors, even in those less encyclopedic such as Doctorow and Cortázar. In the works of latter, this tendency appears as the search for visionary images and epiphanic revelations of totality that obsess many of his characters. It is also found in the self-referential metaphor of the book that the characters of Cortázar's last novel are preparing for Manuel. In the works of Doctorow, the novel is presented as "total" privileged discourse for the representation of human experience, an idea that first appears in *The Book of Daniel* and is taken to higher levels of virtuosity in *Ragtime*. The "Theater of Memory" in *Terra Nostra* and "The Book of Thoth" in *Mumbo Jumbo* also function as totalizing metaphors (*speculum mundi*) analogous to Borges's "Aleph."

However, in the works of none of these authors might the complexity of historical phenomena be accounted for by master narratives. The myth of a "total history" is obviously utopian, as the postmodern philosophers of history have concluded. What the works of Fuentes, Reed, Cortázar, and Doctorow present in a concrete and dramatic form is the impasse in which historiography and literature find themselves in the postmodern world, and the difficulty of positioning oneself temporally and spatially in a universe in which all the great metanarratives have collapsed. These authors tend to identify the concept of totality not with the monolithic force of traditional historical and literary narratives, but with the fragmentation and pluralism characteristic of postmodern thought. Fuentes's "Theater of Memory" articulates a framework of virtually infinite possibilities ultimately associated with the equally infinite number of interpretations of historical or literary reality. As with "The Book of Thoth," this metaphorical "theater" functions as a desirable utopia, nevertheless unreachable within the framework of written texts. In a similar fashion, the books of Manuel and Daniel in the works of Cortázar and Doctorow aspire to a totality through their formal inclusion and distribution of a multiplicity of perspectives and their signifying potential.

This aspiration to totalizing polyphonic forms leads these authors to penetrate the microhistory of anonymous beings. Their works are often centered around marginal individuals or alternative movements that appear in the interstices of the official register. In *Terra Nostra*, Fuentes contrasts the monolithic power of El Señor with the marginal and eccentric universe that he places at the vanguard of historical change in Hispanic societies. A similar vision is implicit in *Mumbo Jumbo*, in which Reed celebrates the creative power of pan-African culture through some of the figures that have escaped the attention of canonical historiography. Finally, Cortázar and Doctorow pay special attention to the impact of anonymous beings on the history of the Americas through polyvocal and discontinuous narratives. These last two authors often identify their historiographic utopia with the ideal novel. They see the latter as a global construction embracing the greatest possible number of voices and perspectives, a privileged meeting place for those who have traditionally been excluded from history.

NARRATIVE SELF-CONSCIOUSNESS AND METAFICTION

While the historiographic component tends to expand the referential spectrum of these novels, their intensive use of self-consciousness often causes them to fold in upon themselves. Although the resulting interior gaze differs according to the objectives of each novelist, we can make some general observations as to the metafictional component of these works through textual analysis. The fourfold division of the following analysis corresponds to the four levels of self-reflexivity that have been discussed in each of the above chapters: 1) the reflections of the utterance as a unifying recourse; 2) the theory of reading that is presented by the reflections of the enunciation; 3) the new aesthetics of the open work that emanates from the reflections of the code; and 4) the mythologization of both the novel and the figure of the novelist that is exposed through fictions of origin.

Reflections of the Utterance

The reflections of the utterance tend to unify not only the aesthetic, but also the historiographic component of these works. The inclusion of self-referential quotations and summaries of the novel within the novel itself direct the reader's attention to the central characteristics of each text. Such specular devices are especially useful in works that are highly discontinuous and intertextually dense. Fuentes, for example, begins *Terra Nostra* with a list of characters grouped according to function. This technique, which mimics the cast list of dramatic works, helps the reader orient him or herself in the novel's formidable entanglement of characters and events. Similar devices are used in *Mumbo Jumbo*, *Libro de Manuel*, and *The Book of Daniel*, by way of prologues and narrative segments that introduce the action and present the characters. References to the content of the novel itself are also made by means of condensing significant aspects of the novelistic project into highly compact metaphors. The nightmares of El Señor in *Terra Nostra*, the Egyptian legend in *Mumbo Jumbo*, Andrés's mysterious dream in *Libro de Manuel*, and the network of electric metaphors in *The Book of Daniel*, not only reinforce crucial ideas in the text, but also counteract its natural tendency toward dispersion, lending a surprising and exemplary unity and coherence to these novels as a whole.

This cohesive dimension of the reflections of the utterance is also observable in historiographic terms. In *Terra Nostra*, the so-called "Superfuck" consists of a card game that encapsulates the entire history of Latin America. Significantly, the players are chosen from among the protagonists of some of the greatest Latin American novels. This episode compresses into a few lines an enormous number of historical events that are alluded to, directly or indirectly, at other points in the novel, and are furthermore represented as being under the omniscient control of characters from the fictional works that constitute the novel's intertextual framework. There are two reasons for this episode's specular complexity. First, it condenses the historical and literary referents of the work in which it itself is immersed. Second, it questions the ontological rift between fiction and history, as well as among author, character, and reader. A similar function is played by the mythical tale of Papa LaBas in chapter 52 of *Mumbo Jumbo*. Reed uses a spiral of quotations to advance the central theme of LaBas's digression (the blackness of universal origin myths), which in turn is a summary and explanation of the novel's major events.

In many cases, the reflections of the utterance serve to install these novels in the sociohistorical context of their production by transgressing the traditional logic of narrative "levels," a process known as "metalepsis."[9] This helps to explain the structured ruptures that occur at the end of the novels of Cortázar and Doctorow. The enigmatic final episode of *Libro de Manuel* (the scene at the morgue) represents one of the news clippings or files that the characters of the novel have placed in the album they are preparing for Manuel. *The Book of Daniel* ends when the writing of the novel by one of its characters is interrupted by an omniscient voice situated at a level superior to that of the central events. Nevertheless, the transgression of the structural framework of these novels goes beyond mere narrative artifice. As Patricia Waugh has pointed out, metafiction constantly collates the organization of the literary work with the organization of sociohistorical reality, so that all of the transgressions of the novel's ontological and structural hierarchies have explicit repercussions in that other sphere with which the literary work is in permanent dialogue.[10] Implicit in the violation of the rules of traditional realist narratives is the violation of the social norms that sustain those narratives. Indeed, many of these works suggest the possibility—if not the necessity—of such social transgression. By revealing the reversibility of their texts' hierarchic structures, these authors suggest the artificiality—and therefore, the vulnerability—of the cultural construction that legitimates the status quo.

Reflections of the Enunciation

In contrast to previous literary trends that privileged the author, the extratextual referent, or the text itself, postmodernist literature explicitly celebrates the creative power of the reader in the creation of the aesthetic object.[11] There is a tendency in these works to channel the reflexivity of the enunciation toward a description of the mechanisms and possibilities of the act of reading. The central metaphor of *Terra Nostra* is in fact a metaphor of reading: Valerio Camillo's Theater of Memory is a magisterial summary of Fuentes's historiographic and aesthetic theories. The theater's openness reflects the aesthetic flexibility that Fuentes seeks, and inverts the customary relationship between reader and text. In this theater, the reader does not passively contemplate the action taking place on stage, but rather is summoned onto the stage, and transformed into an actor in his or her own work, an agent of his or her own destiny.

In *Mumbo Jumbo*, Reed makes use of the Yoruba and voodoo religious in order to metaphorically express his participatory vision of culture and art. He perceives the relationship between reader and work in spiritual and experiential—rather than in rational and objective—terms. Cortázar makes use of a different strategy, but demands a no less active participation from the reader. While Cortázar has always emphasized the reader's "active" role, in *Libro de Manuel* he invests said role with a clear political meaning. We discover the aesthetic and political evolution of Andrés—an evolution parallel to Cortázar's—through that character's dream, and we are witness to his final critical compromise with the historical reality of Latin America. The reader's participation is encouraged by means of Brechtian "alienation effects" that oblige him or her to adopt a critical attitude toward the narrated events and to seek a political alternative to them. The active reader is thus converted into an "activist reader," implicated not only in the creative process of the work, but also in the process of the transformation of the reality to which the work belongs. Doctorow's novel similarly posits a necessity for the reader's collaboration in both the coupling of the discontinuous segments that form *The Book of Daniel* and the radical political project advocated by the author.

The poetics of reading that emanate from all of these works also help us understand their intrinsic tendency toward totalization. The utopian concept of the total novel—a text that would encompass all possible perspectives, while remaining open to future variations—is obviously unachievable in reality. An undertaking of such dimensions only becomes possible when the act of reading is understood as an integral part of a novel's creative process. In fact, Fuentes, Reed, Cortázar, and Doctorow all find similar solutions to this theoretical problem. In *Terra Nostra*, the anti-utopian "totalizing text"—devoid of transformational possibilities—is embodied in the mausoleum of El Señor; a monument that aspires to totality, but fails because of its rigidity and closure. The only work that comes close to this amalgamating ideal is Valerio Camillo's Theater of Memory, in which totality is not the result of a unique genesic source, but subject to new revisions by the spectators/actors. A similar idea is communicated in the Villa Lewaro scene in *Mumbo Jumbo*, in which LaBas presents the Book of Thoth to the characters. The idea of "the Book" as origin, essence, and cipher of African-American culture is simply impossible, as its disappearance symbolically illustrates. On the other hand, the Book becomes a utopian paradigm for the construction of a genuinely autochthonous culture. The Book is also a collective work that materializes only by means of incessant variations that guarantee its multiple utilities and openness. In *Libro de Manuel*, Cortázar also insists on this collective and broad concept of "book," which in this case results from the participation of all the members of the revolutionary group. Manuel is the book's immediate beneficiary because he represents the incarnation of the new humanity to which the author and characters aspire. However, in addition to this inscribed reader, the novel suggests a potential reader who will participate in a similar fashion in the book's construction. This idea is consolidated through a use of metalepsis that converts the characters of *Libro de Manuel* into protagonists of the other "book" that the future reader of the novel will have to reconstruct. The militant role of the reader proposed in Cortázar's work is also invoked by Doctorow in *The Book of Daniel*. Here a critical revision of individual and collective memory constitutes a preliminary step toward political action. Just as the protagonist is involved in an unending struggle to establish connections between historical reality and the form in which this reality is textualized, the reader of the novel is forced to produce systems of coherence in a text that is largely discontinuous and fragmentary.

Reflections of the Code

If the reflections of the utterance function principally as summaries of content, and the reflections of the enunciation allude to the process of production or reception, the reflections of the code explore the underlying aesthetics of each novel. Such explorations are undertaken through discussions and declarations that unmask the mechanisms that sustain both the articulation and philosophical foundations of the works.

Among the most recurrent configurative elements of the code present in these novels are fierce antirealism, narrative discontinuity, self-referentiality, and openness. In *Terra Nostra*, the aesthetic discussions are channeled through the writer who is alluded to as the Chronicler, the Renaissance painter Fray Julián, the theology student Ludovico, and the Venetian humanist Valerio Camillo. By means of their dialogues and interior monologues, these characters give voice to Fuentes's own aesthetic ideas. In the majority of the cases, Fuentes's pluralistic views are defined by their opposition to the ideas represented by the authoritarian figure of El Señor and his somber mausoleum. The contrast between the historic and aesthetic visions embodied by these two forces is explored in numerous digressions and culminates in the passage in which the novel provides a set of contrasting characteristics for each of these two worldviews (761–62).

The monolithic and dogmatic power embodied by El Señor in *Terra Nostra* corresponds to that which Reed attributes to Judeo-Christian culture in general. In *Mumbo Jumbo*, the aesthetic and political equivalent of El Señor and Julián is represented by the figures of Set, Moses, Von Vampton, and the social realist critics. In opposition to the rigidity of the forms that conscript these characters, Reed proposes the openness and heterogeneity that characterize the aesthetics of Osiris, Thoth, Jethro, and LaBas.

Another comparative element in the works of Reed and Cortázar is represented by their prediction of the eventual reaction of the critics. From the beginning, *Mumbo Jumbo* and *Libro de Manuel* warn the reader about the inevitable negative critiques to which they will be subjected. The objections of an editor concerning the translation of the Book of Thoth, or those of a Marxist critic following the conference of Papa LaBas, are only two of the most obvious examples of reflections of the code that inscribe the potential reception of the text within the text itself. In a similar fashion, Cortázar anticipates in his prologue that the "proponents of reality in literature" will label his novel "fantastic," while the proponents of art for art's sake will view his political content as incongruous and out of place (7). In the presentation of such contradictory criticism, Reed and Cortázar unmask the personal interests that lie behind each one of these positions. The technique is therefore an effective method of neutralizing such criticism, while dialectically exploring the novel within the framework of its reception.

Two other recurring elements that are innovatively employed in all of these works are the techniques of artistic collage and cinematic montage. In every case, heterogeneous narrative materials, diverse forms of documentation, and mobile narrative perspectives are superimposed upon one another. The resultant hybrid is not decontextualized, however, as would be the case in ahistoric forms of modernist collage, but rather imbued with ideological and historical overtones. Of all of these novels, *Mumbo Jumbo* and *Libro de Manuel* present the most aggressive use of collage. Reed's work combines the narrative text with reproductions of photographs, posters, pamphlets, and etchings that are directly related to the central action. Cortázar's text deals mainly with newspaper clippings that are usually commented on (and occasionally translated) by its fictional characters. The materials inserted into both novels do not have a purely aesthetic function, but are instead politically motivated. In the case of *Mumbo Jumbo*, their goal is to invert stereotypes referring to the cultural inferiority of the black world. In *Libro de Manuel*, they provide testimony to the political violence in Latin America and to the proliferation of insurgent movements in the 1970s.

The textual fragments and multiple perspectives that compose these novels usually require of the reader a labor similar to that of a film editor. They stimulate a cohesive impulse that will activate the work and allow the perception of a final synthesis. The use of narrative techniques that derive from cinema is also reinforced by numerous allusions to films, and by the use of cinematic metaphors. Such is the case in Valerio Camillo's Theater of Memory in *Terra Nostra*, in the use of language commonly associated with movie scripts in *Mumbo Jumbo*, in the central episode of *Libro de Manuel* (Andrés's dream), and in the images taken from surrealist cinema in *The Book of Daniel*.

Fictions of the Origin

One of the most characteristic forms of self-referentiality in the postmodern historical novel consists of the mythologization of both the genre of the novel and the figure of the novelist. In some cases, this mythologization is achieved through narratives that imaginatively re-create the origins of writing and the aesthetic project of their respective authors. The mythical framework of *Terra Nostra* centers on the story of Quetzalcoatl. From among the numerous characteristics that the various versions of the myth attribute to the multifaceted hero-god of the Nahuas, Fuentes focuses on his representation as cultural hero. In Fuentes's amalgamating version Quetzalcoatl becomes a benevolent god and the founder or patron of the arts; a reformer of religious ritual and a guarantor of peace for his people. His characterization is surprisingly similar to that of Osiris in *Mumbo Jumbo*. Like Quetzalcoatl, Osiris is described as the inventor of writing, patron of the arts, and innovator of religious ceremonies. As with the Nahua god, the government of Osiris coincides with a period of splendor, peace, and prosperity of his people. Even the tales of the fall of these two mythical beings hold clear parallels with one another. The hero-gods are tricked as a result of the astuteness of their enemies Tezcatlipoca and Set, respectively. The struggle between these two groups of divinities clearly evokes the cultural confrontation articulated in the novels of Fuentes and Reed, since both works describe the battle between a hybrid, open, and flexible vision and a monolithic, closed, and dogmatic one.

In addition to the use of extant mythical narratives in order to idealize their own aesthetics, some of these authors tend to overvalue the genre of the novel itself, elevating it to the category of a total system of knowledge. In "False Documents" and *Geografía de la Novela*, Doctorow and Fuentes portray the novel as the ideal genre for the expression of the heterogeneous and changing reality of the Americas. In this sense, the positions of both authors are explained as reactions to canonical forms and to the concept of mimesis in the traditional historical novel. In the "reflectionist" vision of theorists such as Georg Lukács, fiction lacks specific cognitive power. For Lukács, "fiction tells nothing that history cannot."[12] From this perspective, literature was always formulated for the purpose of mirroring social reality, and therefore lacked creative potential at the margin of that reality. As we have seen, the postmodernist historical novel inverts these theoretical suppositions. From the perspective of the postmodernist novel, fiction tells us that which history silences, both for ideological reasons and because of its limitations. Although these novels never deny the influence of the sociohistorical context, they view the relationship between society and fiction in reciprocal terms. Social reality conditions literary creation which, in turn, contributes to the shaping of social reality. Finally, the literary imagination and the sociohistorical framework materialize textually in dialogic discursive forms, in which it is difficult to establish the dividing line between fiction and history.

RECONTEXTUALIZING POSTMODERN FICTION IN THE AMERICAS

The characteristics that emanate from the texts here analyzed facilitate an understanding of the particular forms that historiographic metafiction has been adopting in the Americas. As I have recurrently pointed out, the works of Fuentes, Reed, Cortázar, and Doctorow propose a revisionist vision of postmodernism. While they do share the historical relativism and the epistemological skepticism characteristic of postmodern thought, these historiographic metafictions also react against the nihilism created by the radicalization of these tendencies. In these texts, the formal techniques of postmodernism and its methodology are placed in the service of a political agenda that sees the transformation of cultural forms as a first step toward long-term social transformation.

In this last section, I will recapitulate the four features that demonstrate the cultural project of resistance inherent in each of these works within a New World context: 1) a vision of the Americas as a utopian space in which the writer is called upon to carry out the role of political and cultural leader; 2) the configuration of autochthonous cultural systems based on the parodic appropriation of hegemonic forms of expression; 3) the use of hybridity and amalgamation within semiotic constructs that are inclusive, open, and heterogeneous; and 4) the creation of a pedagogical and political culture as an alternative to dominant cultural forms.

America as Utopia

Since its "discovery" and colonization, cultural production in the United States and Latin America has been characterized by utopian idealism. America was quickly conceptualized as an empty slate upon which Europeans would be able to inscribe their overwhelming imaginations.[13] The Mexican historian Edmundo O'Gorman (1958) posits that in 1492 America was not discovered, but "invented," and alludes to the fantasies that in Western Europe led to the first explorations of the New World.[14] In fact, we should not forget that historically speaking, Western utopian discourse is structured and rationalized at the moment America is discovered. America has provided the two basic ingredients necessary to utopia for both Europeans and Americans alike: space and time, a territory in which to establish it, and a history with both a past to recover and a future upon which to easily project oneself. America permitted the abstract utopian dreams of Antiquity and the Middle Ages to materialize, and it served as a concrete reality for the imagining subject of the time in a process of mutual identification.[15] This relationship would survive throughout the centuries. During the Enlightenment, thinkers like Voltaire considered the discovery as a "new creation," and in the nineteenth century, Tocqueville, and Hegel would describe the Americas as future-oriented continents.[16] "Nation of the future," as Hegel would baptize it; the New World is possibility, hope for a new life rooted in a symbolic "starting from scratch." However, as Aínsa points out, the price for this youthful exuberance would be paid with the ignorance, if not the negation, of a past reduced to mere archaeological curiosity regarding pre-Hispanic civilization and the taking of inventory of so many "dead cultures."[17]

During the first half of the nineteenth century, the theories and practices of utopian socialism were played out in the United States rather than in Europe. It has been estimated that upwards of two hundred experimental communities were started in the United States during the 1800s, and that guess is probably on the low side. It was here that the disciples of Owen and Fourier established themselves, and where passionate autarchic experiences such as Icaria, New Harmony, Freedom Colony, Utopia, Brook Farm, Equity, Valley Farm, Nashoba, and so many others that, under different names, to this day have thrived.[18]

The end of the nineteenth and start of the twentieth centuries witnessed vast migratory movements impregnated by the foundational spirit of utopian thought. The utopian function during this period was once again spatial and geographic. They sought to colonize an America they identified with the Promised Land. Suddenly, new dominions available for conquest were discovered, new territories that ethnic, religious, and political groups would be able to inhabit freely. Localities that by their very names invoked the lost Paradise began to fill the new human geography of the continent (Ciudad Paraíso, Valparaíso, Puerto Edén), while the idealization of America as a land of infinite economic promise was revealed in the popular phrase "to make the Americas."

The utopian ideal, which was likewise important during this period for the flamboyant American states, fashioned America's national landscape, and later would necessarily be reflected in its national literatures. America's latent utopian tendency, originally an extension of the utopianism imposed from abroad, progressively transformed itself into a so-called "right to our own utopia," and formed part of the continent's evolution toward cultural autonomy. The essays of Alfonso Reyes (*Última Thule*) and Pedro Henríquez Ureña (*La utopía de América*) are paradigmatic of the renewal of American utopian discourse in the twentieth century. This line of American utopian thought, regardless of the differing models it has proposed, reawakens the concerns of the Americanist projects of José Martí, Eugenio María de Hostos, José Enrique Rodó, as well as the works of Manuel González Prada, Manuel Ugarte, and José Vasconcelos.

To this day, on the eve of a new millennium, we still repeat to ourselves that America is a "New World," a "young continent" whose "virgin territory" is replete with "possibility." And yet the social reality of the Americas remains closer to the anti-utopia that its postmodern writers often re-create in their fictions. The American Dream frequently becomes the American Nightmare. This aspect of the ideal America, the exaggeration of which is so obvious when compared to the real America, becomes all the more evident when the nature of utopian thought as a binary relationship between a real and a desired space is taken into account.[19] The utopian space "that is not here" presupposes an effort to create another world, an alterity that recovers the virtues of the past, a space that is projected upon the future or, more simply, is represented as already existing in another place. That *other* place, in its alterity, represents the critical counterimage to the reality it wishes to redeem by modifying the unjust aspects of its structure.

The historical tension between utopian theory and dystopian praxis distinguishes American literary production from that of other cultural traditions. In no other geographical zone do we find such an obsessive and recurrent meditation on the encounter between individual hopes and collective reality. No other space has been the target of such a disproportionate number of utopian fantasies, that in turn have been so systematically subverted. Logically, this dynamic effects the region's literary production. Historiographic metafiction in the New World completely contradicts the postulates of theoreticians such as Linda Hutcheon who deny the existence of a utopian impulse within postmodernism.[20] And more importantly, it is precisely in the works of postmodern writers such as those studied in this book, where utopianism is presented in its most intensely critical form.

In each of the novels analyzed here, this utopian dimension manifests itself in a vision of the Americas as a laboratory in which the postmodern writer experiments with new projects as a force for change. Both Fuentes and Reed are particularly explicit in their descriptions of perfect societies that, transported to a mythical past, are converted into models of these authors' cultural agendas. In *Terra Nostra*, the Toltec nation under the leadership of the hero-god Quetzalcoatl constitutes the first great utopia of the New World. This utopia initiates a cycle in which Latin Americans see their hopes for access to a just and egalitarian society alternately renewed and frustrated. Quetzalcoatl's ideal community is also a cultural utopia in which artists and intellectuals enjoy an effective power. The return to a society such as that described in the mythical pre-Hispanic past must be carried out, according to Fuentes, by means of a struggle in which those same artists and intellectuals occupy an important role. Similarly, in *Mumbo Jumbo*, the Egypt of Osiris is an ideal society in which the plastic arts, literature, and music play a major role. For Reed, this lost cultural paradise also constitutes the origin of a dynamic in which the forces of obscurantism, repression, and authoritarianism are periodically imposed on the successors of the spirit of Osiris.

In the work of Cortázar, the vision of the writer as a cultural hero is more critical and subtle. In *Libro de Manuel*, utopianism manifests itself through the hopes of revolutionary changes that still existed in Latin America during the 1970s. Manuel himself—the recipient of the album of clippings—is often presented as the archetype of the "new mankind" whom the protagonists aspire to create. The communal society toward which the main characters of the novel orient their struggle is identified with a critical form of socialism that may be placed within the global project of the New Left. Like a great many of the neo-leftist movements contemporaneous to the novel, the political vision of Andrés and Marcos synthesizes a variety of currents such as Marxism, anarchism, surrealism, psychoanalysis, and counterculture. As we pointed out earlier, Cortázar's cultural utopia appears as a geopolitical reality in the form of the Sandinista revolution in Nicaragua. In fact, the manner in which Cortázar describes the cultural gains of this revolution is similar to that used by Fuentes and Reed in the creation of their utopias; although the Argentine's emphasis on a pluralistic, all-encompassing culture is much stronger.

A similar form of utopianism is found in "False Documents," in which Doctorow locates his concept of a Golden Age for the world of culture on a vague primigenial past. In remote times, the storyteller had the power to educate and transmit the collective memory of the nations; in the present industrialized era, the writer no longer exercises a decisive social influence. Subjected to progressive isolation, the modern novelist has been transformed into entertainer with little power over people's lives. According to Doctorow, the moral obligation of the fiction writer today is to struggle in order to restore fiction to its former utopian condition.

Cultural Cannibalization

The postcolonial nature of most of the literary production in the Americas has led to a systematic search for its cultural identity. It has been repeatedly noted that the rise of the novel coincided with the formation of national identity in the New World and with the development of modern historical consciousness in Western nations.[21] Consequently, in nineteenth-century America a historical literature appeared which attempted to construct cultural identity based on those models within reach. Whereas the modernity of the majority of European aesthetic currents resided explicitly in their violent break with tradition, in the New World it would be more precise to speak not of a radical rejection but rather of a reworking of the past within an inclusive conception of fiction and history. Zamora develops two concepts of great interest when comprehending this process of remodeling tradition: "the anxiety of origins" and "the usable past." According to Zamora, the cultural histories of the Americas are dominated by a restless search for precursors as well as attempts at connecting or inventing "flexible" historical traditions. This leads to an overwhelming appetite for the conglomeration of historical elements within an open and inclusive cultural system. Moreover, this remodeling of the past implied a recontextualization of European cultural models. Often, the cultural autonomy of the New World has been created by the appropriation of hegemonic forms placed at the service of oppositional ends. The postmodern historical novel of the Americas tends to invert the analytical models of the metropolis. European history and historiography are placed in an autochthonous context in order to investigate the peculiar character of American history. It is this compulsive need to define itself that distinguishes the literary production of the Americas from that of Western Europe.

Historiographically speaking, this impulse led to the reinvention of a communal past that would enable the articulation of individual histories. These "contingent modes of historic discovery" as Zamora calls them, imply an awareness and acceptance of the creative qualities of historiographic production. The mirage of historiographic objectivity is henceforth replaced by a "narrative" concept of history. This acknowledgment of the narrative, and therefore rhetorical, quality of historical discourse has become widely accepted in both the theory and practice of international postmodern fiction. What makes New World postmodernism stand out among other literary traditions is precisely its acceptance—or better yet, appropriation—of previous models within a new cultural order in which they are invested with fresh meaning, often in contradiction with that meaning originally associated with the co-opted model. We could name this phenomenon "cultural cannibalism" on two levels: first, of European models by Spanish American literature; and second, of dominant cultural forms by the racial or ethnic "minority" literature of North America. In the latter case, this process is doubly complex insofar as it implies the modification of cultural elements of the United States that, in turn, are fashioned from numerous previous appropriations.

The literary metaphor best suited to this concept of a past susceptible to infinite revision is once again the Theater of Memory. Valerio Camillo's theater embodies the aforementioned impulse to reorganize the past from multiple perspectives in an attempt to bring about utopian projects. Faced with the mass amnesia of contemporary society in which the past is often erased or idealized, the theater (and by extension the postmodern novel as it is understood by the four authors analyzed in this book) offers the possibility of a reencounter with our origins; not in a transcendent or metaphysical sense, but rather historic and cultural. We should not forget that the theaters of memory that thrived under the influence of Neoplatonism went beyond their mere mnemotechnic function. They often adopted the form of fantastical mechanisms through which an attempt was made to store in the mind not only the image of all things, but also of all their possible representations. Obviously, this impetus is analogous to the archival reconstruction proposed by the novels in question. These texts do not attempt to erase the past but rather to reinvent it within an alternative discourse that could serve as an instrument in the bringing about of cultural utopias.

The oppositional nature of the authors discussed here is not limited to the creation of new verbal forms, but also includes the use of hegemonic forms of expression in order to express antithetical theses. This is the case of Fuentes and Reed regarding their use of documentary sources. In *Terra Nostra*, for example, Fuentes incorporates obscure chronicles of the life of Philip II in order to offer a sensationalistic tale of the Spanish monarch's personality. Similarly, Reed portrays President Harding according to the gossip of popular history. In both cases, the intention is apparently to offer a "literary" version of these figures. The historical descriptions of Fuentes and Reed priviledge the forceful portrayal of a specific psychological makeup over the tedious objectivity of reproducing economic and political data. Moreover, the selection of documentary sources also implies ideological choices. *Terra Nostra* presents the Spanish king as solitary and doubtful in order to symbolize a tendency in Spanish politics toward isolation and indecision. In much the same way, Reed turns Harding into a black man in his novel—echoing unfounded rumors—principally in order to demonstrate the influence that the black world exercised on North American culture in the 1920s.

Although exaggeration is not a disproportionate recourse in the novels of Cortázar and Doctorow, their works reveal an analogous tendency toward the appropriation of diverse documentary forms of validation. In *Libro de Manuel*, Cortázar uses and abuses the mass media in order to denounce that the new technologies do not merely inform us, but actually manufacture our vision of the world. On the other hand, many of the reproduced clippings are used paradoxically by the novel to denounce the escalation of repression that took place in Latin America at the beginning of the 1970s. In *The Book of Daniel*, Doctorow often makes use of academic formulas and of the objectivist style of traditional historiography in order to examine the hidden history of U.S. radicalism. In both cases we are faced with divergent conceptualizations of reality at the service of the same political function; one paradox among many that can only be understood in the light of the strategies of appropriation that characterize a large part of postmodernist narrative. For critics such as

Hassan and Jameson, it is not possible to escape the dominant cultural logic, but rather, it becomes necessary to find solutions from within that logic.[22] The most viable alternative—and that which we see repeated in each of the authors analyzed—is precisely that of theft, appropriation. The recurrent use of these forms of documentation often aims at subverting the system of values traditionally upheld by them.

Hybridity

Although it is true that postmodern fiction, as it has generally been theorized, tends toward fragmentation and avoids and condemns totalization,[23] the historiographic metafictions of the Americas have been producing global "countersystems" as alternatives to the implicit totalization of the hegemonic grand-narratives. Faced with modernist metanarratives characterized by their homogeneity and exclusiveness,[24] as well as with the dominant micronarratives of international postmodernism, I have been able to show how New World authors, especially those with more obvious encyclopedic intentions such as Reed and Fuentes, attempt to articulate postmodern fragmentation within global analytical models that strive to bring about not only cultural transformation, but social and political change as well. This globalizing tendency is intimately related to an inclusive impulse that is rooted in the cultural traditions of the Americas.

Concepts such as "the marvelous real" or "magic realism" stem from the notion that the most fascinating aspects of the cultural and physical reality of the Americas appear in its inclusive and totalizing capacity. Alejo Carpentier proposes in his now-classic prologue to *El reino de este mundo* that the marvelous nature of Latin America emerges not from imaginary worlds created at the margins of daily life, as in European surrealism, but rather from the heterogeneity and hybrid nature that characterize the very reality of the American continent, a reality that, as Gabriel García Márquez has stated, surpasses the imagination. This vision of the New World as an incommensurable and all-encompassing space where the most varied geographical, political, economic, cultural, racial, religious, and linguistic landscapes coexist is not free of a certain mystification of hybridity that has been brewing for some time in both the Eurocentric primitivism of modernist aesthetics and the eclectic cultural politics of postmodernism.

In the context of Latin America, the rise, dissemination, and continuity of the Baroque serves as irrefutable proof of the syncretic drive so present in the cultural manifestations of the Hispanic New World. Whereas in Europe and North America, Romanticism would be the aesthetic movement to exert the greatest influence, in the Hispanic world this would not be the case. Although this is not the moment to enter into a discussion of the reasons behind this phenomenon, it is important to point out that, although Romanticism barely evolved in Hispanic America and Spain, since the seventeenth century the Baroque has continued to generate one of the most richly varied and influential traditions in the Hispanic world. Since its first manifestations in the work of Sor Juana Inés de la Cruz and Carlos de Sigüenza y Góngora until the intricate visions of José Lezama Lima and Severo Sarduy, and considering its impact on magic realism and a great deal of the new narrative, the Baroque aesthetic has proved to be the most in tune with the amalgamating and polyphonic tendencies of Latin American literary production.[25]

Compared with the heightened individuality of Romantic thought, the Baroque privileges the richness of intertextual and hybrid components above those of individuality and originality. The aesthetic practices of the Baroque likewise favor the globalizing tendencies of Latin American literary production when studied beyond its national context. This impulse toward fusing the individual and the historical has opened the way to many so-called "total" novels in which the characters embody continental drives. Novels such as *Los pasos perdidos* by Carpentier exemplify these elaborate all-encompassing constructions founded on the basis of archetypical characters and supranational spaces and times that surpass even the boundaries of history in order to enter into the realm of myth and visions of the origin.

North American reality is most certainly different in this sense. In *Hijos del limo* Octavio Paz has explored these differences, emphasizing the disparity between the Baroque and Romanticism and their respective impacts on the cultural history of Hispanic America and the United States. According to Paz, the Baroque favors the inclusion of individual differences within a centralized system, while Romanticism favors individual autonomy within a pluralist system. However, the Romantic influence on North American literature should be studied not only in relation to the European origins of the Romantic movement, but also in view of the idiosyncratic nature of Romantic production in the United States since the nineteenth century. As Zamora points out, beginning in the nineteenth century, North American writers who were interested in imagining coherent communities and malleable histories would be forced to dilute Romantic notions of individuality by mean of mythical strategies. Transcendentalism, according to Zamora, was simultaneously derived from European Romanticism and served as its antidote, by imagining shared human traits and hence communal possibilities.[26] As a result, the novels produced in the United States during the nineteenth century are radically different from those produced in England in both their use of archetypical characters and their mythic dimensionality. A repositioning of European Romantic subjectivity occurs in which the utopian structures of the individual are placed above idiosyncratic sentimentality. For these and other reasons, Zamora establishes an original connection between the North American Romantic tradition and contemporary examples of Magic Realism, a comparison that would be incomprehensible in relation to the nineteenth-century European novel.

This inclusive, archetypal, and mythical aspect of recent American fiction helps us to understand its tendency toward totalization. As a result of their inclusive and amalgamating impulse and in consonance with postmodernism's recuperation of multiplicity and difference, New World postmodernist writers blend diverse types and sources of documentation in hybrid discursive forms. Among these authors, Reed and Fuentes demonstrate most clearly the value of hybridity and multiculturalism, to the extent that *Terra Nostra* and *Mumbo Jumbo* often reveal themselves as "genealogies" of American syncretism. *Terra Nostra* explores the origins of racial and cultural crossbreeding in the Hispanic world. On the one hand, Fuentes returns to the era of interethnic coexistence in the Spain of the Middle Ages and, on the other hand, to the period of cultural splendor that took place in Mesoamerica under the Toltecs and Aztecs. Fuentes highlights from the encounter between the Spaniards and the indigenous population the very crossbreeding that, on a cultural level, led to the enrichment of both traditions. *Mumbo Jumbo* follows—and rewrites—the evolution of African-American cultural forms from their Yoruba origins to their final hybridization with popular North American culture. Fuentes and Reed view cultural identity not as an essence, but as a permanent transformation that is enriched through contact and intersection with other cultures. Both authors favor those historical sources that underline this amalgamating concept of cultural identity. Fuentes resorts to the multicultural historical perspective of Américo Castro and to the polyvocal work of Bernardino de Sahagún to explain the consequences of transculturation in Spain and Latin America. Reed makes use of the studies of Zora Neale Hurston for all the material dealing with Caribbean voodoo and North American hoodoo. In both works, the cultural heroes tend to identify themselves with characters who register this syncretic conception of culture: Mijail-Ben-Sama, Fray Julián, and The Chronicler in *Terra Nostra*; Osiris, Thoth, and Papa LaBas in *Mumbo Jumbo*.

Although the works of Cortázar and Doctorow do not directly dwell upon the origins of syncretism in the Americas, their formal recourses respond to the same agglutinating tendency as do the novels of Fuentes and Reed. The discourses that form the narrative collages of *Libro de Manuel* and *The Book of Daniel* range from the language of publicity and the mass media to the new forms of slang. Nevertheless, they still apply traditional omniscient narrative, as well as interior monologues so characteristic of international modernism, epistolary literature, and biographical and confessional diaries. What most characterizes these discursive forms, however, is not so much their heterogeneous nature as the discontinuous form in which they are inserted into the novel. The absence of transitions and of editorial commentary communicates a polyphonic notion by which meaning is constructed upon a collective foundation of multiple perspectives.

Toward a Pedagogical Political Culture

Near the end of his apocalyptic diagnosis of postmodern culture, Fredric Jameson calls for the need to create a pedagogical and political culture capable of resituating the individual within an increasingly global context, in which the elements that would have enabled the development and implementation of projects for social transformation seem to have been lost:

An aesthetic of cognitive mapping—a pedagogical political culture which seeks to endow the individual subject with some new heightened sense of its place in the global system—will necessarily have to respect this now enormously complex representational dialectic and invent radically new forms in order to do it justice. This is not then, clearly, a call for a return to some older kind of machinery, some older and more transparent national space, or some more traditional and reassuring perspective or mimetic enclave: the new political art (if its is possible at all) will have to hold to the truth of postmodernism, that is to say, to its fundamental object—the world space of multinational capital—at the same time at which it achieves a breakthrough to some as yet unimaginable new mode of representing this last, in which we may again begin to grasp our positioning as individual and collective subjects and regain a capacity to act and struggle which is at present neutralized by our spatial as well as our social confusion. The political form of postmodernism, if there is ever any, will have as its vocation the invention and projection of a global cognitive mapping, on a social as well as a spatial scale.[27]

Over the last three decades, the historiographical metafictions produced in Latin America and the United States prove the possibility of political forms within postmodernism. The attempt to represent collective histories in which particular individuals are empowered to function in their singularity and difference is a good example of a renewed effort to draw up that cognitive map that Jameson calls for. Logically, the forms assumed by that cartography have differed in function according to the context in which they have been produced. Obviously, such openly political and oppositional tendencies have been common practice on the Latin American literary scene, and recent trends within postmodern fiction confirm as much. In the United States, these same tendencies have flourished in recent years principally as a result of the rise in collective consciousness as it regards matters of ethnicity, race, and gender, a situation that exists both in the universities and in the society at large. The purely ontological experiments of the postmodern fiction of the seventies (represented primarily in the works of John Barth, Donald Barthelme, Raymond Federman, and William H. Gass) have given way to a new generation of writers that, without abandoning formal experimentation, has made known the reality of ethnic and racial "minorities" within the country. This new consciousness has fueled the development of an entirely new tradition of African-American, Latino and Asian-American authors, who in their majority recontextualize postmodern practices within their historical condition to political and oppositional ends. Individual expression in their works coincides with communal self-definition and culturally legitimizing undertakings.

The works analyzed here openly manifest their opposition by challenging traditional forms of hegemonic representation and seeking flexible alternatives, which, although political in context, are defined in aesthetic rather than ideological terms. These works propose a discourse that has corrective public and moral implications, while simultaneously criticizing the narrow social-realist aesthetic to which political literature traditionally subscribes. The historiographic metafictions discussed here are opposed both to functional political art—devoid of aesthetic ambitions—as well as to the ahistoric aestheticism of high modernism.

In *Terra Nostra*, didacticism is reflected in the extended monologues and digressions in which the characters and multiple narrators of the novel discuss prevalent aesthetic and political realities, as well as viable alternatives to them. The novel challenges hegemonic strategies—presented as monolithic and authoritarian—by means of groups that defend a flexible and participatory ideology with libertarian inclinations. Fuentes presents these groups' activities as part of a continuum dating back to the multicultural experiments of remote periods in Spanish and Mesoamerican history.

Reed's cultural heroes are attacked—in much the same way as those in the other novels analyzed—both by the representatives of power and by the defenders of social-realism. *Mumbo Jumbo* confirms Reed's own aesthetic and political conflict. The dynamic of cultural confrontation that the novel describes leads him to seek his origins in a mythical past of established models that he believes have created the history of relations between the white West and the nations of African descent. He responds to the traditional accusation of the cultural inferiority of the black world with a chronicle of the plundering of the African and African-American systems of representation. In contrast to the essentialism and intolerance of black nationalism, Reed proposes a return to the authentically autochthonous roots of African-American culture characterized by flexibility, hedonism, humor, and tolerance.

Neither Fuentes nor Reed provide specific political alternatives regarding the extratextual reality surrounding the period in which they wrote their novels. *Terra Nostra* and *Mumbo Jumbo* are above all attempts to fathom a past from which several contemporary conflicts may have originated. Nevertheless, the degree of distortion to which they subject the historical register, as well as the extreme use of historical fantasy in Fuentes and satire in Reed, make it difficult to evaluate their ultimate political relevance.

The political dimension is outlined with greater clarity in *Libro de Manuel* and *The Book of Daniel* for a number or reasons. Both novels deal with current events related to their period of production, both focus on the theme of political struggle, and both ponder the New Left that arose as a consequence of the turmoil of the late 1960s and early 1970s. In *Libro de Manuel*, Cortázar denounces the escalation of terror that Latin America experienced as a result of its military regimes. Furthermore, the novel comments on the new paths adopted by guerrilla warfare after the failure of *foquismo*, together with the general ambivalence of political activists of the period. In *The Book of Daniel*, Doctorow summarizes the history of North American radicalism from the period of the Popular Front until the anti–Vietnam War demonstrations. Neither Cortázar nor Doctorow limit themselves to the political chronicle, choosing instead to explore the psychology of the anonymous beings who forge history. The political urgency that Latin America experienced in the 1970s led Cortázar to proclaim the need for engagement in the political struggle. The alternative outlined in *Libro de Manuel* points to active participation in the revolutionary transformation of society, regardless of its personal and aesthetic toll. Doctorow's novel—although politically more skeptical than Cortázar's—ultimately leads to a similar conclusion. The writing of *The Book of Daniel* itself is presented as a first step in a process of participatory political action. Doctorow subjects the strategies and personalities of the North American Left to a critical revision with the intention of discovering the reasons for its failure and thus permitting the articulation of a more effective oppositional model.

The historiographic metafictions of Fuentes, Reed, Cortázar, and Doctorow offer an alternative to the relativist impasse seen by some critics as the key to postmodern culture. Although the modernist rejection of the purely functional and pragmatic value of the work of art lives on in these works, these are rarely inclined toward ahistoricism nor ideological distancing. On the contrary, they try to recontextualize art and culture within a critical conception of political and moral commitment. Opposed to the immobility that characterizes the most nihilistic trends within postmodernism, these works defend the need to act politically in a world dominated by extreme contingency. History and fiction cease being the objective discourses that had formerly aspired to recuperate the past and faithfully reflect reality; instead, they freely recognize their condition as narratives whose form and content are always determined by the subjectivity of the writer and the pressures of the context in which they are produced. Metafiction allows for the exploration of the novel, and of history, as narrative artifice. The historiographic component of these works is reflexive as well. These novels not only expose their documentary sources (a common characteristic of historical works), but criticize these sources and subject them to a permanent dialogue with the realm of fiction. They do not present history as a purely extratextual phenomenon, but as an inextricable part of the discursive practices that create a changing and heterogeneous reality. Rather than the individual isolation that often characterizes literature in the reflexive mode, these novels clearly attempt to return the literary work of art to the sociohistorical framework that determined its production and without which its full understanding will always remain elusive and incomplete.

Conclusion

The historiographic metafictions of Fuentes, Reed, Cortázar, and Doctorow are paradigmatic of the most dramatic paradoxes faced by postmodernism in the Americas. These works fluctuate between self-reflexivity and historical revisionism; between multivocal open forms and totalizing projects of representation; between democratic invitations to the reader's participation and doctrinaire intentions; between an increasing historical relativism and the concomitant need to preserve the past in our memories. This ambivalence is frequently the result of the coexistence of different styles and conflicting ideologies within the works themselves; hence the terms "double view" (Hassan), "double talk" (Hutcheon), and "double coding" (Jencks), used to define postmodernism's ambiguous repertoire.[1] These authors, rather than conceal such paradoxes, bring them to the foreground. Their novels become forums in which conflicting aesthetic and political ideas are debated. In this conclusion, I shall once again address the concepts of postmodernism discussed in chapter 1, contrast them with my readings and, finally, make a determination as to their theoretical effectiveness in an inter-American context.

The works examined in this study respond to what Ihab Hassan considers postmodernism's deconstructionist thrust. Hassan regards the disarticulation of all forms of authority—and especially of all central principles of literature—as the governing principle behind postmodern texts.[2] These works are transgressive in their frequent use of narrative points of view that shatter the basic assumptions of realism. They utilize intrusive narrators who openly discuss the arbitrariness of novelistic conventions and the limitations of any historical perspective. They make use of multiple narrative voices and mobile vantage points that contradict the monologic power of conventional representations, producing a polyphonic effect on the reader ("a democracy of perception," in Doctorow's words). This formal openness is the product of an ideology that is opposed to hegemonic cultural systems and celebrates plurality as a supreme value. Rather than the elitism, monolithism, and centralization that characterize institutionalized culture, these authors foster a difference-based ideology that celebrates the role of marginal groups and local cultures.

There is, however, one important feature of Hassan's postmodern catena that these novels problematize: the rejection of all forms of totalization. Although the assault on organicism in both fiction and history constitutes one of their central motifs, in some of these works—especially those of Fuentes and Reed—there is a tendency toward macrohistorical representations, toward encyclopedic and all-encompassing visions of the cultural history of the Americas. In fact, *Terra Nostra* and *Mumbo Jumbo* may be described as novels searching for a utopian global synthesis of the Indian-Spanish-American and African-American cultures, respectively. This inclination, of course, assumes a postmodern stance due to its ambiguous, plural, and fragmentary nature. Therefore, the proclivity to totalization of these works is often subjected to parody, as happens in *Terra Nostra* with the metaphor of El Escorial and in *Mumbo Jumbo* with the allegorical scene of recognition in Villa Lewaro. However, it would be inappropriate to speak of any synthesis as the "ultimate opprobrium" for these authors.[3]

As for McHale's concept of postmodernism, the texts analyzed contradict his theory of an "ontological dominant" in this movement. In addition to their concern with the materiality of narrative artifacts and their relationship to other discursive universes, these works address with equal (or superior) intensity key epistemological and political questions: What is the nature of the past? How is our knowledge of the past produced? How is that knowledge transmitted? How does a particular vision get sanctioned? How can we produce alternative versions of these vision? How can we make them politically effective? These are questions that go much farther than merely implying an ontological exploration of the text and the world. In cases such as the novels of Cortázar and Doctorow, epistemological problems actually dominate the narrative. *Libro de Manuel* and *The Book of Daniel* explore, above all, the process of production and transmission of historical knowledge, as well as the moral demand placed upon intellectuals engaged in their own political reality. Although these two issues might relate indirectly to ontological questions (any philosophical exploration involves a certain amount of study of the nature of the elements implied by it), they escape what McHale considers to be the specific realm of postmodernism.

McHale's analysis is helpful, however, when examining the historical and literary revisionism that he attributes to postmodernism.

Through apocryphal and fantastic historical narratives, these authors seek both to question the problematic borderline between fiction and reality, and to revise the historical register—if not to replace it all together—with a more flexible and multifaceted vision. As in much contemporary historiography, official history is conceived of as a construct that has traditionally served the interests of the powerful. In removing the focus from official historiographic discourse and bringing it to bear on those groups previously excluded or silenced by it (radicals, heretics, visionaries, "Third World" artists, craftsmen, "minorities"), these works try "to redress the balance of the historical record."[4]

This revisionist tendency in postmodern historical fiction proves the existence of a strong adversary ethos in contemporary culture that could very well constitute what some critics have identified as a "postmodernism of resistance."[5] Confronted by the strategies of simulation that dominate consumer society together with the elitism of institutionalized high culture, the historiographic metafictions of the Americas provide alternatives that evoke those briefly outlined by Fredric Jameson. While in his earlier theorizations Jameson had manifested his skepticism regarding the possibility of any emancipatory trend in postmodernism,[6] in his later contributions he suggests some practical solutions to the present impasse of postmodern culture. He mentions in particular the possibility of undoing the dominant culture homeopathically.[7] This strategy of dissolving from within (described also by Hutcheon, albeit from a different perspective) is put into practice by these authors through their appropriation of the dominant forms of legitimation. Reed, for example, inverts the stereotypes concerning the cultural inferiority of the black world by resorting to precisely those types of documentary validation that had been used to perpetuate such stereotypes. The evidence used to sanction one version of the past is thus creatively reorganized to prove its opposite. In the case of Cortázar, the mass media are used to document a reality that they too often ignore, when they do not deform or pervert it. In a like manner, Fuentes and Doctorow present in their works a dynamic of cultural confrontation in which hegemonic strategies of representation are inscribed and then subverted and in which alternative models are tested. In contrast to the vision of postmodernism as an ahistorical and narcissistic movement, the works of these authors offer deep reflections on history and on the textual form in which it is transmitted and recreated.

Of the three conceptualizations of postmodernism that I have been discussing, the poetics of Linda Hutcheon provide the most suitable approach to the analysis of postmodern historical fiction in the Americas. It was, indeed, Hutcheon who coined the term "historiographic metafiction" and provided it with a global theory. In the areas of intertextuality, referentiality, and subjectivity, my readings of the works selected correspond to her vision of a problematizing postmodernism. As in Hutcheon's analysis, intertextuality in these works is not limited to an occasional reference to other texts of the literary and historiographic traditions, but also extends to popular and mass culture. This hybridization of genres and multiple discursive practices tends to problematize the referent in conventional forms of representation, and ultimately aims at establishing the textual nature of our experience of the world. According to the epistemology of realism, the referent is a prelinguistic reality ("the total objective process of life");[8] for historiographic metafiction, every referent is itself always textual and thus mediated by other texts. In contrast to the apocalyptic dismissal of the referent,[9] these works claim that it has not disappeared, but has, in fact, ceased to be simple and unproblematic. It has become unstable and textual. This "textualization" of the referent also implies a questioning of the human subject as knower of an objective and passive world. Hutcheon associates this subject with the Western, bourgeois, white, individual, and male subject who has traditionally obtained his power by masking himself as eternal, universal, and humanistic. In contrast to this subject's pretensions of objectivity and a sense of the common good, historiographic metafiction affirms that any enunciative act is always mediated and serves particular interests.

It is the global character of Hutcheon's approach, however, that sometimes leads to misunderstandings. Works from very dissimilar cultural traditions are interpreted within the same paradigm, ignoring the specific context in which they were produced. Although crucial for understanding the new forms of historical fiction, her conceptualization of postmodernism as a style that articulates self-consciousness and a new sense of history must be complemented by a deeper and more extensive contextual analysis. My reading of the novels of Fuentes, Reed, Cortázar, and Doctorow, has uncovered certain features that call into question two recurrent generalizations in Hutcheon's poetics: the incompatibility of their metafictional and historiographic components; and the consideration of these works as being politically "unmarked."

Although Hutcheon posits a lack of synthesis between the metafictional and the historiographic realms,[10] my analysis reveals a relationship that is not always antagonistic, and, in fact, can often prove to be mutually illuminating. The study of the different levels

of self-reflexivity in these works has revealed how specular metaphors and self-conscious digressions tend to consolidate, rather
than obliterate, their historical vision. Since these fictions deal extensively with history, and regard history itself as an ideologically
constructed fiction, self-referentiality does not imply a solipsistic
withdrawal from the "real" world, but a probing into the very nature of that world. The different varieties of the *mise en abyme* in
these works tend to effect a semantic compression of their own referents, both literary and historical. A frequent shortcoming of this
compressive strategy is the simplification of very complex aesthetic
and historical issues; nevertheless, in no case is it possible to establish a clear-cut distinction—let alone an opposition—between these
two aspects of the novels under discussion. Self-reflexivity and historiography are not invariably separate, as Hutcheon suggests, but
frequently elucidate one another and lead to successful syntheses.

On the other hand, Hutcheon considers that postmodern works
are politically "unmarked," in that they install and subvert the
dominant strategies of representation, while remaining neither completely complicitous nor totally transgressive. This supposed absence of both a concrete political attitude and a clear orientation
toward the future made Hutcheon to deny the existence of utopianism in postmodern thought,[11] a point that my analysis questions, at
least in an inter-American context. As suggested in each chapter,
the possibility of reordering a more just society along idealized
lines has been a conceptual determinant in the development of New
World cultures, and, even in the skeptical context of postmodernism, this determinant still plays an important role. Although all of
the works I have studied present a problematic view of the materialization of these utopian ideas (the New World's current reality is
often described as anti-utopian), these same ideals paradoxically in-
spire the aesthetic and political projects of many contemporary authors of the Americas.

As for the political aim of these works, Hutcheon's generalizations also need clarification. The main political target in Latin
American novels such as *Terra Nostra* and *Libro de Manuel* is not
the "liberal humanism" of bourgeois ideology, but rather the feudal, oligarchic, and totalitarian practices that were dominant in the
Hispanic world in the time of their production. Although in *Libro
de Manuel* Cortázar recognizes the interrelatedness of different
forms of social, sexual, and political control, his diatribe focuses on
the escalation of military repression in Latin America during the
1970s. One of the central historical problems in *Terra Nostra* is the
permanent backwardness of the Hispanic world in relation to mo-

dernity. Rather than confronting humanism, Fuentes values its relative advantages in comparison with the quasifeudal institutions imported from Spain. As far as the novels of Reed and Doctorow are concerned, their political targets are also more specific than Hutcheon's vague concept of "liberal humanism." Although *Mumbo Jumbo* and *The Book of Daniel* undermine the aesthetic postulates that Hutcheon assigns to that ideology (that is, realism, coherent subjectivity, monological narration, centralization, stable historical referents), the names of their political enemies are more specific. Reed's novel aims its biting satire at the cultural imperialism of "white" Western societies and Doctorow attacks the intolerant North America of the Cold War. Although all of these works engage in a similar assault on bigotry, especially on an aesthetic level, their targets can hardly be identified with the same hegemonic practice in politics.

The similarities and differences between textual analysis and the theoretical foundations of the postmodernism debate prove the need for contextualization in literary and cultural studies. All global theories of postmodernism—in order to be truly ecumenical—must take into account the sociocultural conditions not only of the old hegemonic centers (Europe and the United States), but of the periphery as well (Latin America and the rest of what has been traditionally called the Third World). This need for respecting difference is particularly strong in the Americas, where multiple stages of cultural and economic development coexist and produce characteristic literary forms.

Having arrived this far, it is worth reiterating the importance of an inter-American focus in the analysis of postmodern fiction. No doubt that many of the characteristics that have been studied in this book (self-referentiality, experimentation, historiographic revisionism) can be found in novels produced in other geographical areas. The historiographic metafictions of Juan Goytisolo or Salman Rushdie represent but two examples of literary sensibilities analogous to those of the authors studied here. In the present era of increasing globalization, it is no longer possible to posit the existence of pure, impermeable, and stagnant literary traditions. If there is one element that distinguishes international postmodern fiction, it is the ability to absorb—oftentimes indiscriminately—traditions and influences within a fluid concept of culture as an open arena for the exchange of diverse and often contradictory ideas. However, this does not mean that these texts fail to share a significant number of formal and contextual elements that permit their study from a hemispheric perspective. Fuentes, Reed, Cortázar, and Doctorow have generally been studied within their respective national traditions, as well as in relation to their supposed European models. At times this pathological search for European literary influences has led to absurd comparisons, albeit at minimal risk to the academic reputation of the critic. However, every time an inter-American approach is attempted, suspicions arise. That incessant—and at times enervating—question, "Why the Americas?" to which I referred in the introduction, pursues each critic who dares to attempt a comparative analysis of New World literature. On occasion I have been tempted to respond with a similar question: "Why not?" And yet beyond the legitimacy that any comparative focus deserves, there are many reasons that propel me not only to continue adopting this perspective, but that oblige me to do so. The Americas constitute a vast complex of cultural traditions among which similar ideas have flowed, and yet they have never been the object of a continuous and consistent comparative analysis. The differences that exist among the cultural productions of the hemisphere are naturally evident and multiple. They have to be. As Chevigny, Laguardia, and Zamora have emphasized, we are dealing with thirty-five nations and fifteen territories or protectorates, in which four major Indo-European languages are spoken together with innumerable Amerindian tongues, and where 675 million inhabitants, who practice an incalculable number of religions, inhabit more that sixteen million square miles of territory.[12] The truly surprising reality is the existence of common ground among so many national, linguistic, demographic, and religious contexts. This basic fact is in and of itself sufficient to justify a New World perspective.

In the final section of chapter 5 I summarized the common traits among postmodern fiction in the Americas. Above all, the cultural traditions of the United States and Latin America were founded on utopian thought, a factor that has undoubtedly effected their literary production, including that analyzed today within the context of postmodernism. Contrary to the militant anti-utopianism of international postmodernism, American writers have not ceased to produce an oppositional discourse in which they tend to present cultural utopias that serve as alternatives to the dystopic realities of their nations. Moreover, the postcolonial condition of a considerable part of the literature produced in the New World has led to a long process of construction and reconstruction of identity on the basis of a respect for difference. This obsessive search for identity has often led to the appropriation of hegemonic forms of representation within amalgamating semiotic systems that fuse with a rich multicultural tradition. Although it is true that the fundamentally hybrid nature of the cultures of the Americas has too often become an easy postmodern cliché, it is also true that racial, religious and cultural hybridity constitute an undeniable aspect of the reality of the United States and Latin America. As a counterpart to the divergent states of economic development among its nations, we may add their culturally heterogeneous constitution in which the most varied forms of expression turbulently coexist.

The historiographic metafictions of Fuentes, Reed, Cortázar, and Doctorow make such heterogeneity the basis of their historical and aesthetic visions. All of these works share a similar penchant for impure forms, albeit in differing degrees. They favor the historiographic pastiche of multiple and ideologically heterogeneous documentary sources that communicate an emotional and intuitive vision of history. In opposition to the old ethnocentric paradigm of purity as a condition for the flowering of civilizations, these works see in crossbreeding and transculturation an endless source of richness. In their enthusiastic celebration of multiculturalism, these authors seek forms capable of respecting the amalgamating latencies in the cultures of the Americas. Because of its flexibility, formal eclecticism, and visionary potential, the genre of the novel is treated as a privileged scenario for a revision of the past. Through a mixture of myth, academic and popular histories, esoteric doctrines, and their own respective literary traditions, these writers convey through their novels an alternative vision to that inherited from the official register.

Unlike the traditional forms of the historical novel, these metafictions discuss the past in a self-reflexive manner. This is not an insoluble contradiction, as some critics have suggested. That the novel can refer to itself does not mean that it cannot also refer to the outside world. Indeed, this self-reflexivity is contemplated as a necessary element effecting all of the novel's referents. History is not conceived of as an objective realm that can be "encapsulated" by a purely denotative language, but as a problematic and shifting discourse that reflects on the past from the writer's ideologically positioned present. This revision of the nature and function of historical discourse is not limited to a questioning of the legitimating principles of the officially sanctioned historical truth, but also has a liberating value present in the very act of its production. The opening of a new space for the creation of alternative histories facilitates the access of marginal groups to the register. Moreover, the self-consciousness of this discursive space allows for a critical knowledge of both the dominant discourses and their possible alternatives; something that is essential in effecting any cultural or political change.

The articulation of self-reflexivity and historiography in the works studied results in hybrid forms that represent and celebrate the cultural heterogeneity of the Americas. Hegemonic forms of validation are often inverted and placed in the service of an alternative worldview. These works create new representational structures that seek to complement or to displace dominant mimetic systems. Although their novels are essentially documentaries in which past and present historical realities are debated, these four authors open new prospects of change for the future. In this sense, they are particularly interested in the critical analysis of the current postmodern condition with the intention of exploring the possibility of its integral democratization. In contrast to the dominant epistemological skepticism that has too often led to political passivity and nihilism, these authors propose a radical and resistant culture that could well serve as a model for the political transformation of their respective societies. Through their self-conscious narratives, Fuentes, Reed, Cortázar, and Doctorow aim at reinventing history and fiction as open and fluid systems that offer alternative ways of perceiving and experiencing the New World.

Notes

In citing primary sources in the notes, short titles have generally been used. Works frequently cited have been identified by the following abbreviations:

AAAC	*Argentina: años de alambradas culturales* (Julio Cortázar)
CCL	*Cervantes o la crítica de la lectura* (Carlos Fuentes)
EE	*El espejo enterrado* (Carlos Fuentes)
LM	*Libro de Manuel* (Julio Cortázar)
BD	*The Book of Daniel* (E. L. Doctorow)
EC	*Essays and Conversations* (E. L. Doctorow)
MJ	*Mumbo Jumbo* (Ishmael Reed)
NCP	*New and Collected Poems* (Ishmael Reed)
NNH	*La nueva novela hispanoamericana* (Carlos Fuentes)
NTVD	*Nicaragua tan violentamente dulce* (Julio Cortázar)
SIONO	*Shrovetide in Old New Orleans* (Ishmael Reed)
TN	*Terra Nostra* (Carlos Fuentes)
UR	*Último Round* (Julio Cortázar)
VAUM	*Viaje alrededor de una mesa* (Julio Cortázar)
VDOM	*La vuelta al día en ochenta mundos* (Julio Cortázar)
WIF	*Writin' Is Fightin': Thirty-Seven Years of Boxing on Paper* (Ishmael Reed)

All translations in the book are mine unless otherwise noted.

INTRODUCTION: PROSPECTS FOR AN INTER-AMERICAN APPROACH TO POSTMODERN FICTION

1. Gustavo Pérez Firmat, ed., *Do the Americas Have a Common Literature?* (Durham, N.C.: Duke University Press, 1990), 2. There are, however, a few exceptions to this rule. In recent years some critics have shown an increasing concern for inter-American literary studies. As a result, several comparative books and collections have been published. In addition to Pérez Firmat's anthology, see Bell Gale Chevigny and Gari Laguardia, eds., *Reinventing the Americas: Comparative Studies of Literature of the United States and Spanish America* (New York: Cambridge University Press, 1986); Alfred Mac Adam, *Textual Confrontations: Comparative Readings in Latin American Literature* (Chicago: The University of Chicago Press, 1987); Lois Parkinson Zamora, *Writing the Apocalypse: Historical Vision in Contemporary U.S. and Latin American Fiction* (New York: Cambridge University Press, 1989), and *The Usable Past: The Imagination of History in Recent Fiction of the Americas* (New York: Cambridge University Press, 1997); José

David Saldívar, *The Dialectics of Our America: Genealogy, Cultural Critique, and Literary History* (Durham, N.C.: Duke University Press, 1991); Earl Fitz, *Rediscovering the New World: Inter-American Literature in a Comparative Context* (Iowa City: University of Iowa Press, 1991); and Johnny Payne, *Conquest of the New World: Experimental Fiction and Translation in the Americas* (Austin: University of Texas Press, 1993).

2. To my knowledge, the only meeting of that kind was the 1989 Novel of the Americas Symposium held at the University of Colorado at Boulder. The conference proceedings are available in Raymond Leslie Williams, ed., *The Novel in the Americas* (Boulder: University Press of Colorado, 1992).

3. Roberto González Echevarría, *Myth and Archive: A Theory of Latin American Narrative* (Cambridge, Mass.: Cambridge University Press, 1990), 28.

Chapter 1. Historiographic Metafiction in the Context of Postmodernism Theory

1. Molly Hite's comments on the term summarize its paradoxical nature: "The 'post' in 'postmodernism' signifies both a temporal condition (postmodernism is a period after modernism and thus in certain respects an evolution from it) and an attitude of resistance (postmodernism is a turn away from modernism and thus in certain respects a radical break with it). Postmodernism is thus both a late modernism and an antimodernism." "Postmodern Fiction," in *The Columbia History of the American Novel*, ed. Emory Elliott (New York: Columbia University Press, 1991), 697.

2. Fredric Jameson, *Postmodernism, or the Cultural Logic of Late Capitalism* (Durham, N.C.: Duke University Press, 1991), 1; Linda Hutcheon, *A Poetics of Postmodernism: History, Theory, Fiction* (New York: Routledge, 1988), 8; David Harvey, *The Condition of Postmodernity* (Oxford: Blackwell, 1989), 7.

3. As Charles Jencks points out, Hassan's 1971 article "POSTmodernISM: A Paracritical Bibliography" both "christened" postmodernism and "provided a pedigree" for it. *The Post-Modern Reader* (London: Academy Editions, 1992), 21.

4. Ihab Hassan, *The Dismemberment of Orpheus: Towards a Postmodern Literature* (Madison: University of Wisconsin Press, 1982).

5. Some of the near sixty names include J. Derrida, J. F. Lyotard, M. Foucault, H. White, J. Lacan, J. Baudrillard, T. Kuhn, P. Feyerabend, R. Barthes, J. Kristeva, W. Iser, J. Cage, K. Stockhausen, R. Venturi, S. Beckett, E. Ionesco, J. L. Borges, V. Nabokov, H. Pinter, P. Handke, G. García Márquez, J. Cortázar, A. Robbe-Grillet, J. Barth, W. Burroughs, T. Pynchon, D. Barthelme, and S. Shepard. Hassan, *The Dismemberment of Orpheus*, 260.

6. Ibid. Although Hassan's ascription of works and authors to each of these currents is truly problematic and reflects the typical shortcomings of all pioneering works, he admits being aware of the three major limitations in his study: the artificial character of all literary movements; the inconsistencies inherent in any description of new phenomena; and the difficulty of establishing any deconstructionist canon.

7. Leslie Fiedler, "Close the Border—Close the Gap," in *The Collected Essays of Leslie Fiedler* (New York: Stein and Day, 1971), 2:115–31.

8. Hassan, *The Dismemberment of Orpheus*, 267–68.

9. Ihab Hassan, *The Postmodern Turn: Essays in Postmodern Theory and Culture* (Columbus: Ohio State University Press, 1987), 172.

10. Steven Connor, *Postmodernist Culture: An Introduction to Theories of the Contemporary* (Oxford: Blackwell, 1989), 112.

11. Roman Jakobson, "The Dominant," in *Readings in Russian Poetics: Formalist and Structuralist Views*, eds. Ladislav Matejka and Krystyna Pormorska (Cambridge: MIT Press, 1971), 105–10.

12. Roman Ingarden, *The Literary Work of Art: An Investigation on the Borderlines Between Ontology, Logic, and the Theory of Literature* (Evanston,Ill.: Northwestern University Press, 1973), 30.

13. Brian McHale, *Postmodernist Fiction* (New York: Methuen, 1987).

14. Ibid., 45.

15. Ingarden, *The Literary Work of Art*, 246.

16. McHale, *Postmodernist Fiction*, 9.

17. Fredric Jameson, "Postmodernism and Consumer Society," in *The Anti-Aesthetic: Essays On Postmodern Culture*, ed. Hal Foster (Seattle, Wash.: Bay Press, 1983), 111–25.

18. Ibid., 115.

19. "Postmodernism, or the Cultural Logic of Late Capitalism" (*New Left Review* 146 [1984]: 53–92) consists of a revised and substantially enlarged version of Jameson's seminal work "Postmodernism and Consumer Society." Subsequent parenthetical references refer to the last version (1991), which figures as chapter 1 in the book *Postmodernism, or the Cultural Logic of Late Capitalism*, 1–54.

20. Ibid., 48.

21. Although on this occasion Jameson does not end his essay with a question, he does end it with a proposal that opens new queries. Jameson himself appears to be somewhat skeptical concerning the real possibility of his utopian program ("if there is any," he says laconically). In recent essays and interviews, his attitude is certainly more positive. For example, he suggests the use of "homeopathical techniques"—or techniques of appropriation—in order to fight postmodernism from within: "To undo postmodernism homeopathically by the methods of postmodernism: to work at dissolving the pastiche by using all the instruments of pastiche itself, to reconquer some genuine historical sense by using the instruments of what I have called substitutes for history." Douglas Kellner, ed., *Postmodernism / Jameson / Critique* (Washington D.C.: Maisonneuve Press, 1989), 59. See also Jameson's review of Don DeLillo's *The Names*, in *The Minnesota Review* 22 (1984): 117–22, for a positive evaluation of some postmodernist practices.

22. Linda Hutcheon's criticism reflects the changes experienced by the theory and practice of Anglo-American postmodernism. The publication of *Narcissistic Narrative: The Metafictional Paradox* (New York: Methuen, 1984) coincides with a transitional period between the rise of reception theory and the consolidation of New Historicism. One proof of these changes in the orientation of criticism is the preface that Hutcheon wrote for the second edition of her essay on metafiction. In this preface, she offers a veiled mea culpa for her previous formalist orientation, expressing her new interest in historiographic and cultural studies. The use (albeit still reticent) of the term "postmodernism" instead of metafiction, and the coining of the concept of historiographic metafiction to express what Hutcheon considers the paradigm of postmodernist narrative, also point in this direction.

23. Frank Lentricchia, *After the New Criticism* (Chicago: University of Chicago Press, 1980), xiii.

24. Hutcheon, *A Poetics of Postmodernism*, x.

25. Linda Hutcheon, *The Politics of Postmodernism* (New York: Routledge, 1989), 19.

26. Hutcheon, *A Poetics of Postmodernism*, xiii.

27. Fredric Jameson, "Third-World Literature in the Era of Multinational Capitalism." *Social Text* 15 (1986): 65–88.

28. Ibid., 69.

29. Ibid.

30. Within the Latin American literary context, Jameson's theses have been incisively refuted by Jean Franco, "The Nation as Imagined Community," in *The New Historicism*, ed. H. Aram Veeser (New York and London: Routledge, 1989), 204–12; George Yúdice, "Postmodernity and Transnational Capitalism in Latin America," in *On Edge: The Crisis of Contemporary Latin American Culture*, eds. Yúdice et al. (Minneapolis and London: University of Minnesota Press, 1992), 1–28; and Santiago Colás, *Postmodernity in Latin America: The Argentine Paradigm* (Durham, N.C.: Duke University Press, 1994). For an example of how the concept of the Third World novels as national allegories is parodied in contemporary fiction, see Santiago Juan-Navarro, "The Dialogic Imagination of Salman Rushdie and Carlos Fuentes: National Allegories and the Scene of Writing in *Midnight's Children* and *Cristóbal Nonato*," *Neohelicon* 20, 2 (1993): 257–312.

31. See Octavio Paz, "El romanticismo y la poesía contemporánea," *Vuelta* 11, 127 (1987): 26–27; Nelson Osorio, "The Debate on Postmodernism in Latin America," *Revista de Crítica Literaria Latinoamericana* 29 (1989): 146–48; and Leon Rozitchner, "La postmodernidad es el opio de los pueblos," *Casa de las Américas* 168 (1988): 165–66.

32. An example of the interest that the postmodernism debate has recently awoken in Latin American studies may be found in the special issues published by *Revista de Crítica Literaria Latinoamericana* (1989), *Nuevo Texto Crítico* (1990), and *Boundary* 2 (1993).

33. Julio Ortega, "Postmodernism in Latin America," in *Postmodernist Fiction in Europe and the Americas*, eds. Theo D'Haen and Hans Bertens (Amsterdam: Rodopi, 1988), 193–208.

34. Ibid., 194.

35. This position is taken to hyperbolic extremes by Alfonso de Toro, who affirms that "with *Ficciones* (1939–1944), J. L. Borges inaugurates postmodernity, not only in Latin America, but everywhere." "Postmodernidad y Latinoamérica," *Revista Iberoamericana* 155–56 (1991): 455. For an interpretation of Borges as a bridging figure between modernity and postmodernity, see Jaime Alazraki, "Borges entre la modernidad y la postmodernidad," *Revista Hispánica Moderna* 41, 2 (1988): 175–79.

36. Ortega, "Postmodernism in Latin America," 195.

37. Néstor García Canclini, *Culturas híbridas* (Mexico City: Grijalbo, 1990).

38. For some Anglo-American critics, the coexistence of different ages and aesthetics would make Latin America a cultural utopia for the postmodern thinker. For a defense of this attitude, see McHale, *Postmodernist Fiction*, 51–53. McHale sees Latin America as a postmodernist topos in itself, which leads him to assimilate its literature into mainstream postmodernism. This concept of Latin America's postmodernism *avant la lettre* has been refuted by Yúdice, "Postmodernity and Transnational Capitalism in Latin America," 1–6.

39. García Canclini, *Culturas híbridas*, 20.

40. Ibid., 23.

41. Ibid.

42. Ibid., 25.

43. Yúdice, "Postmodernity and Transnational Capitalism in Latin America," 7.

44. John Beverly, "Postmodernism in Latin America," *Siglo XX/20th Century* 9, 1–2 (1991–92): 9–20.

45. Neil Larsen, "Postmodernismo e imperialismo: Teoría y política en Latinoamérica," *Nuevo Texto Crítico* 3, 6 (1990): 77–94.

46. John Beverly and José Oviedo, "Introduction," *The Postmodernism Debate in Latin America: A Special Issue, Boundary 2* 20, 3 (1993): 1–17.

47. Patricia Waugh, *Metafiction: The Theory and Practice of Self-Conscious Fiction* (London: Methuen, 1984), 2.

48. Ibid., 15.

49. Robert Scholes, *Fabulation and Metafiction* (Urbana: University of Illinois Press, 1970).

50. Gustavo Pérez Firmat also connects metafiction with the didactic tradition and, especially, with the medieval *exemplum*. Pérez Firmat distinguishes between two metafictional modes: discursive metafiction (in which the characteristic moral of the *exemplum* becomes a form of the novel's theory) and narrative metafiction (which, following this same tradition, offers an allegorical representation of characters and events). See Pérez Firmat, "Metafiction Again," *Taller Literario* 1 (1980): 30–38.

51. Robert Alter, *Partial Magic: The Novel as a Self-Conscious Genre* (Berkeley: University of California Press, 1975), x.

52. Ibid., xi.

53. Waugh, *Metafiction*, 2.

54. Ibid., 5.

55. Ibid., 7.

56. Gerald Graff, *Literature Against Itself: Literary Ideas in Modern Society* (Chicago: The University of Chicago Press, 1979).

57. Ibid., 179.

58. Hutcheon, *Narcissistic Narrative*, 5.

59. Robert Spires, *Beyond the Metafictional Mode: Directions in the Modern Spanish Novel* (Lexington: University Press of Kentucky, 1984).

60. For further analysis of the metafictional mode, see John Stark, *The Literature of Exhaustion: Borges, Nabokov and Barthes* (Durham: University of North Carolina Press, 1974); Steven G. Kellman, *The Self-Begetting Novel* (New York: Columbia University Press, 1980); Inger Christensen, *The Meaning of Metafiction: A Critical Study of Selected Novels by Sterne, Nabokov, Barth and Beckett* (Bergen: Universitetsforlaget, 1981); Larry McCaffery, *The Metafictional Muse* (Pittsburgh: University of Pittsburgh Press, 1982); Robert Siegle, *The Politics of Reflexivity: Narrative and the Constitutive Poetics of Culture* (Baltimore: The Johns Hopkins University Press, 1986); Rüdiger Imhof, *Contemporary Metafiction: A Poetological Study of Metafiction in English Since 1939* (Heidelberg: Carl Winter Universitätsverlag, 1986); Brian Stonehill, *The Self-Conscious Novel: Artifice in Fiction from Joyce to Pynchon* (Philadelphia: University of Pennsylvania Press, 1988); Mark Currie, ed., *Metafiction* (London: Longmans, 1995); and Madelyn Jablon, *Black Metafiction: Self-Consciousness in African American Literature* (Iowa City: University of Iowa Press, 1997). Although less influential, all these works focus on different aspects of narrative reflexivity. Of special interest is Kellman's use of the term "self-begetting novel" to designate a subgenre in which the narrative is a record of its own genesis; that is, "an account, usually first-person,

of the development of a character to the point at which he is able to take up his pen and compose the novel we have just finished reading" (*The Self-Begetting Novel*, 3). Siegle also provides an original insight into this subject by considering reflexivity as a fundamental narrative trait with political implications: "reflexivity suggests that narrative derives its authority not from the 'reality' it imitates, but from the cultural conventions that define both narrative and the construct we call 'reality' " (ibid., 225).

61. For a detailed study of this device, see Lucien Dällenbach, *The Mirror in the Text* (Chicago: University of Chicago Press, 1989) and "Reflexivity and Reading," *New Literary History* 11, 3 (1980): 435–49. Other works dealing with this subject include Mieke Bal, "Mise en Abyme et Iconocité," *Littérature* 29 (1978): 116–28; Jacques Derrida, "Living On: Border Lines," in *Deconstruction and Criticism*, eds. Harold Bloom et al. (London: Routledge and Kegan Paul, 1979), 75–176; Jean Ricardou, "The Story within the Story," *James Joyce Quarterly* 18, 3 (1981): 323–38; Ann Jefferson, "*Mise en abyme* and the Prophetic in Narrative," *Style* 17, 2 (1983): 196–208; and David Carroll, *Paraesthetics: Foucault, Lyotard, Derrida* (New York: Routledge, 1987).

62. In his *Journal 1889–1939*, André Gide mentions the *mise en abyme* for the first time: "In a work of art, I rather like to find thus transposed, at the level of the characters, the subject of the work itself. Nothing sheds more light on the work or displays the proportions of the whole work more accurately . . . what would explain what I'd wanted to do in my *Cahiers*, in *Narcisse* and in *La Tentative*, would be a comparison with the device from heraldry that involves putting a second representation of the original shield 'en abyme' within it" (Dällenbach, *The Mirror*, 7).

63. Ibid., 36.

64. Ibid., 55.

65. Ibid., 98.

66. Ibid., 99.

67. Carroll, *Paraesthetics*.

68. Keith Jenkins, *Re-thinking History* (New York: Routledge, 1991).

69. Some of the historians who have acknowledged their leanings toward postmodernism include Hayden White, Dominick LaCapra, Hans Kellner, F. R. Ankersmit, and Keith Jenkins, whose positions stem from previous investigations about narrativity and history as well as from the theory and practice of poststructuralism.

70. Jenkins, *Re-thinking History*, 66.

71. See Jorge Lozano, *El discurso histórico* (Madrid: Alianza, 1987), 12.

72. See Paul Feyerabend, *Contra el método* (Barcelona: Ariel, 1981), 11; and Corina Yturbe, "El conocimiento histórico," in *Filosofía de la historia*, ed. Reyes Mate, (Madrid: Trotta, 1993), 207–28.

73. Jenkins, *Re-thinking History*, 71.

74. Paul Veyne, *Cómo se escribe la historia* (Madrid: Fragua, 1972), 48.

75. The word *documentum*, Jorge Lozano recalls, did not have the juridical value of proof that it has today, but its etymology derived from *docere* "to teach" (*El discurso histórico*, 66).

76. For a development of the detective metaphor in relation to historical enunciation, see Robin W. Winks's collection of essays *The Historian as Detective: Essays on Evidence* (New York: Harper & Row, 1968).

77. Michel Foucault, *Discipline and Punish* (New York: Pantheon, 1977); "Nietzsche, Genealogy, History," in *The Foucault Reader*, ed. Paul Rabinow (New York: Pantheon, 1984); and *History of Sexuality* (New York: Pantheon, 1978).

78. Mark Poster, *Foucault, Marxism & History: Mode of Production versus Mode of Information* (Cambridge, Mass.: Polity Press, 1984), 76.

79. Foucault, "Nietzsche, Genealogy, History," 76.

80. Poster, *Foucault, Marxism & History*, 89–90.

81. Foucault, "Nietzsche, Genealogy, History," 93.

82. Ibid., 88.

83. See Hayden White, *Metahistory: The Historical Imagination in Nineteenth-Century Europe* (Baltimore: The Johns Hopkins University Press, 1973), ix; and *Tropics of Discourse: Essays in Cultural Criticism* (Baltimore: The Johns Hopkins University Press, 1978), 82.

84. White, *Tropics,* 90–91.

85. White, *Metahistory*, 7.

86. Arthur C. Danto, *Analytic Philosophy of History* (Cambridge, Mass.: Cambridge University Press, 1965), 116.

87. White, *Metahistory*, xii.

88. Dominick LaCapra, *History & Criticism* (Ithaca: Cornell University Press, 1985), 35. LaCapra recognizes, however, White's evolution toward a more critical formalism. See "Method and Ideology in Intellectual History," in *Modern European Intellectual History: Reappraisals and New Perspectives*, ed. Dominick LaCapra and Steven L. Kaplan (Ithaca: Cornell University Press, 1982), 280–310, where White considers ideology, and not rhetoric, as the determinant level of discourse.

89. For different appraisals of this phenomenon, see Jorge Lozano, *El discurso histórico*, and Manuel Cruz, "Narrativismo," in *Filosofía de la Historia*, ed. Reyes Mate, 253–69.

90. Roland Barthes, "The Discourse of History," in *Comparative Criticism: A Yearbook* 3, ed. E. S. Shaffer (Cambridge, Mass.: Cambridge University Press, 1981), 7–20.

91. It is not a matter, therefore, of an infinite freedom of choice that we can exert from a neutral ground. As Keith Jenkins claims, there is no such ground. The only possibility of election is between a history that is aware of what it is doing and a history that is not: "All history is theoretical and all theories are positioned and positioning" (*Re-thinking History*, 69–70).

CHAPTER 2. HERETICAL HISTORY: CARLOS FUENTES'S THEATER OF MEMORY

1. Carlos Fuentes, "Discurso inaugural," in *Simposio Carlos Fuentes: Actas*, eds. Isaac Jack Lévy and Juan Loveluck (Columbia: University of South Carolina Press, 1978), 13.

2. For an acknowledgment of the importance of Dos Passos and Faulkner, see Carlos Fuentes, *La nueva novela hispanoamericana* (Mexico City: Joaquín Mortiz, 1969), 88; and Emmanuel Carballo, "Carlos Fuentes," in *Diecinueve protagonistas de la literatura mexicana del siglo XX* (Mexico City: Empresas Editoriales, 1965), 434.

3. However, Fuentes omits any reference to its most immediate intertexts: Ariel Dorfman's *La última canción de Manuel Sendero* (1982) and Salman Rushdie's *Midnight's Children* (1980). Among many other elements (narrative techniques, themes, etc.), Fuentes borrows from these novels the motifs of the

biological metaphor and the transcendental birth of a character endowed with the power of a transindividual consciousness. For a comparative study of *Cristóbal Nonato* and *Midnight's Children* see Santiago Juan-Navarro, "The Dialogic Imagination."

4. Fuentes's fondness of both *Todos los gatos son pardos* and the subject of the conquest led to successive rewritings that have culminated in the revision of the play under a new title, *Ceremonias del alba* (1991).

5. Fuentes, *NNH*, 11–12.

6. Ibid., 32.

7. Spanish novelist Juan Goytisolo refers to the novel's historical context of production in these terms: "When *Terra Nostra* was published in 1975, the panorama offered by the Spanish-speaking world was not one that inspired much hope. Let us refresh our memories a bit. Spain: dictatorship, repression, censorship, the total absence of any of the timidly progressive institutional structures that had been permitted by even the most conservative government of the past century; Latin America (with the exception of Cuba): hunger, wretched poverty, exploitation, illiteracy" ("Our Old New World," *Review* 19 [1976]: 11). Goytisolo continues his diagnosis of the Hispanic political labyrinth by alluding to the executions of political prisoners, Fascist demonstrations, and Franco's grotesque agony in Spain; the institutional terrorism practiced by governments in Chile, Argentina, Uruguay, Bolivia, Peru, Guatemala, and the Dominican Republic; the corruption and power monopoly of the PRI in Mexico; as well as political and economic dependency on a great power (the United States or the USSR) by all the Caribbean countries. In short, Goytisolo presents a group of nations that had been deprived of the right to determine their own destiny.

8. Ibid., 7.

9. Carlos Fuentes, *Cervantes o la crítica de la lectura*, (Mexico City: Joaquín Mortiz, 1976), 36.

10. Ibid., 39.

11. See J. H. Elliott, *Imperial Spain, 1469–1716* (Harmondsworth, Eng.: Pelican Books, 1970), 128.

12. Carlos Fuentes, *CCL*, 53–60; *El espejo enterrado*, (Mexico City: Fondo de Cultura Económica, 1992), 153–54.

13. Ibid, 88.

14. Fuentes, *CCL*, 53.

15. Fuentes, *EE*, 159–65.

16. Ibid., 165. John Lynch refutes this legendary view of the king's final isolation. Lynch contends that Charles V maintained a strong interest in foreign affairs and continued advising and helping his son Philip II. *Spain 1516–1598: From Nation State to World Empire* (Oxford: Blackwell, 1991), 135.

17. Fuentes, *CCL*, 63.

18. Elliott repeatedly outlines the Spanish-American character of Philip II's empire, as opposed to Charles V's European empire, *Imperial Spain,* 211, 291. It is precisely this Spanish-American projection that makes the figure of Philip II especially attractive for Fuentes's inquiry into the origins of the complex relationship between Spain and Spanish America.

19. Elliott, *Imperial Spain,* 291–93.

20. Fuentes, *EE*, 167.

21. As in the case of Charles V, Fuentes's view of the sovereign cloistered in El Escorial is, most likely, an exaggeration of what were probably occasional retreats. Both Elliott (*Imperial Spain,* 254) and Lynch (*Spain 1516–1598,* 258–59),

although admitting Philip II's lonely and reserved nature, refer also to the king's journeys throughout the peninsula and underline the shortness of his stays in El Escorial. Lynch goes even further in suggesting that the image of the sovereign living in permanent seclusion is just a legend (ibid., 258). In any case, Philip II's private life has numerous dark areas that could logically have inflamed the novelist's imagination. Elliott has pointed to the fact that there is not yet a satisfactory biography of the king (*Imperial Spain*, 394).

22. For a similar view about this paradoxical relationship between political decadence and cultural splendor in Golden Age Spain, see Elliott, *Imperial Spain,* 382–86. Jonathan Tittler has studied this paradox in relation to Fuentes's work. In "De siglos dorados y leyendas negras," Tittler suggests that in the periods of political and social stagnation, art has a compensatory function. *La obra de Carlos Fuentes: Una visión múltiple*, ed. Ana María Hernández de López (Madrid: Pliegos, 1988), 197.

23. Apart from several history primers and handbooks, Fuentes mentions the biographies of Philip II written by Luis Cabrera de Córdoba, *Historia de Felipe II, Rey de España* (Madrid: Aribau, 1876) and Louis Bertrand, *Philippe II à l'Escorial* (Paris: L'Artisan du Livre, 1929), as well as the essays about El Escorial by José Fernández Montaña, *Los arquitectos escurialenses* (Madrid: Hijos de Gregorio del Amo, 1924); José M. Pla Dalmau, *El Escorial y Herrera* (Gerona: Dalmau, 1952); and Fray José de Sigüenza, *La fundación del monasterio del Escorial* (Madrid: Aguilar, 1963). In *Un Teatro de la Memoria: Análisis de "Terra Nostra" de Carlos Fuentes* (Leuven: Leuven University Press, 1990), 177–201, Luz Rodríguez Carranza has traced the presence of some of these documentary sources in *Terra Nostra*.

24. The allusion to Francisco Franco's actual death seems improbable since he died the very same year the novel was published. However, some surprising coincidences can be noted, such as the fact that Franco's final agony lasted thirty-three days, the same period of time that Fuentes concedes to El Señor's. Moreover, in his last moments El Señor is mysteriously transported to the Valley of the Fallen, the other huge Castilian necropolis where Franco's mortal remains are interred.

25. For literary and ideological reasons, Fuentes emphasizes Philip II's fight against millennial movements and heresies over campaigns against military powers. The novel proves to be more interested in the battle of ideas, rather than in the confrontations between powers.

26. El Señor's platonic love does not have any historical justification. In fact, Philip II married three times and had several children, among them, Philip III, his successor to the throne.

27. Michel Foucault, *Discipline and Punish*, (New York: Pantheon, 1977), 26.

28. Fuentes, *CCL*, 33.

29. Although Thomist philosophy had its origin in the twelfth century, it has reappeared periodically in moments of intellectual and institutional crisis. In his introduction to Aquinas's *Compendium of Theology*, Francisco J. Fortuny refers to the revival of Thomism as a reaction to the two foundational periods of modernity in Western thought: on the one hand, the sixteenth and seventeenth centuries, when baroque scholasticism combated inwardness in religion and secularization in politics; and, on the other, the nineteenth and twentieth centuries, when a univocal and fixed truth was erected against the social and intellectual mutations of the age. *Compendio de teología* (Barcelona: Orbis, 1985), 11.

30. The first chapter of the novel presents an enigmatic vision of the origin of

the world: "Increíble el primer animal que soñó con otro animal. Monstruoso el primer vertebrado que logró incorporarse sobre dos pies . . . " (13) ["Incredible the first animal that dreamed of another animal. Monstrous the first vertebrate that succeeded in standing on two feet"] (9). The paragraph that follows refers, with no transition, to the inexplicable events that take place in 1999 Paris. The situation will be reversed in the last chapter, reaffirming the characteristic spiral design of the novel.

31. See, for example, Tittler, "De siglos dorados," 201, and Rodríguez Carranza, *Un Teatro de la Memoria*, 86. Fuentes himself has insisted on this same interpretation. See Alfred MacAdam and Alexander Coleman, "An Interview with Carlos Fuentes," *Book Forum* 4 (1978–79): 684.

32. Lucien Dällenbach, *The Mirror in the Text*, Jeremy Whiteley and Emma Hughes, trans. (Chicago: University of Chicago Press, 1989), 55–75.

33. A similar list is reproduced in the last chapter of *Terra Nostra* ("The Thirty-three Steps") in a logical culmination of this binary obsession that parallels Ihab Hassan's *The Dismemberment of Orpheus: Towards a Postmodern Literature*, (Madison: University of Wisconsin Press, 1982), 267–68, and Charles Jencks's *The Post-Modern Reader*, (London: Academy Editions, 1992), 34, anachronistic taxonomies regarding modernism vs. postmodernism.

34. Fuentes, *EE*, 192. This same aspect of Velázquez's work has been extensively discussed by Michel Foucault in the first chapter of *The Order of Things* (New York: Pantheon, 1970), a text that Fuentes mentions in his "Bibliografía conjunta" (*CCL* 112).

35. The only attempt at changing the nature of the palace into a participatory space is firmly rejected by El Señor. The humanist Ludovico proposes that the sovereign transform the palace into a utopian Theater of Memory: "Sumemos nuestro saber para transformar este lugar en un espacio que verdaderamente los contenga todos y en un tiempo que realmente los viva todos: un teatro donde nosotros ocupemos el escenario, donde hoy está tu altar, y el mundo se despliegue, se represente a sí mismo en todos sus símbolos, relaciones, tramas y mutaciones, ante nuestra mirada: los espectadores en el escenario, la representación en el auditorio" (620) ["We will add together all our knowledge in order to transform this place into a space that truly contains all spaces, into a time which truly embodies all times: a theater in which we occupy a stage, where your altar stands today, and the world will unfold before our eyes, express itself in all its symbols, relations, stratagems, and mutations: the spectators on the stage, the performance in the auditorium"] (614).

36. José Ortega y Gasset, "Meditación del Escorial," in *Meditaciones sobre la literatura y el arte* (Madrid: Castalia, 1987), 358. Ortega underlines the self-reflexive and narcissistic character of El Escorial and considers it characteristic of the superlative style of late Renaissance: "The Monastery of El Escorial is an effort without name, without dedication, without transcendence. It is an effort that reflects upon itself, disdaining all that is outside of itself. Satanically, this effort worships and sings to itself. It is an effort consecrated to effort" (Ibid., 356).

37. The palace receives, among several others, the names of "Basílica del Poder" ["Basilica of Power"] and "Icono inmutable del Honor del Poder y de la Virtud de la Fe" ["immutable icon of the honor of Power and the Virtue of Faith"] (755 [750]). Regarding the textual basis of El Señor's power, the king confesses to Ludovico: "El poder se funda en el texto. La legitimidad única es reflejo de la posesión del texto único" (605) ["Power is founded upon the text. The only legitimacy is the reflection of one's possession of the unique text"] (611).

38. See, in this sense, the dialogue between El Señor and Ludovico in chapter 131 ("Cuarta jornada"):

> —¿Los libros se reproducen?
> —Sí, ya no son el ejemplar único, escrito sólo para ti y por tu encargo, iluminado por un monje, y que tú puedes guardar en tu biblioteca y reservar para tu sola mirada . . .
> —Entonces, mísero de mí, la realidad es de todos, pues sólo lo escrito es real (610).
> ["Books reproduce themselves?"
> "Yes, there is no longer a single copy, commissioned by you, written only for your, and illuminated by a monk, which you can keep in your library and reserve for your eyes alone" [. . .]
> "Then, wretch that I am, reality belongs to everyone, for only what is written is real"] (605).

Fuentes expresses this same thesis in his work on Cervantes (*CCL*, 33), in terms that evoke Irving A. Leonard's *Los libros del conquistador* (México: Fondo de Cultura Económica, 1953), 27. For a more skeptical position about the immediate democratizing effect of the printing press, see Maxime Chevalier, *Lectura y lectores en la España del siglo XVI* (Madrid: Ediciones Turner, 1976), 71–72.

39. The most influential of these critical interpretations of *Terra Nostra* have been those written by Robert Coover, "A Myth of Creation, Spanning 20 Centuries and 778 Pages," *New York Times Book Review* 7 (November 1976): 30, 48–50; Lucille Kerr, "The Paradox of Power and Mystery: Carlos Fuentes's *Terra Nostra*," *PMLA* 95.1 (1980): 91–102; and Roberto González Echevarría, "*Terra Nostra*: Theory and Practice," in *Carlos Fuentes: A Critical View*, eds. Robert Brody and Charles Rossman (Austin: University of Texas Press, 1982), 132–45.

40. Coover, "A Myth of Creation," 3.

41. Carlos Fuentes, *Aura. Cuerpos y ofrendas* (Madrid: Alianza, 1973), 140. Trans. Lysander Kemp (New York: Farrar, Straus and Giroux, 1965), 34.

42. The connection between El Señor's historiographic project and *Terra Nostra*, as its antithesis, has been made by several critics. See, for example, Alexis Márquez Rodríguez, "Aproximación preliminar a *Terra Nostra*," in *La obra de Carlos Fuentes: una visión múltiple,* ed. Ana María Hernández de López (Madrid: Pliegos, 1988), 186. Fuentes himself refers to this same relationship in an interview with Jason Weiss published in *The Kenyon Review* 5, 4 (1983): 106.

43. Hutcheon, *The Politics of Postmodernism*, 63.

44. Raymond Leslie Williams, *The Writings of Carlos Fuentes* (Austin: University of Texas Press, 1996). For a description and evaluation of Williams's book, see Santiago Juan-Navarro's review in *Latin American Literary Review* 48 (1996): 94.

45. Raymond Leslie Williams, *The Writings of Carlos Fuentes*, 48–49, 53, 57, 58–59. This disturbing idealization of the architecture of El Escorial perhaps is a result, as Williams himself admits, of the fact that the book was conceived during an international seminar that took place at the site and at which Fuentes himself was present. Fuentes's fondness for praising his hosts and cultural patrons (especially when the praise is mutual) is well known, and it wouldn't be overtly risky to suggest that within this very framework the Mexican novelist's vision of El Escorial could have taken a new turn. In fact, Fuentes apparently has become one of El Escorial's most frequent guests of honor. The mausoleum of the Spanish Kings was one of the preferred historical relics under Franco; in democratic Spain, especially during thirteen years of Socialist rule, it has become one of the favorite sites

for reuniting intellectuals. Some of its halls have been converted into university classrooms and Fuentes has not ceased to appear in them, both as part of the so-called Summer University of El Escorial and as part of the Summer seminars organized by the Universidad Complutense of Madrid. See, for example, the newspaper articles of Héctor Perea, "La obra en el tiempo de Carlos Fuentes," *El país* (10 July 1992); Diego Muñoz, "Carlos Fuentes y Juan Goytisolo elogian el mestizaje como antídoto contra el racismo," *El país* (15 July 1992); and Fietta Jarque, "Carlos Fuentes subraya la importancia de la imaginación literaria ante los cambios históricos," *El país* (19 August 1995). It's ironic that the fortress of faith of the "prudent" King has been converted into one of the most active forums for intellectual debate during summer courses in Spain.

46. The relationship between these two architectural sites and totalitarian regimes is made explicit in Fuentes's novel, first when El Señor is presented with some of the physical and psychological traits of Franco himself, and later when the character ascends, at the moment of his death, a fantastical staircase that connects El Escorial with the Valley of the Fallen. In his review of *Terra Nostra* Spanish novelist Juan Goytisolo insists on this same interpretation: "A rotting-chamber, a necropolis, a pantheon, a mausoleum, the beauty of El Escorial is intimately linked with the obscene cult of death and its works which for the reign of Ferdinand and Isabella onward slowly stifled Spanish culture and culminated in that Fascist cry of *Viva la muerte!*" ("Our Old New World," *Review* 19 [1976]: 16).

47. In referring to another of Fuentes's novels (*La región más trasparente*), Hanne Zech-Gedeon has suggested Fuentes's difficulty in representing the working masses: "Although the masses are never absent from Fuentes's description of social life, they rarely appear in all their magnitude. On the contrary, they are relegated to the background against which the representation of the bourgeoisie stands out" ("Carlos Fuentes," *Lateinamerikanische Literatur der Gegenwart in Einzeidarstellungen* [Stutgart: Wolfgang Eitel, 1976], 409).

48. Fuentes, *CCL*, 43–44.

49. Hutcheon, *The Politics of Postmodernism*, 63.

50. Fuentes, *CCL*, 96.

51. The feasibility of this program will be discussed in the analysis of the novel's third part, in which all these same ideas are expressed by Fuentes through the metaphor of Valerio Camillo's Theater of Memory.

52. For an interpretation of *Terra Nostra* as an inquiry into the origins of the Hispanic American dictator, see Jaime Alazraki, "*Terra Nostra*: Coming to Grips with History," *World Literature Today* 57.4 (1983): 551–58.

53. See note 23.

54. The reasons for such a harsh rejection of this genre are rooted in the "lying" nature of novels, as opposed to the "veracity" of historiography. Since the Renaissance, historiographic theory had been based on a system of valuation of history as a useful truth and condemnation of fiction as a useless and dangerous lie. See William Nelson, *Fact or Fiction: The Dilemma of the Renaissance Storyteller* (Cambridge: Harvard University Press, 1973).

55. For a thorough study of such attacks, see the essays by Leonard, *Los libros del conquistador*; Nelson, *Fact or Fiction*; and B. W. Ife, *Reading and Fiction in Golden-Age Spain: A Platonist Critique and Some Picaresque Replies* (Cambridge: Cambridge University Press, 1985).

56. Fuentes's position fluctuates between an overvaluation of fiction and a more sensible consideration of the novel not as an epistemological model that excels history, but one that complements it.

57. The discussion of pre-Cortesian Mexico will use four related terms—Aztec, Mexica, Nahua, and Nahuatl—whose applicability should be distinguished in order to avoid confusion. Eloise Quiñones Keber proposes to use "Aztec" to refer to "the tribute empire dominated by Mexico Tenochtitlan at the time of European contact." "Mexica," on the other hand, applies more specifically to the inhabitants of the two cities of the island in Lake Texcoco (Mexico Tenochtitlan and Tlatelolco). Finally, Nahua is the generic term by which we refer to the Aztecs in their cultural practices, while Nahuatl is the name of the language they spoke. See Eloise Quiñones Keber, "Aztecs Before and After the Conquest," *Colonial Latin American Review* 1, 1–2 (1992): 225.

58. Davíd Carrasco, *Quetzalcoatl and the Irony of the Empire* (Chicago: The University of Chicago Press, 1982), 3.

59. H. B. Nicholson, "Ehecatl Quetzalcoatl vs. Topiltzin Quetzalcoatl: A Problem in Mesoamerican Religion and History," *Actes du XLII Congrès International des Américanistes*, Paris, vol. VI (1976): 35. This Toltec-Aztec custom of using the name of this god as a title has led to an endless series of confusions that has affected both the oral evolution of the legend and its recollection by modern historians. Thus, in the descriptions of the historical hero it is not surprising to find the concepts that are more properly associated with the god. See also Quiñones Keber, "The Aztec Image of Topiltzin Quetzalcoatl," in *Smoke and Mist: Mesoamerican Studies in Memory of Thelma D. Sullivan*, eds. J. Kathryn Josserand and Karen Dakin (Oxford: BAR International Series 402, 1988), 337.

60. According to Nahua cosmogony, the world had been created and destroyed several times. To be exact, four suns preceded the current era. Each of these suns had been destroyed in a different manner: the first by jaguars, the second by the wind, the third by the rain, and the fourth by a flood. Since the fifth sun, or current era, had been created by the sacrifice of gods, the Nahuas felt that a continuous human sacrifice was necessary to appease the divinities.

61. Eloise Quiñones Keber, "From Tollan to Tlapallan: The Tale of Topiltzin Quetzalcoatl in the Codex Vaticanus A," *Latin American Indian Literatures Journal* 3, 1 (1987): 77.

62. The six documents that form the "core sources" of Nicholson's essay are: *Historia de los Mexicanos por sus Pinturas* (c. 1531–1537), the Juan Cano *Relaciones (Relación de la genealogía y linaje de los Señores que han señoreado esta tierra de la Nueva España* and *Origen de los Mexicanos*) (c. 1532), *Histoyre du Mechique* (c. 1535–1543), *Leyenda de los soles* (c. 1558), Fray Bernardino de Sahagún's *Historia General de las Cosas de Nueva España* (c. 1547–1585), and *Anales de Cuauhtitlan* (c. 1570). These documents offer the most complete and sustained narrative about Topiltzin Quetzalcoatl. For a detailed analysis of these sources regarding the myth of Quetzalcoatl see Nicholson, "Topiltzin Quetzalcoatl of Tollan: A Problem in in Mesoamerican Ethnohistory," Ph.D. diss., Harvard University, Cambridge, 1957. In *Quetzalcoatl de Tula: Mitogénesis de una leyenda postcortesiana* (Nuevo León: Facultad de Filosofía y Letras, 1991) Werner Stenzel offers a summary of similar sources from a more skeptical, although less rigorous, perspective.

63. One of the religious reforms, supposedly introduced by Quetzalcoatl and the one sources mention more frequently, is the practice of self-sacrifice. Several sixteenth-century documents (*Codex Vaticanus A, Codex Telleriano-Remensis*, and *Anales de Cuauhtitlan*), allude to this representation of Quetzalcoatl as a penitent. For a detailed analysis of this aspect of Topiltzin Quetzalcoatl's personality see Alfredo López Austin, *Hombre-Dios: Religión y política en el mundo náhuatl* (México: UNAM, 1973), 143–60.

64. Nicholson, "Topiltzin," 360–61; "Ehecatl," 38–39.

65. Jacques Lafaye, *Quetzalcoatl and Guadalupe: The Formation of Mexican National Consciousness (1531–1813)* (Chicago: The University of Chicago Press, 1976); Anthony Pagden, ed., *Letters from Mexico* (New Haven: Yale University Press, 1986); J. H. Elliott, "The Mental World of Hernán Cortés," *Transactions of the Royal Historical Society* 17 (London: Offices of the Royal Historical Society, 1967), 41–58; Victor Frankl, "Imperio particular e imperio universal en las Cartas de Relación de Hernán Cortés," *Cuadernos Hispanoamericanos* 163–64 (1963): 443–82; Susan D. Gillespie, *The Aztec Kings: The Construction of Rulership in Ancient Mexico* (Tucson: University of Arizona Press, 1989); Werner Stenzel, *Quetzalcoatl de Tula: Mitogénesis de una leyenda postcortesiana* (Nuevo León: Facultad de Filosofía y Letras, 1991).

66. Lafaye, *Quetzalcoatl*, 153.

67. Anthony Pagden and J. H. Elliott go further than Lafaye in pointing out that there are no evidences of a pre-Hispanic tradition about the legend of a hypothetical return of Quetzalcoatl to claim back his throne. Yet, both omit an important fact that has been pointed out above: the oral nature of Nahua culture, which has hindered our knowledge of its history and mythology. What does exist is archeological evidence that proves the extension of Quetzalcoatl's cult throughout Mesoamerica and that contradict Pagden's restrictive view of the myth. For a detailed analysis of the role of prophecies in the fall of Aztec empire see Nicholson, "Topiltzin Quetzalcoatl of Tollan," and Carrasco, *Quetzalcoatl and the Irony of the Empire*.

68. Pagden, ed., *Letters from Mexico*, 467; Gillespie, *The Aztec Kings*, 181.

69. There is also the possibility that native writers saw their history in a different light after the conquest. Quetzalcoatl is a mediating figure not only for the Spaniards but also for the Nahuas. Rather than seeing the Quetzalcoatl myth as a Spanish imposition we should also allow for Indian participation in the (re)writing of their own history.

70. Fuentes, *EE*, 107; 99.

71. Ibid., 99.

72. A substantial part of this prologue has been reprinted in essay form as part of his collection *Tiempo mexicano* (Mexico City: Joaquín Mortiz, 1970) and became also integrated into Fuentes's last version of his play *Todos los gatos son pardos*, published under the title of *Ceremonias del alba* (Madrid: Mondadori, 1991). The quoted passage comes from Fuentes, *Todos los gatos*, 1153.

73. Fuentes, *Tiempo mexicano*, 17; *Todos los gatos*, 1154.

74. The prophecy of the god's return is mentioned by Sahagún in chapter 7, book VIII (2:293), and in chapter 2, book XII (4:25) of his *Historia general de las cosas de Nueva España*, ed. Angel María Garibay (Mexico City: Porrúa, 1956).

75. As noted, in *Todos los gatos son pardos* (*Obras completas*, vol. 2. [Mexico City: Aguilar, 1980], 1154) and *Tiempo mexicano* (17), Fuentes attributes Quetzalcoatl's horror to the fact that he ignored his human appeareance. In *The Buried Mirror* Fuentes takes this personal interpretation even further: "He thought that being a god, he had no face. Now, reflected in the mirror, he saw his own face. It was, after all, a man's face, the face of his own creature. Since he had a human face, he realized that he must also have a human destiny" (*EE*, 116). The same explanation can be found in his play *Ceremonias del alba*, where, just as Quetzalcoatl lets out a yell, Tezcatlipoca says: "Reconócete en un rostro humano, oh Gran Dios, y teme poseer también un destino humano" ["Recognize yourself in a human face, oh Great God, and fear to have a human destiny as well"] (Madrid:

Mondadori, 1991), 15. But, according to the *Anales*, Topiltzin Quetzalcoatl's terror is actually due to the opposite reason: to the inhuman—because aged and deformed—character of his face.

76. Angel María Garibay, *Historia de la literatura náhuatl* (Mexico City: Porrúa, 1954), I: 313. The indirect and lyrical representation of the seeming incest in the *Anales* contrasts with Fuentes's rude reconstruction of the incident in *Tiempo mexicano* (17) and *El espejo enterrado* (116), where he uses the verb "to fornicate" (from "fornix," brothel) to describe their sexual transgression. In *Terra Nostra* and *Ceremonias del alba* Fuentes goes even further, portraying the episode as a rape.

77. Fuentes, *EE*, 116.

78. In the *Anales*, although there is mention of a series of disasters that follow the death and resurrection of the Toltec ruler culminating with the total destruction of Tollan there is no trace of such omens or prophecy like the one Fuentes presents. Most of the references to the legend of the god's return come either from sources in which it is difficult to establish the borderline between the properly indigenous narrative and evangelizing discourse, or from authors who used Cortés's *Letters* as the basis for their chronicles. Versions of the former can be found in Fray Diego Durán, *Historia de las Indias de Nueva España* (Mexico City: Porrúa, 1967), 2: 507, 514, 541; and Fray Jerónimo de Mendieta, *Historia eclesiástica indiana* (Mexico City: Porrúa, 1971), 93. For examples of the second case, see Francisco López de Gómara, *Historia general de las Indias y vida de Hernán Cortés* (Caracas: Biblioteca Ayacucho, 1979), 2: 47.

79. See Bernardino de Sahagún, *Historia general de las cosas de Nueva España*, ed. Angel María Garibay (Mexico City: Porrúa, 1956), chapter 1, book XII (4: 23–4).

80. Miguel León-Portilla, *Visión de los vencidos: Relaciones indígenas de la conquista* (México: UNAM, 1959), 67; Bernardino de Sahagún, *Historia general*, 4: 43.

81. As noted by Elliott ("The Mental World of Hernán Cortés," in *Transactions of the Royal Historical Society*, vol. 17 [London: Offices of the Royal Historical Society, 1967], 54–55), the Franciscans wanted to find a way out of the apocalyptic impasse that Christianity was experiencing in the sixteenth century. They turned to the New World to create a new church based on the communal ideals of the first Christians. Fuentes also conceives the New World as a space for utopian experiments, away from a corrupted Europe. His utopianism is critical and manifests itself in his view of Latin American history as a succession of subverted Edens. In *Cervantes* he discusses the connections between the humanist friars who traveled to the New World and the utopian thought of the Renaissance (*CCL*, 89).

82. The name of the Pilgrim itself evokes Quetzalcoatl's condition as a self-exile, whose journey to Tlapallan—"the city of the sun"—is mentioned in many accounts. See, for example, chapters 12–14, book III, in Sahagún's *Historia General*, 1:288–91.

83. See Cristóbal Colón, "Diario del primer viaje," in *Textos y documentos completos*, ed. Consuelo Valera (Madrid: Alianza, 1982), 15–138; Américo Vespucio, *El nuevo mundo: Cartas relativas a sus viajes y descubrimientos*, ed. R. Levillier (Buenos Aires: Nova, 1951); Pedro Mártir de Anglería, *Décadas del Nuevo Mundo*, ed. Joaquín Torres Asensio (Buenos Aires: Bajel, 1944); and Hernán Pérez de Oliva, *Historia de la invención de las Indias*, ed. José Juan Arroum (Bogotá: Instituto Caro y Cuervo, 1965).

84. Compare section 63 in *Terra Nostra* ("The Beyond") with the story inter-

polated by the Inca Garcilaso de la Vega in chapter 8, book I of his *Comentarios reales*, ed. José de la Riva-Agüero (México: Porrúa, 1990), 18–20.

85. Fuentes alludes to Amerigo Vespucci's commentaries in his *Mundus Novus* (1503). The Indian groups described by Vespucci in his work lived in harmony with nature, with no concept of property and no need of any kind of government or authority (*EE*, 133). J. H. Elliott has also pointed out how the discoveries moved Renaissance thinkers both to question fundamental values of European civilization and to project upon America an idyllic scenario in which they could make their dreams come true (*The Old World*, 25–27). It is necessary to keep in mind that only a few years after *Mundus Novus* came out, Thomas Moore published his *Utopia* (1516) and both Franciscans and Jesuits tried to put Moore's ideas into practice on American soil. For a study of the influence of Columbus and Vespucci in humanist utopian thought, see Charles L. Sanford, *The Quest for Paradise: Europe and the American Moral Imagination* (Urbana: University of Illinois Press, 1961), 56–73; and J. Martin Evans, *America: The View From Europe.* (New York: W.W. Norton, 1979), 2–12. For a description of the utopian experiment of the Franciscan Vasco de Quiroga in Michoacán, see Fuentes, *EE* 144: 134; and Fernando Aínsa, *De la Edad de Oro a El Dorado: Génesis del discurso utópico americano* (Mexico City: Fondo de Cultura Económica, 1992), 156–57.

86. A detail that proves this hypothesis is that in the version selected by Angel María Garibay, *Historia de la literatura náhuatl* (Mexico City: Porrúa, 1954), 462, Tezcatlipoca loses his foot in his struggle with the earth goddess and, when the Pilgrim meets Moctezuma-Tezcatlipoca, we are told that the latter lost his foot on the day of creation (462; 455). See also the chapter "El espejo humeante" in which the Pilgrim also assumes the features of Tezcatlipoca (426–44). For different versions of this myth see Diego Muñoz Camargo, *Historia de Tlaxcala* (Guadalajara: Edmundo Aviña Levy, 1966), 150; and M. Edouard de Jonghe, ed. "Hystoire du Méchique." *Journal de la Societe des Americanistes de Paris* 2, 2 (1905): 28ff.; and Andrés de Olmos, ed., *Historia de los mexicanos por sus pinturas* (México City: Porrúa, 1965), 25ff.

87. We are again dealing with a Sahaguntine manuscript as an intertext of "The New World." The *Códice Matritense* was written circa 1564 by Sahagún using native informants. The myth of the Fifth Sun is also told in book VII of Sahagún's later *Historia general.*

88. Miguel León-Portilla, *Literaturas de Mesoamérica* (México: SEP, 1984), 61.

89. Laurette Séjourné, *Burning Water: Thought and Religion in Ancient Mexico* (Berkeley, Calif.: Shambhala, 1976), 66.

90. In the Nahuas' ritual practice, the chosen impersonator of Tezcatlipoca was offered a year of pleasure, after which he was sacrificed to the god on his feast day Cecilio A. Robelo, *Diccionario de mitología nahoa* (Mexico City: Porrúa, 1982).

91. As noted above, Fuentes fuses the myth of the creation of the Fifth Sun with that of the creation of the new men through the legend of the sacrifice of the leprous god. This manipulation allows him to establish a close tie between the origin of mestizaje and the utopian value associated with Quetzalcoatl.

92. This device may also be understood as a declaration of faith in the need that Latin Americans have to be the makers of their own history. In the "Prólogo del autor" to *Todos los gatos son pardos*, Fuentes comments on this historical enterprise of contemporary Mexico in the context of anticolonialism: "It will be the role of the new mestizo world, the children of La Malinche, to invent new historical projects, and the struggle, even in our times, will be between colonizers and

decolonizers. If Mexico does not destroy colonialism, both foreign and that exercised by some Mexicans against millions of Mexicans, the conquest will continue to be our historical trauma and nightmare: the mark of an insuperable fatality and of a frustrated will." *Obras completas*, Vol. II (Mexico City: Aguilar, 1980), 1164.

93. The two elements of this double axis (pre-Hispanic myths and conquest of the Aztec empire) maintain a permanent dialogue. For example, the structure of the "initiation" trials that was discussed above also serves a more earthly and secular purpose. In this part of *Terra Nostra* Fuentes describes the rational cunning of the conquistador facing a supernatural world. This idea is confirmed as we recognize in many of the Pilgrim's movements and reactions those of Cortés, as they are described by Bernal Díaz in his *Historia Verdadera* and by Sahagún in his *Historia General*.

94. Several of the moments in which the Pilgrim is welcomed in these terms are his encounters with the ancient of memories, with the old woman who gives him shelter in the middle of the forest, with the Indians after his fall and ascent from the depths of the *cenote*, with the Lords of the Underworld, with Moctezuma (represented as Tezcatlipoca and Tlacaelel), and finally with the ancient of memories in the Plaza of Tlatelolco.

95. On different levels, Fuentes's text imitates the style of the sixteenth-century *cartas relatorias*, chronicles and histories. In its description of the omens, the narrative repeats ideas, expressions, and even whole passages from Sahagún's *Historia General*. From the stylistic point of view, several episodes, such as the description of the market of Mexico Tenochtitlan, follow Bernal Díaz's tortuous syntax, with its endless sentences and long sequences, linked by a large number of copulative conjunctions (*TN*, 460).

96. The passage in which Bernal compares his view of Tenochtitlan with the enchantments of the chivalric romances, is even more literally reproduced by Fuentes in *Todos los gatos son pardos* and *Ceremonias del alba*.

97. This encounter, which confirms the Pilgrim-Quetzalcoatl in his role of Messianic cultural hero and gives rise to a reflection upon the role of the writer in Latin America, is analyzed below in the section on self-reflexive motifs in "The New World."

98. The Pilgrim's departure freely follows Sahagún's version of Quetzalcoatl's myth. But, although it coincides with the *Historia General* in some basic elements (he heads eastward in a barge of serpents), it differs in many details. In "The New World" the twenty mestizos created by the Pilgrim bid him farewell. He sails away from the city and behind him the lagoon turns into a barren field. The Pilgrim is finally swallowed by "the great serpent of dust and water of the Mexican lagoon"(*TN*, 492; 484). Venus shines at the end of his journey.

99. Fuentes bases his vision of the myth on Séjourné's interpretation, an approach of mystical and symbolic overtones that shows a particular aversion toward historicist interpretations and that converts Quetzalcoatl into a totalizing compendium of all Nahua mythology. References to Séjourné can be found in *TM*, 18, and *EE*, 371.

100. Dällenbach, *The Mirror*, 101.

101. These devices will be addressed in the discussion of the novel's central *mise en abyme*: Valerio Camillo's Theater of Memory.

102. Jaime Alazraki, *La prosa narrativa de Jorge Luis Borges* (Madrid: Gredos, 1983), 92.

103. Ibid., 141.

104. The quality of the character's words makes of the passage an example of what Lucien Dällenbach calls a *mise en abyme* of the code. This new level of reflection alludes to all those metatextual indicators (artistic or literary metaphors, aesthetic theories or debates, manifestoes or credos) that the text adopts to facilitate and guide the reader's interpretation. See *The Mirror*, 99–100.

105. A Spanish selection from this document is included in Garibay's *Historia*. The first three lines come from a poem that Garibay attributes to the king-poet Nezahualcoyotl (1:244). Lines 4–7 are part of a poem from Chalco in which the poet sings about the ephemerality of life and songs (1:184). Lines 8–10 have their origin in the work that another poet from Chalco dedicates to a colleague (1:181). Finally, the last three lines are part of a piece that Garibay entitles "The poet's mission" (*La literatura de los aztecas,* 67).

106. The title for the Aztec ruler was in reality Tlatoani, which means "the speaker" or "he who speaks."

107. Aztec poetry could hardly be seen as a threat by the dominant class, since it was one of the favorite vehicles of expression of that class. David Damrosch has shown that not only is there not a contradiction between the delicate aestheticism of Mesoamerican poetry and the cruel practices of the Aztec empire, but that aestheticism was an intrinsic part of those practices. Damrosch also points to the difficulty of separating those purely indigenous elements from those that could have been received from the Europeans as a consequence of the process of transculturation that took place in the sixteenth century, when most of these poems were composed. "The Aesthetics of Conquest: Aztec Poetry Before and After Cortés," *Representations* 33 (1991): 101–2.

108. Angel María Garibay, *La literatura de los aztecas,* 67.

109. Fuentes, *CCL*, 106.

110. For a study of the connections of *Terra Nostra* with Castro's thought, see Goytisolo, "Our Old New World"; González Echevarría, "*Terra Nostra*: Theory and Practice"; and Rodríguez Suro, "La huella de Américo Castro en *Terra Nostra*."

111. Fuentes, *CCL*, 41.

112. Ibid., 44.

113. González Echevarría, "*Terra Nostra*," 135–36.

114. Guillermo Araya, *El pensamiento de Américo Castro: Estructura intercastiza de la historia de España* (Madrid: Alianza, 1983), 33.

115. Moved by his interest in the influence of the Arabs on the formation of Hispanic culture, Castro literally inverts the traditional view of the Visigothic world as the origin of Spanish identity. In an essay published in 1949, Castro justified the methodological reasons that made him exclude the Visigoths from the history of Spain.

116. González Echevarría, "*Terra Nostra*," 136. We could say that, since the publication of *España en su historia* in 1948, the whole of Castro's intellectual production conforms to the concept of a work in progress. From that moment on, several revisions and new editions with new prologues and appendixes appear. Fuentes mentions three titles that represent three different stages in Castro's thought. It is not clear whether he follows the early or the late Castro. González Echevarría suggests arbitrariness, if not ignorance, as the answer to these questions ("*Terra Nostra*," 134–36). However, as mere speculation, we could simply see in this gesture Fuentes's homage to a historian with whom he deeply identifies.

117. See Fuentes, *NNH*, 11. In one of the prologues to *La realidad histórica de España*, Castro begins by highlighting his sharp rejection of positivistic historiog-

raphy: "For years I have been running into the problem that Spaniards have been portrayed as if they were biological or psychological objects, and not as a collective unity of human lives, existing in time and space, and with a clear recognition of their social dimension" (xi). The title of this prologue, "Let us be masters and not servants of our history," is an accurate summary of Fuentes's historiographic underpinnings.

118. See Castro, *La realidad*, 38–41; and Fuentes, *EE*, 79–80. Although both writers recognize the intellectual merit of this king, who was dubbed in his own time "the Wise," Fuentes goes much further than Castro in his idealization of the Spanish sovereign, to the extent of making of him another of the cultural heroes he honors in his works. Fuentes seems to be especially attracted by Alfonso X's encyclopedic drive. One of the king's most ambitious projects was the writing of a "monumental summa of the Spanish Middle Ages," a compilation of the knowledge of the times, which Fuentes considers "a sort of encyclopedia, before encyclopedias came into vogue in the eighteenth century" (*EE*, 79).

119. See Fuentes, *CCL*, 22–23. In fact, Fuentes compares the heretics' recycling of theology with the rewriting of the literary tradition that postmodernist authors have carried out in the last decades. In both cases, tradition is submitted to an endless series of metamorphoses with the purpose of celebrating the multifarious nature of reality (*CCL*, 23–24).

120. Norman Cohn, *The Pursuit of the Millennium* (Fairlawn: Essential Books, 1957), xiii.

121. See Fuentes, *CCL*, 20, 24. A change in Fuentes's treatment of these movements can be appreciated in his most recent works. In *Cristóbal Nonato* (1987), for example, proletarian millenarianism reemerges under the form of the wild fundamentalism headed by the "Ayatola Guadalupano" Matamoros Moreno. Fuentes's idealization of these movements in *Terra Nostra* yields here to a more critical view of political violence and fanaticism.

122. José Antonio Maravall, *Las Comunidades de Castilla: Una primera revolución moderna* (Madrid: Revista de Occidente, 1970), 16.

123. Ibid., 17. Maravall suggests that the major bodies of the Western modern state were already present embryonically in medieval Spain.

124. See Fuentes, *CCL*, 59–60.

125. Ibid., 56.

126. Ibid., 57.

127. Elliott, *Imperial Spain*, 151–59. According to Elliott, the echoes of the *comunero* movement were heard throughout all of the Spain of the Hapsburgs, but in a very different sense from that attributed by Fuentes to the revolt. Thus, for Elliott, the Spanish court in the reign of Philip II was divided between the closed nationalist mentality of the *comuneros*, represented by the Duke of Alba, and the open, enlightened and Europe-oriented Spain of the Mendozas (261).

128. Fuentes, *CCL*, 26.

129. Fuentes, *EE*, 10.

130. "¿Cómo voy a cambiar la mezclada sangre de mi cuerpo? Y sangre impura, de árabe y de judío, algún día te la cobra el mundo cristiano" (252) ["What can I do to change my mixed blood? Eventually, the Christian world will make a man pay for his Jewish or Moorish blood"] (246); "héroe impuro, héroe de todas las sangres y de todas las pasiones" (253) ["the impure hero, the hero in whom all bloods and all passions flowed"] (247); "la impureza, la mezcla de todas las sangres, todas las creencias, todos los impulsos espirituales de una multitud de culturas" (568) ["impurity, the mixture of all bloods, all beliefs, all the spiritual

impulses of a multitude of cultures"] (562); "mézclese mi sangre con la de todos" (762) ["let my blood be mixed with that of all other men"] (757); "renazca mi cuerpo enriquecido por la sangre mezclada" (762) ["let my body be reborn enriched by mixed bloods"] (757).

131. As a result of the expulsion, some of the key members of the financial system emigrated to those European powers that later wrested imperial hegemony from Spain (*EE*, 95; 88).

132. This same idea is paradoxically confirmed by El Señor in one of his dialogues with Guzmán: "Multiplica las dudas, Guzmán, relata todas las posibles historias y pregúntate otra vez por qué escogimos una sola versión entre esa baraja de posibilidades y sobre ella fundamos una Iglesia inmortal y cien Reinos pasajeros" (207) ["Multiply your doubts, Guzmán, tell all the possible stories, and ask yourself once more why we chose one single version among that pack of possibilities, and then upon that choice founded an immortal Church and a hundred transitory kingdoms"] (202).

133. However, Fuentes tends to idealize what Cohn presents with critical detachment. Indeed, Cohn studies the mystical anarchism of this Brotherhood in the light of Freudian psychoanalysis, pointing to the megalomaniac and paranoid character of their leaders (*The Pursuit of the Millennium*, 185–94). As Marteen Van Delden has incisively pointed out: "In Cohn the millenarian movements are the forerunners of Hitler and Stalin, whereas in Fuentes they are the precursors of Copernicus and Cervantes (and himself). A more striking difference in interpretation is difficult to imagine." *Carlos Fuentes, Mexico, and Modernity* (Nashville: Vanderbilt University Press, 1998), 131.

134. See Cohn, *The Pursuit of the Millennium*, 11; and Carlos Fuentes *CCL*, 24; *TN*, 583; 577.

135. The conversation between El Señor and Ludovico (60; 54) repeats the dialogue between Suso and the spirit: " 'Whence have you come?' The image answers: 'I come from nowhere.'—'Tell me, what are you?'—'I am not.'—'What do you wish.'—'I do not wish.'—'This is a miracle!'—'Tell me, what is your name?'—'I am called Nameless Wildness.' 'Where does your insight lead to?'—'Into untrammeled freedom.'—'Tell me, what do you call untrammeled freedom?'—'When a man lives according to all his caprices without distinguishing between God and himself, and without looking before or after' " Cohn, *The Pursuit of the Millennium*, 186.

136. Malcolm Lambert, *Medieval Heresy: Popular Movements from Gregorian Reform to the Reformation* (Oxford: Blackwell, 1992), 398.

137. There are several reasons to assume the historical authenticity of the *comunero* documentation presented in the novel. On the formal level, it is reproduced in italics, while the rest of the text appears in regular characters. Italics are frequently used to indicate that the author is quoting a particular paragraph. In fact, many older historians such as Prudencio de Sandoval, author of *Historia de la vida y hechos del emperador Carlos V* (a work that includes numerous records about the *comunero* movement), favored this method. Regarding the contents, the self-styled *comunero* documents lack many of the fantastic elements present in the dialogues between the fictional characters and allude to historical places such as the battles of Medina and Villalar.

138. Most of the actual documents from which Fuentes draws to create his historiographic collage are included in the appendices to Antonio Ferrer del Río, *Decadencia de España: historia del levantamiento de las comunidades de Castilla*

(Madrid: Establecimiento tipográfico de Mellado, 1850): the first is a letter from the city of Toledo that appears in Appendix V, 359–61, and is reproduced almost entirely in the novel (*TN*, 633–46; 628–41); the second is a letter written by the council of Medina del Campo to the city of Valladolid complaining about the destruction caused by the royalist Antonio de Fonseca (Appendix IV, 355–56), who in the novel appears as Guzmán (*TN*, 646–49; 642–44); the third letter, sent by the city of Segovia to Medina del Campo, expresses its full support of the rebels' cause (Appendix IV, 356–58 and *TN*, 652; 647); the last is a letter from Antonio de la Torre to the Marquis of Vélez, briefly informing him of the defeat of the rebels (Appendix XIII, 380 and *TN* 655; 650). All documents are modified in one way or another. Some omit references to the participation of principal prelates or nobles in the revolt, others incorporate allusions to the fictional character Guzmán or are intersected by other historical and/or apocryphal passages that emphasize Fuentes's own interpretation of this movement.

139. Maravall, *Las comunidades de Castilla*, 192–93.

140. The author of the letter addressed to a "Marquis, kinsman" outlines the services of Captain Don Guzmán in the final battle of Villalar (655; 650), something that, of course, does not happen in the actual document reproduced by Ferrer del Río, *Decadencia de España*, 380. All references to Guzmán, and the most dramatic parts of the letter, are entirely fictional.

141. In this proclamation the rebels state that "no serán más perseguidos los conversos que con su trabajo acrecientan la riqueza de España, ni los mudéjares integrados en las comunidades cristianas, ni se seguirá proceso alguno por origen de la sangre" (*TN* 639) ["those converts will no longer be persecuted who with their labor enrich the coffers of Spain, nor mudejares already integrated into Christian communities, nor shall any prosecution continue because of the blood"] (634). Everything suggests that this is an apocryphal passage that serves Fuentes to idealize even more the *comuneros*. Maravall himself, on whom Fuentes bases his views, discards any connection between the *comunidades* and the converts. The Spanish historian even highlights the influence of anti-Semitism on the popular and middle classes (the protagonists of the revolt, according to both Maravall and Fuentes). Due to their persecution by the masses, Jews tended to look for protection among aristocrats. Hence, antiaristocratic feelings were usually associated with anti-Semitism among the urban low classes (*Las comunidades*, 240). See also in this regard Julio Caro Baroja, *Los judíos en la España moderna y contemporánea* (Madrid: Arión Caro Baroja), I: 115.

142. Placing the final battle in El Escorial is one more example of the creative anachronisms that are found *Terra Nostra*. On this occasion, such anachronism serves to stress the encounters between the two above-mentioned discursive groups that intersect in this chapter: the supposedly historic, which places the final battle in its real setting (Villalar), and the purely fictional, which takes place in an impossible scenario (El Escorial).

143. Guzmán's role as initial instigator and final repressor of the revolt dramatizes the treachery of those sectors of the low nobility that supported the upheaval in defense of their own feudal interests, but deserted and crushed it as soon as the movement developed into a revolution.

144. Frances Yates, *The Art of Memory* (Chicago: The University of Chicago Press, 1966). In her essay Yates traces the history of the memory arts from their origin in ancient Greece to their final manifestations in seventeenth-century Europe. Originally conceived of as a way of improving the psyche's memory by means of the manipulation of images, they progressively acquired a more complex

functionality and were eventually incorporated into the hermetic tradition of the Renaissance.

145. With this term ("scene of reading") I refer to that textual scenario in which the act of reading is primarily thematized, that is, a space where all its elements (even some of the most apparently trivial) tend to underscore different aspects of that act. The term may be regarded as a counterpart to Michael Fried's "scene of writing," which he discusses in *Realism, Writing, Disfiguration* (Baltimore: The Johns Hopkins University Press, 1987), 117–18, 127–29.

146. Yates, *The Art of Memory*, 163. This emphasis on translation on both the textual and intertextual levels constantly refers us to the postmodernist realm of writing, understood not as original creation, but as the rewriting of previous texts. As noted in the previous chapter, postmodernism tends to undermine the notion of the unique and the original work of art, stressing instead its intertextual nature through parodical rewriting. See Umberto Eco, *Postcript to The Name of the Rose* (New York: Harcourt Brace Jovanovich, 1983), 20; Hassan, *The Postmodern Turn*, 170; and Hutcheon, *A Poetics of Postmodernism*, 93. Roland Barthes has taken this position to the limit, stating that there is no possible life outside the "infinite text" that constitutes reality (*The Pleasure of the Text*, 20), and Hassan has adapted this view to his concept of history as a palimpsest where past, present and future texts cohabit (*The Postmodern Turn*, 88).

147. Some of the details in the description of the erudite that are presented in *Terra Nostra* seem to have their origin in Viglius's letter to Erasmus. For example, Viglius alludes to Camillo's stammering, saying that he has nearly lost his use of speech "through continually using his pen" (Yates, *The Art of Memory*, 131). In attributing this physical defect to the character's feverish reading, rather than his writing, the novel insists on the interchangeability between these two acts and also sets the basis for an interpretation of Camillo's theater as a "scene of reading."

148. There are many references in this chapter that highlight the similarity between Ludovico's position in relation to Camillo's invention and that of the reader regarding Fuentes's novel. Ludovico is compelled to decipher Camillo's manuscript by patient reading and research, and so is the reader of *Terra Nostra*. Sometimes Camillo hides information in order to make his disciple discover things for himself, as happens with Simonides's story. This concealment repeats Fuentes's recurrent postulation of indeterminacy as an activator of the reader's response (*CCL*, 109), as well as his authorial prerogative "of not clarifying mysteries" (*TN*, 660; 655).

149. Of the three worlds in which the cabala divides the universe (supercelestial, middle celestial, and subcelestial or elementary), Camillo's theater bases his system of memory on the Sephiroths or divine emanations, which correspond in the Platonic hierarchy to the world of ideas (Yates, *The Art of Memory*, 137).

150. Saul Sosnowski, "Entrevista a Carlos Fuentes," *Hispamérica* 9, 27 (1980): 96.

151. As discussed in the first chapter, historiographic metafiction moves away from the solipsistic dead end of late modernism. Unlike the *nouveau roman* or the most radical experiments of North American surfiction, postmodernist historical fiction returns literature to the historical milieu (Hutcheon, *A Poetics of Postmodernism*, xii; Connor, *Postmodernist Culture*, 127).

152. Umberto Eco, *Obra abierta* (Barcelona: Ariel, 1979), 39.

153. The location of these final events in Paris could not have been more appropriate for underscoring Fuentes's ideas about the transforming power of fiction. The suggestive combination of utopia and apocalypse that rule over Paris at the

end of the millennium inevitably evokes Fuentes's description of the student uprisings of May 1968, which he experienced firsthand and recorded in his book *París, la revolución de mayo* (Mexico City: Era, 1968). As Enrique Krauze points out, in 1968 Fuentes "saw reality impersonating fiction" ("The Guerrilla Dandy: The Literary and Political Illusions of Carlos Fuentes, everybody's favorite Mexican." *The New Republic* 27 Jun. 1988: 28–38). The world of literature was in the streets, covering the walls in the form of graffiti, and inspiring the actions of the student leaders. Those events may have prefigured for Fuentes the brief materialization of the same hoped-for kingdom of joy, justice, and power of imagination that the heretical and millennial movements would proclaim a few years later in *Terra Nostra*.

154. These characters belong to works that Fuentes considers the foundation of new Spanish American narrative: "Pierre Menard, autor del Quijote" (1939), *Rayuela* (1963), *Cien años de soledad* (1967), *Tres tristes tigres* (1965), *El obsceno pájaro de la noche* (1970), *El siglo de las luces* (1962), and *Conversación en la catedral* (1969). See in this respect his literary essays *La nueva novela hispanoamericana* (1969) and *Valiente Mundo Nuevo* (1990).

155. Carlos Fuentes, *Geografía de la novela*, 33.

CHAPTER 3. DISPLACING THE OFFICIAL RECORD: ISHMAEL REED'S REINVENTION OF WESTERN HISTORY AND MYTH

1. Robert Elliot Fox, *Conscientious Sorcerers: The Black Postmodernist Fiction of LeRoi Jones, Amiri Baraka, Ishmael Reed, and Samuel R. Delany* (New York: Greenwood Press, 1987). 42.

2. See Fox, *Conscientious Sorcerers*, 40; Henry Louis Gates, "The Blackness of Blackness: A Critique of the Sign and the Signifying Monkey," in *Black Literature and Literary Theory* (New York and London: Methuen, 1984), 297; Keith E. Byerman, *Fingering the Jagged Grain: Tradition and Form in Recent Black Fiction* (Athens: University of Georgia Press, 1985), 219; and Reginald Martin, *Ishmael Reed and the New Black Aesthetic Critics* (Houndmills: The MacMillan Press, 1988), 66. Martin alludes to Reed's use of colloquial diction, emotionalism, various perspectives on the improvement of social conditions for blacks, and automatic writing as some of the elements that were debated in African-American cultural circles during the sixties, and that are the target of satire in *Pallbearers*.

3. Reed himself has frequently commented on the influence of the visual media (especially television editing and film montage) in his work. See John O'Brien, "Ishmael Reed: An Interview," in *The New Fiction: Interviews with Innovative American Writers*, ed. Joe David Bellamy (Chicago: University of Illinois Press, 1972), 175–76.

4. For a discussion of the impact of cartoons and comic books on the writing of *Pallbearers*, see Peter Nazareth, "An Interview with Ishmael Reed," *The Iowa Review* 13, 2 (1982): 117.

5. Houston A. Baker points out that Louisiana Red is modeled on the same patterns used in *Mumbo Jumbo*, but it lacks the interest and ambition of the previous novel ("The Last Days of Louisiana Red," *Black World* 24 [June 1975]: 51–52). For other negative reviews of *Louisiana Red* see Peter Dreyer, "New Fiction: Brautigan, Gold and Reed," *San Francisco* 16 (December 1974): 86–87; George E. Kent, "Notes on the 1974 Black Literary Scene," *Phylon* 36 (1975): 182–203; Christopher Herron Lee, "A Gumbo of Black Humor: Voodoo and a Red Rooster,"

Louisville Defender 19 (1072); and Neil Schmitz, "The Gumbo That Jes Grew." *Partisan Review* 42 (1975): 311–16.

   6. This probably explains what provoked some of the most hostile attacks on the novel. Houston Baker, in his review of *Louisiana Red* for the journal *Black World*, underscores the lack of originality and ambition of Reed's novel in comparison with his previous work. Reviews like Baker's set a controversy into motion. See Martin, *Ishmael Reed and the New Black Aesthetic Critics.*

   7. Steven Kellman, *The Self-Begetting Novel,* (New York: Columbia University Press, 1980), 3.

   8. For a greater understanding of the discussion that follows, see the works of Zora Neale Hurston, *Tell My Horse: Voodoo and Life in Haiti and Jamaica* (New York: Harper Perennial, 1990); Maya Deren, *Divine Horsemen: The Divine Gods of Haiti* (New York: McPherson & Co., 1988); Alfred Métraux, *Voodoo in Haiti* (New York: Schocken Books, 1972); as well as Ishmael Reed. In his essays "I Hear You, Doc" (*SIONO*, 259–85) and "Shrovetide in Old New Orleans" (*SIONO*, 9–33) Reed offers a comprehensive view of both Haitian voodoo and North American hoodoo, and in his poem "Neo-HooDoo Manifesto" (*NCP*, 20–25) he explains his personal synthesis of these religious and cultural forms.

   9. It is this vision of voodoo as a collective creation from different cultures (Deren, *Divine Horsemen*, 59) that has led Reed to make it into "the perfect metaphor for the multiculture" (*SIONO*, 232). Regarding the sources of Haiti's slave trade see Philip D. Curtin's *The Atlantic Slave Trade: A Census* (Madison: University of Wisconsin Press, 1969).

   10. Deren, *Divine Horsemen*, 58.

   11. Hurston, *Tell My Horse*, 116.

   12. Ishmael Reed, *New and Collected Poems* (New York: Atheneum, 1989), 20.

   13. Ishmael Reed, *Shrovetide in New Orleans* (New York: Atheneum, 1989), 31–32.

   14. Reed, *NCP*, 24.

   15. Ibid., 26.

   16. Martin, *Ishmael Reed and the New Black Aesthetic Critics*, 107.

   17. Judeo-Christian dogmas are the ongoing target of Reed's criticism in all of his works, and he frequently aims his satire against their most sacred myths. Thus, the God of the Hebrews is described as "a dangerous paranoid pain-in-the-neck a CopGod from the git-go, Jeho-vah was the successful law and order candidate in the mythological relay of the 4th century A.D. Jeho-vah is the God of punishment. The H-Bomb is a typical Jeho-vah 'miracle.' " Jeho-vah is why we are in Vietnam. He told Moses to go out and 'subdue' the world" (*NCP*, 24). The figure of Christ, whom Reed considers to be an "impostor" (*MJ*, 97), is subjected to a similar treatment in his irreverent style: "Neo-HooDoo tells Christ to get lost (Judas Iscariot holds an honorary degree from Neo-HooDoo)" (*NCP*, 21).

   18. See Byerman, *Fingering the Jagged Grain: Tradition and Form in Recent Black Fiction*, 219; Mark Shadle, "A Bird's-Eye View: Ishmael Reed's Unsettling of the Score by Munching and Mooching on the *Mumbo Jumbo* Work of History," *North Dakota Quarterly* 54, 1 (1986): 18; Fox, *Conscientious Sorcerers*, 49; Martin, *Ishmael Reed and the New Black Aesthetic Critics*, 93; and Bernard John De Filippo, "HooDoo, Voodoo, and Conjure: The Novels of Ishmael Reed," Ph.D. diss. Carnegie-Mellon University, Pittsburgh, 1989, 112.

   19. These complex intertextual and intratextual networks have led Henry Louis Gates, Jr. to define *Mumbo Jumbo* as, "a book about texts and a book of

texts, a composite narrative composed of sub-texts, pre-texts, post-texts, and narratives-within-narratives" ("The Blackness of Blackness, 299).

20. See Gates, "The Blackness of Blackness," 300; Byerman, *Fingering the Jagged Grain*, 225; and Shadle, "A Bird's-Eye View," 20.

21. According to Gates, Legba is invoked through the phrase "eh là-bas" in New Orleans jazz recordings of the twenties and thirties ("The Blackness," 300). In a self-interview, Reed himself has identified LaBas as the name by which Legba is identified in North America. (*SIONO*, 132).

22. Donald Cosentino, "Who is that Fellow in the Many-colored Cap?: Transformations of Eshu in Old and New World Mythologies," *Journal of American Folklore* 100, 397 (1987): 265.

23. Unless otherwise indicated, all the quotes from *Mumbo Jumbo* come from the Atheneum edition (1988).

24. See Métraux, *Voodoo in Haiti*, 101; Hurston, *Tell My Horse*, 129.

25. See De Filippo, "HooDoo, Voodoo, and Conjure," 125. Gates has also proposed German engraver Hermann Knackfuss as another possible historical model for Von Vampton ("The Blackness of Blackness," 302–3). In fact, page 155 of *Mumbo Jumbo* reproduces Knakfuss's famous heliogravure "People of Europe, protect that which is most holy to you," in which the German artist justified European domination over Asia.

26. Bruce Kellner, ed., *The Harlem Renaissance* (Westport, Conn.: Greenwood Press, 1984),368. On Carl Van Vechten and his relations with Harlem, see Edward Lueders, *Carl Van Vechten* (New York: Twayne, 1965); Nathan Huggins, *Harlem Renaissance* (New York: Oxford University Press, 1971); and Carl Van Vechten, *Fragments from an Unwritten Autobiography* (New Haven: Yale University Press, 1955).

27. Roi Ottley and William Weatherby, eds., *The Negro in New York* (New York: The New York Public Library, 1967), 246.

28. Ibid., 255.

29. Most details in the description of this scene—e.g. the name of the villa created by Caruso or the luxurious 24-karat-gold-decorated piano—are taken from the description that Ottley and Weatherby give of Madame Walker's palace (ibid., 254). Reed also mentions Madam Walker in his article "Harlem Renaissance Day" (*SIONO*, 256). For more information on Madam Sarah Walker and Harlem's middle-class tastes with its predilections for hair straighteners and skin lighteners, see Jervis Anderson, *This Was Harlem* (New York: Farrar, Strauss and Giroux, 1982).

30. See Ottley and Weatherby, eds., *The Negro in New York*, 257; and Bruce Kellner, ed., *The Harlem Renaissance*, 371–72.

31. See De Filippo, "HooDoo, Voodoo, and Conjure," 132.

32. Gates, "The Blackness of Blackness," 302.

33. See Ottley and Weatherby, eds., *The Negro in New York*, 252; and Kellner, ed., *The Harlem Renaissance*, 150–51.

34. The life and personality of the historical Hamid must have fascinated Reed. Both Claude McKay (*Home to Harlem* [Boston: Northeastern University Press, 1987]) and Kellner (*The Harlem Renaissance*) provide many details about Hamid that define him as a novelistic figure very much attuned to Reed's penchant for the eccentric. Like the characters of LaBas's "Egyptian legend," Hamid claimed to be born in Sudan (when in fact he was a native of the U.S. South). His death trying to demonstrate his mystical powers while aloft in an airplane seems to have been taken from Reed's novel, rather than from real life.

35. De Filippo, "HooDoo, Voodoo, and Conjure," 125.

36. For Reed's views on multiculturalism in North American forms of expression, see his essays "America: The Multinational Society" (*WIF*, 49–56) and "The Multi-Cultural Artist: A New Phase in American Writing" (*SIONO*, 252–54).

37. O'Brien, "Ishmael Reed: An Interview," 179.

38. Reed, *SIONO*, 130.

39. E. A. Wallis Budge, *Osiris and the Egyptian Resurrection* (New York: Dover Publications, 1973), 1–23. Budge's work is one of the sources that Reed acknowledges in his "Partial Bibliography" (*MJ*, 219).

40. Budge, *Osiris*, 11.

41. Concerning Budge's colonialist and racist ideology, see Martin Bernal, *Black Athena: The Afroasiatic Roots of Classical Civilization* (New Brunswick, N.J.: Rutgers University Press, 1987), 261–62. In relation to the intuitive and not very rigorous character of his work, see Leonard H. Lesko, "Egyptian Religion: History of Study," *The Encyclopedia of Religion*, ed. Mircea Eliade (New York: MacMillan, 1987), 67.

42. Quoted in Bernal, *Black Athena*, 261.

43. Ibid., 262.

44. De Filippo, "HooDoo, Voodoo, and Conjure," 152.

45. Plutarch's version ends here. Diodorus offers a very similar version, but other texts provide an alternative ending. According to some Egyptian legends, Isis revived Osiris's body and then conceived Horus (Angela D. Thomas, *Egyptian Gods and Myths* [Aylesbury: Shire Publications, 1986], 46).

46. Fox, *Conscientious Sorcerers*, 54.

47. Ishmael Reed, *Mumbo Jumbo* (Garden City, N.Y.: Doubleday, 1972), 161.

48. Furthermore, the quoted passage is part of a section in Higgins's work that is entitled "Christ Black" (I, 138), and elsewhere Higgins states that Christ came from a black Jewish tribe (I, 751). In order to substantiate his theory, Higgins refers to the many sculptures and paintings in which Christ has Negroid features. The problem with Higgins's thesis is that he does not seem to discriminate between the representation and the object of the representation, between the symbolic and the literal. The fact that there are many examples of black Madonnas does not necessarily mean that the Virgin Mary and her Child were black, although it may demonstrate the influence of African cults and religions on the imagery of Christianity. See Danita Redd, "Black Madonnas of Europe: Diffusion of the African Isis," *African Presence in Early Europe*, ed. Ivan Van Sertima (New Brunswick, N.J.: Transaction Publisher, 1985).

49. Apart from the obvious differences between Bernal's and Reed's projects, one a scientific essay and the other a work of satirical fiction, the two share a similar provocative intention. Both Bernal's rigorous work and Reed's circuslike novel seek to contest the historical visions that we accept as natural, but which too frequently have been built on the basis of political, religious, and/or national interest. Bernal ends the introduction to his work stating that "the political purpose of Black Athena is, of course, to lessen European cultural arrogance" (*Black Athena* I, 73). In a similar way, Reed mentions in an interview that his first novels aimed "to humble Judeo-Christian culture" (*SIONO*, 133). If not in their nature and tone, both Bernal and Reed coincide at least in their declared oppositional attitude in relation to many of what they regard as the stereotypes of Western civilization.

50. Bernal reminds us, for example, how the great classical authors like Aeschylus and Plato invariably placed Hellenistic culture in a lower position than those of the Egyptian and the Phoenician (*Black Athena*, 22–23).

51. Ibid., 1:24.

52. Besides all these authors, Bernal also mentions W. E. B. Du Bois and Ali Mazrui, who, although more moderate than those mentioned above, defended a more multicultural, and therefore less restrictive, perspective in the history of civilizations.

53. In the same tradition as Van Sertima's controversial *They Came Before Columbus* (New York: Random House, 1976), scholars such as Joan Covey, R. A. Jairazbhoy, Keith Jordan, Harold Lawrence, Beatrice Lumpkin, and Alexander Von Wuthenau defend the existence of African contacts with Americans before the Europeans' arrival. Their contributions have been collected by Van Sertima himself in *African Presence in Early America.*

54. As in Fuentes's cultural utopia, what is perhaps being expressed through these myths of the fall is the contemporary artist's desire to recuperate spaces of power and privilege occupied in the past.

55. This view of the relationship between art and power is not exclusive to this episode of *Mumbo Jumbo*; on the contrary, it is repeated throughout Reed's works. In fact, in his definition of Neo-HooDooism Reed uses the same terms as he did in depicting Osiris's Egypt: "Neo-HooDoo believes that every man is an artist and every artist a priest" (*NCP*, 21).

56. Reed has often expressed his admiration for Hurston's work. Examples of this recognition can be found in his prologue to a recent edition of *Tell My Horse* (xi–xvi), as well as in several interviews. In his "Neo-HooDoo Manifesto" Reed refers to Hurston as "our theoretician" (*NCP*, 21), and two of Hurston's works (*Voodoo* Gods and *Mules and Men*) appear in his "Partial Bibliography."

57. Zora Neale Hurston, *Mules and Men* (Bloomington: Indiana University Press, 1978), 195.

58. For a critical evaluation of Hurston's *Moses* on these terms, see Robert E. Hemenway, *Zora Neale Hurston: A Literary Biography* (Urbana: University of Illinois Press, 1977), 256; Lillie P. Howard, *Zora Neale Hurston* (Boston: Twayne, 1980), 113; and Blyden Jackson, "Moses, Man of the Mountain: A Study of Power," in *Zora Neale Hurston*, ed. Harold Bloom (New York: Chelsea House, 1986), 152.

59. Robert Bone, *The Negro Novel in America* (New Haven: Yale University Press, 1958), 114.

60. With regard to the dispersion of these legends, Hurston has noted in *Tell My Horse*: "whenever the Negro is found, there are traditional tales of Moses and his supernatural powers that are not in the Bible, nor can they be found in any written life of Moses" (116). Reed reproduces this same passage in the Doubleday edition of *Mumbo Jumbo*, as part of the above-mentioned spiraling quotation (161).

61. Hemenway, *Zora Neale Hurston*, 257.

62. See chapter XVI in Zora Neale Hurston, *Moses, Man of the Mountain* (New York: Harper Perennial, 1991).

63. Hemenway (*Zora Neale Hurston*, 262) points out the humorous use of speech as one of the ways in which Hurston humanizes the figure of Moses. Although endowed with supernatural powers, Moses behaves and speaks like a black from the U.S. rural South—especially after his experience with Jethro.

64. The only exception is probably Gates, who in "The Blackness of Blackness" (296) mentions some of the similarities between the works of both writers, alluding especially to their reconstruction of the Mosaic legends.

65. Deborah E. McDowell, "Foreword: Lines of Descent / Dissenting Lines," in *Moses*, xxii.

66. See, for example, Richard Wright's devastating review of *Their Eyes Were Watching God*, "In Between Laughter and Tears," *New Masses*, (5 October 1937), 22, 25.

67. Hurston, *Moses*, 116.

68. Although Reed adopts voodoo as the essential base of his aesthetic theory and world view, he does not acknowledge the fact that in Haiti Damballah, the highest figure in the voodoo pantheon, is often identified with Moses (Hurston, *Tell My Horse*, 116; *Moses*, xxiv).

69. David Annan, "The Assassins and the Knights Templar," in *Secret Societies*, ed. Norman MacKenzie (New York: Holt, Rinehart and Winston, 1967), 106–29.

70. Malcolm Barber offers what is considered the most rigorous discussion of the persecution of the Templars. In his examination of this obscure event, he categorically affirms the need to explain it "in terms of factors external to the Order," such as "the financial needs of Philip the Fair" and "the weakness of the papacy" (*The Trial of the Templars* [Cambridge, Mass.: Cambridge University Press, 1978], 247). For a similar interpretation see Ioan Petru Culianu, "Sacrilege," in *The Encyclopedia of Religion*, ed. Eliade.

71. Mark Sullivan, *Our Times: 1900–1925*, 6 vols. (New York: Charles Scribner's Sons, 1972); Robert K. Murray, *The Harding Era: Warren G. Harding and His Administration* (Minneapolis: University of Minnesota Press, 1969). As Reed himself has acknowledged in the novel, the portrayal of the Harding era is based mostly on Mark Sullivan's *Our Times* (*MJ*, 20, 21, 146, 223). For references to Murray's work in the novel, see *MJ*, 17, 146, 222.

72. Randolph Downes, "Negro Rights and White Backlash in the Campaign of 1920," *Ohio History* 75, 2–3 (1966): 101. Downes, who offers an exhaustive coverage of Harding's presidential campaign, is particularly thorough in his treatment of the "Negro blood story" and the pressures of the civil rights movement.

73. Murray, *The Harding Era*, 64.

74. Downes, "Negro Rights," 100–101.

75. Ibid., 102–03. As Downes points out, the Republican National Committee was already prepared for an incident like this and had ordered the making of a dossier containing authentic genealogical data (ibid., 101). As a consequence of the escalation of attacks from Chancellor and other democrats, Will Hays made the dossier public (Murray, *The Harding Era*, 64).

76. Sullivan, *Our Times*, 6: 135–36.

77. Ibid., 6: 134.

78. In fact, Chancellor was immediately expelled from Wooster College and emigrated to Canada. Before leaving the States he published a book in which he expanded his thesis. This is, without question, the book that Reed mentions in his novel. As noted, chapter 46 in *Mumbo Jumbo* mentions three works about Harding's Negro blood. However, all three, as described by Reed, correspond to different aspects of—or anecdotes related to—Chancellor's essay. For a detailed description of the trajectory of Chancellor and his book, see Adams's article "Annals of Politics: A Case of Bibliocide," *The New Yorker*, (21 October 1939), 39–46. According to Murray (65) and Adams (41–42), virtually all copies of this work, which circulated underground, were confiscated by Harry Daugherty, who was by then attorney general.

79. Sullivan, *Our Times*, 6:136.

80. Apart from his declared anti-black feelings, Chancellor was known for his anti-Semitic ideas and for his unconditional support of Wilson's imperialist poli-

tics. Before issuing the letter against Harding, Chancellor had disclosed his opinions against the candidate's antiinterventionist politics and also against the high commissaries of the Soviet Union whom he considered a group of Jews seeking revenge for past discriminations (Downes, "Negro Rights and White Backlash in the Campaign of 1920," 103).

81. In a conversation with his friend, journalist James Faulkner, the Republican candidate said about this issue: "How do I know, Jim? One of my ancestors may have jumped the fence" (Murray, *The Harding Era*, 64). In *Mumbo Jumbo*, Reed reproduces Harding's statement as one of the grounds on which the Wallflower Order condemns him (*MJ*, 146).

82. Downes, "Negro Rights," 107.

83. Reed, *SIONO*, 269.

84. For a study of the role of voodoo in the social history of Haiti, see Dantes Bellegarde, *Histoire du peuple haïtien (1492–1952)* (Port-au-Prince: Collection du cent-cinquant enaire de l'indépendence d'Haiti, 1953), and Métraux, *Voodoo in Haiti*. Both authors point out how, in addition to being a religion, voodoo became a political association, a fraternity aimed at the liberation of blacks. The influence of voodoo in the struggle for the independence of Haiti is dramatically exemplified by Métraux's description of the Oath of Bois Caiman, the blood pact that, according to tradition, set the Haitian revolution in motion on August 14,1791 (42–43). Many of the anecdotes related to voodoo are, however, fictional. For example, Reed attributes President Wilson's final illness to a voodoo curse for the U.S. invasion. In support of this idea, Reed mentions Murray's essay. Of course, Murray does not offer such a fantastic theory. On the contrary, he attributes Wilson's progressive paralysis to two brain seizures that he suffered at the end of his presidential term. What Reed does borrow from Murray is the description of the symptoms of Wilson's sickness (*The Harding Era*, 76–79).

85. For an introduction to the pillage suffered by all Caribbean countries, see Eduardo Galeano, *Open Veins of Latin America: Five Centuries of the Pillage of a Continent* (New York and London: Monthly Review Press, 1973); and Suzy Castor, "The American Occupation of Haiti (1915–34) and the Dominican Republic (1916–24)." *The Massachusetts Review* 15, 1 (1974): 253–75.

86. Johanna Von Grafenstein, *Haití* (Mexico City: Alianza Editorial Mexicana, 1988), 267.

87. For a detailed list of articles published in opposition to the occupation, see Richard G. Frederick, *Warren G. Harding: A Bibliography* (Westport, Conn: Greenwood Press, 1992), 205–10. If news about the occupation of Haiti was scarce during the Wilson administration, it was mainly due to the fact that interventions of the same sort were part of the habitual expansionist practices in U.S. foreign policy.

88. Political agitation under the rule of General Vilbrun Guillaume Sam was merely an excuse to carry out a plan that the U.S. Department of State had been hatching for many years. Since the construction of the Panama Canal, the United States had shown great interest in Haiti's strategic position and was just waiting for the right moment to initiate a military intervention. See Arthur Link, *La política de Estados Unidos en América Latina* (Mexico City: Fondo de Cultura Económica, 1960), 258; and Castor, "The American Occupation," 262.

89. Suzy Castor, "The American Occupation," 267.

90. Von Grafenstein, *Haití*, 271.

91. After the president's death it was discovered that corruption had affected the executive branch, including the departments of Justice, the Interior, the Navy, "the Veterans Bureau," and "The Alien Property Custodian."

92. Sullivan, *Our Times*, 6:365; Adams, "Annals of Politics," 43.

93. Means also insinuated that Jesse W. Smith's death was not a suicide but rather another assassination (Murray, *The Harding Era*, 490). In *Mumbo Jumbo* Reed retakes this same idea and turns Smith into another victim of the Wallflower Order's conspiracy.

94. Sullivan, *Our Times*, 6: 364. References to Harding's "mysterious" death can still be found today. See Charles and Robert McHenry, *Webster's Guide to American History* (Springfield, Ill.: G. & C. Merriam Co., 1971), 1003; and Marshall Smelser and Joan R. Gundersen, *American History at a Glance* (New York: Harper & Row, 1975), 189. For a complete list of the historical works that discuss Harding's death, see Frederick, *Warren G. Harding*, 305–08.

95. The expression is not originally Reed's, but Carl G. Jung's, who, after his visit to the United States wrote "Your Negroid and Indian Behaviour," *The Forum* 83, 4 (1930): 193–99. Jung saw in the cultural expression and behavior of North Americans an expression of "contagion" with the African-American population. The use of expressions such as "infection" and "contagion" to talk about the impact of black culture on U.S. society is a major influence in *Mumbo Jumbo*, where the African-American renaissance is explained through the metaphor of an epidemic (Jes Grew) that some seek to combat and others to perpetuate. For a discussion of Jung's views on North America and its African heritage, see Ann Douglas, *Terrible Honesty: Mongrel Manhattan in the 1920s* (New York: Farrar, Strauss and Giroux, 1995), 165–66.

96. Kellner, ed., *The Harlem Renaissance*, xv; *Terrible Honesty*, 73.

97. John Hope Franklin, *From Slavery to Freedom: A History of Negro Americans* (New York: Alfred A. Knopf, 1980), 364; Douglas, *Terrible Honesty*, 18.

98. Arnold Shaw, *The Jazz Age: Popular Music in the 1920s* (New York: Oxford University Press, 1987), 59; Douglas, *Terrible Honesty*, 74.

99. Ottley and Weatherby, eds., *The Negro in New York*, 257. The name "The Dark Tower" was adopted from a column that Countee Cullen—one of the habitués of Mme. Walker's cultural parties wrote in the magazine *Opportunity*.

100. Ottley and Weatherby, eds., *The Negro in New York*, 249.

101. Like Cullen, Brown writes about "the Black Christ"—the title of Cullen's greatest poem—"commingles Death and Nature," and resides "solidly in the Western tradition" (*MJ*, 116). Von Vampton's criticism of Brown's work in *Mumbo Jumbo* re-creates many of the critical stereotypes about Cullen. For an analysis of these stereotypes, see Douglas, *Terrible Honesty*, 340–44.

102. As Gates points out, the phrase "jes' grew" (from *Uncle Tom's Cabin*) was appropriated by James Weldon Johnson to refer to the compositions of ragtime that were so popular in the 1890s. Gates also mentions Ellison's commentaries about the importance that ragtime had on the development of African-American popular music (Gates, "The Blackness," 302).

103. Among many other popular black musicians, the novel also mentions W. C. Handy ("the father of the blues"), Louis Armstrong, and Fats Waller.

104. Ishmael Reed, *SIONO*, 258. In his brief essay "Harlem Renaissance Day" (*SIONO*, 255–58) Reed rejects the criticisms launched against the movement by some dogmatic intellectuals. According to Reed, critics such as Addison Gayle had accused the renaissance of the twenties of lack of engagement with the cause of black people. The origin of Reed's essay is a speech given at a New York secondary school, a situation very similar to the one presented in the epilogue of *Mumbo Jumbo*, where LaBas reflects on the Harlem Renaissance before an audience of students.

105. For another positive evaluation of the role played by Van Vechten in the Harlem Renaissance, see Richard Barksdale and Kenneth Kinnamon, ed., *Black Writers of America: A Comprehensive Anthology* (New York: Macmillan Co., 1972), 475: "No one on the New York literary and social scene did more to bring Black writers and singers to the attention of whites than this highly sophisticated novelist and critic."

106. See Reed, *SIONO*, 256; Kellner, ed., *The Harlem Renaissance*, xxiii; and Barksdale and Kinnamon, ed., *Black Writers of America*, 475.

107. At the time of the Great Depression Andrew Mellon was the Secretary of the Treasury and, according to some historians, his role in the economic disaster has not yet been clarified. See Hugh Brogan, *The Penguin History of the United States of America* (London: Penguin Books, 1990), 507.

108. Bellamy, ed., *The New Fiction*, 134; Reed, *SIONO*, 131.

109. Reed submitted the manuscript of *Mumbo Jumbo* to the publisher in January 1971. The conspiracy began to go public on 17 June 1972, when five members of the Gemstone team (a White House undercover group) were caught in the act of spying on Democratic Party headquarters. See Jonathan Schell, "Watergate." *A History of Our Time: Readings on Postwar America*, ed. William H. Chafe and Harvard Sitkoff (New York: Oxford University Press, 1991), 421.

110. Reed, *NCP*, 101.

111. Gates, "The Blackness of Blackness," 311.

112. Byerman, *Fingering the Jagged Grain*, 227.

113. For a detailed study of the postmodernist use of allegory, see McHale, *Postmodernist Fiction*, 140–47). In "The Blackness of Blackness," Gates has also examined the allegorical dimension of *Mumbo Jumbo* in relation to the acts of writing and reading.

114. Reginald Martin is probably the only exception. In *Ishmael Reed and the New Black Aesthetic Critics*, he points out: "*Mumbo Jumbo* is itself the Text, and it appears in 1972 as a direct response to the assertion that there is no 'black' way of doing things; that black contributions to world culture have been insignificant at best" (93).

115. McHale, *Postmodernist Fiction*, 142.

116. Reed, *NCP*, 26.

117. For examples of a misreading of Reed's works as mere entertainment, see reviews written by John Alfred Avant, "*Mumbo Jumbo*," *Library Journal* (1 October 1972), 3182; Robert Lee, "Cultures Clash in *Mumbo Jumbo*," *Los Angeles Times* (10 December 1972), 78; and Roger Whitlow, "Ishmael Reed," *Black American Literature: A Critical History* (Chicago: Nelson Hall, 1973), 154–57.

118. Gates, "The Blackness of Blackness," 312.

119. The Afrocentric perspective of history has become increasingly popular in the last decades. Regarding this issue, see George O. Cox, *African Empires and Civilizations—Ancient and Medieval* (Washington D.C.: African Heritage Studies Publishers, 1974); Cheik A. Diop, *The African Origin of Civilization: Myth or Reality* (New York: Lawrence Hill, 1974); George G. G. M. James, *Stolen Legacy* (New York: Philosophical Library, 1954); Jones, *Black Zeus* (Seattle, Wash.: Frayn Printing Co., 1971), and *Profiles in African Heritage* (Seattle, Wash.: Frayn Printing Co., 1972); Van Sertima, *They Came Before Columbus, African Presence in Early Europe* (New Brunswick, N.J.: Transaction Publisher, 1985), and *African Presence in Early America* (New Brunswick, N.J.: Transaction Books, 1987); Joseph E. Harris, ed. *Africa and Africans as Seen by Classical Writers: The William Leo Hansberry African Notebook* (Washington, D.C.: Howard University Press,

1977); C. Tsehloane Keto, *The Africa Centered Perspective of History and Social Sciences in the Twenty First Century* (Blackwood: K.A. Publications, 1989); and Bernal, *Black Athena*.

120. Henry Louis Gates Jr., *The Signifying Monkey: A Theory of Afro-American Literary Criticism* (New York: Oxford University Press, 1988), 4.

121. About Reed's supposed lack of social and political responsibility, see Ernest Kaiser "The Last Days of Louisiana Reed," *Freedomways* (1974): 379; Addison Gayle Jr., "Black Women and Black Men: The Literature of Catharsis," *Black Books Bulletin* 4 (1976): 48–52; and Amiri Baraka, "Afro-American Literature and Class Struggle," *Black American Literature Forum* 14, 1 (1980): 5–14.

122. In relation to *Pallbearers*, see reviews written by John Greenya (*Washington Star*, 5 November 1967), William Hogan (*San Francisco Chronicle*, 29 November 1967), and Allan Katzman (*East Village Other,* 16 July 1967); Hoke Norris (*Chicago Daily News*,16 August 1969), Webster Scott (*Life*, 15 August 1969) and W. J. Nesbitt (*Northern Echo*, 21 May 1971), about *Radio*; and Stephen Hunter (*Baltimore Sun*, 13 August 1972), George Lane (*Patriot Ledger*, 22 August 1972), and Gary Pearce (*News and Observer*, September 1972) about *Mumbo Jumbo*.

123. See John Alfred Avant, "*Mumbo Jumbo*," 3182; Christopher Herron Lee, "A Gumbo of Black Humor: Voodoo and a Red Rooster," *Louisville Defender* 19 (31 January 1972); and Roger Whitlow, "Ishmael Reed," *Black American Literature: A Critical History* (Chicago: Nelson Hall, 1973), 154–57.

124. This attitude is dramatized in the novel through the ultraconservative Biff Musclewhite (chapter 29) and the Marxist critic who harasses LaBas after his lecture in the epilogue. From apparently antithetical positions, both characters support a return to the great classics of the Western tradition.

125. Lawrence Lipton, "Robin the Cock and Doopeyduk Doing the Boogaloo in Harry Sam with Rusty Jethroe and Letterhead America," *Cavalier* 18 (1968): 70–74; Toni Cade, "The Free-Lance Pallbearers," *Liberator* 9 (1969): 20; Kenneth Kinnamon, "The Free-Lance Pallbearers," *Negro American Literature* Forum 1 (1967): 18; Bob H. Singer, "Yellow Back Radio Broke-Down," *New York Herald Tribune* (28 September 1969), 12; Edward M. White, "Story of Black Power Overcoming Evil," *Los Angeles Times Book Review* (25 January 1970), 2; Roger Whitlow, "Ishmael Reed." *Black American Literature: A Critical History* (Chicago: Nelson Hall, 1973), 154–57; Roland E. Bush, "Werewolf of the Wild West: On a Novel by Ishmael Reed," *Black World* 23 (1974): 64–66; Avant, "*Mumbo Jumbo*," 3182.

126. Lucien Dällenbach, *The Mirror in the Text*, trans. Jeremy Whiteley and Emma Hughes (Chicago: University of Chicago Press, 1977), 101.

127. Gates, "The Blackness of Blackness," 296.

128. Bernal, *Black Athena*, 1: 139; Jean-Pierre Mahé, "Hermes Trismegistos," *The Encyclopedia of Religion*, ed. Eliade, 287.

129. For a complete study of this Egyptian institution, see Alan H. Gardiner, "The House of Life," *The Journal of Egyptian Archaeology* 24 (1938): 157–79.

130. In some traditions the trickster is the agent who introduces fire, agriculture, and tools into the human community. He is therefore the bringer of culture (Lawrence E. Sullivan, "Tricksters: An Overview," *The Encyclopedia of Religion*, 45).

131. Robert D. Pelton, "African Tricksters," *The Encyclopedia of Religion*, ed. Eliade, 46.

132. Gates, *The Signifying Monkey*, 6.

133. Gates also points to Legba's representation as the god of generation and fecundity (ibid., 6).

134. Ibid., 26.

135. Gates has also insisted on this pan-African quality of both the mythical Legba and the fictional LaBas: "His surname, of course, is French for 'over there,' and his presence unites 'over there' (Africa) with 'right here.' He is indeed the messenger of the gods, the divine Pan-African interpreter, pursuing, in the language of the text, 'The Work,' which is not only Voudou but also the very work (and play) of art itself" ("The Blackness," 301).

136. Ibid.

Chapter 4. Between Political Commitment and Epistemological Skepticism: Julio Cortázar and E. L. Doctorow

1. Hayden White, *Tropics of Discourse: Essays in Cultural Criticism* (Baltimore: The Johns Hopkins University Press, 1978), 82.

2. Fredric Jameson, *Postmodernism or the Cultural Logic of Late Capitalism* (Durham, N.C.: Duke University Press, 1991), 48, 54.

3. Jaime Alazraki, "Los últimos cuentos de Julio Cortázar," *Revista Ibero-americana* 130- 31 (1985): 21.

4. Jean Franco, "Julio Cortázar: Utopia and Everyday Life," *Inti* 10–11 (1979–80): 108–18.

5. In spite of being more politically engaged, Cortázar's late work is openly critical of this Messianic view of the poet espoused by the Romantics. See Ernesto González Bermejo, *Revelaciones de un cronopio: conversaciones con Cortázar* (Buenos Aires: Contrapunto, 1986), 146; and Julio Cortázar, *Viaje alrededor de una mesa* (Buenos Aires: Cuadernos de Rayvela, 1970), 25; *Agentina: años de alambradas culturales* (Barcelona: Muchnik, 1984), 86, 92.

6. See Omar Prego, *La fascinación de las palabras: Conversaciones con Julio Cortázar* (Barcelona: Muchnik, 1985), 130; and Ernesto González Bermejo, *Revelaciones de un cronopio*, 136.

7. In his interview with Omar Prego (*La fascinación de las palabras*, 67), Cortázar has stressed the major importance of "El Perseguidor" in the construction of his characters' psychology: "the first time that I reflected on . . . the dialogue, the confrontation with a fellow man, with someone who is not my double, but rather another human being who is not at the service of a fantastic story— where the story is the character, contains the character and is determined by the character—was in 'El Perseguidor.' "

8. Julio Cortázar, "Corrección de pruebas," in *Convergencias/Divergencias/Incidencias*, ed. Julio Ortega (Barcelona: Tusquets, 1973), 20.

9. Cortázar has referred to *Rayuela* as the "philosophy" of his short stories: "*Hopscotch* is in a sense the philosophy of my stories, an investigation of what for many years determined their subject matter and stimuli" (*La vuelta al día en ochenta mundos* [Mexico City: Siglo XXI, 1967], 1: 41; 22).

10. Prego, *La fascinación de las palabras*, 127.

11. Ernesto González Bermejo, *Revelaciones de un cronopio*, 132. For a description of the impact of the Cuban revolution on Cortázar, see his open letter to Fernández Retamar (*Último Round* [Mexico City: Siglo XXI, 1969], 265–80).

12. *62 / modelo para armar* is the novel that chronologically follows *Rayuela*. It is an experiment in pure fiction where the historical background is again absent.

Although political subjects invade Cortázar's essays from the late sixties on, his fiction continues to be predominantly experimental.

13. Cortázar alludes to the bad reviews of "Reunion" in his "Corrección de Pruebas en Alta Provenza," 36.

14. Cortázar, *VDOM*, 2: 185–93.

15. Cortázar, *UR*, 2: 265–80.

16. The National Commission on the Desaparecidos (CONADEP) was appointed by President Alfonsín in December 1983. Throughout a period of nine months this commission chaired by Sábato collected thousands of statements from those who survived the Dirty War. In September 1984 it published its conclusions with the title *Nunca más* (Nevermore). The document amassed evidence accusing one thousand three hundred members of the armed forces, confirmed the deaths of many of the *desaparecidos* (people abducted by the military forces during the Dirty War), and revealed chilling details about their tortures. It also demonstrated that many of the victims had absolutely nothing to do with the guerrillas. The publication of *Nunca más* had a great impact on public opinion and played an important part in the trials against the *Junta* members.

17. Prego, *La fascinación de las palabras*, 134.

18. With the return of democracy to Argentina in late 1983, and as a result of national and international pressure, the nine military commanders who had ruled the country between 1976 and 1983 were brought before a court of law and tried for their crimes. Although the trials were carried out, most of the active partici pants in the repression (its hundreds of executioners) were cleared of all charges claiming that they acted in "due obedience." For information about these trials, see *Argentina: The Military Juntas and Human Rights. Report of the Trial of the Former Junta Members, 1985* (London: Amnesty International Publications, 1987).

19. Cortázar, *AAAC*, 100.

20. Ibid., 75.

21. Julio Cortázar, *Nicaragua tan violentamente dulce* (Barcelona: Muchnik, 1984), 92.

22. For an analysis of the ideology of the Sandinistas, see David Hodges, *The Intellectual Foundations of the Nicaraguan Revolution* (Austin: University of Texas Press, 1986).

23. The main difference, however, stems from the "historical" character of the Nicaraguan utopia. While the brotherhood of Nahua poets and Osiris's court of artists are mere fantasies, the cultural achievements of Sandinista Nicaragua are an undeniable reality.

24. In his late work Cortázar tends to abandon the old modernist identification between everyday life and the banal, in order to contemplate the relationship between art and historical reality in a more productive way. See Franco, "Julio Cortázar," 111. Everyday reality is not only the "Gran Costumbre" of the bourgeoisie in Paris or Buenos Aires. Daily life also manifests itself through the forms of popular art that are produced in a small Central American country. Unlike the clear-cut separation between art and reality in his early works, daily experiences can now also be a source of utopian pleasure.

25. See Jaime Alazraki, "From Bestiary to Glenda: Pushing the Short Story to its Utmost Limits," *Review of Contemporary Fiction* 3, 3 (1983): 96–97; and "Los últimos cuentos de Julio Cortázar," 4–29.

26. Phil Gunson, ed., *The Dictionary of Contemporary Politics of South America* (New York: Macmillan Publishing Co., 1989), 96. Two of the clippings,

for example, allude to French police violence (19, 43; 14, 38), while two others mention U.S. military aid to dictatorships in Central and South America (364, 383; 367, 386).

27. Timothy P. Wicham-Crowley, *Guerrillas and Revolution in Latin America: A Comparative Study of Insurgents and Regimes Since 1956* (Princeton: Princeton University Press, 1992), 313.

28. Robert Moss, *Urban Guerrillas: The New Face of Political Violence* (London: Temple Smith, 1972), 159.

29. For a discussion of U.S. interventionism in Latin America and human rights violations during the 1970s, see Tom J. Farer, *The Grand Strategy of the United States in Latin America* (New Brunswick, N.J.: Transaction Books, 1988). U.S. government and corporate aid to the coup against Chilean president Salvador Allende in 1973 is also well documented. See Gunson, ed., *The Dictionary of Contemporary Politics of South America*, 5.

30. Rather than comment on these facts, the words Trelew and Munich are simply placed side by side in *Libro de Manuel*, leaving the readers to make the necessary connection and arrive at their own conclusions concerning manipulation by the mass media.

31. However, Cortázar does not reject the media per se, but rather the alienation they cause. Indeed, he uses popular and mass culture for his own ends. The potential value that Cortázar attributes to the media is evidenced by his use of the press in *Libro de Manuel* and comic strips in *Fantomas*.

32. Theo D'Haen, *Text to Reader: A Communicative Approach to Fowles, Barth, Cortázar and Boon* (Amsterdam: John Benjamins, 1983), 92.

33. See Randolph Pope, "Dos novelas álbum: *Libro de Manuel* de Cortázar y *Figuraciones en el mes de marzo* de Díaz Valcárcel," *Bilingual Review* 1, 2 (1974): 170–84; Ellen M. McCraken, "*Libro de Manuel* and *Fantomas contra los vampiros multinacionales*: Mass Culture, Art, and Politics," in *Literature and Popular Culture in the Hispanic World: A Symposium* (Gaithersburg: Hispamérica, 1981), 69–77; and Myrna Solotorevsky, *Literatura—Paraliteratura: Puig, Borges, Donoso, Cortázar, Vargas Llosa* (Gaithersburg: Hispamérica, 1988).

34. Ihab Hassan, *The Right Promethean Fire: Imagination, Science, and Cultural Change* (Urbana: University of Illinois Press, 1980), 17.

35. Barbara Foley, *Telling the Truth: The Theory and Practice of Documentary Fiction* (Ithaca: Cornell University Press, 1986), 221.

36. In *Narrative Irony in the Contemporary Spanish-American Novel* (Ithaca: Cornell University Press, 1984), 188, Jonathan Titler uses the term "schizoid narration" to refer to the novel's heterogeneity of perspectives.

37. At the very beginning of the narrative segment that follows the prologue, the narrator (Andrés), refers to the role played by "the-one-I-told-you" as the first narrator who tries to record the history of the Joda: "Por lo demás era como si el que te dije hubiera tenido la intención de narrar algunas cosas, puesto que había guardado una considerable cantidad de fichas y papelitos, esperando al parecer que terminaran por aglutinarse sin demasiada pérdida" (*LM* 11) ["Otherwise, it was as if the one I told you had intended to recount some things, for he had gathered together a considerable amount of notes and clippings, waiting, it would seem, for them to end up all falling into place without too much loss"] (6).

38. Another narrative agency present is the voice that sets the novel in motion. The opening segment is delivered by a voice that announces the novel's subject and the circumstances surrounding its writing. This narrative voice—clearly related to the author's—reflects upon some of the values and limitations of *Libro de Manuel* and helps to place the novel in the context of its production.

39. Andrés's and Cortázar's processes of growing historical consciousness are explicitly identified and established in the novel's prologue: "Ese hombre sueña algo que yo soñé tal cual en los días en que empezaba a escribir y, como tantas veces en mi incomprensible oficio de escritor, sólo mucho después me di cuenta de que el sueño era también parte del libro y que contenía la claves de esa convergencia de actividades hasta entonces disímiles" (*LM* 7) ["This man is dreaming something I had dreamed in a like manner during the years when I was just beginning to write and, as happens so many times in my incomprehensible writer's trade, only much later did I realize that the dream was also part of the book and that it contained the key to that merging of activities which until then had been unlike"] (3).

40. See Santiago Juan-Navarro, "El espectador se rebela: 'Instrucciones para John Howells' de Julio Cortázar o la estética de la subversión," *MIFLC Review* 1 (1991): 149–58; "Un tal Morelli: teoría y práctica de la lectura en *Rayuela*," *Revista Canadiense de Estudios Hispánicos* 16, 2 (1992): 235–52; and "77 ó 99 / modelos para desarmar: claves para una lectura morelliana de 'Continuidad de los parques' de Julio Cortázar," *Hispanic Journal* 13, 2 (1992): 241–49.

41. See D'Haen, *Text to Reader*; and Linda Hutcheon, *A Poetics of Postmodernism: History, Theory, Fiction* (New York: Routledge, 1989).

42. Given the political nature and avant-gardism of *Libro de Manuel*, the reference to Fritz Lang is especially relevant. As Lois Parkinson Zamora has suggested, Fritz Lang was a member of the German film avant-garde movement that confronted problems that, in a historical and political sense, were similar to those issues Cortázar dealt with in his novel. Both Lang and Cortázar are artists who seek to harmonize aesthetic innovation and political content. Both also wrote in a period in which the rise of Fascism was seen as an increasing threat to their respective countries: "By alluding to Lang, Cortázar allies his novel to a tradition of formal experimental and politically committed art. . . . He also allies his work to a highly problematic historical and national context in which artistic commitment was both difficult and essential, as Cortázar feels it to be in contemporary Latin America as well" ("Movement and Stasis, Film and Photo: Temporal Structures in the Recent Fiction of Julio Cortázar," *Review of Contemporary Fiction* 3, 3 [1983]: 59).

43. The preceding segment, in which members of the Joda discuss the making of Manuel's manual, ends with Andrés's passing on to Patricio of a final clipping to be included in the album. According to Andrés, this clipping "empieza con una jarra de agua" (*LM* 385) ["begins with a pitcher of water"] (388). Similarly, the final scene begins with these words: "Lonstein llenó despacio la jarra de agua y la puso sobre una de las mesas vacías" (386) ["Lonstein slowly filled the water pitcher and put it on one of the empty tables"] (386).

44. Cortázar, *AAAC*, 107.

45. See White, *The Content of the Form*, ix.

46. See T. V. Reed "Genealogy / Narrative / Power: Questions of Postmodernity in Doctorow's *The Book of Daniel*," *American Literary History* 4, 2 (1992): 303; and Saldívar, *The Dialectics of Our America*, 538.

47. See Victor S. Navasky, "E. L. Doctorow: I Saw a Sign," *The New York Times Book Review* (29 September 1980), 40; and Larry MacCaffery, "A Spirit of Transgression," *E. L. Doctorow: Essays and Conversations*, ed. Richard Trenner (Princeton: Ontario Review Press, 1983), 37.

48. Navasky, "E. L. Doctorow," 40.

49. Ibid., 44. The novel's opening paragraphs have been misread by some critics who refer to Doctorow's vision as nostalgic, when in fact that nostalgia is one

of the targets of Doctorow's critique. In a first version of his "Postmodernism, or the Cultural Logic of Late Capitalism," Jameson referred to *Ragtime* as "the most peculiar and stunning monument to the aesthetic situation engendered by the disappearance of the historical referent" ("Postmodernism," 70). This was systematically contested by Hutcheon, who alleged that "it is just as easy to argue that, in that very novel, the historical referent is very present—and in spades" (*A Poetics of Postmodernism*, 89). Jameson's position has evolved throughout the years. In later essays he has declared his "fascination for Doctorow's novels" and has regarded the U.S. author as "a radical left-wing novelist who has seized the whole apparatus of nostalgia, art, pastiche and postmodernism in order to work himself through them instead of attempting to resuscitate some older forms of social realism" (Kellner, *Postmodernism*, 61–62). This last interpretation is, in fact, prevalent in Jameson's revised version of his seminal essay on postmodernism (*Postmodernism*, 1–54) and is the one that informs the present analysis of Doctorow's previous novel, *The Book of Daniel*.

50. George Stade, Review of *Ragtime*, *New York Times Book Review* (6 July 1975), 2.

51. Although pointing out differences in tone and content, Doctorow has acknowledged the formal similarities between *The Book of Daniel* and *Loon Lake*. See McCaffery, "A Spirit of Transgression," 29.

52. George Stade, "Types Defamiliarized," *Nation* 231, (27 September 1980), 286.

53. Herwig Friedl and Dieter Schulz, "A Multiplicity of Witnesses: E. L. Doctorow at Heidelberg," in *E. L. Doctorow: A Democracy of Perception* (Essen, Germany: Blaue Eule, 1988), 184.

54. E. L. Doctorow, *EC*, 24. The works of some contemporary philosophers of history (Louis O. Mink, Hayden White, and Dominick LaCapra) stem from the assumption that any historical work is, above all, a narrative construction, susceptible, therefore, to be analyzed by means of linguistic and rhetorical criteria, like any literary work.

55. Doctorow, *EC*, 18.

56. Ibid.

57. Ibid., 21.

58. Doctorow's theses about the nature of history are fully corroborated by the views expressed in many other essays and interviews: "I think history is made; it's composed. There is an objective event, but until it is construed, until it is evaluated, it does not exist as history. As Nietzsche said, you need meaning before you know what the fact is." Herwig Friedl and Dieter Schulz, "A Multiplicity of Witnesses: E. L. Doctorow at Heidelber," in *E. L. Doctorow: A Democracy of Perception*, 184.

59. Ibid., 26.

60. Geoffrey Galt Harpham, "E. L. Doctorow and the Technology of Narrative," *PMLA* 100, 1 (1985): 82.

61. The same confusing tendency can be appreciated in some of his later nonfiction. In "The Belief of Writers" (1985) and "Ultimate Discourse" (1986), he continues to equate storytelling and novel writing, fiction and narrative.

62. Doctorow, *EC*, 19.

63. Ibid.

64. Walter Benjamin, *Illuminations: Essays and Reflections* (New York: Schocken Books, 1969), 87.

65. Ibid., 88.

66. Doctorow, *EC*, 26.

67. Doctorow has advanced similar views in other essays and interviews. In "The Belief of Writers" (1985) and "Ultimate Discourse" (1986), he deplores again the lessening of the novelist's authority and the need for U.S. writers to participate more actively in the political life of their country.

68. Harpham, "E. L. Doctorow," 82; Christopher Morris, *Models of Misrepresentation: On the Fiction of E. L. Doctorow* (Jackson: University Press of Mississippi, 1991), 180–81.

69. Morris himself does not hesitate to refer to it as "a major manifesto of American postmodernism" (*Models of Misrepresentation*, 177).

70. White, *Tropics*, 122.

71. Critics differ when describing the specific field of Daniel's dissertation. While most consider it to be historical, Jerry O. Powell ("The Structure of Narrative: Facts and Fiction in the Rosenberg Case," Ph.D. diss. Indiana University, 1981, 208) places it in political science, and T. V. Reed ("Genealogy / Narrative / Power," 291) suggests it is literary. The intentional ambiguity of this core fact stresses the recurrent intermingling of history, social science, and fiction in *The Book of Daniel*.

72. Because of its diverse and all-encompassing nature, *The Book of Daniel* exemplifies Doctorow's concept of ideal fiction: "fiction is the discipline that includes all the others. Its language is indiscriminate, it accepts the diction of science, theology, journalism, poetry, myth, history, everything" (Morris, "Fiction," 446).

73. Doctorow, *EC*, 67–68.

74. As Daniel himself acknowledges, William Appleman Williams's *The Tragedy of the American Diplomacy* (New York: Dell Publishing Co., 1959) is his major source about the period. Williams's basic assumption is that the Cold War was not merely an incident between the two superpowers that emerged after World War II, but "only the most recent phase of a more general conflict between the established system of Western capitalism and its internal and external opponents" (10). Nearly all documents quoted in Daniel's discussion of the Cold War come from Williams's book.

75. Daniel portrays Henry Stimson, senior member of the cabinet, as the only sensible voice in the Truman administration. The novel reproduces his letter to president Truman (11 September 1945), asking him to reopen negotiations with the Soviet Union (*BD*, 284; see also Williams, *The Tragedy of American Diplomacy*, 276). However, Truman ignored Stimson's advice and leaned more and more toward the aggressive position held by the new conservative Secretary of State James F. Byrnes.

76. Williams, *The Tragedy of the American Diplomacy*, 15.

77. Daniel's parodic intentions frequently become evident by his abuse of academic formulae such as the expression "many historians have noted this phenomenon" (*BD*, 28–29), repeated excessively throughout certain historiographic discussions.

78. The parallel between the repressive practices of the two great superpowers is reinforced by continuous allusions to the Bukharin trials (*BD*, 18–19, 65–67), which strongly evoke those of the Isaacsons's. Like the Isaacsons of the novel, Bukharin was accused of espionage, convicted through false proofs, and finally executed. Political dissidence in the two cases was interpreted as a conspiracy

against state interests. Furthermore, Daniel's discussion of the Bukharin trials follows the same formal pattern as his analysis of the Truman administration. Written in the conventional style of a dissertation and citing authorities like George Kennan and E. H. Carr, Daniel's discussion moves from the specifics of the case to generalizations that try to explain the rationale of the Soviet betrayal of international radicalism. On two occasions the digression is violently interrupted by Daniel's subjective voice in one case to present a list of "subjects to be taken up" later in his book, in another to insert "A Note to the Reader" (*BD*, 67) protesting against the reductionism of historiographic analysis.

79. Paul Buhle, *Marxism in the United States: Remapping the History of the American Left* (London: New Left Books, 1987), 179.

80. Bernard K. Johnpoll and Harvey Klehr, eds., *Biographical Dictionary of the American Left* (New York: Greenwood Press, 1986), 51.

81. The influence of Browder's ideas on the party's militancy is reflected in Daniel's indoctrination by his father: "He told me about using imported Chinese labor like cattle to build the West and of breeding Negroes and working them to death in the South. Of their torture. Of John Brown and Nat Turner. Of Thomas Paine, whose atheism made him an embarrassment to the leaders of the American Revolution" (43).

82. Robert Cottrell, "The Portrayal of American Communists in Doctorow's *The Book of Daniel*," *McNeese Review* 31 (1984–86): 63.

83. Leslie Fiedler, "Afterthoughts on the Rosenbergs," in *An End to Innocence* (Boston: Beacon Press, 1955), 25–45.

84. A minor character in the novel, journalist Jack Fein, provides an explanation that has been popular among some historians: "Your folks were framed but that doesn't mean they were innocent babes. I don't believe they were a dangerous conspiracy to pass defense secrets, but I don't believe either that the U.S. Attorney, and the Judge, and the Justice Department, and the President of the United States conspired against them. . . . In this country people don't get picked out of a hat to be put on trial for their lives. . . . They were little neighborhood commies probably with some kind of third-rate operation that wasn't of use to anyone except maybe it made them feel important" (*BD*, 260). In *The Great Fear: The Anti-Communist Purge Under Truman and Eisenhower* (New York: Simon and Schuster, 1978), historian David Caute quotes this passage from *The Book of Daniel* as a very suggestive explanation of the mystery surrounding the Rosenberg case. However, this is just one among many of the versions collected by Daniel, which also include dissenting views provided by Robert Lewin, Fanny Ascher, Artie Sternlicht, and Linda Mindish.

85. See Gerald Markowitz, "How Not to Write History," *Science and Society* 48, 1 (1984): 74–89. In his review Markowitz dismantles the theses presented by Radosh and Milton. As an example of the favorable media coverage of *The Rosenberg File*, see Alan Dershowitz's review (*New York Times Book Review* [27 August 1983], 1). For works arguing the innocence of the Rosenbergs, the most convincing continues to be Walter and Miriam Schneir's *Invitation to an Inquest* (New York: Pantheon Books, 1983). In addition to Doctorow's novel, the Rosenberg case has inspired two other literary works, Robert Coover's *The Public Burning* (1977) and Donald Freed's *Inquest: A Play* (1969), both of which portray them as victims of the hysterical political climate of the era.

86. Doctorow, *EC*, 23.

87. Daniel's focus on Sternlicht responds to literary demands for contrast and tension. Although critics have wrongly identified Doctorow's character with the

New Left as a whole, Sternlicht represents only one of its many tendencies. What came to be known as the New Left was never a homogeneous movement but in fact a very diverse conglomerate of groups that evolved throughout the 1960s.

88. Taking advantage of the media coverage of the Democratic convention, the Yippies and several New Leftist organizations demonstrated in Chicago. As a consequence of the ensuing disturbances and confrontations with police, Rubin and the rest of the organizers were charged with conspiracy to incite a riot.

89. Jerry Rubin, *Do It! Scenarios of the Revolution* (New York: Simon and Schuster, 1970), 21.

90. Ibid., 116.

91. For a discussion of the influence of Cuban political aesthetics on the New Left, see Norman Mailer's *Armies of the Night* (New York: New American Library, 1968). Mailer explains this "idea of a revolution that preceded ideology" as the result of the New Left's contempt for all forms of authority: "authority could not comprehend nor contain nor finally manage to control any political action whose end was unknown" (104–5).

92. As Todd Gitlin points out in *The Sixties: Years of Hope, Days of Rage*, (New York: Bantam Books, 1987), 235, the Yippies "collaborated with the media, became celebrities . . . Abbie (Hoffman) and Jerry (Rubin) wanted to go through the channels, use them for good ends, take the theater to the enemy camp." Considering their uncritical celebration of the media revolution, it is no surprise that Hoffman and Rubin received job offers from advertising companies.

93. Rubin, *Do It!*, 106.

94. Gitlin, *The Sixties*, 233.

95. Rubin, *Do It!*, 132.

96. Herwig Friedl and Dieter Schulz, "A Multiplicity of Witnesses: E. L. Doctorow at Heidelberg," in *E. L. Doctorow: A Democracy of Perception*, 184.

97. As Susan E. Lorsch has noted, *The Book of Daniel* falls into the tradition of the *Künstlerroman*. As in other examples of this novelistic form, Doctorow's novel describes the process that leads to its protagonist's discovery of the value of art as a response to alienation in the contemporary world. ("Doctorow's *The Book of Daniel* as Künstlerroman: The Politics of Art." *Papers on Language and Literature* 18, 3 [1982]: 384–97).

98. Doctorow, *EC*, 63.

99. Ibid.

100. Ibid., 40.

101. In this sense, *Libro de Manuel* and *The Book of Daniel* are more comprehensive than other works by Cortázar and Doctorow (*62 / modelos para armar* and *Loon Lake*), where radical disconnectedness makes a lineal reconstruction of the plot impossible.

102. One of the more evident chronological disarrangements occurs when Daniel evokes his childhood in the Bronx: "We moved there in 1945 when I was four years old. Or maybe in 1944 when I was five years old" (118). In Christopher Morris's view these lapses help to create a "teasing chronology" that undermine the reader's attempts to establish sequence *(Models of Misrepresentation*, 236). However, these slight errors seem more directed at Daniel's limitations as a narrator (whether historian or novelist) and do not seriously affect the novel's continuity.

103. McCaffery, "A Spirit of Transgression," 40.

104. Ibid., 41.

105. As seen in Cortázar's *Libro de Manuel*, cinematic techniques—whether

classical or avant-garde—inevitably acquire an antirealistic dimension when transposed onto a literary text. Although shifts in the narrative point of view do not affect the viewer's empathy in a film, they have an alienating effect in literature.

106. Even more violent are the words that an anonymous voice introduces between Daniel's description of a demonstration in favor of the Isaacsons and one of his digressions about the Cold War: "Oh baby, you know it now. We done played enough games for you. You smart lil fucker. . . . This is the story of a fucking, right? You pullin' out yo lit-er-ary map, mutha? You know where we goin', right muthafuck?" (27). It is impossible to determine the origin of this voice. It could be Daniel addressing the reader with street slang, or it could be an interior voice talking to Daniel himself. In any case, the result is the reader's alienation, and the problematization of the two discourses that flank those words: the realistic and sentimental recollection of Daniel's childhood memories (that "David Copperfield kind of crap" he alludes to somewhere else) and the analytic language of academic historiography that follows ("Many historians have noted an interesting phenomenon" [28]).

107. Brian McHale explores this aspect of contemporary metafiction in works by John Barth, William Gass, Thomas Pynchon, and Gilbert Sorrentino (*Postmodernist Fiction*, 222–27).

108. Doctorow, *EC*, 215.

109. Michel Foucault, *Discipline and Punish*, trans. Alan Sheridan (New York: Pantheon, 1977), 112. Doctorow's concept of power differs from Foucault's in other respects. In fact, the naive dualism that contrasts individual freedom with the repressive state does not seem compatible with Foucault's more relativistic positions. On the other hand, Doctorow sometimes claims for fiction a criterion of truth that would be illegitimate from the point of view of Foucault's theories. Both do share, however, the problematization of the concept of power as it has been traditionally conceived by Marxist and conservative positions.

110. One of the most conflictive aspects of the political ideas of Doctorow and Foucault results from the elaboration of alternative forms of power that could go beyond a negative epistemology. While Doctorow has tried to accommodate his views of power to an idealistic theory of fiction, Foucault's concept of *pouvoir* evolved into a metaphysical and all-encompassing principle that allowed no space for resistance. For a criticism of Foucault's ideas from a radical perspective, see Nicos Poulantzas, *State, Power, Socialism* (London: New Left Books, 1978), 96–107; and Edward W. Said, *The World, the Text, and the Critic* (Cambridge: Harvard University Press, 1983), 243–47.

111. Doctorow, *EC*, 23.

112. In this way the novel's conclusions dramatize the inevitable—though arbitrary—nature of closure. As Geoffrey G. Harpham points out, "closure provides the consolation of narrative, without which we are trapped in an unmasterable flux, perpetual victims of sequence or of repetition" ("E. L. Doctorow and the Technology of Narrative," *PMLA* 100, 1 [1985]: 87).

113. The occupation of Columbia during the spring of 1969 was one of the most spectacular actions led by SDS and followed by New Left groups, from Maoist parties to anarchist organizations. The occupation began as a protest over two specific issues: the university's sponsorship of war-related research and the construction of a segregated gymnasium on city land adjoining Harlem; however, it soon became a mass protest against the military-industry complex.

114. Said, *The World*, 245.

115. Waugh, *Metafiction*, 125.

Chapter 5. Toward a Pedagogical Political Culture: Historical Revisionism, Fiction, and Resistance in the Americas

1. Linda Hutcheon, *A Poetics of Postmodernism: History, Theory, Fiction* (New York: Routledge), 106.

2. Claude Lévi-Strauss, *Le Pensée sauvage* (Paris: Plon, 1962), 28–33, 49–50.

3. Jorge Lozano, *El discurso histórico* (Madrid: Alianza, 1987), 122.

4. Lévi-Strauss examines the differences between magical and scientific thought by comparing the "primitive" thinker with the "bricoleur" (or handyman), and the modern scientist with the engineer. Magical thought operates much as the bricoleur in that it deals with intellectual problems by manipulating preexisting concepts. When faced with a new problem, the mythmaker goes back through the community's collective experience and rearranges existing elements to produce a pattern that may account for the new situation (*Le Pensée sauvage*, 28–33).

5. Roberto González Echevarría, "*Terra Nostra*: Theory and Practice," in *Carlos Fuentes: A Critical View*, eds. Robert Brody and Charles Rossman (Austin: University of Texas, 1982).

6. Roland Barthes, *Mythologies* (New York: The Noonday Press, 1972), 142.

7. Myrna Solotorevsky, *Literatura—Paraliteratura: Puig, Borges, Donoso, Cortázar, Vargas Llosa* (Gaithersburg, Md.: Hispamerica, 1988), 123.

8. David Pace, *Claude Lévi-Strauss: The Bearer of Ashes* (London: Routledge, 1983), 140.

9. Gérard, Genette, *Figuras III* (Barcelona: Lumen, 1989), 289.

10. Patricia Waugh, *Metafiction: The Theory and Practice of Self-Conscious Fiction* (London: Methuen, 1984), 48–61.

11. See Linda Hutcheon, *Narcissistic Narrative: The Metafictional Paradox* (London: Methuen, 1984), 138–52; and Brian McHale, *Postmodernist Fiction* (London: Methuen, 1987), 222–27.

12. Barbara Foley, *Telling the Truth: The Theory and Practice of Documentary Fiction* (Ithaca: Cornell University Press, 1986), 79.

13. See Anthony Pagden, *The American Indian and the Origins of Comparative Ethnology* (Cambridge: Cambridge University Press, 1982); and Eduardo Subirats, *El continente vacío: La conquista del Nuevo Mundo y la conciencia moderna* (Madrid: Anaya, 1994).

14. Edmundo O'Gorman, *La invención de América: Investigación acerca de la estructura histórica del Nuevo Mundo y del sentido de su devenir* (México: Fondo de Cultura Económica, 1958), 9. Alfonso Reyes pointed out in a now-celebrated phrase that America "prior to being experienced as a presence, was felt as an absence," in reference to the idea that America was solely a virtual space where Europeans wished to realize their dreams and frustrated ideals. Before having been discovered, America had been imagined, and it became necessary to adjust reality to correspond to the dream, for the latter was not the reality of America, as of yet unknown, but rather the ideal of constructing an imaginary topography to negate the extant topography of Europe. See Horacio Cerutti Guldberg, *De Varia Utópica: Ensayos de Utopía III* (Bogotá: Publicaciones Universidad Central, 1989), 227.

15. Fernando Aínsa, *De la Edad de Oro a El Dorado: Génesis del discuros utópico americano* (Mexico City: Fondo de Cultura Económica, 1992), 10.

16. Alexis de Tocqueville, *Democracy in America* (New York: Anchor Books,

1969), 507; Georg Wilhelm Friedrich Hegel, *Introduction to "The Philosophy of History"* (Indianapolis: Hackett, 1988), 90.

17. Aínsa, *De la Edad de Oro a El Dorado*, 11.

18. Communal utopian movements have been the object of numerous studies. David E. Pitzer's recent collection of essays covers both the communal experiences of millenarian religious sects and those of the socialist utopians. For a deeper analysis of the socialist utopias of the nineteenth century, see the works of Arthur E. Bestor, *Backwood Utopias: The Sectarian Origins and the Owenite Phase of Communitarian Socialism in America, 1663–1829* (Philadelphia: University of Pennsylvania Press, 1950); and Carl J. Guarneri, *The Utopian Alternative: Fourierism in Nineteenth-Century America* (Ithaca: Cornell University Press, 1991).

19. Aínsa, *De la Edad de Oro a El Dorado*, 10.

20. Hutcheon, *A Poetics of Postmodernism*, 215.

21. See Bell Gale Chevigny and Gari Laguardia, eds., *Reinventing the Americas: Comparative Studies of Literature of the United States and Spanish America* (Cambridge, Mass.: Cambridge University Press, 1986), 18; Lois Parkinson Zamora, *The Usable Past*, 2.

22. Ihab Hassan, *The Right Promethean Fire: Imagination, Science, and Cultural Change* (Urbana: University of Illinois Press, 1980), 17; Fredric Jameson, *Postmodernism or the Cultural Logic of Late Capitalism* (Durham, N.C.: Duke University Press, 1991), 54.

23. See McHale, *Postmodernist Fiction*, 190–96; and Hutcheon, *A Poetics of Postmodernism*, 37–60.

24. Andreas Huyssen, *After the Great Divide: Modernism, Mass Culture, Postmodernism* (Bloomington: Indiana University Press, 1986), vii.

25. For a study of the impact and continuity of the Baroque in Hispanic literature, see González Echevarría, *Celestina's Brood: Continuities of the Baroque in Spanish and Spanish American Literature* (Durham, N.C.: Duke University Press, 1993). González Echevarría offers an interesting explanation for the presence of Baroque motifs in the foundational texts of Latin America's new narrative.

26. Lois Parkinson Zamora, *The Usable Past: The Imagination of History in Recent Fiction of the Americas* (Cambridge, Mass.: Cambridge University Press, 1997), 204–5.

27. Jameson, *Postmodernism*, 54.

Conclusion

1. Ihab Hassan, *The Dismemberment of Orpheus: Towards a Postmodern Literature* (Madison: University of Wisconsin, 1982), 264; Linda Hutcheon, *A Poetics of Postmodernism: History, Theory, Fiction* (New York: Routledge, 1988), 201–21; Charles Jencks, ed., *The Postmodern Reader* (London: Academy Editions, 1992), 12.

2. Ihab Hassan, *The Postmodern Turn: Essays in Postmodern Theory and Culture* (Columbus: Ohio State University Press, 1987), 169.

3. Ibid., 168.

4. Brian McHale, *Postmodernist Fiction* (London: Methuen, 1987), 90.

5. Hall Foster, ed. *The Anti-Aesthetic: Essays on Postmodern Culture* (Seattle, Wash.: Bay Press, 1983), 12; Santiago Colás, *Postmodernity in Latin America: The Argentine Paradigm* (Durham, N.C.: Duke University Press, 1994), 161–72.

6. Fredric Jameson, "Postmodernism and Consumer Society," in *The Anti-Aesthetic: Essays on Postmodern Culture*, 125.

7. Fredric Jameson, *Postmodernism, or the Cultural Logic of Late Capitalism* (Durham, N.C.: Duke University Press, 1991), 54.

8. Georg Lukács, "Art and Objective Truth," in *Writer and Critic and Other Essays*, ed. Arthur D. Kahn (New York: Grosser & Dunlap, 1971), 41.

9. Jean Baudrillard, *Cultura y simulacro* (Barcelona: Kairós, 1978), 11.

10. Linda Hutcheon, *A Poetics of Postmodernism*, 106; *The Politics of Postmodernism* (New York: Routledge), 72.

11. Hutcheon, *A Poetics of Postmodernism*, 215, 218, 230.

12. Bell Gale Chevigny and Gari Laguardia, eds., *Reinventing the Americas: Comparative Studies of Literature of the United States and Spanish America* (Cambridge, Mass.: Cambridge University Press, 1986), ix; Lois Parkinson Zamora, "The Usable Past: The Idea of History in Modern U.S. and Latin American Fiction," in *Do the Americas Have a Common Literature?* (Durham, N.C.: Duke University Press, 1990), ed. Gustavo Pérez Firmat, 11.

Bibliography

Adams, Samuel Hopkins. "Annals of Politics: A Case of Bibliocide." *The New Yorker* (21 October 1939), 39–46.

Aguado Bleye, Pedro. *Manual de Historia de España*. Madrid: Espasa Calpe, 1954.

Aínsa, Fernando. *De la Edad de Oro a El Dorado: Génesis del discurso utópico americano*. Mexico City: Fondo de Cultura Económica, 1992.

Alazraki, Jaime. "Borges entre la modernidad y la postmodernidad." *Revista Hispánica Moderna* 41, 2 (1988): 175–79.

———. "From Bestiary to Glenda: Pushing the Short Story to its Utmost Limits." *Review of Contemporary Fiction* 3, no. 3 (1983): 94–99.

———. "Imaginación e historia en Julio Cortázar." In *Los ochenta mundos de Cortázar: ensayos*. Edited by Fernando Burgos. Madrid: EDI-6, 1987.

———. *La prosa narrativa de Jorge Luis Borges*. Madrid: Gredos, 1983.

———. "*Terra Nostra*: Coming to Grips with History." *World Literature Today* 57, 4 (1983): 551–58.

———. "Los últimos cuentos de Julio Cortázar." *Revista Iberoamericana* 130–31 (1985): 21–46.

Alter, Robert. *Partial Magic: The Novel as a Self-Conscious Genre*. Berkeley: University of California Press, 1975.

Anderson, Jervis. *This Was Harlem*. New York: Farras, Strauss and Giroux, 1982.

Anglería, Pedro Mártir de. *Décadas del Nuevo Mundo*. Edited by Joaquín Torres Asensio. Buenos Aires: Bajel, 1944.

Annan, David. "The Assassins and the Knights Templar." In *Secret Societies*. Edited by Norman MacKenzie. New York: Holt, Rinehart and Winston, 1967.

Antin, David. "Modernism and Postmodernism: Approaching the Present in American Poetry." *Boundary 2* 1 (1972): 106.

Aquino, Tomás de. *Compendio de teología*. Edited by Francisco José Fortuny. Translated by León Carbonero y Sol. Barcelona: Orbis, 1985.

Araya, Guillermo. *El pensamiento de Américo Castro: Estructura intercastiza de la historia de España*. Madrid: Alianza, 1983.

Argentina: The Military Juntas and Human Rights. Report of the Trial of the Former Junta Members, 1985. London: Amnesty International Publications, 1987.

Avant, John Alfred. "Mumbo Jumbo." *Library Journal* 97 (1 October 1972), 3182.

Baker, Houston A. "The Last Days of Louisiana Red." *Black World* 24 (June 1975): 51–53.

Bal, Mieke. "Mise en Abyme et Iconocité." *Littérature* 29 (1978): 116–28.

Baraka, Amiri. "Afro-American Literature and Class Struggle." *Black American Literature Forum* 14, 1 (1980): 5–14.

Barber, Malcolm. *The Trial of the Templars*. Cambridge, Mass.: Cambridge University Press, 1978.

Barksdale, Richard, and Kenneth Kinnamon, eds. *Black Writers of America: A Comprehensive Anthology*. New York: Macmillan Co., 1972.

Barthes, Roland. "The Discourse of History." In *Comparative Criticism: A Yearbook 3*. Edited by E. S. Shaffer. Cambridge, Mass.: Cambridge University Press, 1981.

———. *Mythologies*. Translated by Richard Miller. New York: The Noonday Press, 1972.

———. *The Pleasure of the Text*. Translated by Richard Miller. New York: The Noonday Press, 1975.

Baudrillard, Jean. *Cultura y simulacro*. Translated by Antoni Vicens and Pedro Rovira. Barcelona: Kairós, 1978.

Bazin, André. "The Evolution of the Language of Cinema." In *Film Theory and Criticism*. Edited by Gerald Mast and Marshall Cohen. New York: Oxford University Press, 1979.

Bellegarde, Dantes. *Histoire du peuple haïtien (1492–1952)*. Port-au-Prince: Collection du cent- cinquantenaire de l'indépendance d'Haiti, 1953.

Benjamin, Walter. *Illuminations: Essays and Reflections*. New York: Schocken Books, 1969.

Bernal, Martin. *Black Athena: The Afroasiatic Roots of Classical Civilization*. 2 vols. New Brunswick, N.J.: Rutgers University Press, 1987.

Bertrand, Louis. *Philippe II à l'Escorial*. Paris: L'Artisan du Livre, 1929.

Bestor, Arthur E., Jr. *Backwood Utopias: The Sectarian Origins and the Owenite Phase of Communitarian Socialism in America, 1663–1829*. Philadelphia: University of Pennsylvania Press, 1950.

Beverly, John. "Postmodernism in Latin America." *Siglo XX/20th Century* 9, 1–2 (1991–92): 9–20.

Beverly, John, and José Oviedo. "Introduction." In *The Postmodernism Debate in Latin America: A Special Issue. Boundary 2* 20, 3 (1993): 1–17.

Bleeker, C. Jouco. *Hathor and Thoth: Two Key Figures of the Ancient Egyptian Religion*. Leiden: E. J. Brill, 1973.

Bone, Robert. *The Negro Novel in America*. New Haven: Yale University Press, 1958.

Borges, Jorge Luis. *El Aleph*. Madrid: Alianza, 1971.

Brecht, Bertolt. *Brecht on Theatre: The Development of an Aesthetic*. Edited and translated by John Willett. New York: Hill and Wang, 1964.

Brogan, Hugh. *The Penguin History of the United States of America*. London: Penguin Books, 1990.

Budge, E. A. Wallis. *The Gods of the Egyptians: Studies in Ancient Egyptian Mythology*. 2 vols. London: Methuen, 1904.

———. *Osiris and the Egyptian Resurrection*. New York: Dover Publications, 1973.

Buhle, Paul. *Marxism in the United States: Remapping the History of the American Left*. London: New Left Books, 1987.

Bürger, Peter. *Theory of the Avant-Garde*. Translated by Michael Shaw. Minneapolis: University of Minnesota Press, 1984.

Bush, Roland E. "Werewolf of the Wild West: On a novel by Ishmael Reed." *Black World* 23 (1974): 64–66.

Byerman, Keith E. *Fingering the Jagged Grain: Tradition and Form in Recent Black Fiction*. Athens: The University of Georgia Press, 1985.

Cabrera de Córdoba, Luis. *Historia de Felipe II, Rey de España*. Madrid: Aribau, 1876.

Cade, Toni. "*The Free-Lance Pallbearers*." *Liberator* 9 (1969): 20.

Carballo, Emmanuel. "Carlos Fuentes." In *Diecinueve protagonistas de la literatura mexicana del siglo XX*. Mexico City: Empresas Editoriales, 1965.

Caro Baroja, Julio. *Los judíos en la España moderna y contemporánea*. 3 vols. Madrid: Arión, 1961.

Carrasco, Davíd. *Quetzalcoatl and the Irony of the Empire*. Chicago: The University of Chicago Press, 1982.

Carroll, David. *Paraesthetics: Foucault, Lyotard, Derrida*. New York: Routledge, 1987.

Caso, Alfonso. *El pueblo del sol*. Mexico City: Fondo de Cultura Económica, 1953.

Castañeda, Jorge G. *Utopia Unarmed: The Latin American Left After the Cold War*. New York: Knopf, 1993.

Castor, Suzy. "The American Occupation of Haiti (1915–34) and the Dominican Republic (1916–24)." *The Massachusetts Review* 15, 1 (1974): 253–75.

Castro, Américo. *España en su historia*. Buenos Aires: Losada, 1948.

———. *El pensamiento de Cervantes*. Barcelona: Noguer, 1972.

———. *La realidad histórica de España*. Mexico City: Porrúa, 1966.

Caute, David. *The Great Fear: The Anti-Communist Purge Under Truman and Eisenhower*. New York: Simon and Schuster, 1978.

Cerutti Guldberg, Horacio. *De Varia Utópica (Ensayos de Utopía III)*. Bogotá: Publicaciones Universidad Central, 1989.

———. "Para una filosofía política indo-iberoamericana: América en las utopías del Renacimiento." In *Hacia una filosofía política de la liberación latinoamericana*. Buenos Aires: Bonum, 1974.

Chevalier, Maxime. *Lectura y lectores en la España del siglo XVI*. Madrid: Ediciones Turner, 1976.

Chevigny, Bell Gale, and Gari Laguardia, eds. *Reinventing the Americas: Comparative Studies of Literature of the United States and Spanish America*. Cambridge, Mass.: Cambridge University Press, 1986.

Christensen, Inger. *The Meaning of Metafiction: A Critical Study of Selected Novels by Sterne, Nabokov, Barth and Beckett*. Bergen: Universitetsforlaget, 1981.

Clearfield, Andrew M. *These Fragments I Have Shored: Collage and Montage in Early Modernist Poetry*. Ann Arbor, Mich.: UMI Research Press, 1984.

Cohn, Norman. *The Pursuit of the Millennium*. Fairlawn: Essential Books, 1957.

Colás, Santiago. *Postmodernity in Latin America: The Argentine Paradigm*. Durham, N.C.: Duke University Press, 1994.

Colón, Cristóbal. *Textos y documentos completos*. Edited by Consuelo Valera. Madrid: Alianza, 1982.

Colón, Hernando. *Historia del Almirante*. Edited by Luis Arranz. Madrid: Historia 16, 1984.

Connor, Steven. *Postmodernist Culture: An Introduction to Theories of the Contemporary*. Oxford: Blackwell, 1989.

Coover, Robert. "A Myth of Creation, Spanning 20 Centuries and 778 Pages." *New York Times Book Review* (7 November 1976), 3, 50.

Cortázar, Julio. *Alguien que anda por ahí*. Madrid: Alfaguara, 1977.

———. *Argentina: años de alambradas culturales*. Barcelona: Muchnik, 1984.

———. *Las armas secretas*. Buenos Aires: Sudamericana, 1959.

———. *Around the Day in Eighty Worlds*. Translated by Thomas Christensen. San Francisco: North Point Press, 1986.

———. *Los autonautas de la cosmopista*. Barcelona: Muchnik, 1983.

———. *Bestiario*. Buenos Aires: Sudamericana, 1951.

———. "Corrección de pruebas." In *Convergencias/Divergencias/Incidencias*. Edited by Julio Ortega. Barcelona: Tusquets, 1973.

———. *Deshoras*. Mexico City: Nueva Imagen, 1983.

———. *Fantomas contra los vampiros multinacionales: una utopía realizable, narrada por Julio Cortázar*. Mexico City: Excelsior, 1975.

———. *Final del juego*. Mexico City: Los Presentes, 1956.

———. *Libro de Manuel*. Buenos Aires: Sudamericana, 1973.

———. *A Manual for Manuel*. Translated by Gregory Rabassa. New York: Pantheon, 1978.

———. *Nicaragua tan violentamente dulce*. Barcelona: Muchnik, 1984.

———. *Los premios*. Buenos Aires: Sudamericana, 1960.

———. *Prosa del observatorio*. Barcelona: Lumen, 1972.

———. *Queremos tanto a Glenda*. Mexico City: Nueva Imagen, 1980.

———. *Rayuela*. Buenos Aires: Sudamericana, 1963.

———. *Los reyes*. Buenos Aires: Gulab y Aldabahor, 1949.

———. *Salvo el crepúsculo*. Mexico City: Nueva Imagen, 1984.

———. *62: Modelo para armar*. Buenos Aires: Sudamericana, 1968.

———. *Territorios*. Mexico City: Siglo XXI, 1978.

———. *Todos los fuegos el fuego*. Buenos Aires: Sudamericana, 1966.

———. *Último Round*. Mexico City: Siglo XXI, 1969.

———. *Viaje alrededor de una mesa*. Buenos Aires: Cuadernos de Rayuela, 1970.

———. *La vuelta al día en ochenta mundos*. Mexico City: Siglo XXI, 1967.

Cortínez, Verónica. "Crónica, épica y novela: *La Historia verdadera de la conquista de la Nueva España* y 'El mundo nuevo' de *Terra Nostra*." *Revista Chilena de Literatura* 38 (1991): 59–72.

Cosentino, Donald. "Who is that Fellow in the Many-colored Cap?: Transformations of Eshu in Old and New World Mythologies." *Journal of American Folklore* 100, 397 (1987): 261–75.

Cottrell, Robert. "The Portrayal of American Communists in Doctorow's *The Book of Daniel*." *McNeese Review* 31 (1984–1986): 63–8.

Cox, George O. *African Empires and Civilizations—Ancient and Medieval*. Washington D.C.: African Heritage Studies Publishers, 1974.

Cruz, Manuel. "Narrativismo." In *Filosofía de la Historia*. Edited by Reyes Mate. Madrid: Trotta, 1993.

Culianu, Ioan Petru. "Sacrilege." In *The Encyclopedia of Religion*. Edited by Mircea Eliade. 16 vols. New York: MacMillan, 1987.

Currie, Mark , ed. *Metafiction*. London: Longmans, 1995.

Curtin, Philip D. *The Atlantic Slave Trade: A Census*. Madison: University of Wisconsin Press, 1969.

Dällenbach, Lucien. *The Mirror in the Text*. 1977. Translated by Jeremy Whiteley and Emma Hughes. Chicago: University of Chicago Press, 1989.

———. "Reflexivity and Reading." *New Literary History* 11, 3 (1980): 435–49.

Damrosch, David. "The Aesthetics of Conquest: Aztec Poetry Before and After Cortés." *Representations* 33 (1991): 101–20.

Danto, Arthur C. *Analytic Philosophy of History*. Cambridge, Mass.: Cambridge University Press, 1965.

De Filippo, Bernard John. "HooDoo, Voodoo, and Conjure: The Novels of Ishmael Reed." Ph.D. diss., Carnegie-Mellon University, Pittsburgh, 1989.

Deren, Maya. *Divine Horsemen: The Divine Gods of Haiti*. New York: McPherson & Co., 1988.

Derrida, Jacques. "Living on: Border Lines." In *Deconstruction and Criticism*. Edited by Harold Bloom et al. London: Routledge and Kegan Paul, 1979.

Dershowitz, Alan. Review of Ronald Radosh and Joyce Milton, *The Rosenberg File: A Search for the Truth* Radosh and Milton's *The Rosembergs File, New York Book Review* (27 August 1983), 1.

D'Haen, Theo. *Text to Reader: A Communicative Approach to Fowles, Barth, Cortázar and Boon*. Amsterdam: John Benjamins, 1983.

Díaz del Castillo, Bernal. *Historia verdadera de la conquista de la Nueva España*. Edited by Joaquín Ramírez Cabañas. Mexico City: Porrúa, 1983.

Diop, Cheikh A. *The African Origin of Civilization: Myth or Reality*. New York: Lawrence Hill, 1974.

Doctorow, E. L. *Big as Life*. New York: Simon & Schuster, 1964.

———. *The Book of Daniel*. New York: Fawcett Crest, 1987.

———. "False Documents." In *E. L. Doctorow: Essays and Conversations*. Edited by Richard Trenner. Princeton, N.J.: Ontario Review Press, 1983.

———. "The Importance of Fiction: Ultimate Discourse." *Esquire* 106 (August 1986): 41.

———. *Loon Lake*. New York: Random House, 1980.

———. "The Passion of Our Calling." *New York Times Book Review* (25 August 1985), 1, 21–23.

———. *Ragtime*. New York: Random House, 1975.

———. *Welcome to Hard Times*. New York: Fawcett Crest, 1988.

———. *World's Fair*. New York: Random House, 1985.

Douglas, Ann. *Terrible Honesty: Mongrel Manhattan in the 1920s*. New York: Farrar, Strauss and Giroux, 1995.

Downes, Randolph. "Negro Rights and White Backlash in the Campaign of 1920." *Ohio History* 75, 2–3 (1966): 85–107.

Dreyer, Peter. "New Fiction: Brautigan, Gold and Reed." *San Francisco* 16 (December 1974): 86–7.

Durán, Fray Diego. *Historia de las Indias de Nueva España*. Mexico City: Porrúa, 1967.

Eagleton, Terry. "Capitalism, Modernism, and Postmodernism." *New Left Review* 152 (1985): 60–73.

Eco, Umberto. *Obra abierta*. Translated by Roser Berdagué. Barcelona: Ariel, 1979.

———. *The Open Work*. Translated by Anna Cancogni. Cambridge: Hutchinson Radius, 1989.

———. *Postcript to The Name of the Rose*. Translated by William Weaver. New York: Harcourt Brace Jovanovich, 1983.

Eisenstein, Sergei. "A Dialectical Approach to Film Form." In *Film Theory and Criticism*. Edited by Gerald Mast and Marshall Cohen. New York: Oxford University Press, 1979.

———. *S. M. Eisenstein: Selected Works*. Edited and translated by Richard Taylor. 2 vols. London: British Film Institute Publishing, 1987–1988.

Elliott, Emory, ed. *The Columbia History of the American Novel*. New York: Columbia University Press, 1991.

Elliott, J. H. *Imperial Spain, 1469–1716*. Harmondsworth, Eng.: Pelican Books, 1970.

———. "The Mental World of Hernán Cortés." In *Transactions of the Royal Historical Society*. London: Offices of the Royal Historical Society, 1967.

———. *The Old World and the New, 1492–1650*. Cambridge, Mass.: Cambridge University Press, 1970.

Ercilla y Zúñiga, Alonso de. *La araucana*. Edited by Marcos A. Moríñigo and Isaías Lerner. Madrid: Castalia, 1983.

Evans, J. Martin. *America: The View From Europe*. New York: W.W. Norton, 1979.

Farer, Tom J. *The Grand Strategy of the United States in Latin America*. New Brunswick, N.J.: Transaction Books, 1988.

Fernández, Adela. *Diccionario ritual de voces nahuas*. Mexico City: Panorama, 1988.

Fernández Montaña, José. *Los arquitectos escurialenses*. Madrid: Hijos de Gregorio del Amo, 1924.

Ferrer del Río, Antonio. *Decadencia de España: historia del levantamiento de las comunidades de Castilla*. Madrid: Establecimiento tipográfico de Mellado, 1850.

Feyerabend, Paul. *Contra el método*. Barcelona: Ariel, 1981.

Fiedler, Leslie. "Afterthoughts on the Rosenbergs." In *An End to Innocence*. Boston: Beacon Press, 1955.

———. "Close the Border—Close the Gap." In *The Collected Essays of Leslie Fiedler*. Vol. 2. New York: Stein and Day, 1971.

Fitz, Earl. *Rediscovering the New World: Inter-American Literature in a Comparative Context*. Iowa City: University of Iowa Press, 1991.

Flouret, Michèle. *La guerrilla en Hispanoamérica*. Paris: Masson, 1976.

Foley, Barbara. *Telling the Truth: The Theory and Practice of Documentary Fiction*. Ithaca: Cornell University Press, 1986.

Foster, Hal, ed. *The Anti-Aesthetic: Essays on Postmodern Culture*. Seattle: Bay Press, 1983.

Foucault, Michel. *Discipline and Punish*. Translated by Alan Sheridan. New York: Pantheon, 1977.

———. *The Order of Things: An Archeology of the Human Sciences*. Translated by Alan Sheridan. New York: Pantheon, 1970.

———. "Nietzsche, Genealogy, History." In *The Foucault Reader*. Edited by Paul Rabinow. New York: Pantheon, 1984.

Fox, Robert Elliot. *Conscientious Sorcerers: The Black Postmodernist Fiction of LeRoi Jones / Amiri Baraka, Ishmael Reed, and Samuel R. Delany*. New York: Greenwood Press, 1987.

Franco, Jean. "Julio Cortázar: Utopia and Everyday Life." *Inti* 10–11 (1979–1980): 108–18.

———. "The Nation as Imagined Community." In *The New Historicism*. Edited by H. Aram Veeser. New York and London: Routledge, 1989.

Frankl, Victor. "Hernán Cortés y la tradición de las Siete Partidas: Un comentario jurídico-histórico a la llamada "Primera Carta de Relación" de Hernán Cortés." *Revista de Historia de América* 53–54 (1962): 9–74.

———. "Imperio particular e imperio universal en las Cartas de Relación de Hernán Cortés." *Cuadernos Hispanoamericanos* 163–64 (1963): 443–82.

Franklin, John Hope. *From Slavery to Freedom: A History of Negro Americans*. New York: Alfred A. Knopf, 1980.

Frederick, Richard G. *Warren G. Harding: A Bibliography*. Westport, Conn.: Greenwood Press, 1992.

Freed, Donald. *Inquest: A Play*. New York: Viking Press, 1967.

Fried, Michael. *Realism, Writing, Disfiguration: On Thomas Eakins and Stephen Crane*. Baltimore: The Johns Hopkins University Press, 1987.

Friedl, Herwig and Dieter Schulz. "A Multiplicity of Witnesses: E. L. Doctorow at Heidelberg." In *E. L. Doctorow: A Democracy of Perception*. Essen: Blaue Eule, 1988.

Fuentes, Carlos. *Aura*. Translated by Lysander Kemp. New York: Farrar, Straus and Giroux, 1965.

———. *Aura*. In *Cuerpos y ofrendas*. Madrid: Alianza, 1973.

———. *The Buried Mirror*. New York: Houghton Mifflin Co., 1992.

———. *Cambio de piel*. Mexico City: Joaquín Mortiz, 1967.

———. *Ceremonias del alba*. Madrid: Mondadori, 1991.

———. *Cervantes o la crítica de la lectura*. Mexico City: Joaquín Mortiz, 1976.

———. *Cristóbal Nonato*. Mexico City: Fondo de Cultura Económica, 1987.

———. *Los días enmascarados*. Mexico City: Los presentes, 1954.

———. "Discurso inaugural." *Simposio Carlos Fuentes: Actas*. Edited by Isaac Jack Lévy and Juan Loveluck. Columbia: University of South Carolina Press, 1978.

———. *El espejo enterrado*. Mexico City: Fondo de Cultura Económica, 1992.

———. *La muerte de Artemio Cruz*. Mexico City: Fondo de Cultura Económica, 1962.

———. *La nueva novela hispanoamericana*. Mexico City: Joaquín Mortiz, 1969.

————. *París, la revolución de mayo*. Mexico City: Era, 1968.

————. *La región más transparente*. Mexico City: Fondo de Cultura Económica, 1958.

————. *Terra Nostra*. Mexico City: Joaquín Mortiz, 1975.

————. *Terra Nostra*. Translated by Margaret Sayers Peden. New York: Farrar, Straus and Giroux, 1976.

————. *Tiempo mexicano*. Mexico City: Joaquín Mortiz, 1970.

————. *Todos los gatos son pardos*. In *Obras completas*. Vol. 2. Mexico City: Aguilar, 1980.

————. "La tradición literaria latinoamericana." In *La obra de Carlos Fuentes: Una visión múltiple*. Edited by Ana María Hernández de López. Madrid: Pliegos, 1988.

————. *El tuerto es rey*. Mexico City: Joaquín Mortíz, 1970.

————. *Valiente mundo nuevo: Épica, utopía y mito en la novela hispanoamericana*. Madrid: Mondadori, 1990.

Galeano, Eduardo. *Open Veins of Latin America: Five Centuries of the Pillage of a Continent*. New York: Monthly Review Press, 1973.

García Canclini, Néstor. *Culturas Híbridas: Estrategias para entrar y salir de la modernidad*. Mexico City: Grijalbo, 1990.

Gardiner, Alan H. "The House of Life." *The Journal of Egyptian Archaeology* 24 (1938): 157- 79.

Garfield, Evelyn Picon. *Cortázar por Cortázar*. Veracruz: Universidad Veracruzana, 1978.

Garibay, Angel María. *Historia de la literatura náhuatl*. 2 vols. Mexico City: Porrúa, 1954.

————. *La literatura de los aztecas*. Mexico City: Joaquín Mortiz, 1964.

Gass, William H. *Fiction and the Figures of Life*. New York: Alfred A. Knopf, 1970.

Gates, Henry Louis, Jr. "The Blackness of Blackness: A Critique of the Sign and the Signifying Monkey." In *Black Literature and Literary Theory*. London: Methuen, 1984.

————. *The Signifying Monkey: A Theory of Afro-American Literary Criticism*. New York: Oxford University Press, 1988.

Gayle, Addison, Jr. "Black Women and Black Men: The Literature of Catharsis." *Black Books Bulletin* 4 (1976): 48–52.

Genette, Gérard. *Figuras III*. Translated by Carlos Manzano. Barcelona: Lumen, 1989.

Gillespie, Susan D. *The Aztec Kings: The Construction of Rulership in Ancient Mexico*. Tucson: University of Arizona Press, 1989.

Gitlin, Todd. *The Sixties: Years of Hope, Days of Rage*. New York: Bantam Books, 1987.

González Bermejo, Ernesto. *Revelaciones de un cronopio: conversaciones con Cortázar*. Buenos Aires: Contrapunto, 1986.

González Echevarría, Roberto. *Celestina's Brood: Continuities of the Baroque in Spanish and Spanish American Literature*. Durham, N.C.: Duke University Press, 1993.

————. *Myth and Archive: A Theory of Latin American Narrative*. Cambridge, Mass.: Cambridge University Press, 1990.

————. "*Terra Nostra*: Theory and Practice." In *Carlos Fuentes: A Critical View*. Edited by Robert Brody and Charles Rossman. Austin: University of Texas Press, 1982.

Goytisolo, Juan. "Our Old New World." *Review* 19 (1976): 5–24.

Graff, Gerald. *Literature Against Itself: Literary Ideas in Modern Society*. Chicago: The University of Chicago Press, 1979.

Grafenstein, Johanna Von. *Haití*. Mexico City: Alianza Editorial Mexicana, 1988.

Greenya, John. "A Novel of Satire But It's Overdone." *Washington Star* (5 November 1967).

Guarneri, Carl J. *The Utopian Alternative: Fourierism in Nineteenth-Century America*. Ithaca: Cornell University Press, 1991.

Gunson, Phil, ed. *The Dictionary of Contemporary Politics of South America*. New York: Macmillan Publishing Co., 1989.

Harpham, Geoffrey Galt. "E. L. Doctorow and the Technology of Narrative." *PMLA* 100, 1 (1985): 81–95.

Harris, Joseph E., ed. *Africa and Africans as Seen by Classical Writers: The William Leo Hansberry African Notebook*. Vol. 2. Washington, D.C.: Howard University Press, 1977.

Harvey, David. *The Condition of Postmodernity*. Oxford: Blackwell, 1989.

Hassan, Ihab. *The Dismemberment of Orpheus: Towards a Postmodern Literature*. Madison: University of Wisconsin Press, 1982.

————. *The Postmodern Turn: Essays in Postmodern Theory and Culture*. Columbus: Ohio State University Press, 1987.

————. *The Right Promethean Fire: Imagination, Science, and Cultural Change*. Urbana: University of Illinois Press, 1980.

Hegel, Georg Wilhelm Friedrich. *Introduction to "The Philosophy of History."* Translated by Leo Rauch. Indianapolis, Ind.: Hackett, 1988.

Hemenway, Robert E. *Zora Neale Hurston: A Literary Biography*. Urbana: University of Illinois Press, 1977.

Higgins, Godfrey. *Anacalypsis, An Attempt to Draw Aside the Veil of the Saitic Isis; or, An Inquiry into the Origin of Languages, Nations and Religions*. London: Longmans, 1836.

Hodges, David. *The Intellectual Foundations of the Nicaraguan Revolution*. Austin: University of Texas Press, 1986.

Hogan, William. "New Novelists and Old Problems." *San Francisco Chronicle* (29 November 1967).

Howard, Lillie P. *Zora Neale Hurston*. Boston: Twayne, 1980.

Huggins, Nathan. *Harlem Renaissance*. New York: Oxford University Press, 1971.

Hunter, Stephen. "*Mumbo Jumbo* Hoo-doos America." *Baltimore Sun* (13 August 1972).

Hurston, Zora Neale. *Moses, Man of the Mountain*. New York: Harper Perennial, 1991.

————. *Mules and Men*. Bloomington: Indiana University Press, 1978.

————. *Tell My Horse: Voodoo and Life in Haiti and Jamaica*. New York: Harper Perennial, 1990.

Hutcheon, Linda. *Narcissistic Narrative: The Metafictional Paradox*. London: Methuen, 1984.

———. *A Poetics of Postmodernism: History, Theory, Fiction*. New York: Routledge, 1988.

———. *The Politics of Postmodernism*. New York: Routledge, 1989.

Huyssen, Andreas. *After the Great Divide: Modernism, Mass Culture, Postmodernism*. Bloomington: Indiana University Press, 1986.

Ife, B. W. *Reading and Fiction in Golden-Age Spain: A Platonist Critique and Some Picaresque Replies*. Cambridge, Mass.: Cambridge University Press, 1985.

Imhof, Rüdiger. *Contemporary Metafiction: A Poetological Study of Metafiction in English Since 1939*. Heidelberg: Carl Winter Universitätsverlag, 1986.

Ingarden, Roman. *The Literary Work of Art: An Investigation on the Borderlines Between Ontology, Logic, and the Theory of Literature*. Translated by George G. Grabowicz. Evanston, Ill.: Northwestern University Press, 1973.

Jablon, Madelyn. *Black Metafiction: Self-Consciousness in African American Literature*. Iowa City: University of Iowa Press, 1997.

Jacson, Blyden. "Moses, Man of the Mountain: A Study of Power." In *Zora Neale Hurston*. Edited by Harold Bloom. New York: Chelsea House, 1986.

James, George G. G. M. *Stolen Legacy: The Greeks Were Not the Authors of Greek Philosophy, but the People of North Africa, Commonly Called the Egyptians*. New York: Philosophical Library, 1954.

Jameson, Fredric. "Postmodernism and Consumer Society." In *The Anti-Aesthetic: Essays On Postmodern Culture*. Edited by Hal Foster. Seattle, Wash.: Bay Press, 1983.

———. *Postmodernism, or the Cultural Logic of Late Capitalism*. Durham, N.C.: Duke University Press, 1991.

———. "Postmodernism, or the Cultural Logic of Late Capitalism." *New Left Review* 146 (1984): 53–92.

———. "Review of Don DeLillo's *The Names* and Sol Yurick's *Richard A.*" *The Minnesota Review* 22 (1984): 117–22.

———. "Third-World Literature in the Era of Multinational Capitalism." *Social Text* 15 (1986): 65–88.

Jarque, Fietta. "Carlos Fuentes subraya la importancia de la imaginación literaria ante los cambios históricos," *El país* (19 August 1995), 21.

Jefferson, Ann. "*Mise en abyme* and the Prophetic in Narrative." *Style* 17, 2 (1983): 196–208.

Jencks, Charles, ed. *The Post-Modern Reader*. London: Academy Editions, 1992.

Jenkins, Keith. *Re-thinking History*. New York: Routledge, 1991.

Johnpoll, Bernard K., and Harvey Klehr, eds. *Biographical Dictionary of the American Left*. New York: Greenwood Press, 1986.

Jones, Edward L. *Black Zeus*. Seattle, Wash.: Frayn Printing Co., 1971.

———. *Profiles in African Heritage*. Seattle, Wash.: Frayn Printing Co., 1972.

Jonghe. M. Edouard de, ed. "Hystoire du Méchique." *Journal de la Societe des Americanistes de Paris* 2, 2 (1905): 1–41.

Juan-Navarro, Santiago. "The Dialogic Imagination of Salman Rushdie and Carlos

Fuentes: National Allegories and the Scene of Writing in *Midnight's Children* and *Cristóbal Nonato.*" *Neohelicon* 20, 2 (1993): 257–312.

———. "El espectador se rebela: 'Instrucciones para John Howells' de Julio Cortázar o la estética de la subversión." *MIFLC Review* 1 (1991): 149–58.

———. Review of *The Writings of Carlos Fuentes,* by Raymond Leslie Williams. *Latin American Literary Review* 48 (1996): 94.

———. "77 ó 99 / modelos para desarmar: claves para una lectura morelliana de 'Continuidad de los parques' de Julio Cortázar." *Hispanic Journal* 13, 2 (1992): 241–49.

———. "Un tal Morelli: teoría y práctica de la lectura en *Rayuela.*" *Revista Canadiense de Estudios Hispánicos* 16, 2 (1992): 235–52.

Jung, Carl G. "Your Negroid and Indian Behaviour." *The Forum* 83, 4 (1930): 193–99.

Kaiser, Ernest. "The Last Days of Louisiana Reed," *Freedomways* (1974): 379

Katzman, Allan. "Books." *East Village Other* (16 July 1967), 14.

Kellman, Steven. *The Self-Begetting Novel.* New York: Columbia University Press, 1980.

Kellner, Bruce, ed. *The Harlem Renaissance: A Historical Dictionary for the Era.* Westport, Conn.: Greenwood Press, 1984.

Kellner, Douglas, ed. *Postmodernism / Jameson / Critique.* Washington D.C.: Maisonneuve Press, 1989.

Kent, George E. "Notes on the 1974 Black Literary Scene." *Phylon* 36 (1975): 182–203.

Kerr, Lucille. "The Paradox of Power and Mystery: Carlos Fuentes' *Terra Nostra. PMLA* 95, 1 (1980): 91–102.

Keto, C. Tsehloane. *The Africa Centered Perspective of History and Social Sciences in the Twenty First Century.* Blackwood: K.A. Publications, 1989.

Kinnamon, Kenneth. "The Free-Lance Pallbearers." *Negro American Literature* Forum 1 (1967): 18.

Krakauer, Siegfried. "Basic Concepts." In *Film Theory and Criticism.* Edited by Gerald Mast and Marshall Cohen. New York: Oxford University Press, 1979.

Krauze, Enrique. "The Guerrilla Dandy: The Literary and Political Illusions of Carlos Fuentes, Everybody's Favorite Mexican." *The New Republic* (27 June 1988), 28–38.

Krishan Kumar. *Utopia & Anti-utopia in Modern Times.* Oxford: Blackwell, 1987.

LaCapra, Dominick. *History & Criticism.* Ithaca: Cornel University Press, 1985.

Lafaye, Jacques. *Quetzalcoatl and Guadalupe: The Formation of Mexican National Consciousness (1531–1813).* Chicago: The University of Chicago Press, 1976.

———. *Mesías, cruzadas, utopías: El judeo-cristianismo en las sociedades ibéricas.* Translated by Juan José Utrilla. Mexico City: Fondo de Cultura Económica, 1984.

Lambert, Malcolm. *Medieval Heresy: Popular Movements from Gregorian Reform to the Reformation.* Oxford: Blackwell, 1992.

Lane, George. "For Browsing and Drowsing." *Patriot Ledger,* (22 August 1972), 12.

Larsen, Neil. "Postmodernismo e imperialismo: Teoría y política en Latinoamérica." *Nuevo Texto Crítico* 3, 6 (1990): 77–94.

Lee, Christopher Herron. "A Gumbo of Black Humor: Voodoo and a Red Rooster." *Louisville Defender* 19 (31 January 1972).

Lee, Robert. "Cultures Clash in *Mumbo Jumbo*." *Los Angeles Times* (10 December 1972), 78.

Lentricchia, Frank. *After the New Criticism*. Chicago: University of Chicago Press, 1980.

Leonard, Irving A. *Los libros del conquistador*. Translated by Mario Monteforte Toledo. Mexico: Fondo de Cultura Económica, 1953.

León-Portilla, Miguel. *Literaturas de Mesoamérica*. Mexico City: SEP, 1984.

———. *Visión de los vencidos: Relaciones indígenas de la conquista*. Mexico City: UNAM, 1959.

Lesko, Leonard H. "Egyptian Religion: History of Study." *The Encyclopedia of Religion*. Edited by Mircea Eliade. 16 vols. New York: MacMillan, 1987.

Levine, Paul. *E. L. Doctorow*. London: Methuen, 1985.

———. "The Writer as Independent Witness." In *Essays and Conversations*. Edited by Richard Trenner. Princeton: The Ontario Review, 1983.

Lévi-Strauss, Claude. *Le Pensée sauvage*. Paris: Plon, 1962.

Link, Arthur. *La política de Estados Unidos en América Latina*. Mexico City: Fondo de Cultura Económica, 1960.

Lipton, Lawrence. "Robin the Cock and Doopeyduk Doing the Boogaloo in Harry Sam with Rusty Jethroe and Letterhead America." *Cavalier* 18 (1968): 70–74.

Lorsch, Susan. "Doctorow's *The Book of Daniel* as Künstlerroman: The Politics of Art." *Papers on Language and Literature* 18, 3 (1982): 384–97.

López Austin, Alfredo. *Hombre-Dios: Religión y política en el mundo náhuatl*. Mexico City: UNAM, 1973.

López de Gómara, Francisco. *Historia general de las Indias y vida de Hernán Cortés*. Caracas: Biblioteca Ayacucho, 1979.

Lozano, Jorge. *El discurso histórico*. Madrid: Alianza, 1987.

Lueders, Edward. *Carl Van Vechten*. New York: Twayne, 1965.

Lukács, Georg. "Art and Objective Truth." In *Writer and Critic and Other Essays*. Edited and translated by Arthur D. Kahn. New York: Grosset & Dunlap, 1971.

Lynch, John. *Spain 1516–1598: From Nation State to World Empire*. Oxford: Blackwell, 1991.

Mac Adam, Alfred. *Textual Confrontations: Comparative Readings in Latin American Literature*. Chicago: The University of Chicago Press, 1987.

Mac Adam, Alfred, and Alexander Coleman. "An Interview with Carlos Fuentes." *Book Forum* 4 (1978–9): 672–85.

McCaffery, Larry. *The Metafictional Muse*. Pittsburgh: University of Pittsburgh Press, 1982.

———. "A Spirit of Transgression." In *E. L. Doctorow: Essays and Conversations*. Edited by Richard Trenner. Princeton, N.J.: Ontario Review Press, 1983.

McCracken, Ellen M. "*Libro de Manuel* and *Fantomas contra los vampiros multinacionales*: Mass Culture, Art, and Politics." In *Literature and Popular Culture in the Hispanic World: A Symposium*. Gaithersburg, Md.: Hispamérica, 1981.

McHale, Brian. *Postmodernist Fiction*. London: Methuen, 1987.

McKay, Claude. *Home to Harlem*. Boston: Northeastern University Press, 1987.

Mahé, Jean-Pierre. "Hermes Trismegistus." In *The Encyclopedia of Religion*. Edited by Mircea Eliade. 16 vols. New York: MacMillan, 1987.

Mailer, Norman. *The Armies of the Night: History as a Novel, the Novel as History*. New York: New American Library, 1968.

Maravall, José Antonio. *Las Comunidades de Castilla: Una primera revolución moderna*. Madrid: Revista de Occidente, 1970.

Markowitz, Gerald. "How Not to Write History: A Critique of Radosh and Milton's *The Rosenberg File*." *Science and Society* 48, 1 (1984): 74–89.

Márquez Rodríguez, Alexis. "Aproximación preliminar a *Terra Nostra*: La ficción como reinterpretación de la historia." In *La obra de Carlos Fuentes: una visión múltiple*. Edited by Ana María Hernández de López. Madrid: Pliegos, 1988.

Martin, Reginald. *Ishmael Reed and the New Black Aesthetic Critics*. Houndmills: The MacMillan Press, 1988.

Matejka, Ladislav, and Krystyna Pormorska, eds. *Readings in Russian Poetics: Formalist and Structuralist Views*. Cambridge: MIT Press, 1971.

Mendieta, Fray Jerónimo de. *Historia eclesiástica indiana*. Mexico City: Porrúa, 1971.

Métraux, Alfred. *Voodoo in Haiti*. New York: Schocken Books, 1972.

Metz, Christian. *Language and Cinema*. Paris: Mouton, 1974.

Morris, Christopher. "Fiction Is a System of Knowledge: An Interview with E. L. Doctorow." *Michigan Quarterly Review* 30 (1991): 439–56.

———. *Models of Misrepresentation: On the Fiction of E. L. Doctorow*. Jackson: University Press of Mississippi, 1991.

Moss, Robert. *Urban Guerrillas: The New Face of Political Violence*. London: Temple Smith, 1972.

Muñoz, Diego. "Carlos Fuentes y Juan Goytisolo elogian el mestizaje como antídoto contra el racismo," *El país* (15 July 1992).

Muños Camargo, Diego. *Historia de Tlaxcala*. Guadalajara: Edmundo Aviña Levy, 1966.

Murray, Robert K. *The Harding Era: Warren G. Harding and his Administration*. Minneapolis: University of Minnesota Press, 1969.

Navasky, Victor S. "E. L. Doctorow: I Saw a Sign." *The New York Times Book Review* (29 September 1980), 44–45.

Nazareth, Peter. "An Interview with Ishmael Reed." *The Iowa Review* 13, 2 (1982): 117–31.

Nelson, William. *Fact or Fiction: The Dilemma of the Renaissance Storyteller*. Cambridge: Harvard University Press, 1973.

Nesbitt, W. J. "Satire Time." *Northern Echo* (21 May 1971).

Nicholson, H. B. "Topiltzin Quetzalcoatl of Tollan: A Problem in Mesoamerican Ethnohistory." Ph.D. diss., Harvard University, Cambridge, Mass., 1957.

———. "Ehecatl Quetzalcoatl vs. Topiltzin Quetzalcoatl: A Problem in Mesoamerican Religion and History." *Actes du XLII Congrès International des Américanistes*, Paris. vol. 6 (2–9 September 1976): 35–47.

Nietzsche, Friedrich. *The Use and Abuse of History*. Translated by Adrian Collins. New York: Liberal Arts Press and Bobbs-Merril, 1957.

Norris, Hoke. "Voodoo on the Range: A Parody." *Chicago Daily News* (16 August 1969).

Núñez Cabeza de Vaca, Alvar. *Naufragios*. Edited by Trinidad Barrera. Madrid: Alianza, 1985.

O'Brien, John. *Interviews with Black Writers*. New York: Liveright, 1973.

————. "Ishmael Reed: An Interview." In *The New Fiction: Interviews with Innovative American Writers*. Edited by Joe David Bellamy. Chicago: University of Illinois Press, 1972.

O'Gorman, Edmundo. *La invención de América: Investigación acerca de la estructura histórica del Nuevo Mundo y del sentido de su devenir*. Mexico City: Fondo de Cultura Económica, 1958.

Olmos, Andrés, ed. *Historia de los mexicanos por sus pinturas: Teogonía e historia de los mexicanos: Tres opúsculos del siglo XVI*. Mexico City: Porrúa, 1965.

Ortega, Julio. "Postmodernism in Latin America." In *Postmodernist Fiction in Europe and the Americas*. Edited by Theo D'Haen and Hans Bertens. Amsterdam: Rodopi, 1988.

Ortega y Gasset, José. "Meditación del Escorial." In *Meditaciones sobre la literatura y el Arte (La manera española de ver las cosas)*. Madrid: Castalia, 1987.

Osorio, Nelson. "The Debate on Postmodernism in Latin America." *Revista de Crítica Literaria Latinoamericana* 29 (1989): 146–48.

Ottley, Roi, and William Weatherby, eds. *The Negro in New York: An Informal Social History*. New York: The New York Public Library, 1967.

Pace, David. *Claude Lévi-Strauss: The Bearer of Ashes*. London: Routledge, 1983.

Pagden, Anthony. *The American Indian and the Origins of Comparative Ethnology*. Cambridge, Mass.: Cambridge University Press, 1982.

Pagden, Anthony, ed. *Letters from Mexico*. New Haven: Yale University Press, 1986.

Payne, Johnny. *Conquest of the New World. Experimental Fiction and Translation in the Americas*. Austin: University of Texas Press, 1993.

Paz, Octavio. *Hijos del limo: Del Romanticismo a la vanguardia*. Barcelona: Seix Barral, 1974.

————. "El romanticismo y la poesía contemporánea." *Vuelta* 11, 127 (1987): 26–27.

Pearce, Gary. "*Mumbo Jumbo*: Is It Brilliance or Garbage?" *News and Observer* 3 (September 1972): 6.

Peavler, Terry J. "*Blow-Up*: A Reconsideration of Antonioni's Infidelity to Cortázar." *PMLA* 94 (1979): 887–93.

Pelton, Robert D. "African Tricksters." In *The Encyclopedia of Religion*. Edited by Mircea Eliade. 16 vols. New York: MacMillan, 1987.

Perea, Héctor. "La obra en el tiempo de Carlos Fuentes." *El país* (10 July 1992).

Pérez de Oliva, Hernán. *Historia de la invención de las Indias*. Edited by José Juan Arroum. Bogotá: Instituto Caro y Cuervo, 1965.

Pérez Firmat, Gustavo. "Metafiction Again." *Taller Literario* 1 (1980): 30–38.

————, ed. *Do the Americas Have a Common Literature?* Durham, N.C.: Duke University Press, 1990.

Perloff, Marjorie. "The Invention of Collage." In *Collage*. Edited by Jeanine Parisier Plottel. New York: New York Literary Forum, 1983.

Phelan, John Leddy. *The Millennial Kingdom of the Franciscans in the New World*. Berkeley: University of California Press, 1970.

Pitzer, Donald E., ed. *America's Communal Utopias*. Chapel Hill: University of North Carolina Press, 1997.

Pla Dalmau, José M. *El Escorial y Herrera*. Gerona: Dalmau, 1952.

Plimpton, George. "The Art of Fiction." *The Paris Review* 28 (winter 1986): 23–47.

Pope, Randolph. "Dos novelas álbum: *Libro de Manuel* de Cortázar y *Figuraciones en el mes de marzo* de Díaz Valcárcel." *Bilingual Review* 1, 2 (1974): 170–84.

Poster, Mark. *Foucault, Marxism & History: Mode of Production versus Mode of Information*. Cambridge, Mass.: Polity Press, 1984.

Poulantzas, Nicos. *State, Power, Socialism*. London: New Left Books, 1978.

Powell, Jerry Owen. "The Structure of Narrative: Facts and Fiction in the Rosenberg Case." Ph.D. diss., Indiana University, 1981.

Prego, Omar. *La fascinación de las palabras: conversaciones con Julio Cortázar*. Barcelona: Muchnik, 1985.

Quiñones Keber, Eloise. "Aztecs Before and After the Conquest." *Colonial Latin American Review* 1, 1–2 (1992): 223–39.

———. "The Aztec Image of Topiltzin Quetzalcoatl." In *Smoke and Mist: Mesoamerican Studies in Memory of Thelma D. Sullivan*. Edited by J. Kathryn Josserand, and Karen Dakin. Oxford: BAR International Series, 1988.

———. "From Tollan to Tlapallan: The Tale of Topiltzin Quetzalcoatl in the Codex Vaticanus A." *Latin American Indian Literatures Journal* 3, 1 (1987): 76–94.

Radosh, Ronald, and Joyce Milton. *The Rosenberg File: A Search for the Truth*. New York: Holt, Rinehart, and Winston, 1983.

Redd, Danita. "Black Madonnas of Europe: Diffusion of the African Isis." In *African Presence in Early Europe*. Edited by Ivan Van Sertima. New Brunswick, N.J.: Transaction Publisher, 1985.

Reed, Ishmael. *Flight to Canada*. New York: Random House, 1976.

———. *The Free-Lance Pallbearers*. Garden City: Doubleday, 1967.

———. *Japanese by Spring*. New York: Atheneum, 1993.

———. *The Last Days of Louisiana Red*. New York: Random House, 1974.

———. *Mumbo Jumbo*. Garden City, NY: Doubleday, 1972.

———. *Mumbo Jumbo*. New York: Atheneum, 1988.

———. *New and Collected Poems*. New York: Atheneum, 1989.

———. *Reckless Eyeballing*. New York: St. Martin's Press, 1986.

———. *Shrovetide in Old New Orleans*. New York: Atheneum, 1989.

———. *The Terrible Threes*. New York: Atheneum, 1989.

———. *The Terrible Twos*. New York: St. Martin's Press, 1982.

———. *Writin' Is Fightin': Thirty-Seven Years of Boxing on Paper*. New York: Atheneum, 1990.

———. *Yellow Back Radio Broke-Down*. Garden City: Doubleday, 1969.

Reed, T. V. "Genealogy / Narrative / Power: Questions of Postmodernity in Doctorow's *The Book of Daniel*." *American Literary History* 4, 2 (1992): 288–304.

Ricardou, Jean. "The Story within the Story." Translated by Joseph Kestner. *James Joyce Quarterly* 18, 3 (1981): 323–38.

Robelo, Cecilio A. *Diccionario de mitología nahoa*. Mexico City: Porrúa, 1982.

Rock, David. *Argentina 1516–1587: Desde la colonización española hasta Alfonsín*. Madrid: Alianza, 1988.

Rodríguez Carranza, Luz. *Un Teatro de la Memoria: Análisis de "Terra Nostra" de Carlos Fuentes*. Leuven, Belgium: Leuven University Press, 1990.

Rodríguez Suro, Joaquín. "La huella de Américo Castro en *Terra Nostra*." In *Américo Castro: The Impact of his Thought. Essays to Mark the Centenary of His Birth*. Edited by Ronald E. Surtz, Jaime Ferrán, and Daniel P. Testa. Madison, Wisc.: The Hispanic Seminary of Medieval Studies, 1988.

Rose, Margaret. *Parody / Metafiction: An Analysis of Parody as a Critical Mirror to the Writing and Reception of Fiction*. London: Croom Hekm Ltd., 1979.

Rozitchner, Leon. "La postmodernidad es el opio de los pueblos." *Casa de las Américas* 168 (1988): 165–66.

Rubin, Jerry. *Do It! Scenarios of the Revolution*. New York: Simon and Schuster, 1970.

Sahagún, Bernardino de. *Historia general de las cosas de Nueva España*. 4 vols. Edited by Angel María Garibay. Mexico City: Porrúa, 1956.

Said, Edward W. *The World, the Text, and The Critic*. Cambridge: Harvard University Press, 1983.

Saldívar, José David. *The Dialectics of Our America: Genealogy, Cultural Critique, and Literary History*. Durham, N.C.: Duke University Press, 1991.

Sanford, Charles L. *The Quest for Paradise: Europe and the American Moral Imagination*. Urbana: University of Illinois Press, 1961.

Schell, Jonathan. "Watergate." In *A History of Our Time: Readings on Postwar America*. Edited by William H. Chafe and Harvard Sitkoff. New York: Oxford University Press, 1991.

Schmitz, Neil. "The Gumbo That Jes Grew." *Partisan Review* 42 (1975): 311–16.

Schneir, Walter and Miriam. *Invitation to an Inquest*. New York: Pantheon Books, 1983.

Scholes, Robert. *Fabulation and Metafiction*. Urbana: University of Illinois Press, 1970.

———. "Metafiction." *Iowa Review* 1, 4 (1970): 100–15.

Scott, Webster. "Antiwestern in a Black Vein." *Life* 67 (15 August 1969), 12.

Séjourné, Laurette. *Burning Water: Thought and Religion in Ancient Mexico*. Berkeley, Calif.: Shambhala, 1976.

Jean Servier. *Histoire de l'utopie*. Paris: Gallimard, 1967.

Shadle, Mark. "A Bird's-Eye View: Ishmael Reed's Unsettling of the Score by Munching and Mooching on the Mumbo Jumbo Work of History." *North Dakota Quarterly* 54, 1 (1986): 18–29.

Shaw, Arnold. *The Jazz Age: Popular Music in the 1920s*. New York: Oxford University Press, 1987.

Siegle, Robert. *The Politics of Reflexivity: Narrative and the Constitutive Poetics of Culture*. Baltimore: The Johns Hopkins University Press, 1986.

Sigüenza, Fray José de. *La fundación del monasterio del Escorial*. Madrid: Aguilar, 1963.

Simson, Ingrid. *Realidad y ficción en "Terra Nostra" de Carlos Fuentes*. Frankfurt: Vervuert, 1989.

Singer, H. Bob. "Yellow Back Radio Broke-Down." *New York Herald Tribune* (28 September 1969), 12.

Smelser, Marshall, and Joan R. Gundersen. *American History at a Glance: From the Earliest Settlements to the Present.* New York: Harper & Row, 1975.

Solotorevsky, Myrna. *Literatura—Paraliteratura: Puig, Borges, Donoso, Cortázar, Vargas Llosa.* Gaithersburg, Md.: Hispamérica, 1988.

Sosnowski, Saul. "Entrevista a Carlos Fuentes." *Hispamérica* 9, 27 (1980): 69–97.

Spires, Robert. *Beyond the Metafictional Mode: Directions in the Modern Spanish Novel.* Lexington: University Press of Kentucky, 1984.

Stade, George. Review of *Ragtime*, by E. L. Doctorow. *New York Times Book Review* (6 July 1975), 1–2.

———. "Types Defamiliarized." Review of *Loon Lake*, by E. L. Doctorow. *Nation* 231 (27 September 1980), 286–86.

Sark, John. *The Literature of Exhaustion: Borges, Nabokov and Barthes.* Durham, N.C.: University of North Carolina Press, 1974.

Stenzel, Werner. *Quetzalcoatl de Tula: Mitogénesis de una leyenda postcortesiana.* Nuevo León: Facultad de Filosofía y Letras, 1991.

Stonehill, Brian. *The Self-Conscious Novel: Artifice in Fiction from Joyce to Pynchon.* Philadelphia: University of Pennsylvania Press, 1988.

Subirats, Eduardo. *El continente vacío: La conquista del Nuevo Mundo y la conciencia moderna.* Madrid: Anaya, 1994.

Sullivan, Lawrence E. "Tricksters: An Overview." In *The Encyclopedia of Religion.* Edited by Mircea Eliade. 16 vols. New York: MacMillan, 1987.

Sullivan, Mark. *Our Times: 1900–1925.* 6 vols. New York: Charles Scribner's Sons, 1972.

Thomas, Angela D. *Egyptian Gods and Myths.* Aylesbury: Shire Publications, 1986.

Tittler, Jonathan. *Narrative Irony in the Contemporary Spanish-American Novel.* Ithaca: Cornell University Press, 1984.

———. "De siglos dorados y leyendas negras." In *La obra de Carlos Fuentes: Una visión múltiple.* Edited by Ana María Hernández de López. Madrid: Pliegos, 1988.

Tocqueville, Alexis de. *Democracy in America.* Edited by J. P. Mayer. New York: Anchor Books, 1969.

Toro, Alfonso de. "Postmodernidad y Latinoamérica." *Revista Iberoamericana* 155–56 (1991): 441–67

Ulmer, Gregory L. "The Object of Post-Criticism." In *The Anti-Aesthetic: Essays on Postmodern Culture.* Edited by Hal Foster. Seattle, Wash.: Bay Press, 1983.

Urbistondo, Vicente. "Cinematografía y literatura en "Las babas del diablo" y en *Blow Up.*" *Explicación de Textos Literarios* 2, 2 (1974): 109–15.

Van Delden, Maarten. *Carlos Fuentes, Mexico, and Modernity.* Nashville, Tenn.: Vanderbilt University Press, 1998.

Van Doren, Charles and Robert McHenry. *Webster's Guide to American History: A Chronological, Geographical and Biographical Survey and Compendium.* Springfield, Ill.: G. & C. Merriam Co., 1971.

Van Sertima, Ivan. *African Presence in Early America*. New Brunswick, N.J.: Transaction Books, 1987.

———. *African Presence in Early Europe*. New Brunswick, N.J.: Transaction Publisher, 1985.

———. *They Came Before Columbus*. New York: Random House, 1976.

Van Vechten, Carl. *Fragments from an Unwritten Autobiography*. New Haven: Yale University Press, 1955.

———. *Nigger Heaven*. New York: Alfred A. Knopf, 1926.

Vega, Inca Garcilaso de la. *Comentarios reales*. Edited by José de la Riva-Agüero. Mexico City: Porrúa, 1990.

Vespucio, Américo. *El nuevo mundo: Cartas relativas a sus viajes y descubrimientos*. Edited by R. Levillier. Buenos Aires: Nova, 1951.

Veyne, Paul. *Cómo se escribe la historia*. Madrid: Fragua, 1972.

Waugh, Patricia. *Metafiction: The Theory and Practice of Self-Conscious Fiction*. London: Methuen, 1984.

Weil, Thomas E., ed. *Area Handbook for Argentina*. Washington, D.C.: Foreign Area Studies, 1974.

Weiss, Jason. "An Interview with Carlos Fuentes." *The Kenyon Review* 5, 4 (1983): 105–18.

White, Edward M. "Story of Black Power Overcoming Evil." *Los Angeles Times Book Review* (25 January 1970), 2.

White, Hayden. *The Content of the Form: Narrative Discourse and Historical Representation*. Baltimore: The Johns Hopkins University Press, 1987.

———. *Metahistory: The Historical Imagination in Nineteenth-Century Europe*. Baltimore: The The Johns Hopkins University Press, 1973.

———. "Method and Ideology in Intellectual History: The Case of Henry Adams." In *Modern European Intellectual History: Reappraisals and New Perspectives*. Edited by Dominick LaCapra and Steven L. Kaplan. Ithaca: Cornell University Press, 1982.

———. *Tropics of Discourse: Essays in Cultural Criticism*. Baltimore: The Johns Hopkins University Press, 1978.

Whitlow, Roger. "Ishmael Reed." In *Black American Literature: A Critical History*. Chicago: Nelson Hall, 1973.

Wicham-Crowley, Timothy P. *Guerrillas and Revolution in Latin America: A Comparative Study of Insurgents and Regimes Since 1956*. Princeton: Princeton University Press, 1992.

Williams, Raymond Leslie. *The Postmodern Novel in Latin America: Politics, Culture, and the Crisis of Truth*. New York: St. Martin's Press, 1995.

———. *The Writings of Carlos Fuentes*. Austin: University of Texas Press, 1996.

———, ed. *The Novel in the Americas*. Boulder: University Press of Colorado, 1992.

Williams, William Appleman. *The Tragedy of American Diplomacy*. New York: Dell Publishing Co., 1959.

Winks, Robin W. *The Historian as Detective: Essays on Evidence*. New York: Harper & Row, 1968.

Wright, Richard. "In Between Laughter and Tears." *New Masses* (5 October 1937), 22, 25.

Yates, Frances. *The Art of Memory*. Chicago: The University of Chicago Press, 1966.

Yturbe, Corina. "El conocimiento histórico." In *Filosofía de la historia*. Edited by Reyes Mate. Madrid: Trotta, 1993.

Yúdice, George, Jean Franco, and Juan Flores, eds. *On Edge: The Crisis of Contemporary Latin American Culture*. Minneapolis: University of Minnesota Press, 1992.

Zamora, Lois Parkinson. "Movement and Stasis, Film and Photo: Temporal Structures in the Recent Fiction of Julio Cortázar." *Review of Contemporary Fiction* 3, 3 (1983): 51–65.

———. "The Usable Past: The Idea of History in Modern U.S. and Latin American Fiction." In *Do the Americas Have a Common Literature?* Edited by Gustavo Pérez Firmat. Durham, N.C.: Duke University Press, 1990.

———. *The Usable Past: The Imagination of History in Recent Fiction of the Americas*. Cambridge, Mass.: Cambridge University Press, 1997.

———. "Voyeur/Voyant: Julio Cortázar's Spatial Esthetic." *Mosaic* 14, 4 (1981): 45–68.

———. *Writing the Apocalypse: Historical Vision in Contemporary U.S. and Latin American Fiction*. Cambridge, Mass.: Cambridge University Press, 1989.

Zech-Gedeon, Hanne. "Carlos Fuentes." In *Lateinamerikanische Literatur der Gegenwart in Einzeidarstellungen*. Stuttgart: Wolfgang Eitel, 1976.